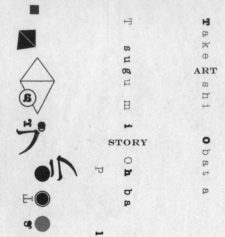

Takeshi Obata

ART

Tsugumi Ohba

STORY

Platinum End

PLATINVM END

12

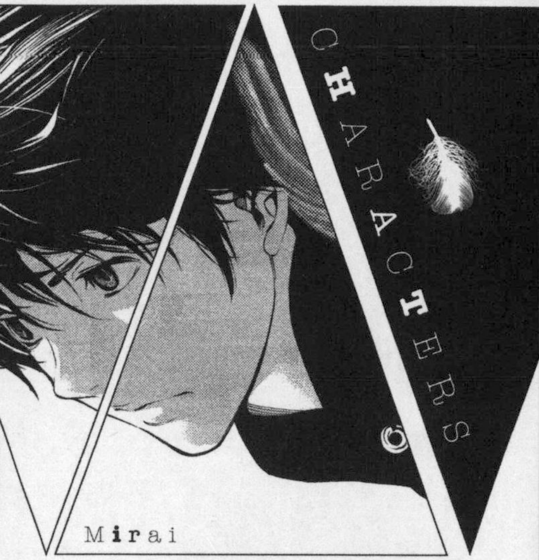
CHARACTERS
Mirai

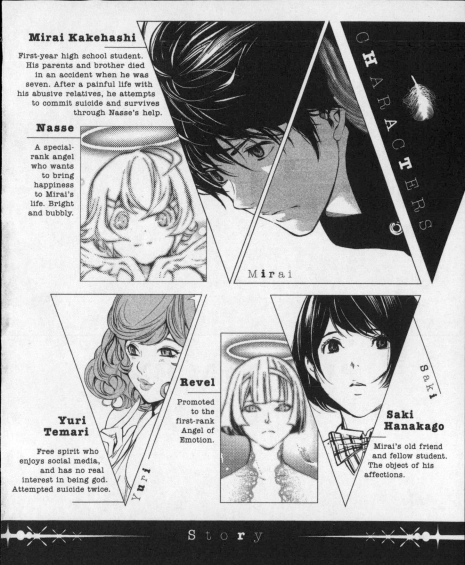

Mirai Kakehashi

First-year high school student. His parents and brother died in an accident when he was seven. After a painful life with his abusive relatives, he attempts to commit suicide and survives through Nasse's help.

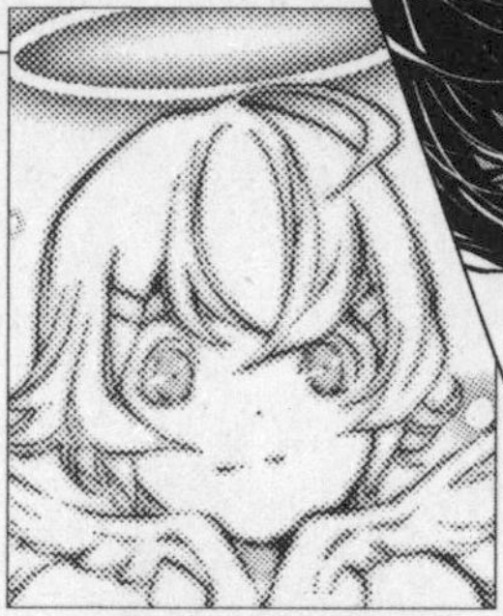

Nasse

A special-rank angel who wants to bring happiness to Mirai's life. Bright and bubbly.

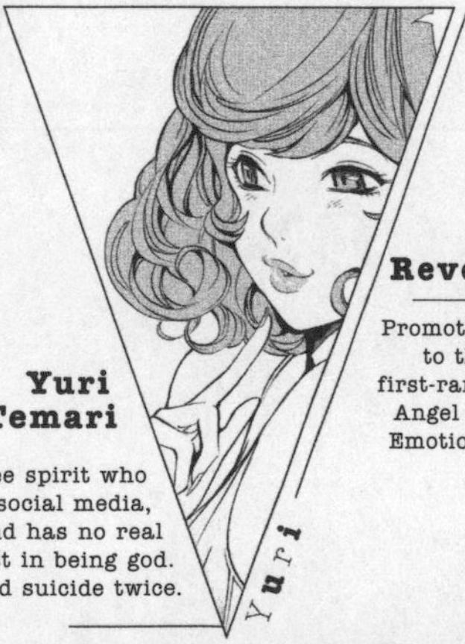
Yuri

Yuri Temari

Free spirit who enjoys social media, and has no real interest in being god. Attempted suicide twice.

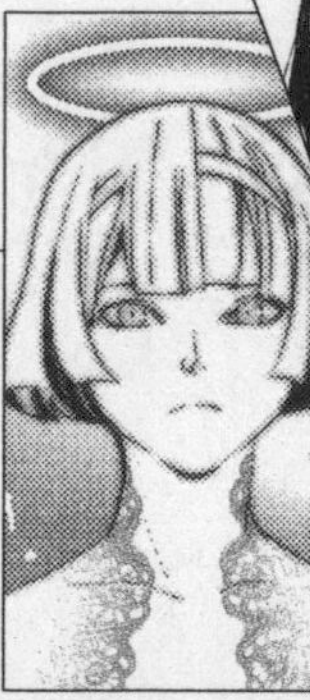

Revel

Promoted to the first-rank Angel of Emotion.

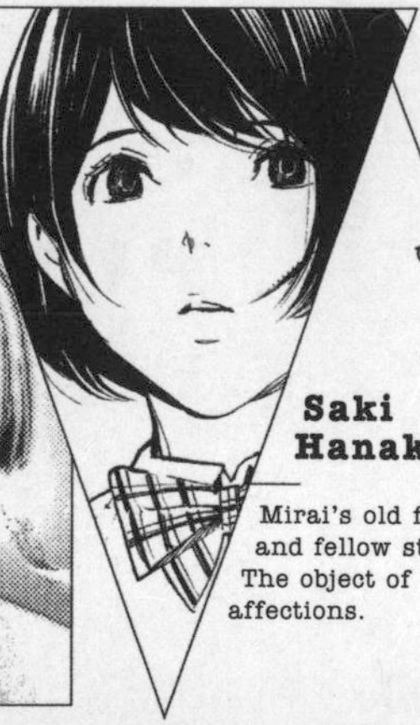
Saki

Saki Hanakago

Mirai's old friend and fellow student. The object of his affections.

Story

"My time has come. I leave the seat of god to the next human. To a younger, fresher power.

The next god shall be chosen from the 13 humans chosen by you 13 angels. When the chosen human is made the next god, your angelic duty is finished, and you may live beside that god in peace.

You have 999 days remaining..."

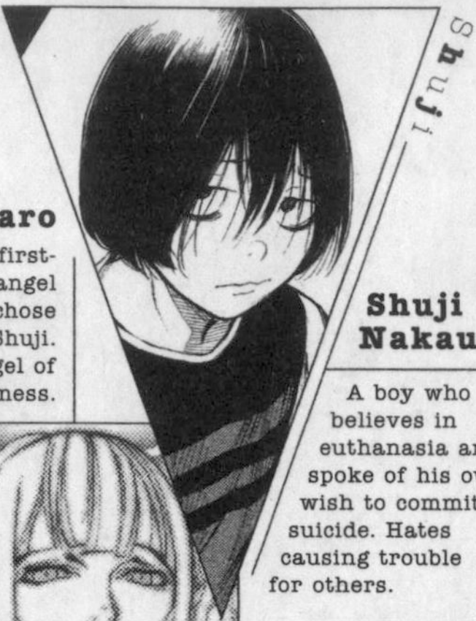
Shuji

Ogaro

The first-rank angel who chose Shuji. Angel of Darkness.

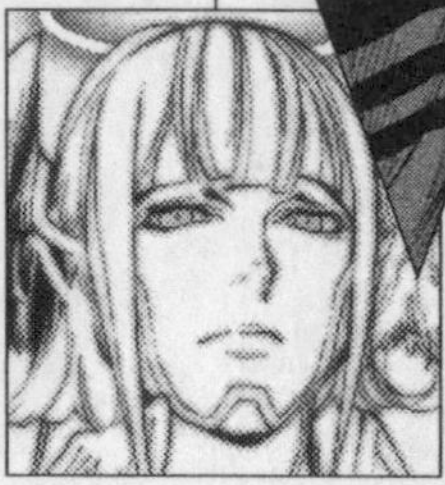

Shuji Nakaumi

A boy who believes in euthanasia and spoke of his own wish to commit suicide. Hates causing trouble for others.

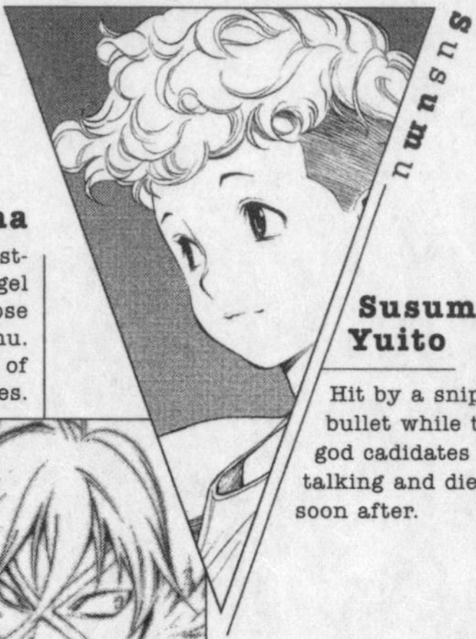
Susumu

Penema

The first-rank angel who chose Susumu. Angel of Games.

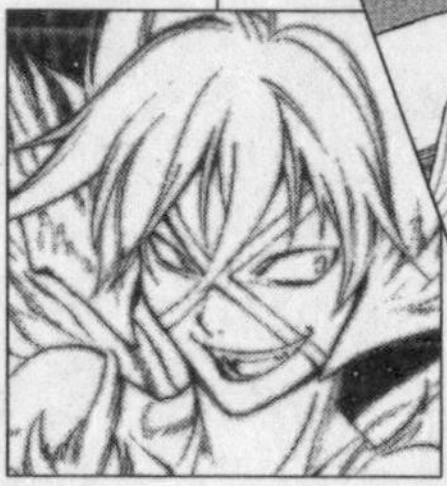

Susumu Yuito

Hit by a sniper's bullet while the god cadidates were talking and died soon after.

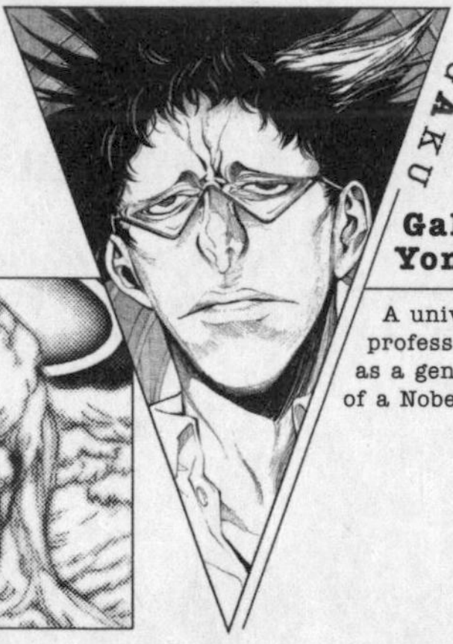
GAKU

Muni

The special-rank angel who chose Yoneda. Angel of Destruction.

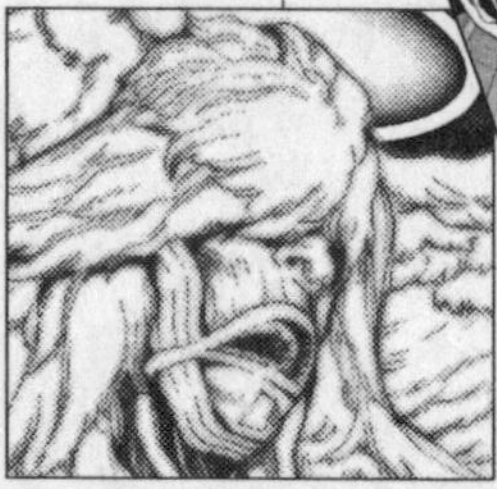

Gaku Yoneda

A university professor hailed as a genius. Winner of a Nobel Prize.

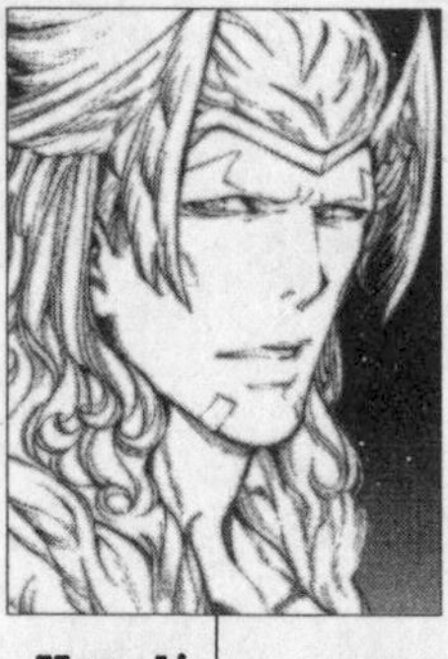

Yazeli

The second-rank angel who chose Yuri. Angel of Truth.

Story

CRUEL BULLET

After Yoneda theorizes that god is unnecessary, a sniper's bullet pierces Susumu's chest without warning.

As the world watches, Yoneda claims that the current "god" is a false creature powered by the mental energy of mankind's prayers.

CONTACT

The group answers the question of what they would do as god, shortly before finally coming into contact with Yoneda, the final candidate.

A GOD WHO EXISTS

CONTENTS

12

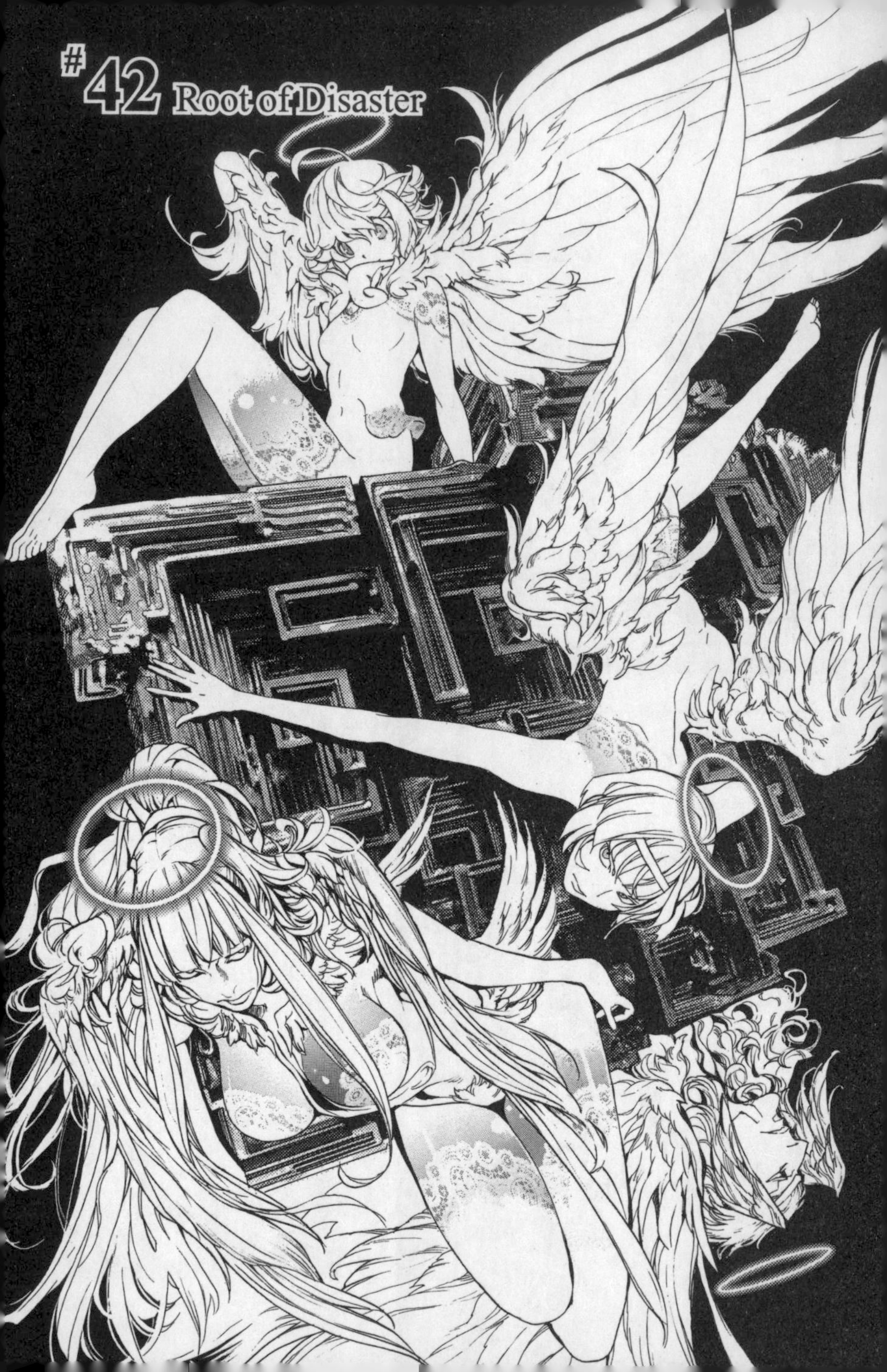
#42 Root of Disaster

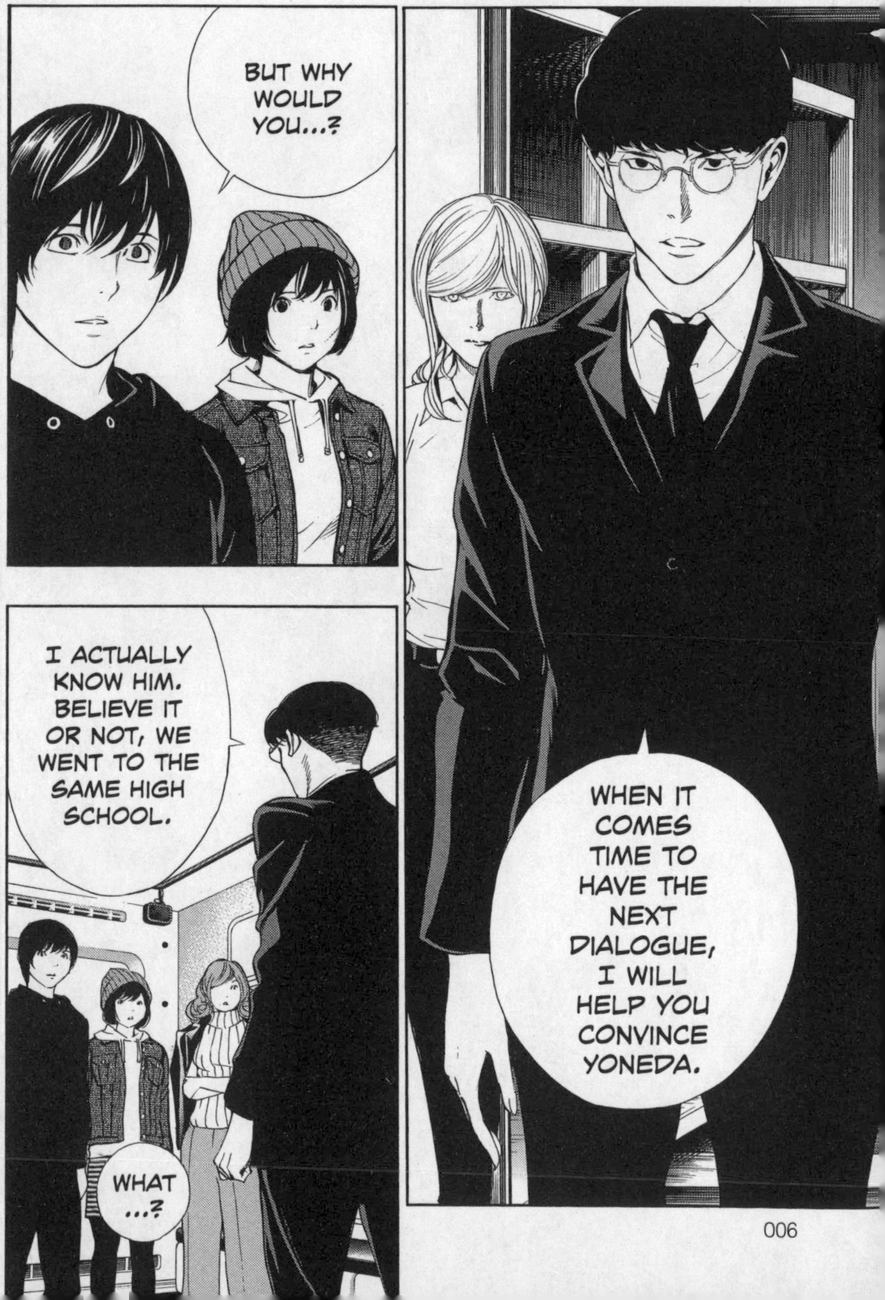
WHEN IT COMES TIME TO HAVE THE NEXT DIALOGUE, I WILL HELP YOU CONVINCE YONEDA.
BUT WHY WOULD YOU...?
I ACTUALLY KNOW HIM. BELIEVE IT OR NOT, WE WENT TO THE SAME HIGH SCHOOL.
WHAT ...?

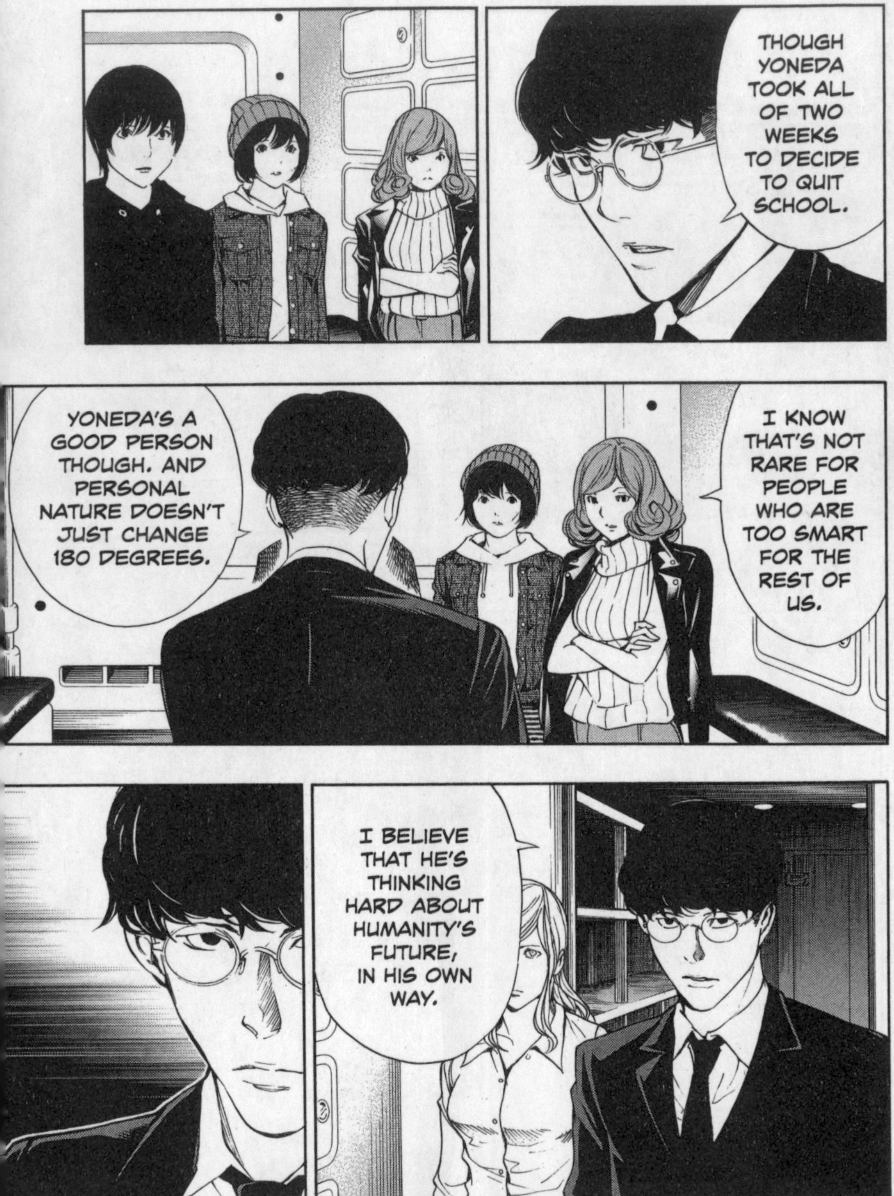
THOUGH YONEDA TOOK ALL OF TWO WEEKS TO DECIDE TO QUIT SCHOOL.
I KNOW THAT'S NOT RARE FOR PEOPLE WHO ARE TOO SMART FOR THE REST OF US.
YONEDA'S A GOOD PERSON THOUGH. AND PERSONAL NATURE DOESN'T JUST CHANGE 180 DEGREES.
I BELIEVE THAT HE'S THINKING HARD ABOUT HUMANITY'S FUTURE, IN HIS OWN WAY.

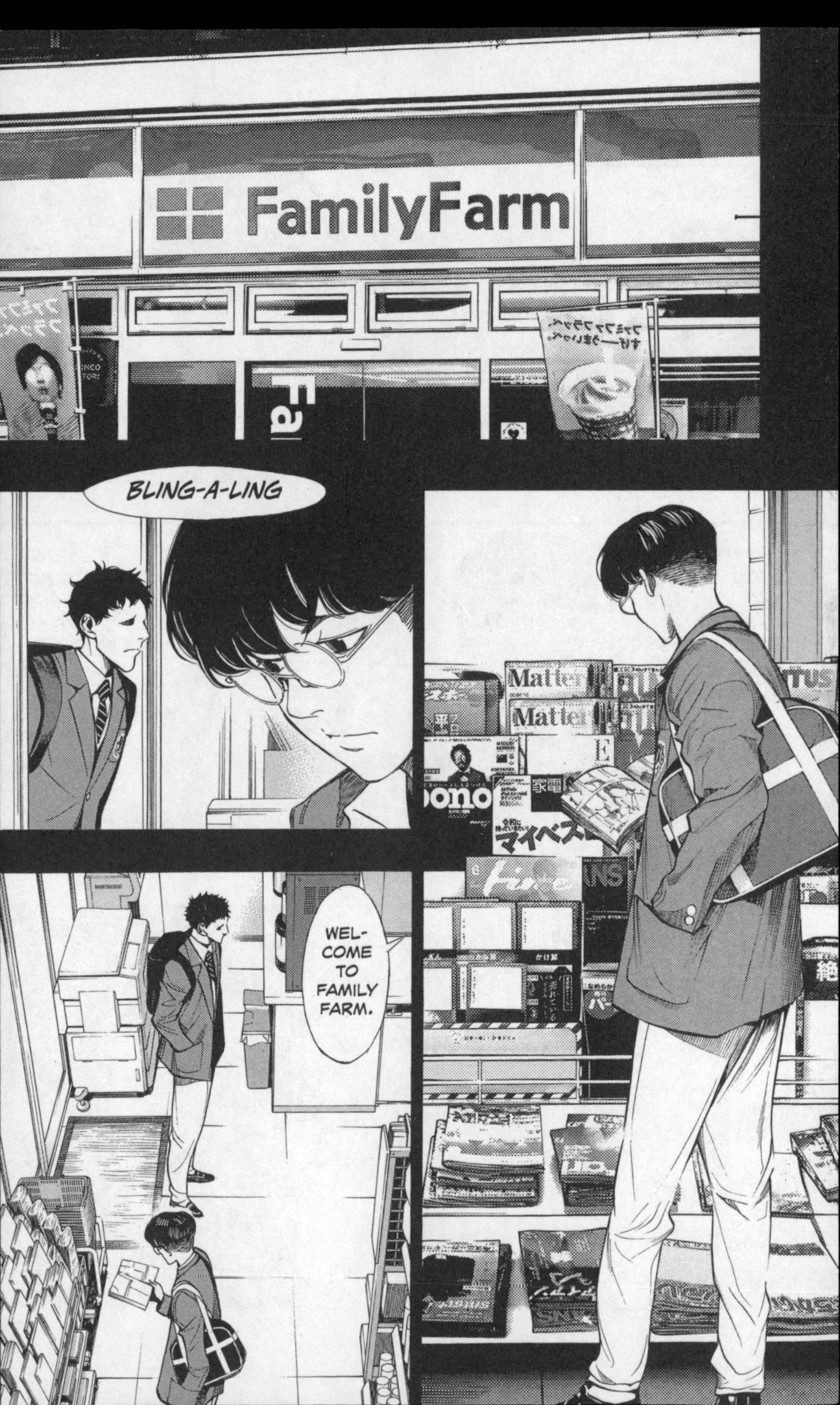
FamilyFarm
BLING-A-LING
WEL-COME TO FAMILY FARM.

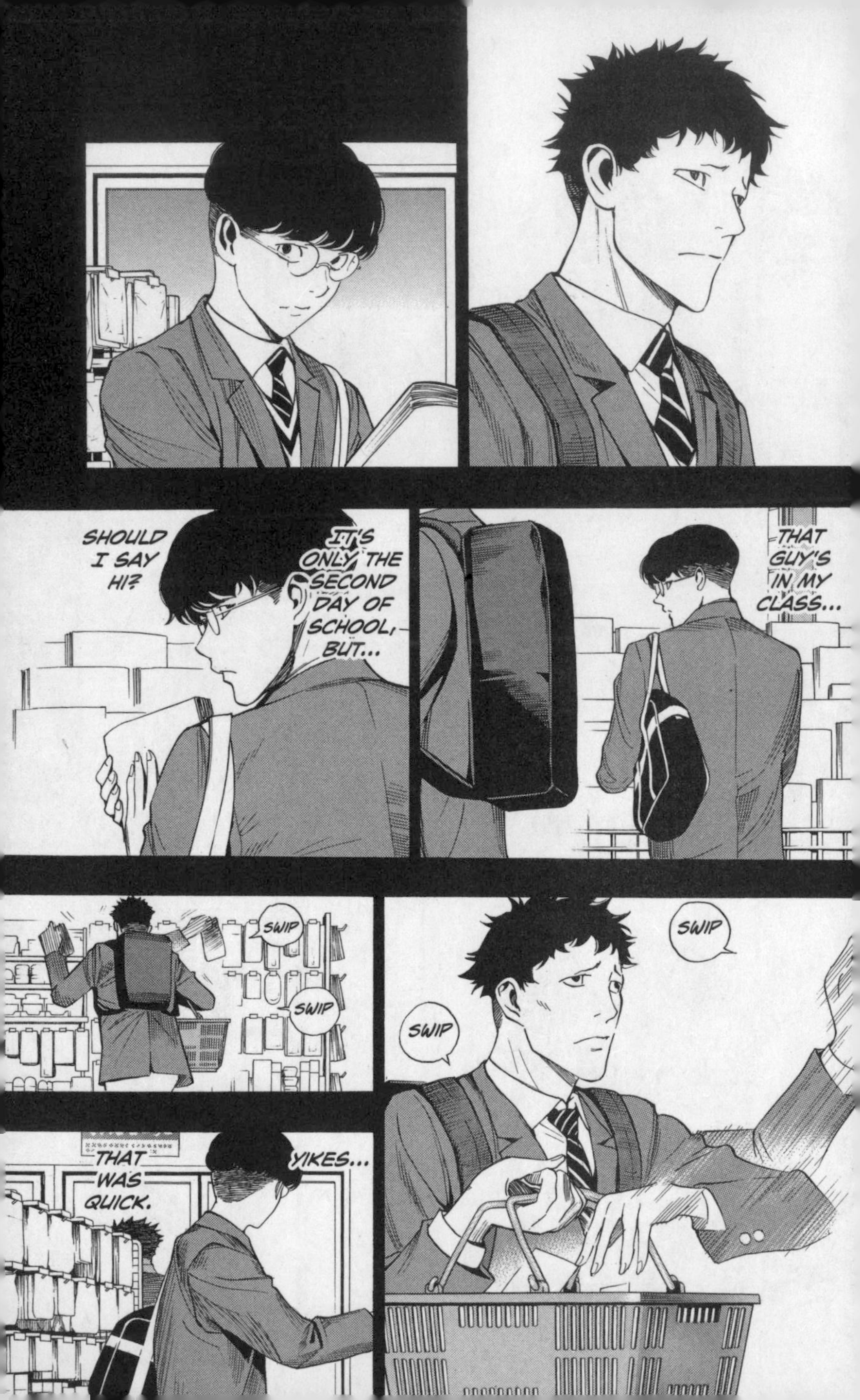
THAT GUY'S IN MY CLASS...
IT'S ONLY THE SECOND DAY OF SCHOOL, BUT...
SHOULD I SAY HI?
SWIP
SWIP
SWIP
SWIP
YIKES...
THAT WAS QUICK.

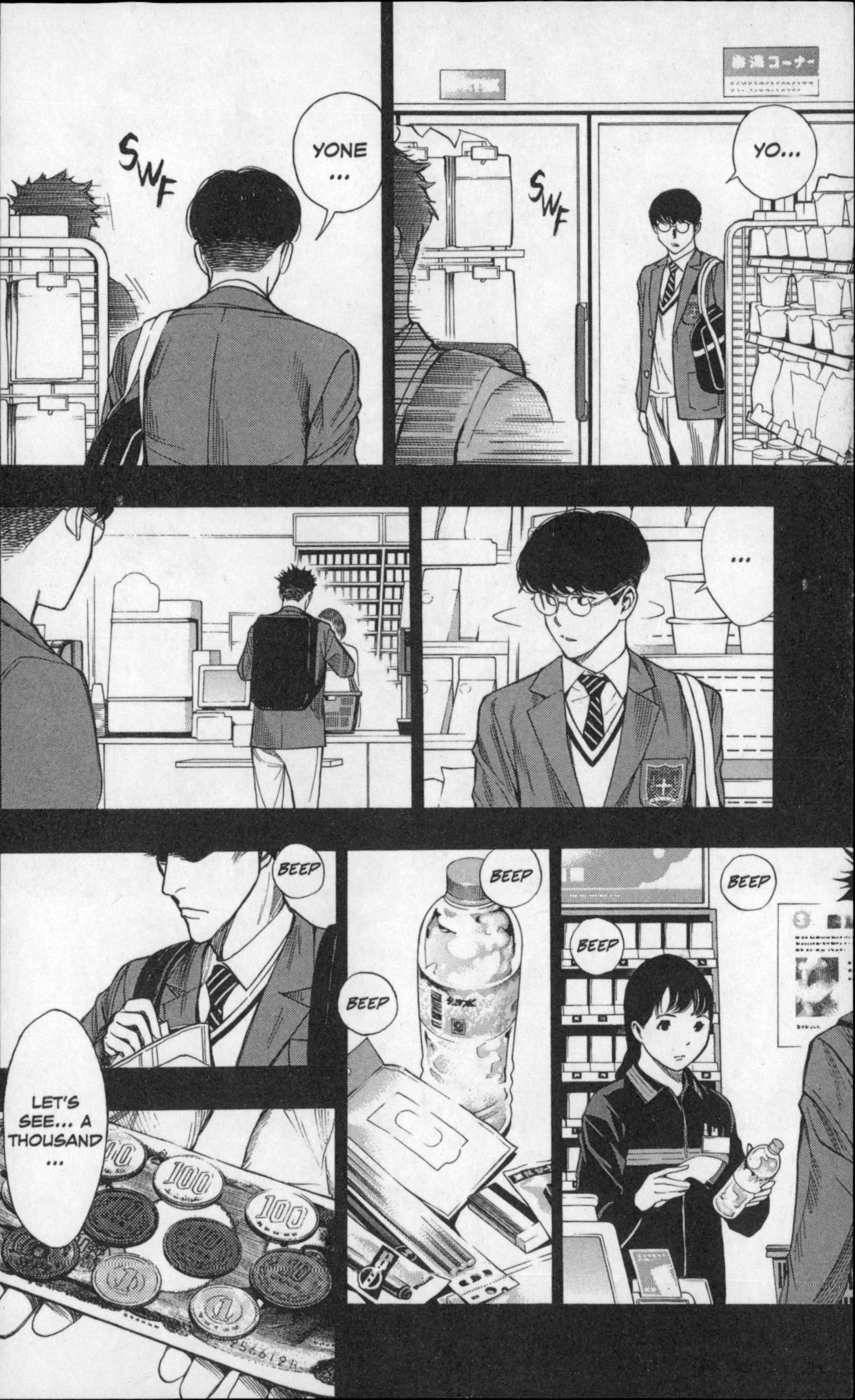
SWF
YO...
SWF
YONE
...
...
BEEP
BEEP
BEEP
BEEP
BEEP
LET'S
SEE... A
THOUSAND
...

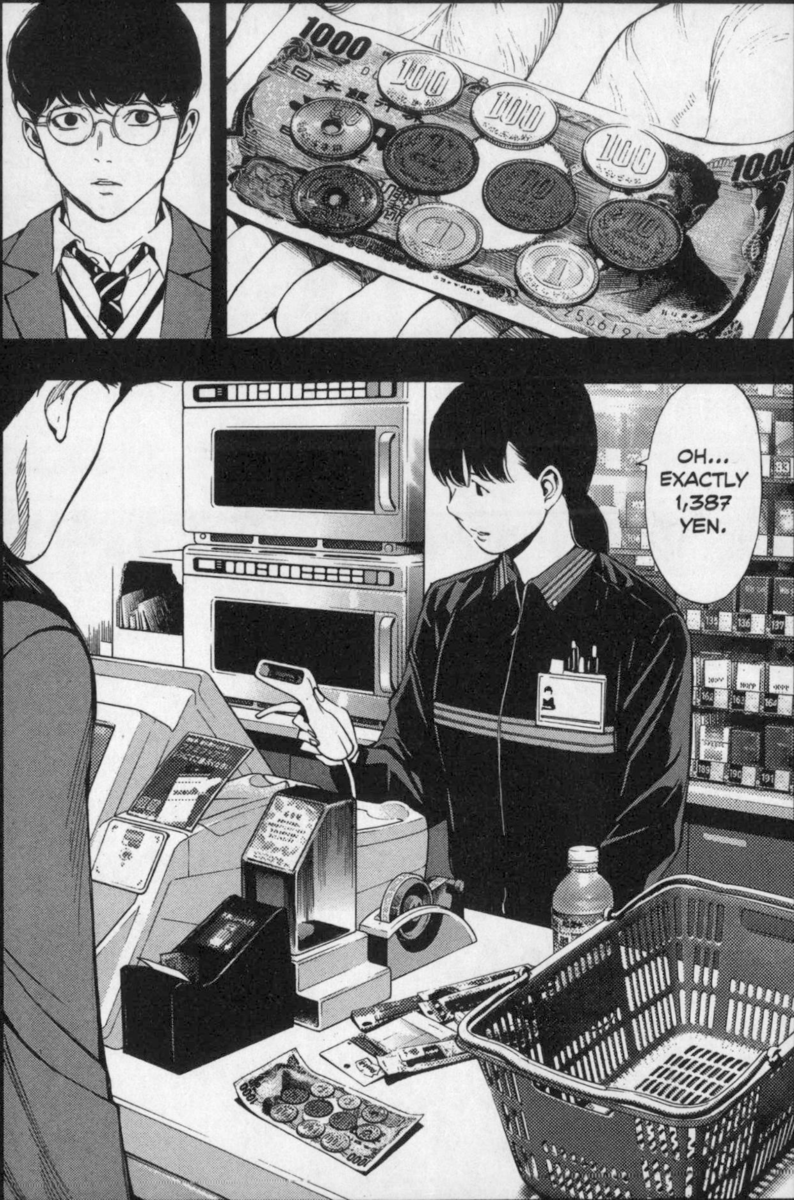
OH... EXACTLY 1,387 YEN.

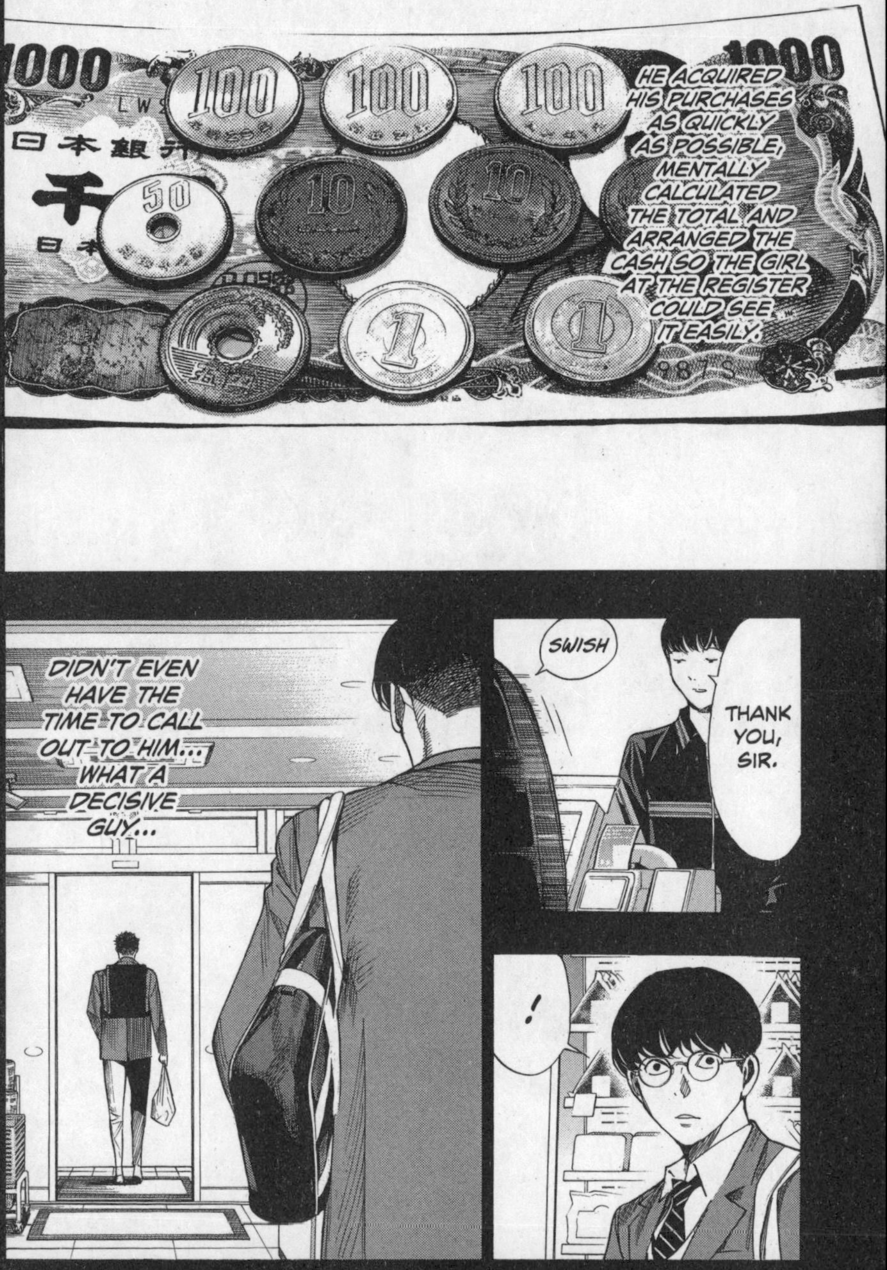
HE ACQUIRED HIS PURCHASES AS QUICKLY AS POSSIBLE, MENTALLY CALCULATED THE TOTAL AND ARRANGED THE CASH SO THE GIRL AT THE REGISTER COULD SEE IT EASILY.
SWISH
THANK YOU, SIR.
!
DIDN'T EVEN HAVE THE TIME TO CALL OUT TO HIM... WHAT A DECISIVE GUY...

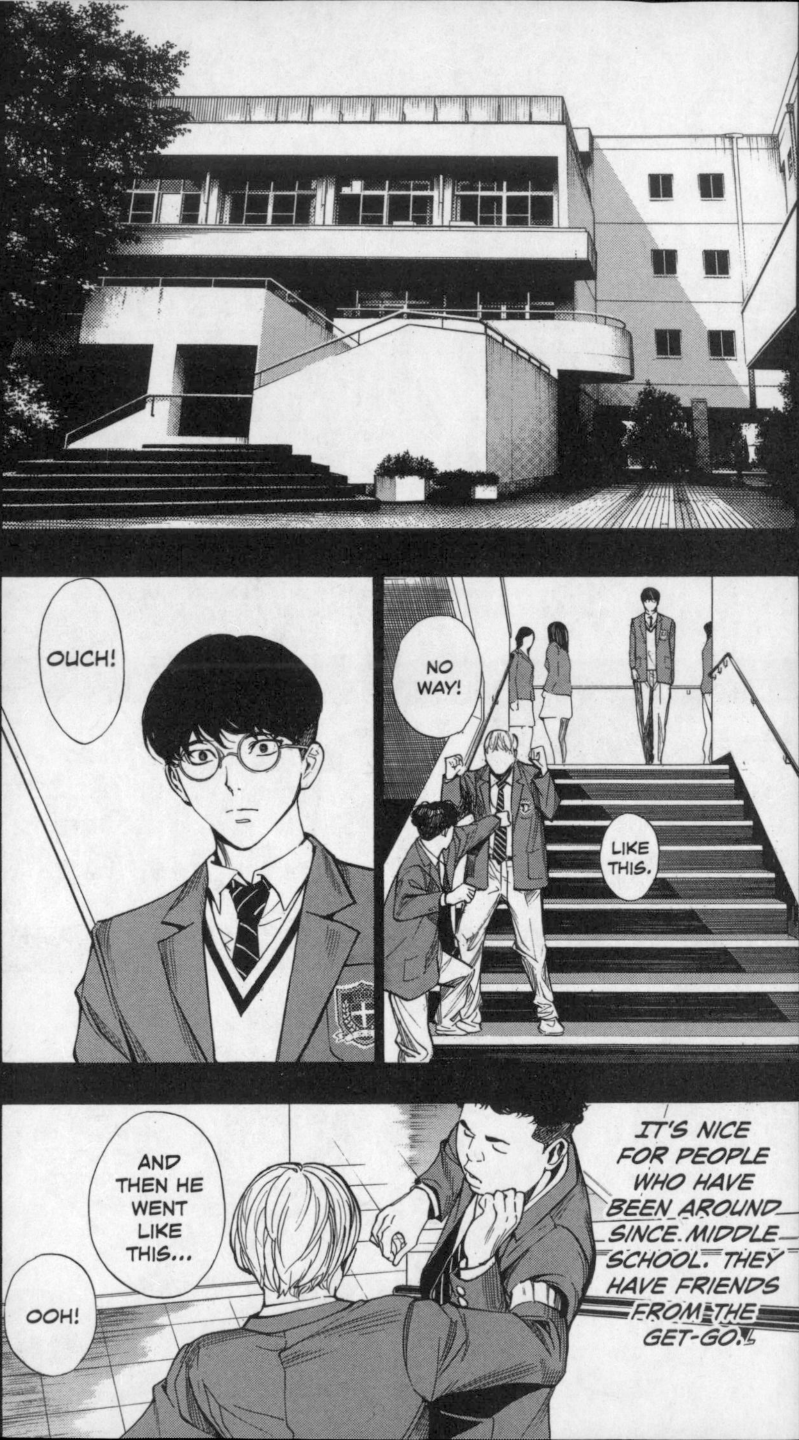
NO WAY!
LIKE THIS.
OUCH!
IT'S NICE FOR PEOPLE WHO HAVE BEEN AROUND SINCE MIDDLE SCHOOL. THEY HAVE FRIENDS FROM THE GET-GO.
AND THEN HE WENT LIKE THIS...
OOH!

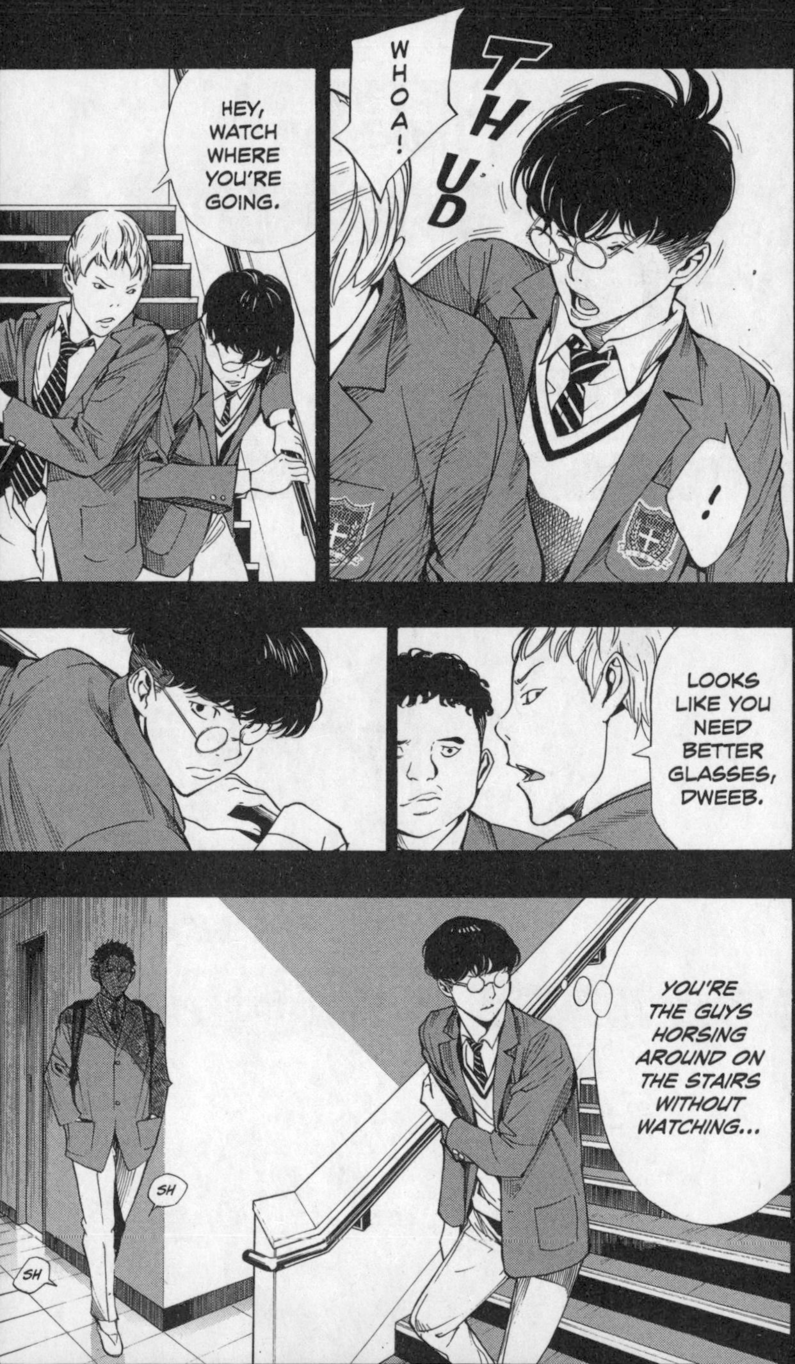
WHOA!
THUD
!
HEY, WATCH WHERE YOU'RE GOING.
LOOKS LIKE YOU NEED BETTER GLASSES, DWEEB.
YOU'RE THE GUYS HORSING AROUND ON THE STAIRS WITHOUT WATCHING...
SH
SH

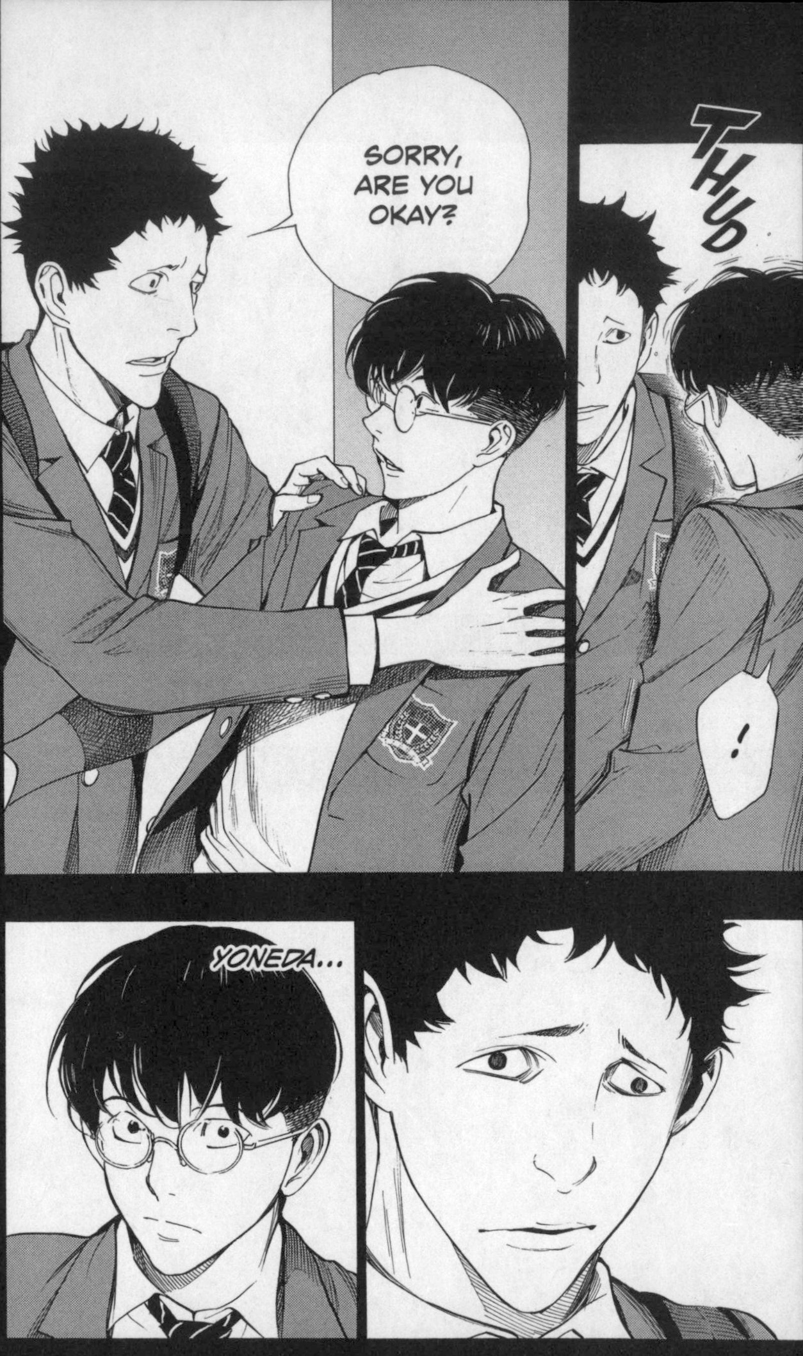
THUD
!
SORRY, ARE YOU OKAY?
YONEDA...

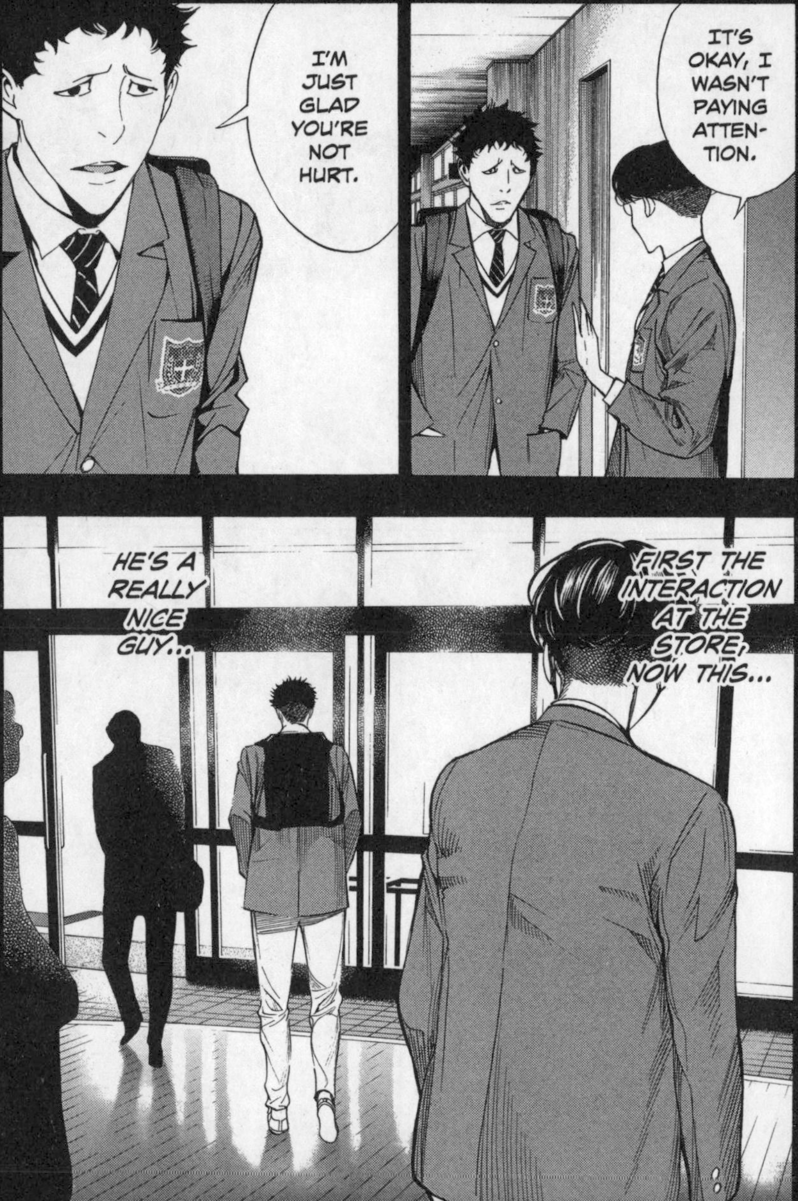
IT'S OKAY, I WASN'T PAYING ATTEN- TION.
I'M JUST GLAD YOU'RE NOT HURT.
FIRST THE INTERACTION AT THE STORE, NOW THIS...
HE'S A REALLY NICE GUY...

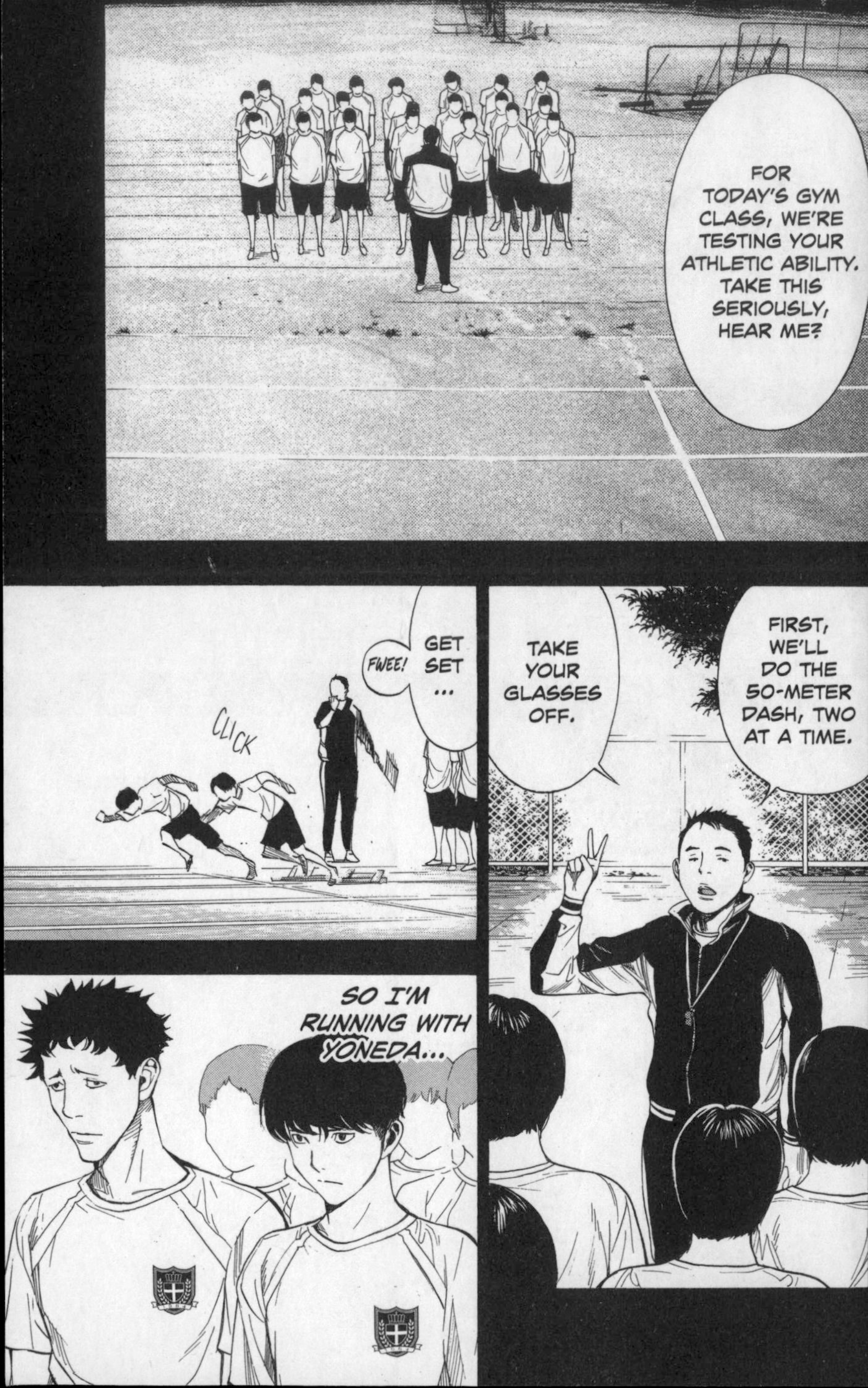
FOR TODAY'S GYM CLASS, WE'RE TESTING YOUR ATHLETIC ABILITY. TAKE THIS SERIOUSLY, HEAR ME?
FIRST, WE'LL DO THE 50-METER DASH, TWO AT A TIME.
TAKE YOUR GLASSES OFF.
GET SET ...
FWEE!
CLICK
SO I'M RUNNING WITH YONEDA...

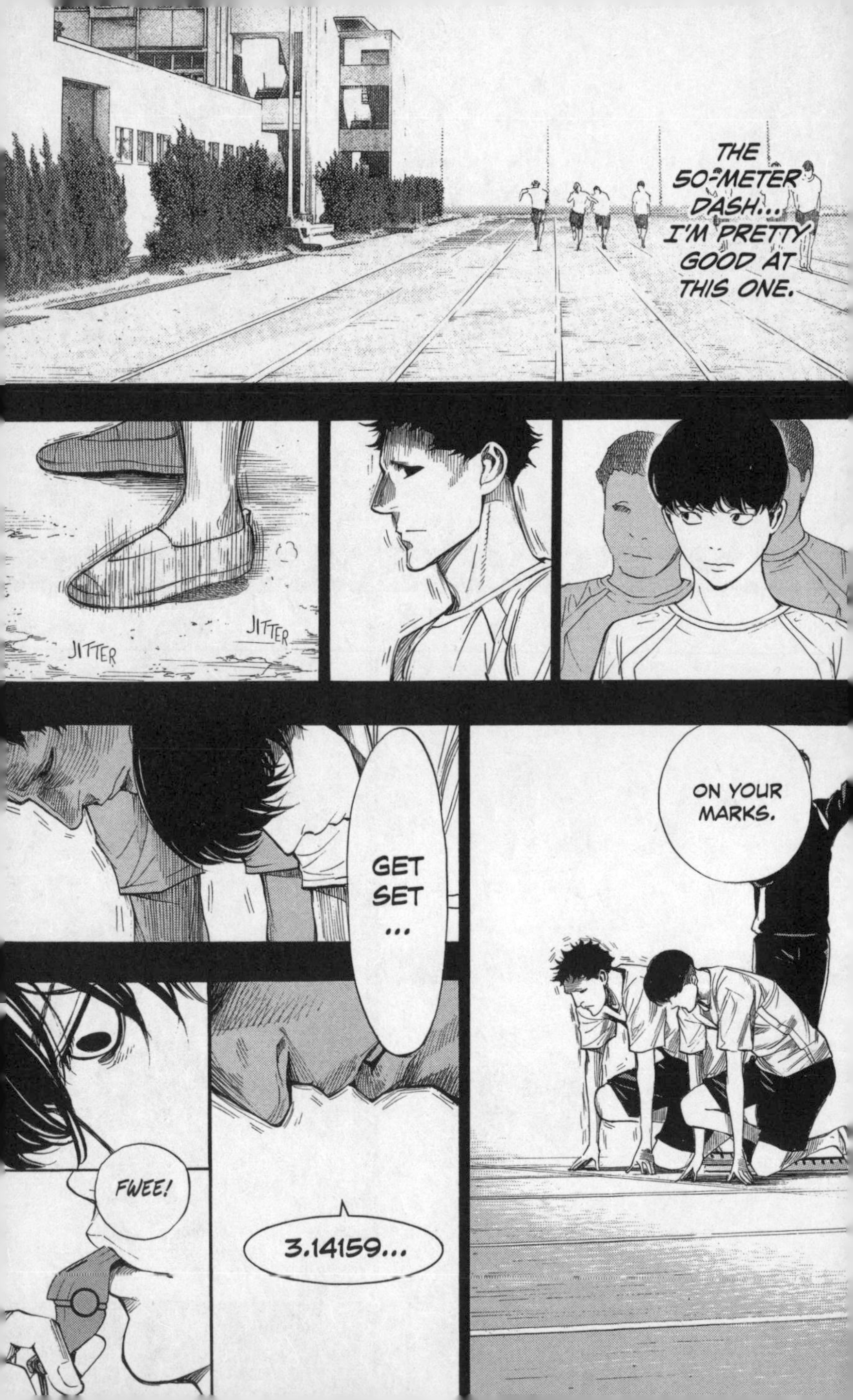
THE 50-METER DASH... I'M PRETTY GOOD AT THIS ONE.
JITTER
JITTER
ON YOUR MARKS.
GET SET ...
3.14159...
FWEE!

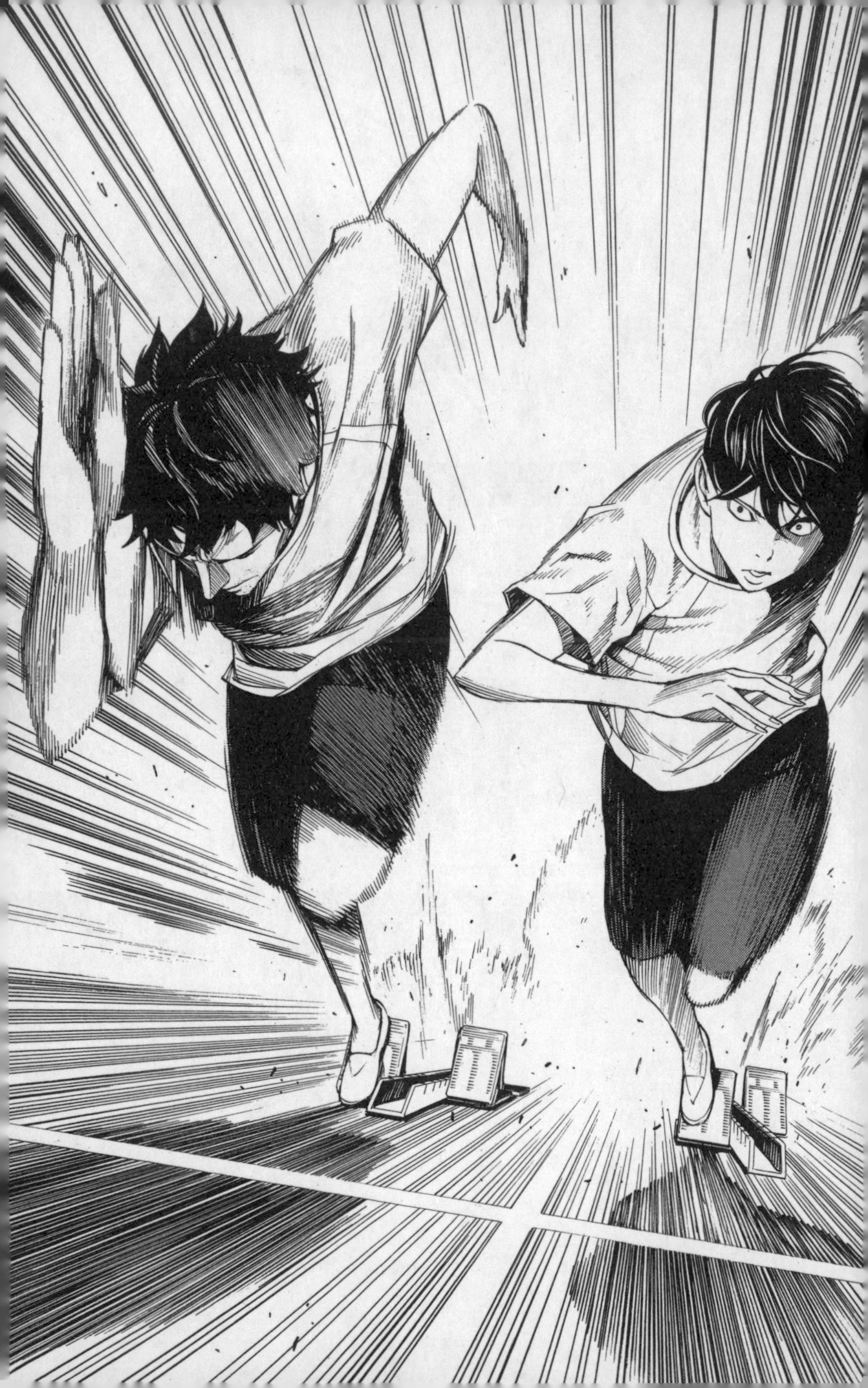

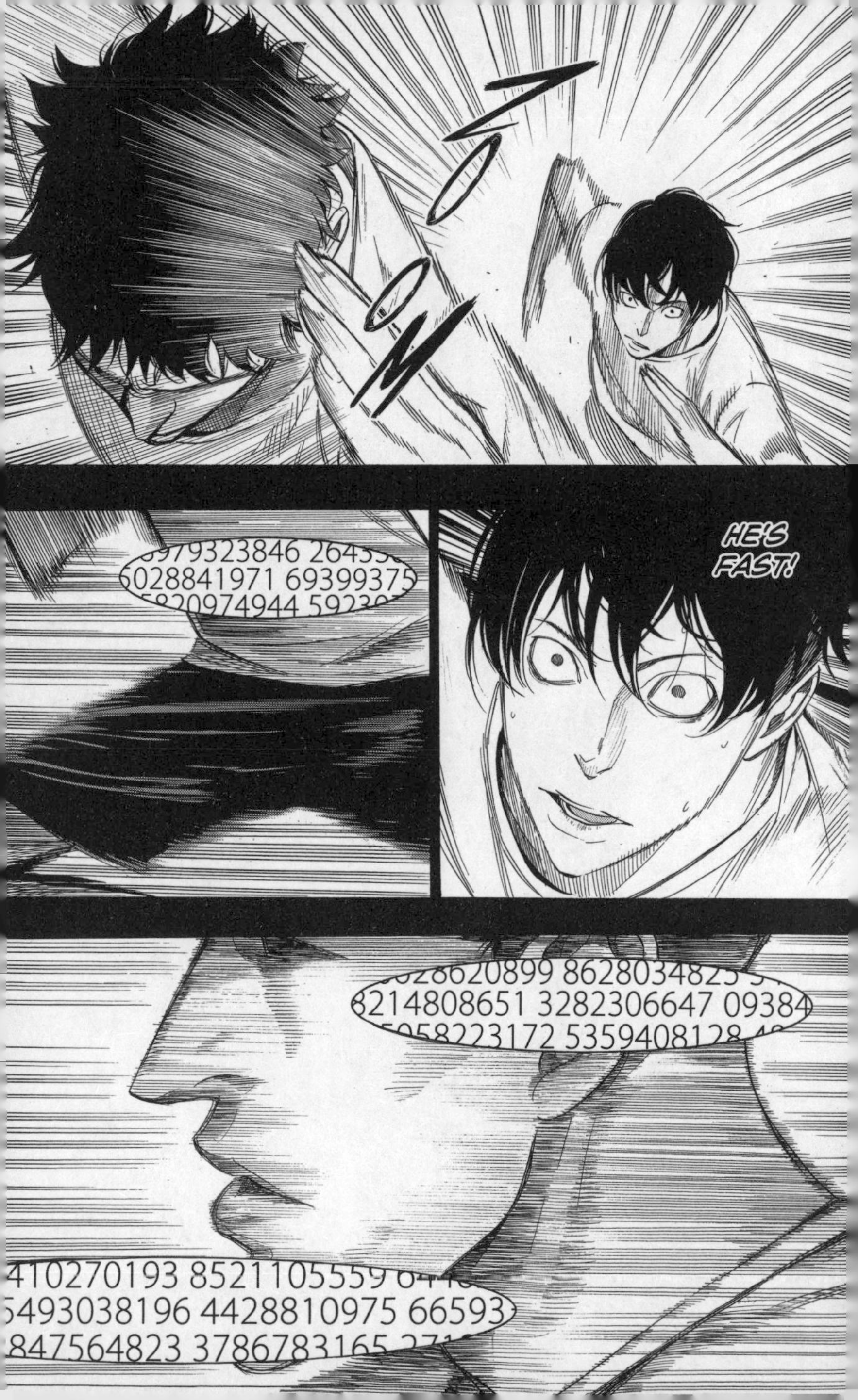
ZOOM
HE'S FAST!
979323846 2643
028841971 6939937
820974944 592
028620899 862803482
214808651 3282306647 09384
058223172 5359408128
410270193 8521105559
493038196 4428810975 66593
847564823 3786783165

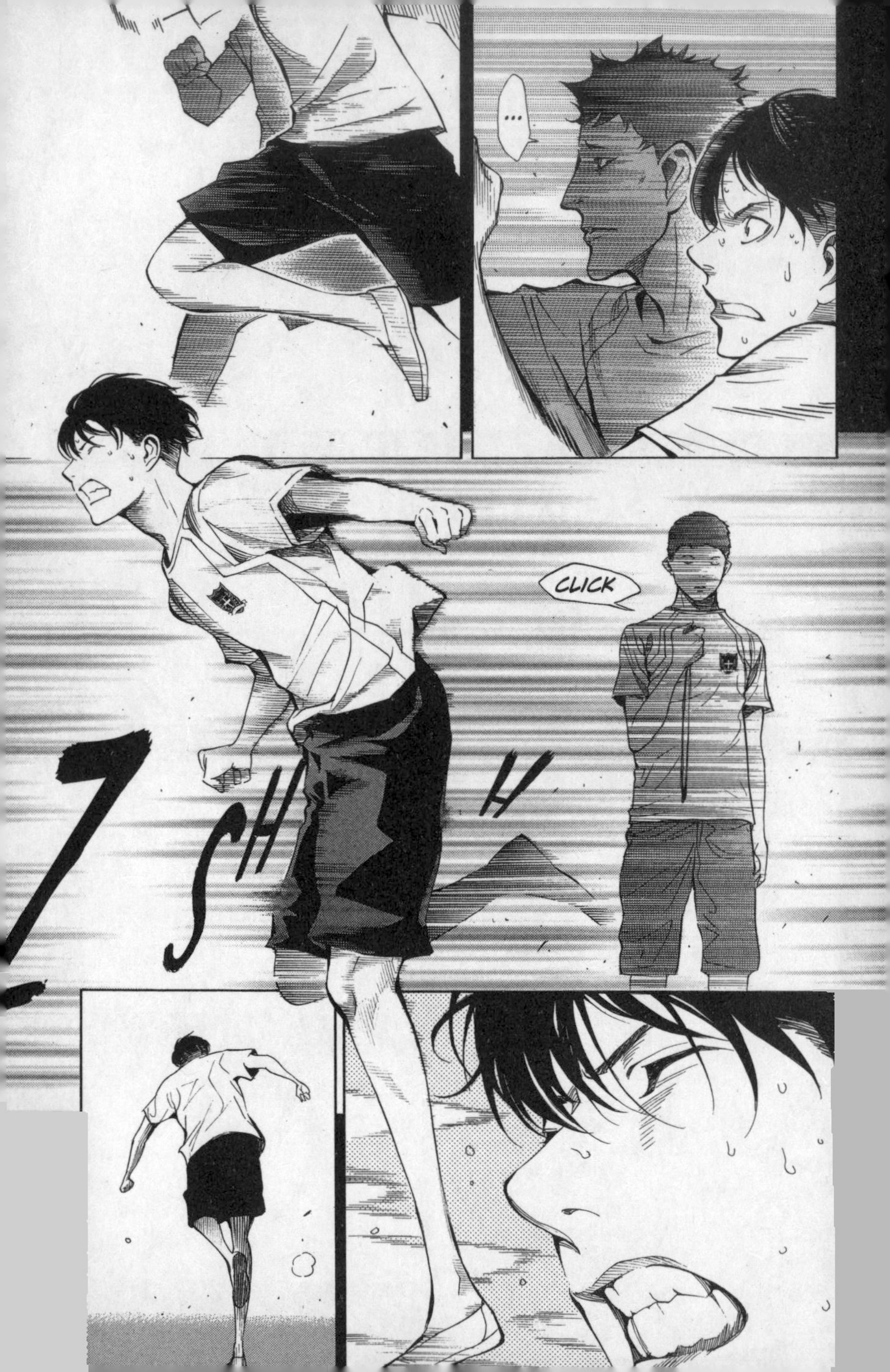
...
CLICK
SHH

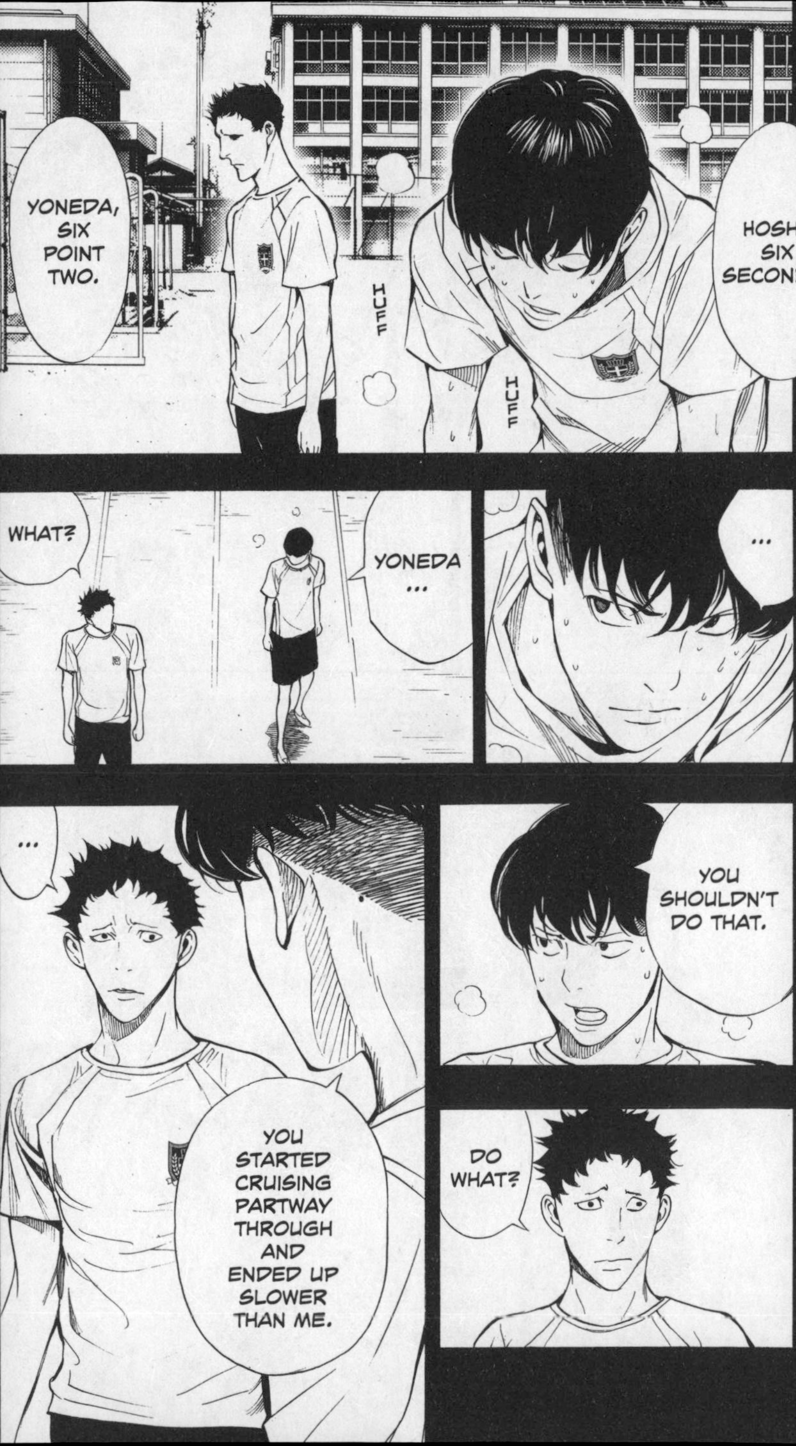
HOSHI, SIX SECONDS.
HUFF
HUFF
YONEDA, SIX POINT TWO.
...
YONEDA ...
WHAT?
YOU SHOULDN'T DO THAT.
DO WHAT?
...
YOU STARTED CRUISING PARTWAY THROUGH AND ENDED UP SLOWER THAN ME.

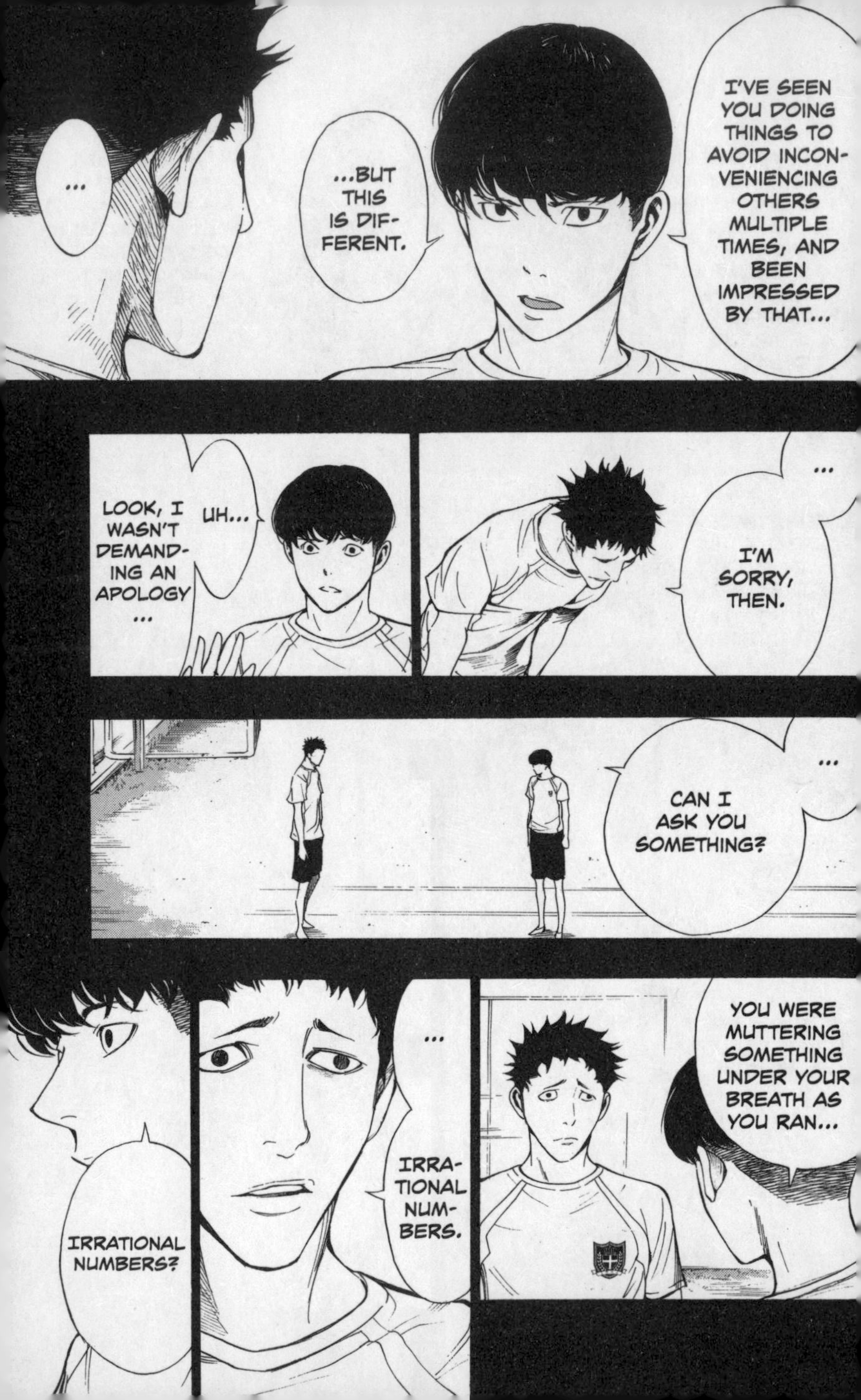
I'VE SEEN YOU DOING THINGS TO AVOID INCONVENIENCING OTHERS MULTIPLE TIMES, AND BEEN IMPRESSED BY THAT...
...BUT THIS IS DIFFERENT.
...
...
I'M SORRY, THEN.
UH...
LOOK, I WASN'T DEMANDING AN APOLOGY...
...
CAN I ASK YOU SOMETHING?
YOU WERE MUTTERING SOMETHING UNDER YOUR BREATH AS YOU RAN...
...
IRRATIONAL NUMBERS.
IRRATIONAL NUMBERS?

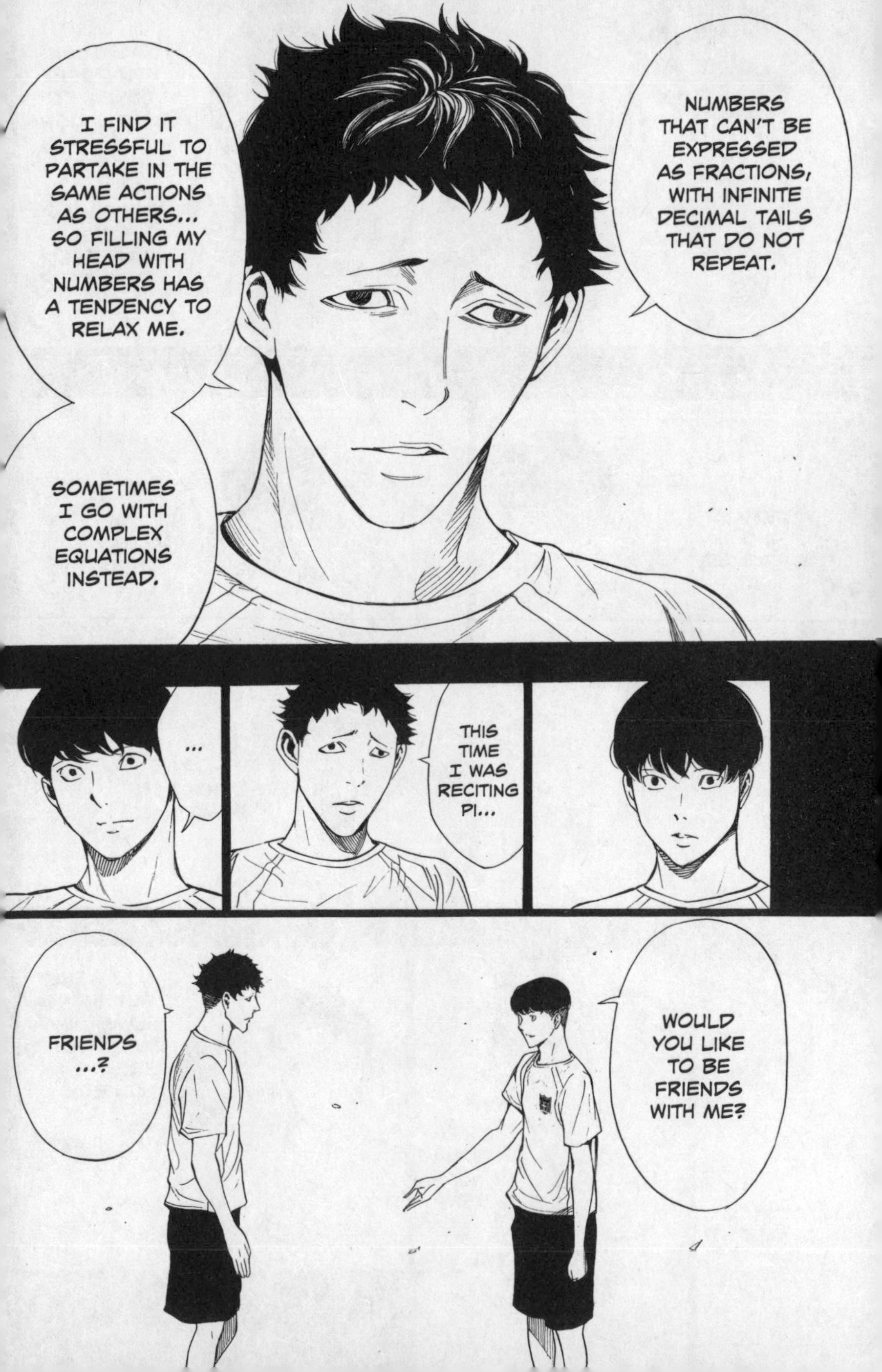
NUMBERS THAT CAN'T BE EXPRESSED AS FRACTIONS, WITH INFINITE DECIMAL TAILS THAT DO NOT REPEAT.
I FIND IT STRESSFUL TO PARTAKE IN THE SAME ACTIONS AS OTHERS... SO FILLING MY HEAD WITH NUMBERS HAS A TENDENCY TO RELAX ME.
SOMETIMES I GO WITH COMPLEX EQUATIONS INSTEAD.
THIS TIME I WAS RECITING PI...
...
WOULD YOU LIKE TO BE FRIENDS WITH ME?
FRIENDS ...?

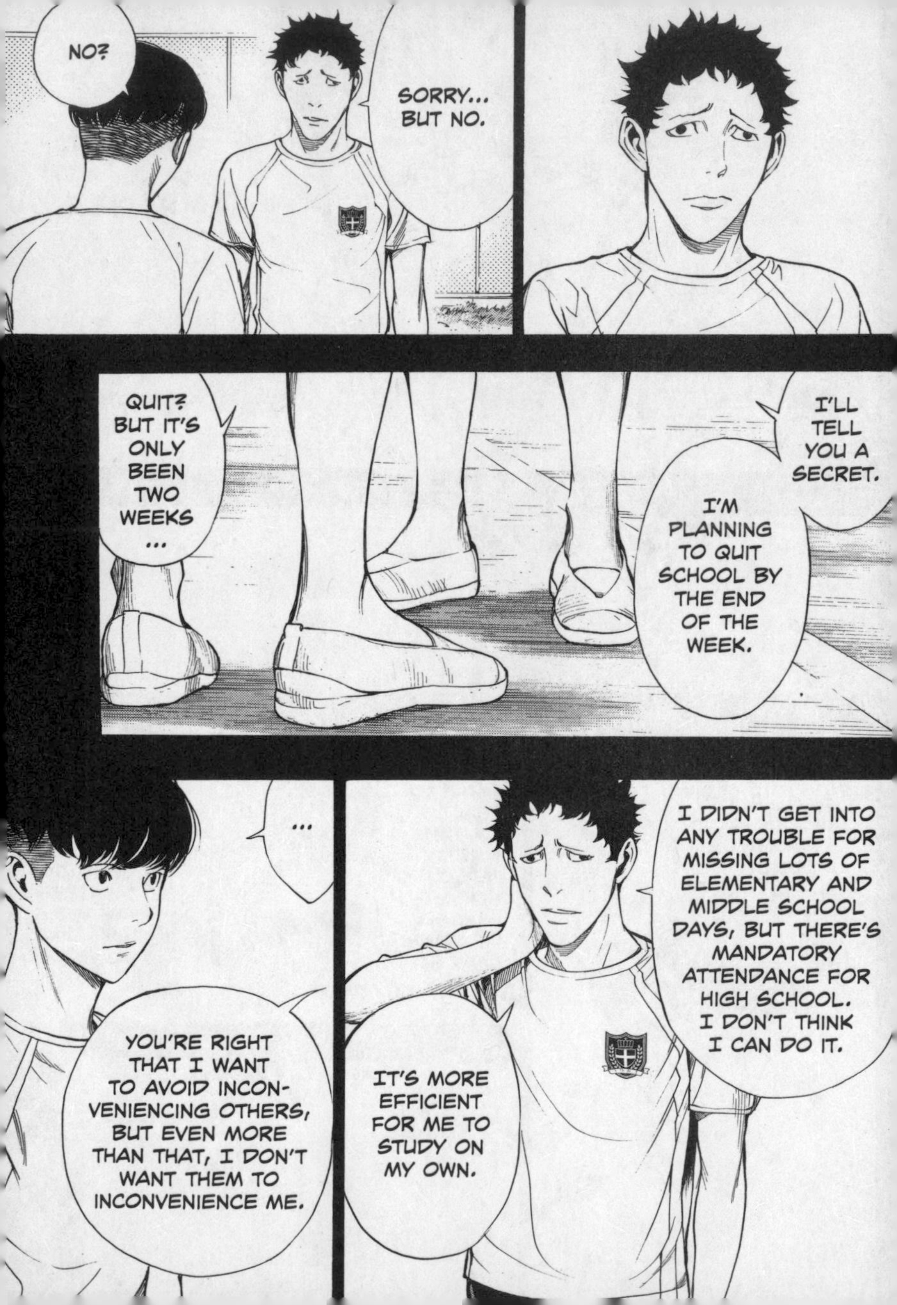
SORRY... BUT NO.
NO?
I'LL TELL YOU A SECRET.
I'M PLANNING TO QUIT SCHOOL BY THE END OF THE WEEK.
QUIT? BUT IT'S ONLY BEEN TWO WEEKS ...
I DIDN'T GET INTO ANY TROUBLE FOR MISSING LOTS OF ELEMENTARY AND MIDDLE SCHOOL DAYS, BUT THERE'S MANDATORY ATTENDANCE FOR HIGH SCHOOL. I DON'T THINK I CAN DO IT.
...
YOU'RE RIGHT THAT I WANT TO AVOID INCON-VENIENCING OTHERS, BUT EVEN MORE THAN THAT, I DON'T WANT THEM TO INCONVENIENCE ME.
IT'S MORE EFFICIENT FOR ME TO STUDY ON MY OWN.

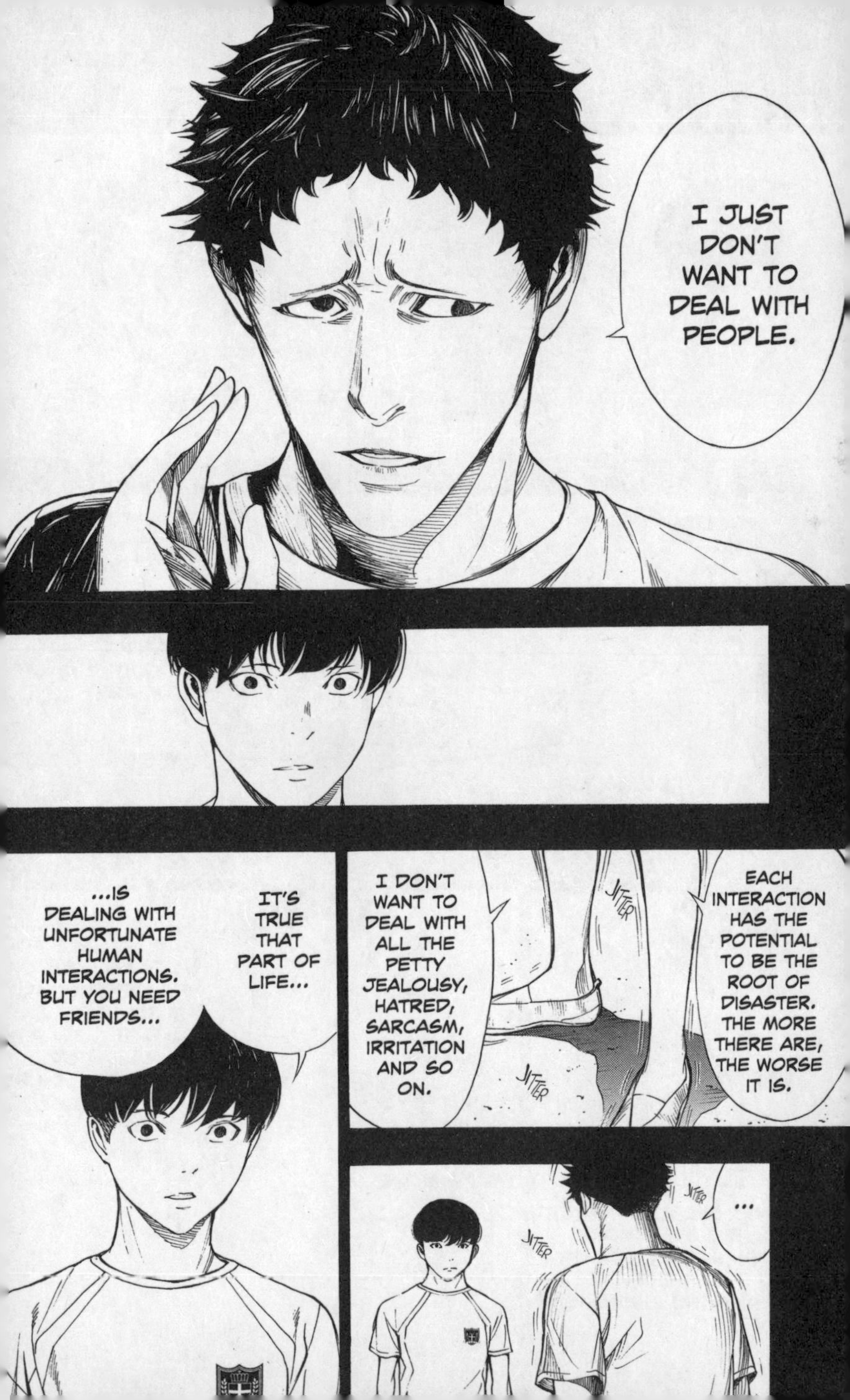
I JUST DON'T WANT TO DEAL WITH PEOPLE.
EACH INTERACTION HAS THE POTENTIAL TO BE THE ROOT OF DISASTER. THE MORE THERE ARE, THE WORSE IT IS.
JITTER
I DON'T WANT TO DEAL WITH ALL THE PETTY JEALOUSY, HATRED, SARCASM, IRRITATION AND SO ON.
JITTER
...
JITTER
JITTER
IT'S TRUE THAT PART OF LIFE...
...IS DEALING WITH UNFORTUNATE HUMAN INTERACTIONS. BUT YOU NEED FRIENDS...

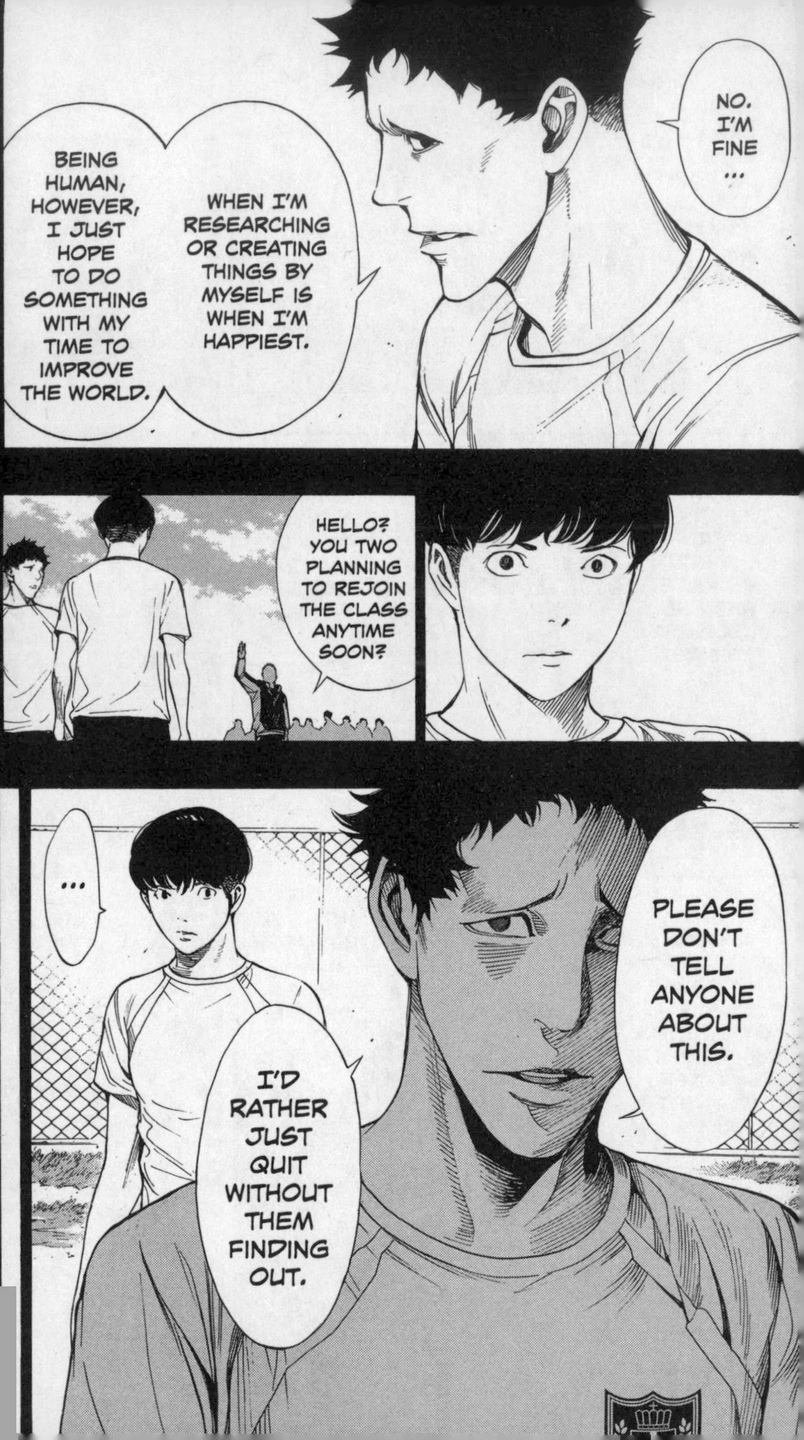
NO. I'M FINE ...
WHEN I'M RESEARCHING OR CREATING THINGS BY MYSELF IS WHEN I'M HAPPIEST.
BEING HUMAN, HOWEVER, I JUST HOPE TO DO SOMETHING WITH MY TIME TO IMPROVE THE WORLD.
HELLO? YOU TWO PLANNING TO REJOIN THE CLASS ANYTIME SOON?
PLEASE DON'T TELL ANYONE ABOUT THIS.
I'D RATHER JUST QUIT WITHOUT THEM FINDING OUT.
...

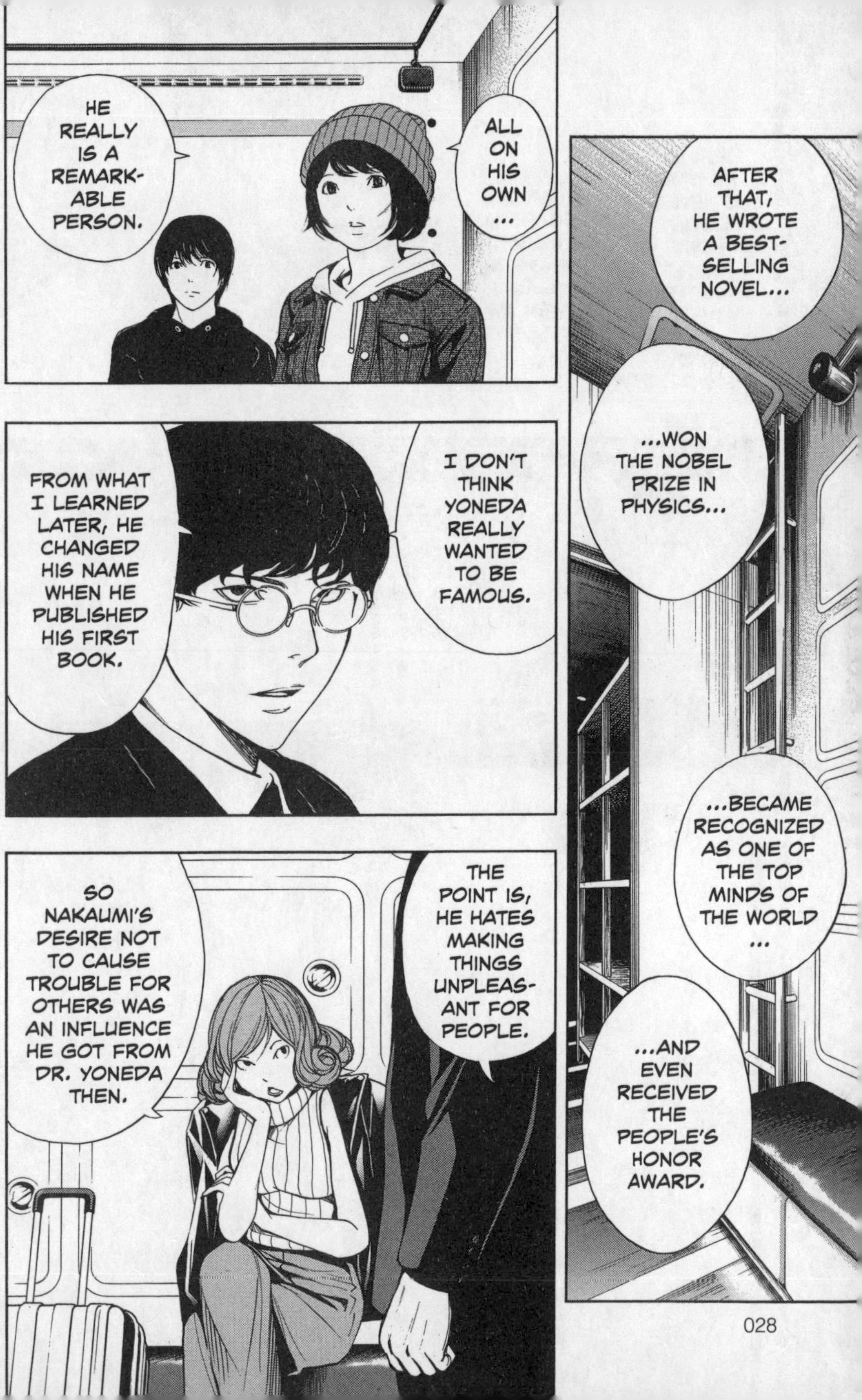
AFTER THAT, HE WROTE A BEST-SELLING NOVEL...
...WON THE NOBEL PRIZE IN PHYSICS...
...BECAME RECOGNIZED AS ONE OF THE TOP MINDS OF THE WORLD ...
...AND EVEN RECEIVED THE PEOPLE'S HONOR AWARD.
ALL ON HIS OWN ...
HE REALLY IS A REMARKABLE PERSON.
I DON'T THINK YONEDA REALLY WANTED TO BE FAMOUS.
FROM WHAT I LEARNED LATER, HE CHANGED HIS NAME WHEN HE PUBLISHED HIS FIRST BOOK.
THE POINT IS, HE HATES MAKING THINGS UNPLEASANT FOR PEOPLE.
SO NAKAUMI'S DESIRE NOT TO CAUSE TROUBLE FOR OTHERS WAS AN INFLUENCE HE GOT FROM DR. YONEDA THEN.

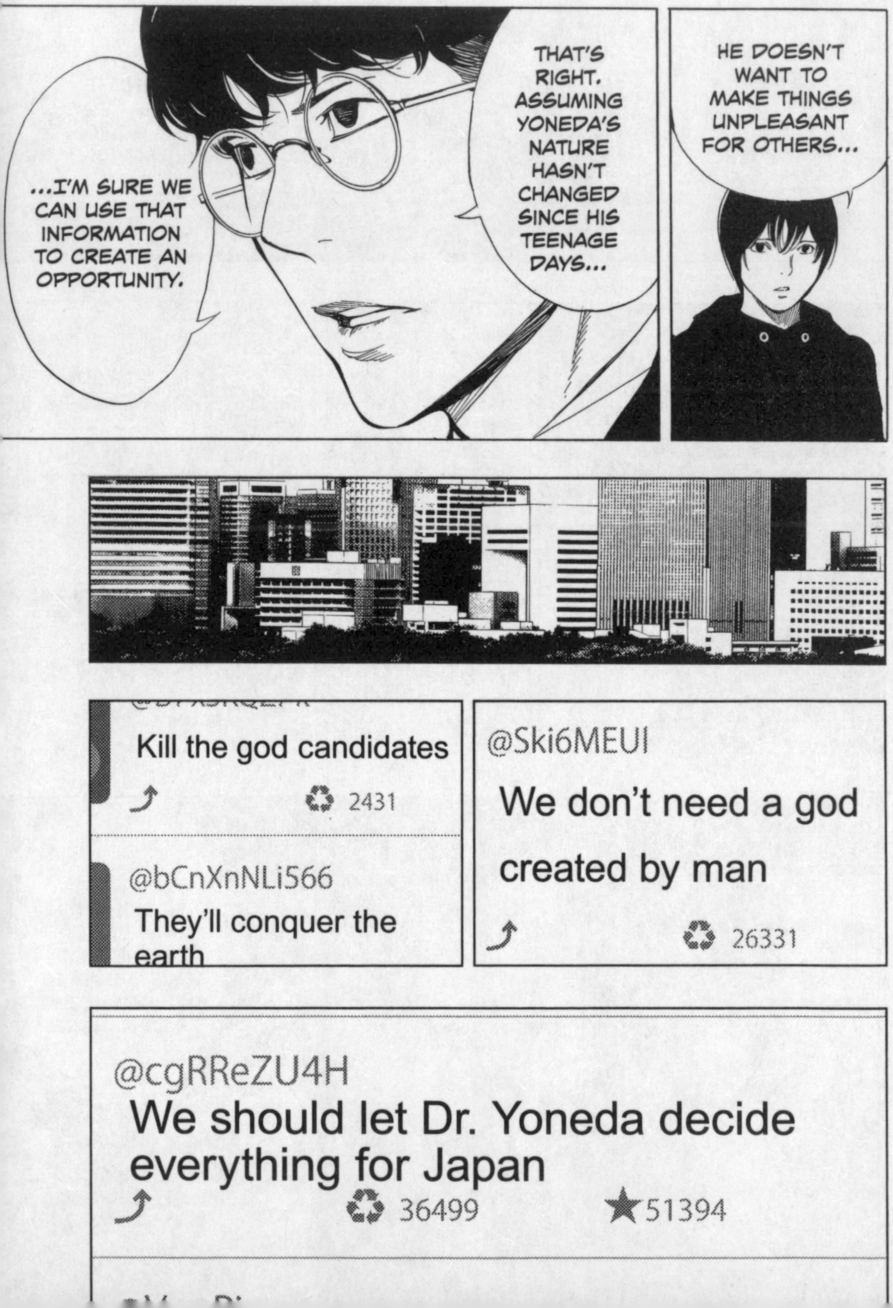
HE DOESN'T WANT TO MAKE THINGS UNPLEASANT FOR OTHERS...
THAT'S RIGHT. ASSUMING YONEDA'S NATURE HASN'T CHANGED SINCE HIS TEENAGE DAYS...
...I'M SURE WE CAN USE THAT INFORMATION TO CREATE AN OPPORTUNITY.
@Ski6MEUI
We don't need a god created by man
26331
Kill the god candidates
2431
@bCnXnNLi566
They'll conquer the earth
@cgRReZU4H
We should let Dr. Yoneda decide everything for Japan
36499
51394

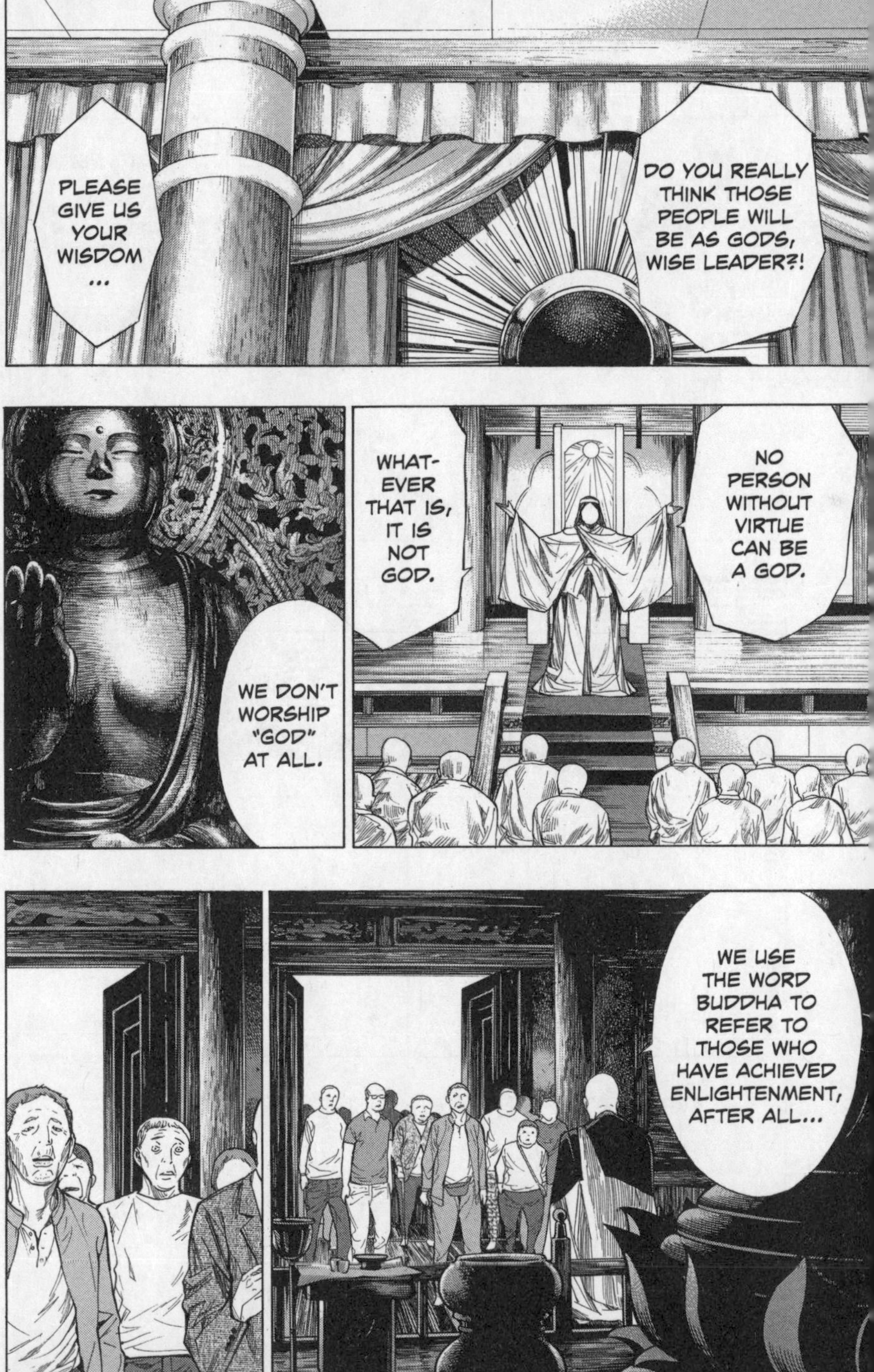
DO YOU REALLY THINK THOSE PEOPLE WILL BE AS GODS, WISE LEADER?!
PLEASE GIVE US YOUR WISDOM ...
NO PERSON WITHOUT VIRTUE CAN BE A GOD.
WHAT-EVER THAT IS, IT IS NOT GOD.
WE DON'T WORSHIP "GOD" AT ALL.
WE USE THE WORD BUDDHA TO REFER TO THOSE WHO HAVE ACHIEVED ENLIGHTENMENT, AFTER ALL...

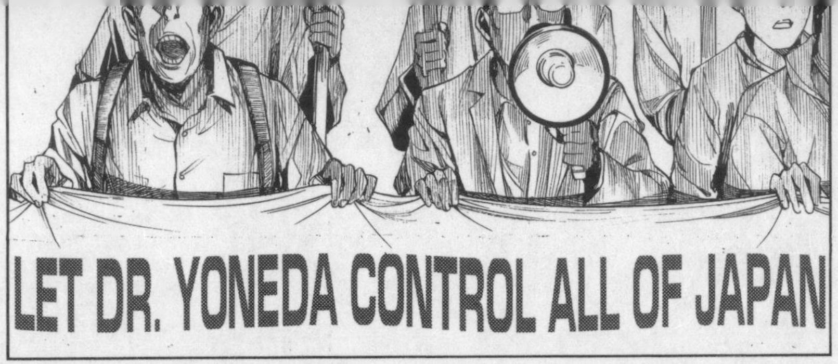
LET DR. YONEDA CONTROL ALL OF JAPAN

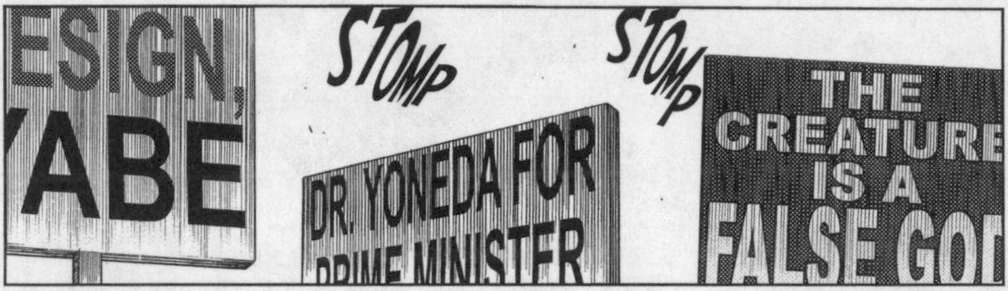
THE CREATURE IS A FALSE GO
STOMP
STOMP
DR. YONEDA FOR PRIME MINISTER
ESIGN, YABE

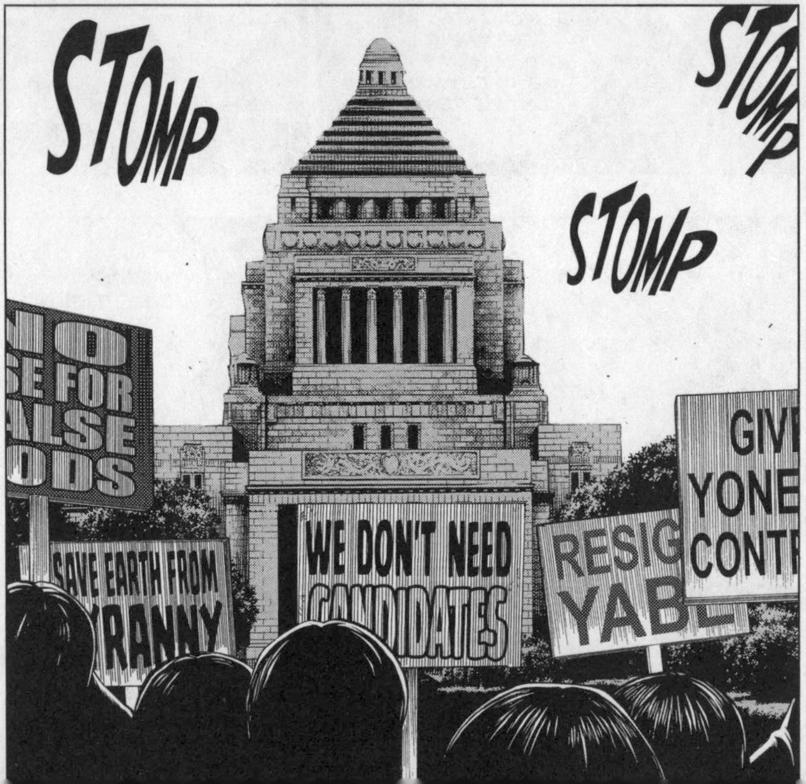
STOMP
STOMP
STOMP
GIV YONE CONTR
RESIG YAB
WE DON'T NEED CANDIDATES
SAVE EARTH FROM YRANNY
N O SE FOR ALSE ODS

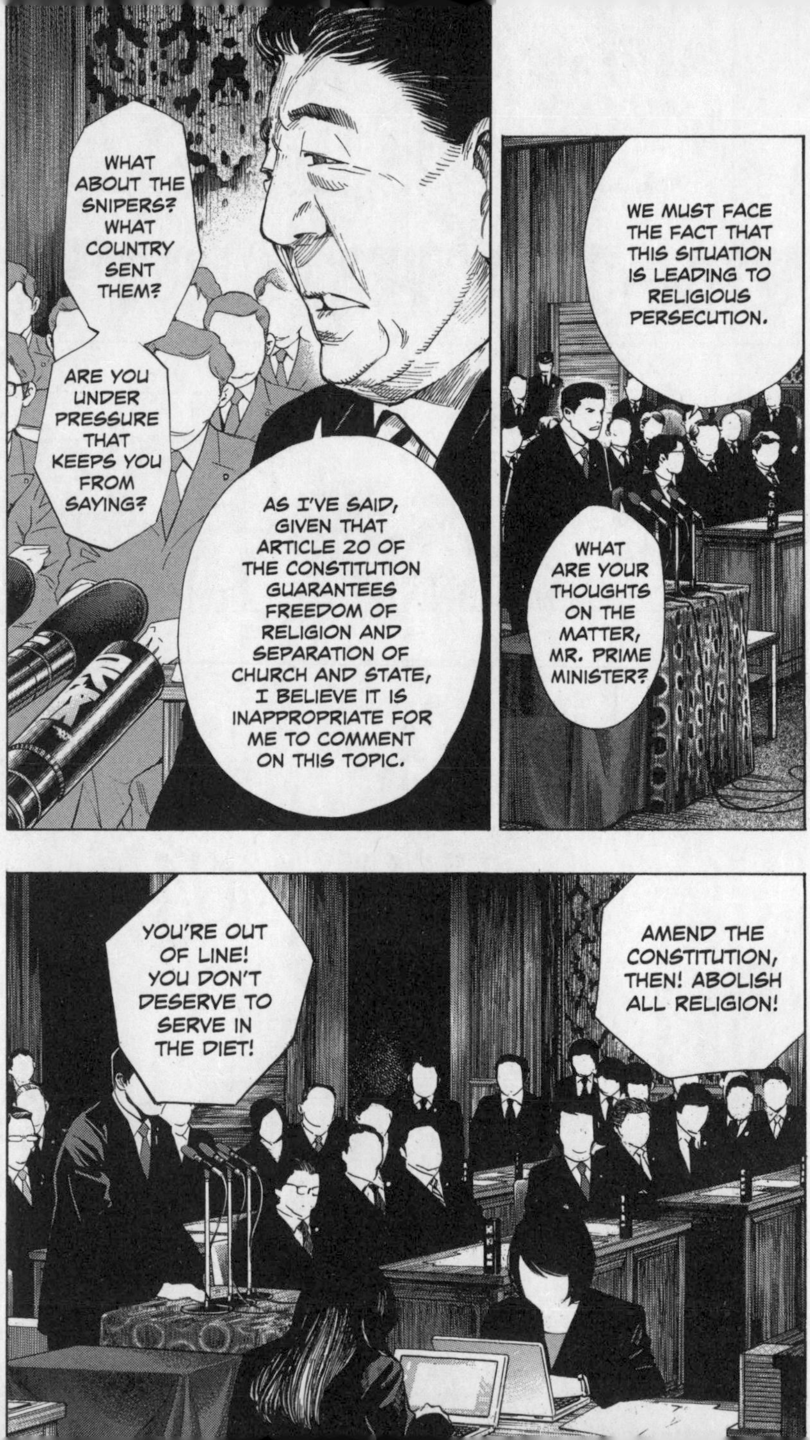
WE MUST FACE THE FACT THAT THIS SITUATION IS LEADING TO RELIGIOUS PERSECUTION.
WHAT ARE YOUR THOUGHTS ON THE MATTER, MR. PRIME MINISTER?
WHAT ABOUT THE SNIPERS? WHAT COUNTRY SENT THEM?
ARE YOU UNDER PRESSURE THAT KEEPS YOU FROM SAYING?
AS I'VE SAID, GIVEN THAT ARTICLE 20 OF THE CONSTITUTION GUARANTEES FREEDOM OF RELIGION AND SEPARATION OF CHURCH AND STATE, I BELIEVE IT IS INAPPROPRIATE FOR ME TO COMMENT ON THIS TOPIC.
AMEND THE CONSTITUTION, THEN! ABOLISH ALL RELIGION!
YOU'RE OUT OF LINE! YOU DON'T DESERVE TO SERVE IN THE DIET!

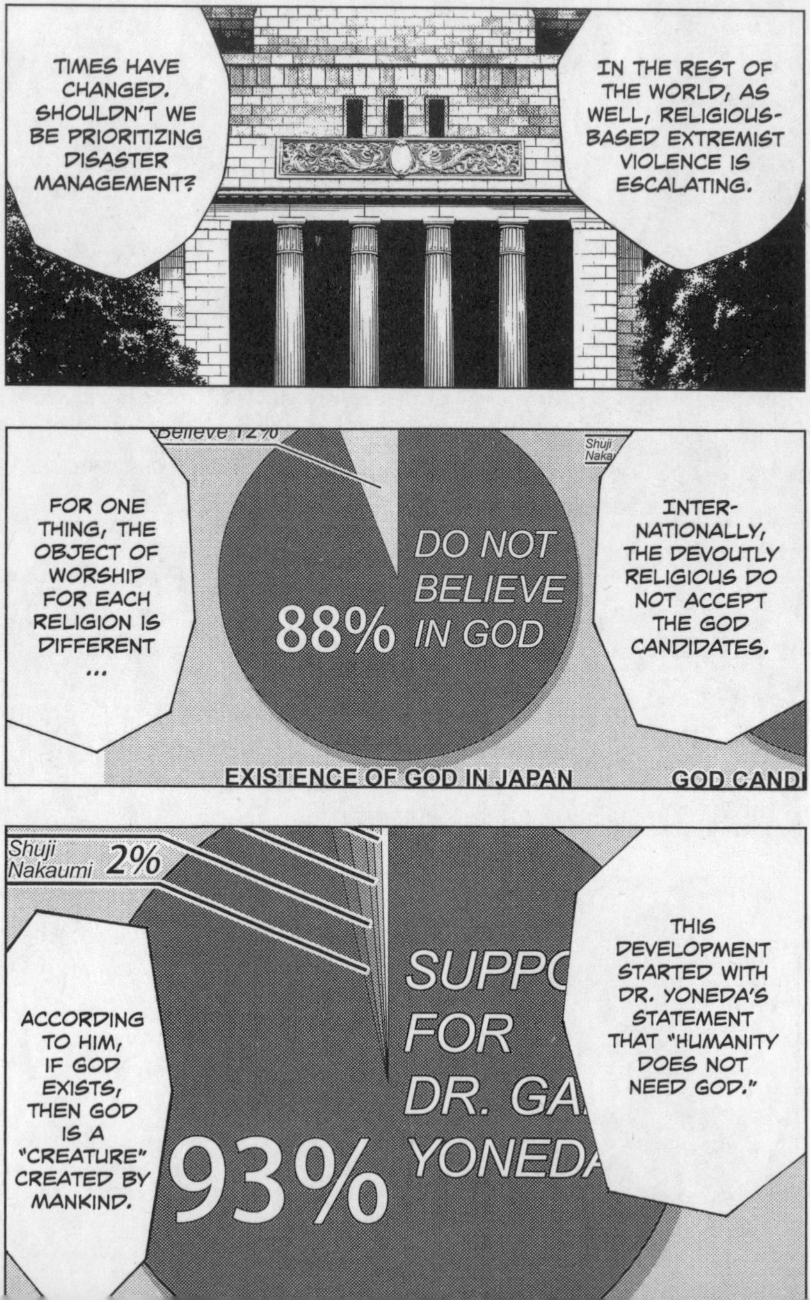
IN THE REST OF THE WORLD, AS WELL, RELIGIOUS-BASED EXTREMIST VIOLENCE IS ESCALATING.
TIMES HAVE CHANGED. SHOULDN'T WE BE PRIORITIZING DISASTER MANAGEMENT?
INTER-NATIONALLY, THE DEVOUTLY RELIGIOUS DO NOT ACCEPT THE GOD CANDIDATES.
FOR ONE THING, THE OBJECT OF WORSHIP FOR EACH RELIGION IS DIFFERENT ...
DO NOT BELIEVE IN GOD
88%
EXISTENCE OF GOD IN JAPAN
THIS DEVELOPMENT STARTED WITH DR. YONEDA'S STATEMENT THAT "HUMANITY DOES NOT NEED GOD."
ACCORDING TO HIM, IF GOD EXISTS, THEN GOD IS A "CREATURE" CREATED BY MANKIND.
Shuji Nakaumi 2%
93%

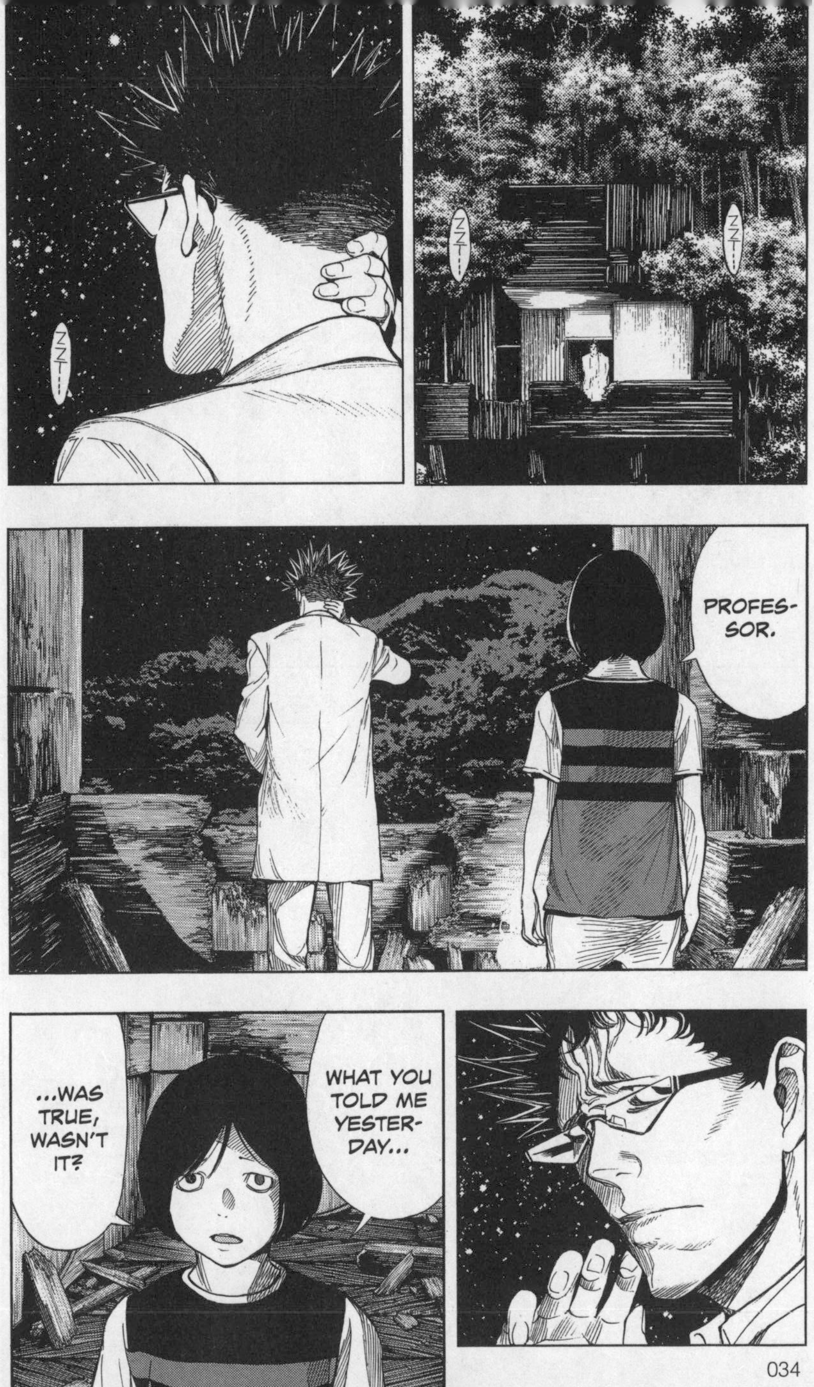
ZZT...
ZZT...
ZZT...
PROFESSOR.
WHAT YOU TOLD ME YESTERDAY...
...WAS TRUE, WASN'T IT?

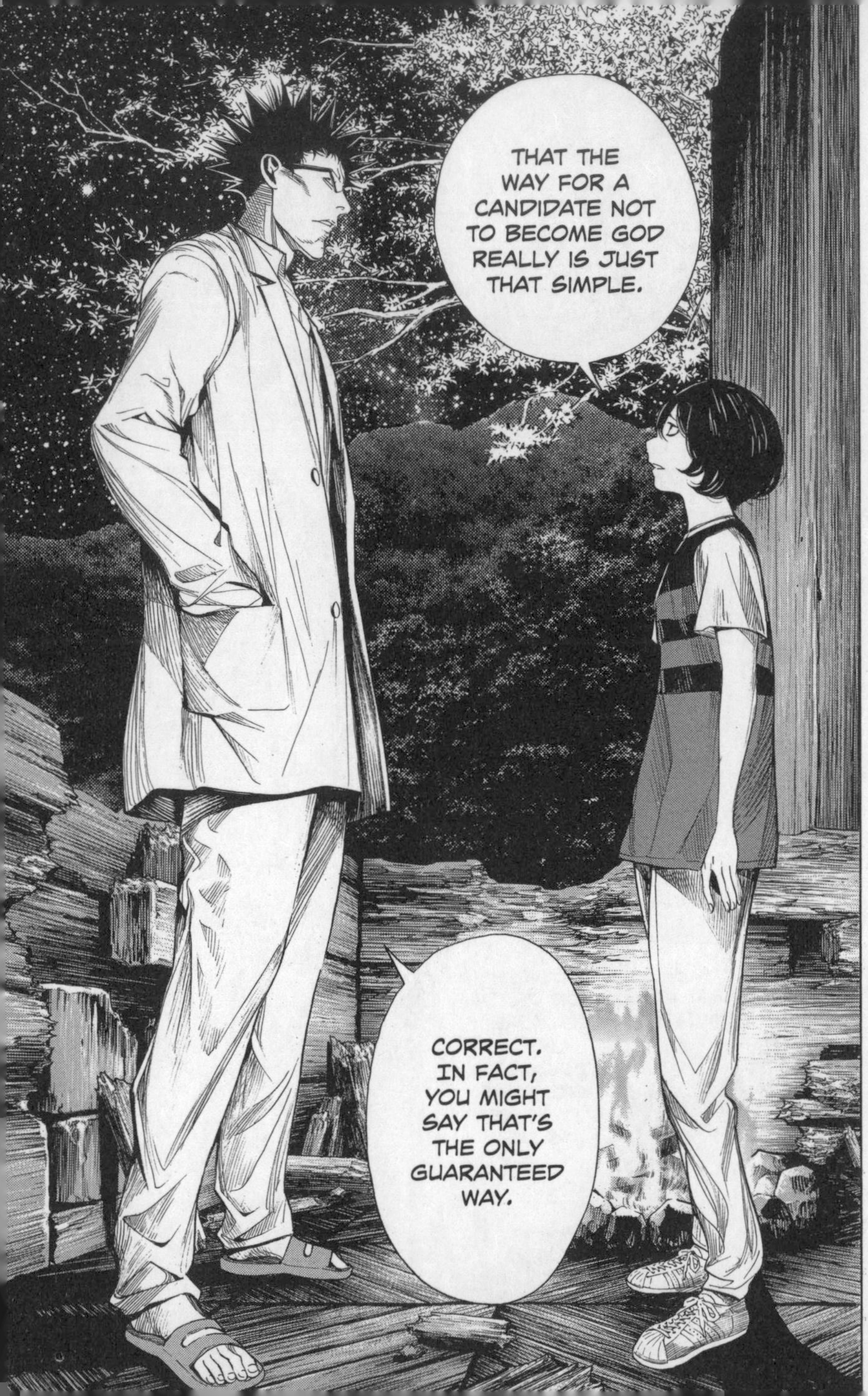
THAT THE WAY FOR A CANDIDATE NOT TO BECOME GOD REALLY IS JUST THAT SIMPLE.
CORRECT. IN FACT, YOU MIGHT SAY THAT'S THE ONLY GUARANTEED WAY.

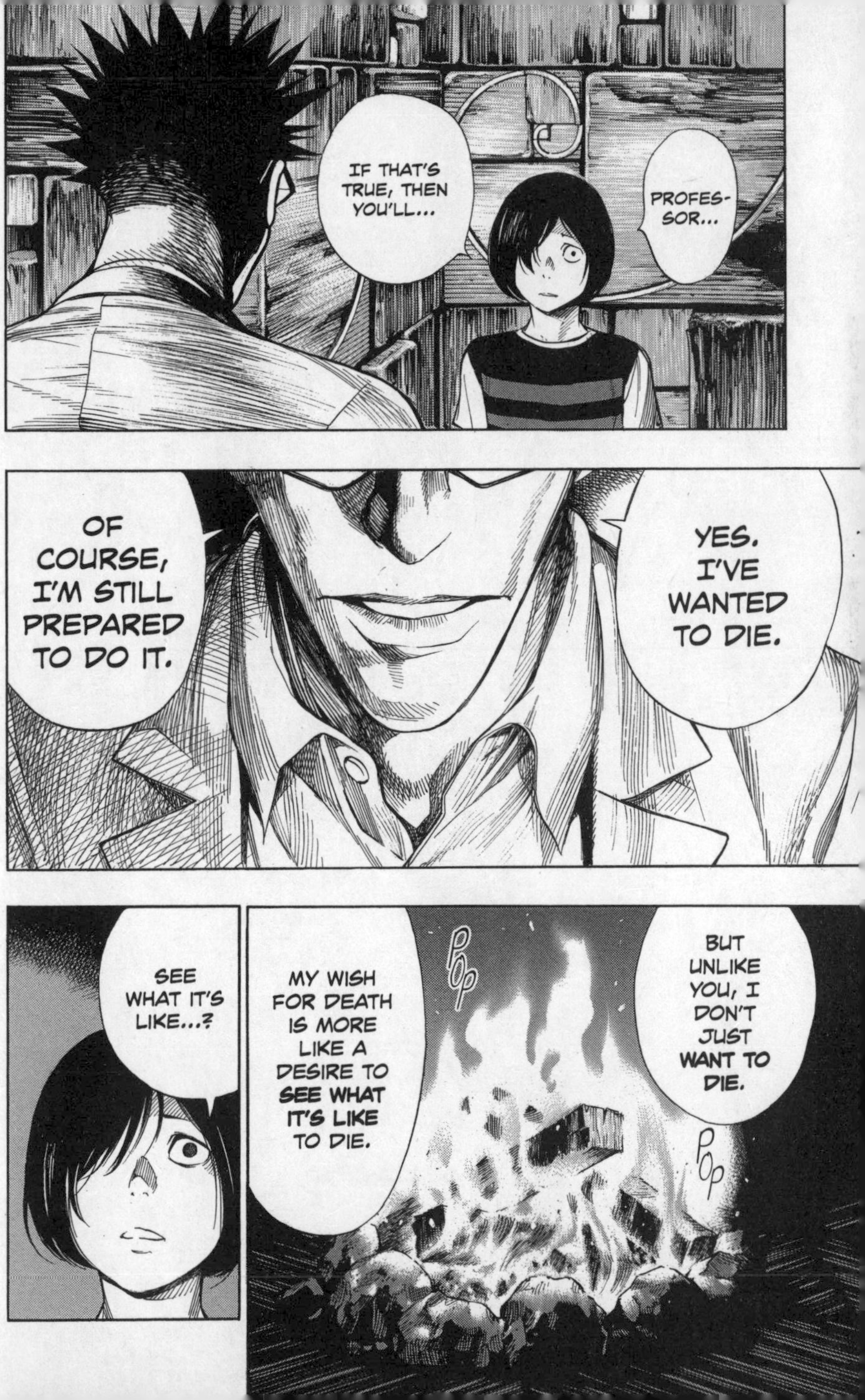
PROFES-SOR...
IF THAT'S TRUE, THEN YOU'LL...
YES. I'VE WANTED TO DIE.
OF COURSE, I'M STILL PREPARED TO DO IT.
BUT UNLIKE YOU, I DON'T JUST WANT TO DIE.
POP
POP
MY WISH FOR DEATH IS MORE LIKE A DESIRE TO SEE WHAT IT'S LIKE TO DIE.
SEE WHAT IT'S LIKE...?

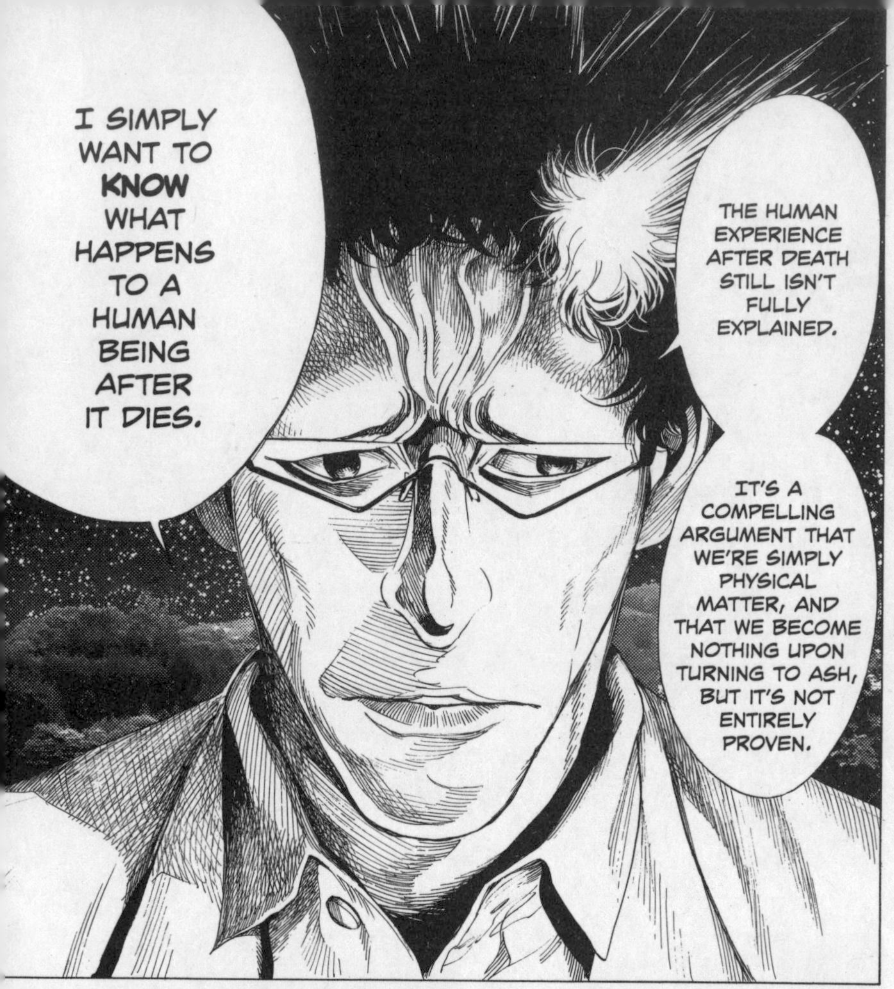
THE HUMAN EXPERIENCE AFTER DEATH STILL ISN'T FULLY EXPLAINED.
IT'S A COMPELLING ARGUMENT THAT WE'RE SIMPLY PHYSICAL MATTER, AND THAT WE BECOME NOTHING UPON TURNING TO ASH, BUT IT'S NOT ENTIRELY PROVEN.
I SIMPLY WANT TO **KNOW** WHAT HAPPENS TO A HUMAN BEING AFTER IT DIES.

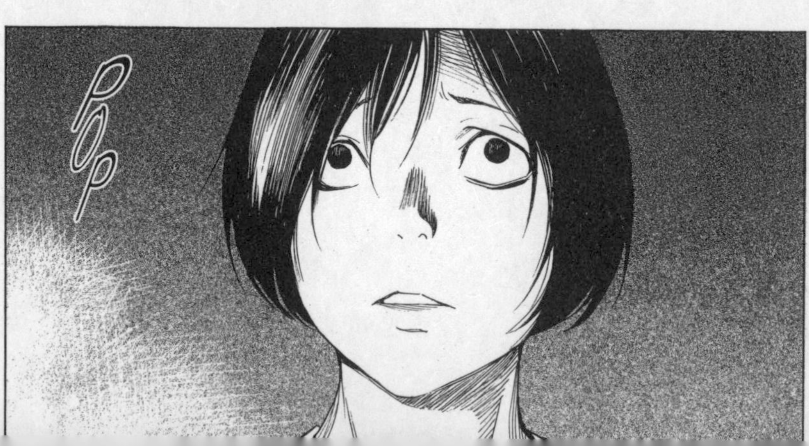
POP

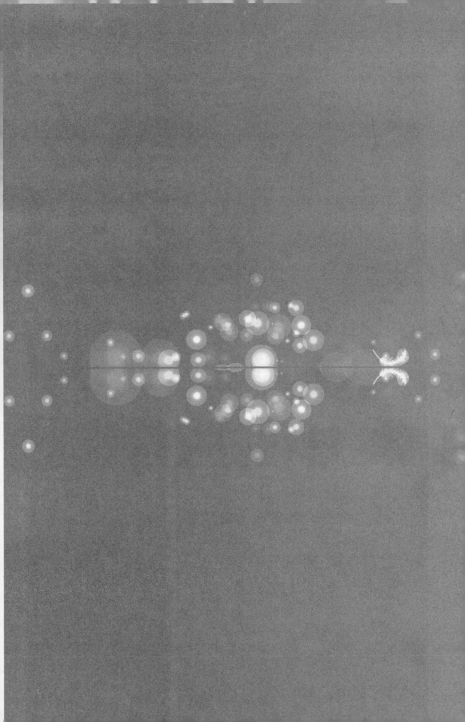

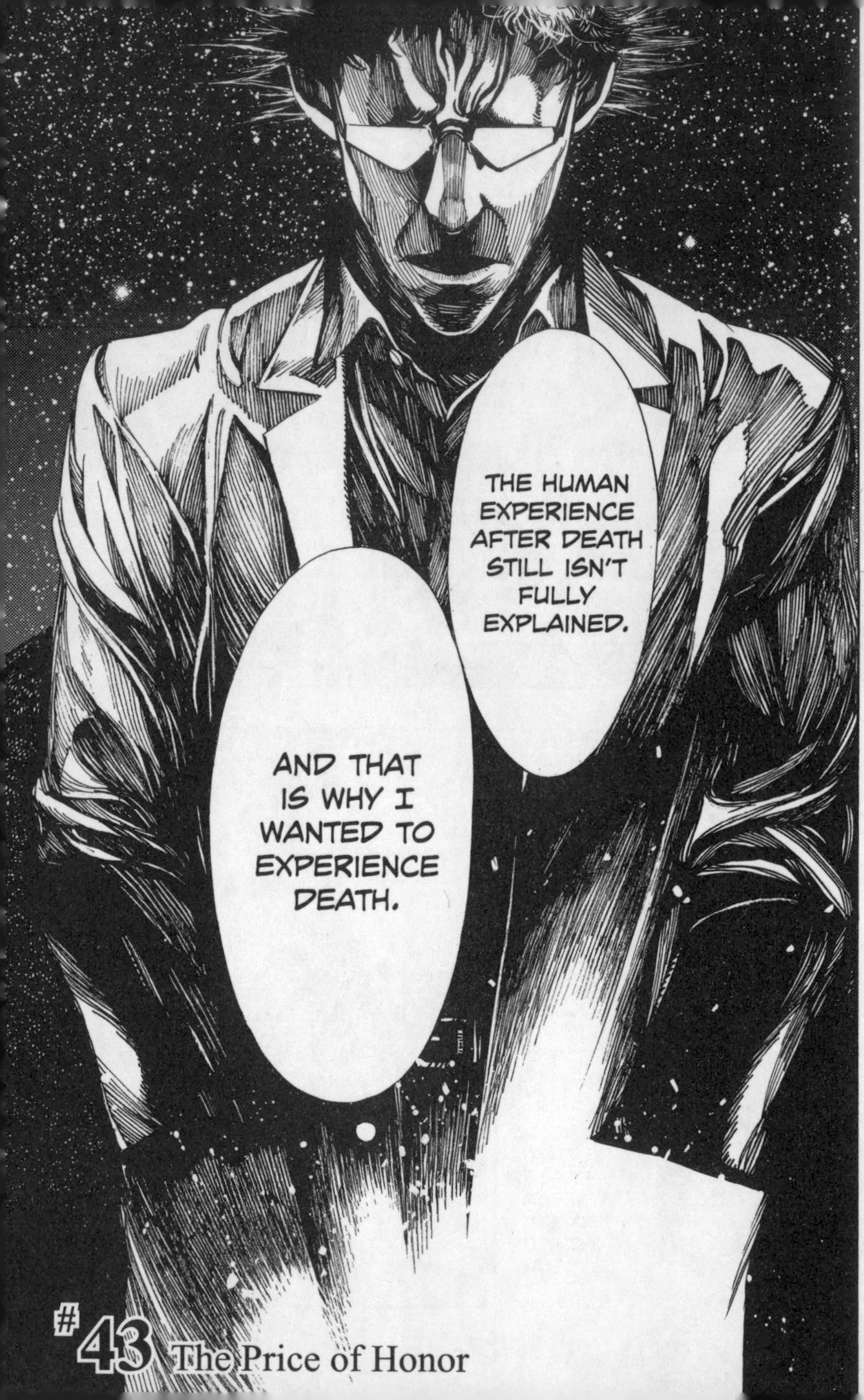
THE HUMAN EXPERIENCE AFTER DEATH STILL ISN'T FULLY EXPLAINED.
AND THAT IS WHY I WANTED TO EXPERIENCE DEATH.

#43 The Price of Honor

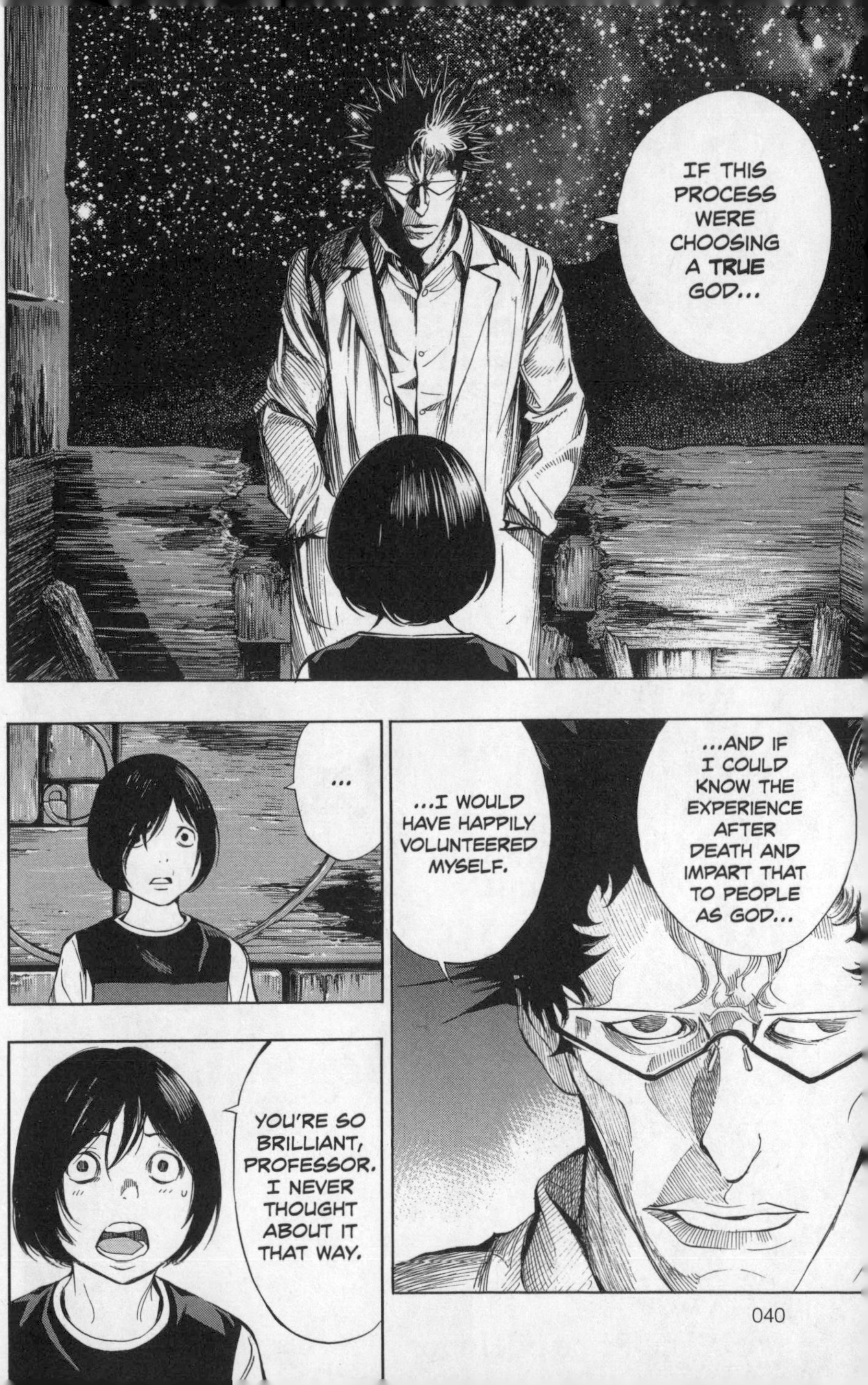
IF THIS PROCESS WERE CHOOSING A **TRUE** GOD...
...AND IF I COULD KNOW THE EXPERIENCE AFTER DEATH AND IMPART THAT TO PEOPLE AS GOD...
...I WOULD HAVE HAPPILY VOLUNTEERED MYSELF.
...
YOU'RE SO BRILLIANT, PROFESSOR. I NEVER THOUGHT ABOUT IT THAT WAY.

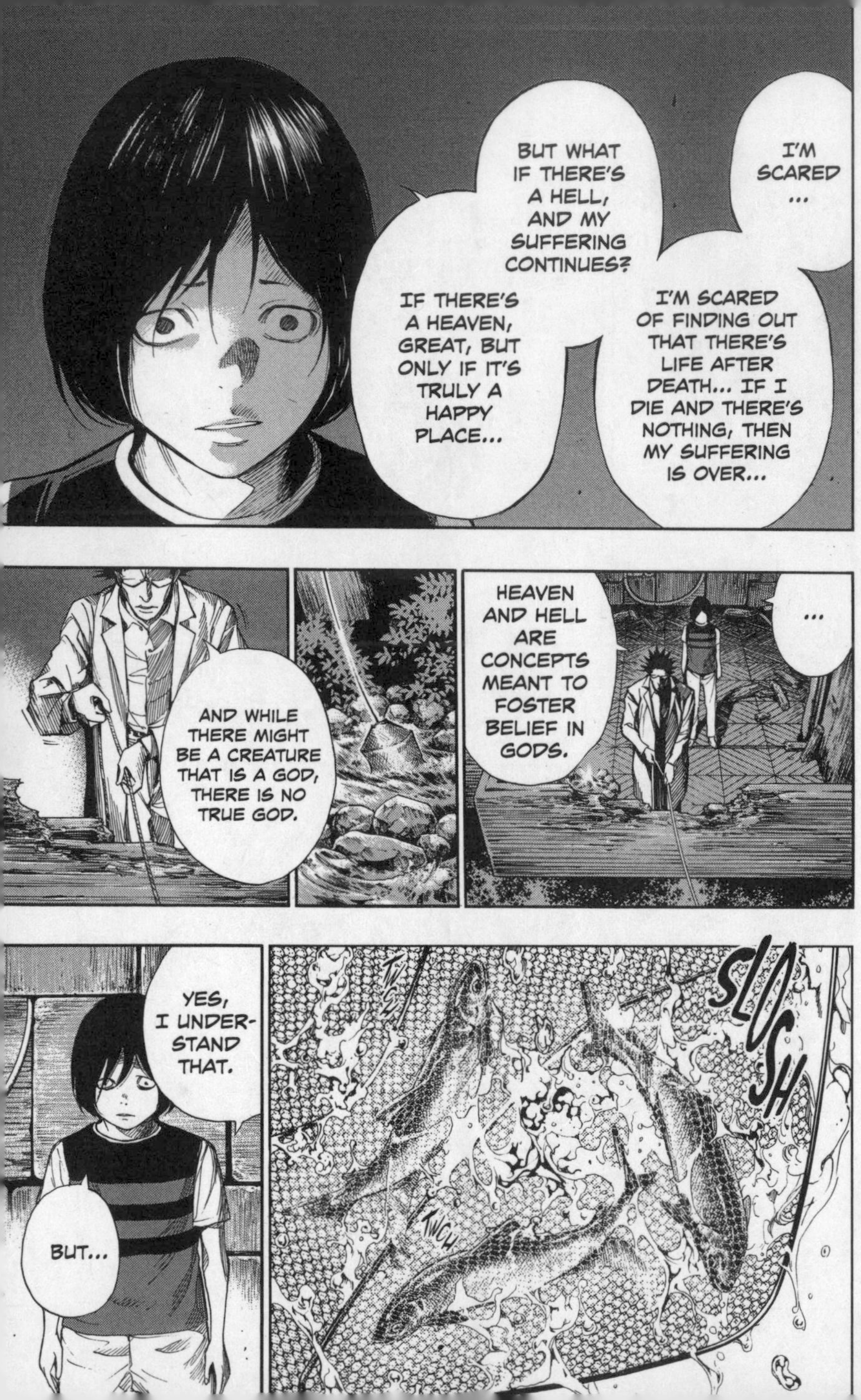
I'M SCARED ...
I'M SCARED OF FINDING OUT THAT THERE'S LIFE AFTER DEATH... IF I DIE AND THERE'S NOTHING, THEN MY SUFFERING IS OVER...
BUT WHAT IF THERE'S A HELL, AND MY SUFFERING CONTINUES?
IF THERE'S A HEAVEN, GREAT, BUT ONLY IF IT'S TRULY A HAPPY PLACE...
...
HEAVEN AND HELL ARE CONCEPTS MEANT TO FOSTER BELIEF IN GODS.
AND WHILE THERE MIGHT BE A CREATURE THAT IS A GOD, THERE IS NO TRUE GOD.
SLOSH
YES, I UNDER-STAND THAT.
BUT...

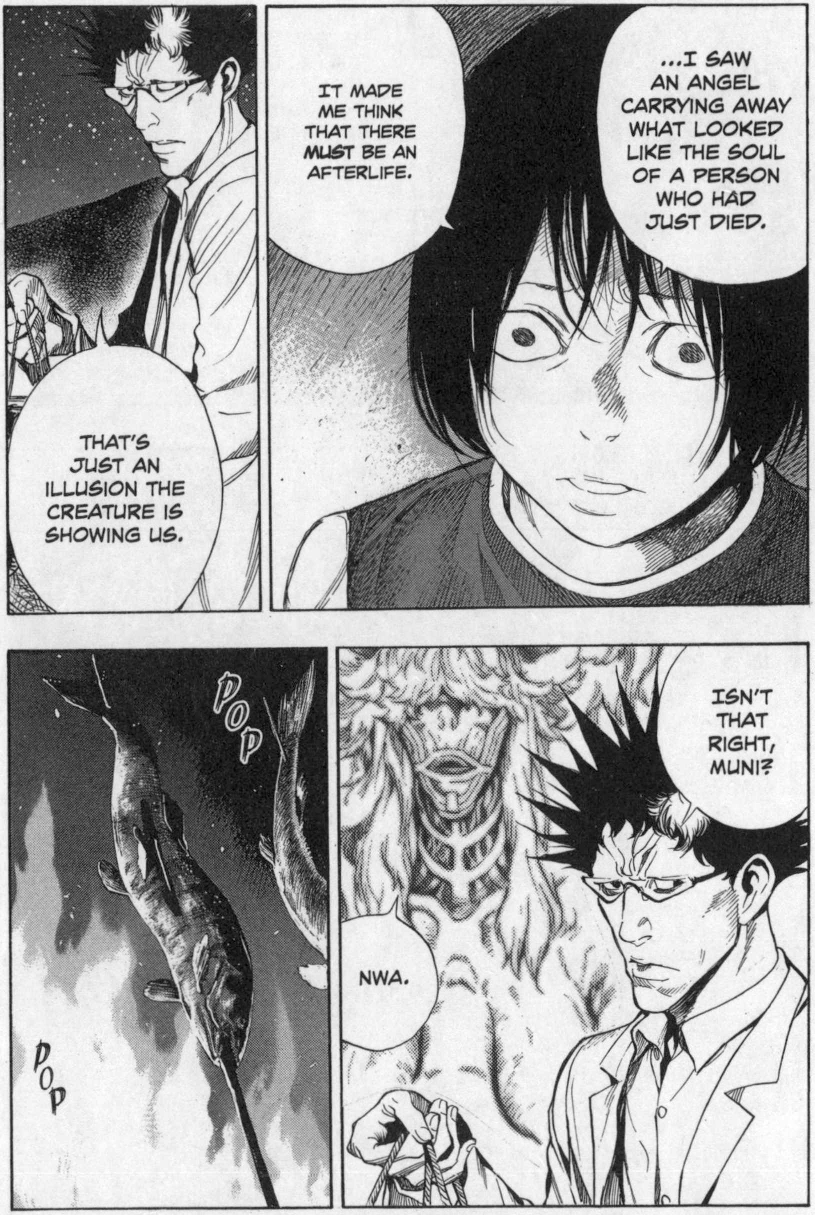
...I SAW AN ANGEL CARRYING AWAY WHAT LOOKED LIKE THE SOUL OF A PERSON WHO HAD JUST DIED.
IT MADE ME THINK THAT THERE MUST BE AN AFTERLIFE.
THAT'S JUST AN ILLUSION THE CREATURE IS SHOWING US.
ISN'T THAT RIGHT, MUNI?
NWA.
POP
POP

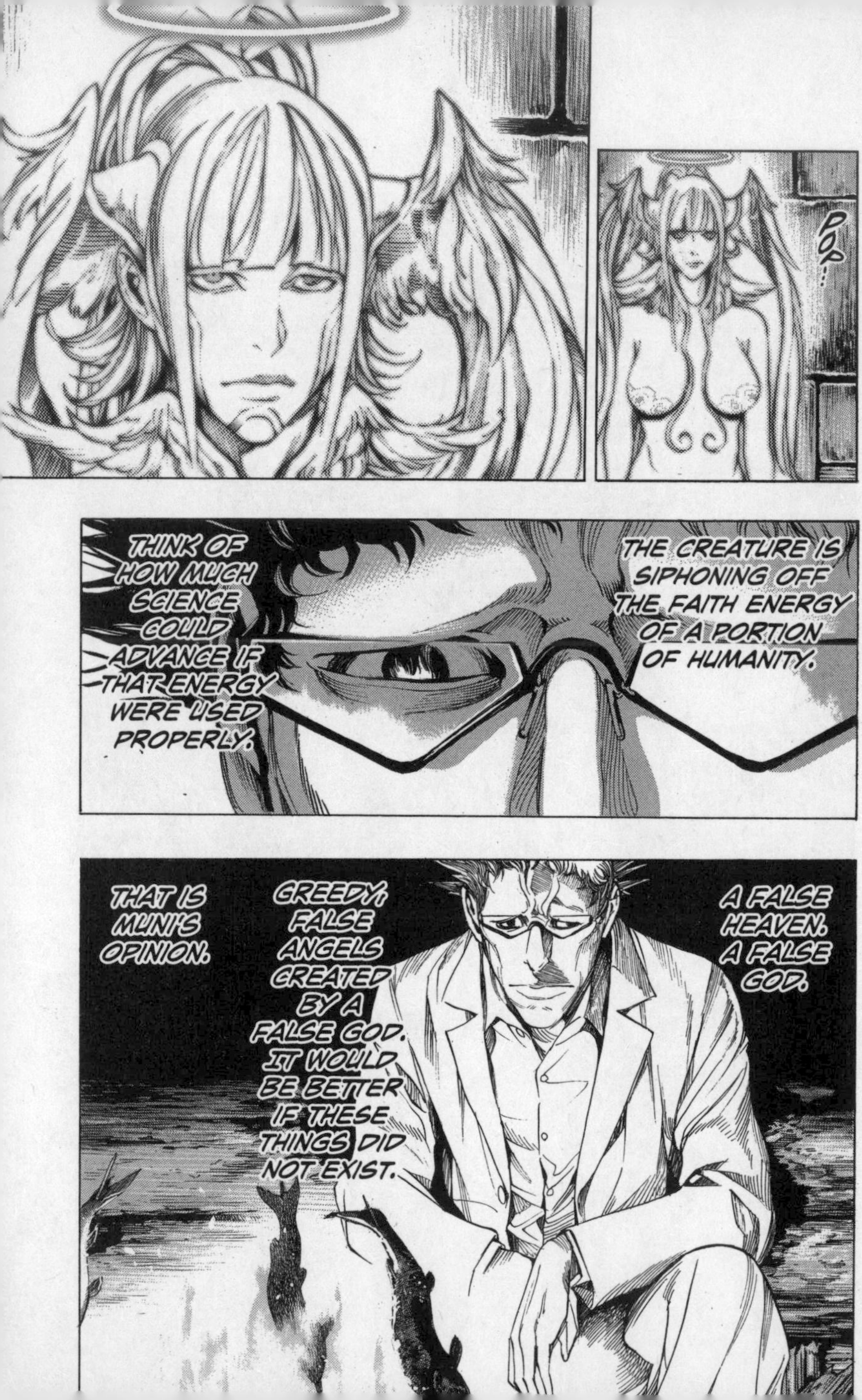
POP...
THE CREATURE IS SIPHONING OFF THE FAITH ENERGY OF A PORTION OF HUMANITY.
THINK OF HOW MUCH SCIENCE COULD ADVANCE IF THAT ENERGY WERE USED PROPERLY.
A FALSE HEAVEN. A FALSE GOD.
GREEDY, FALSE ANGELS CREATED BY A FALSE GOD. IT WOULD BE BETTER IF THESE THINGS DID NOT EXIST.
THAT IS MUNI'S OPINION.

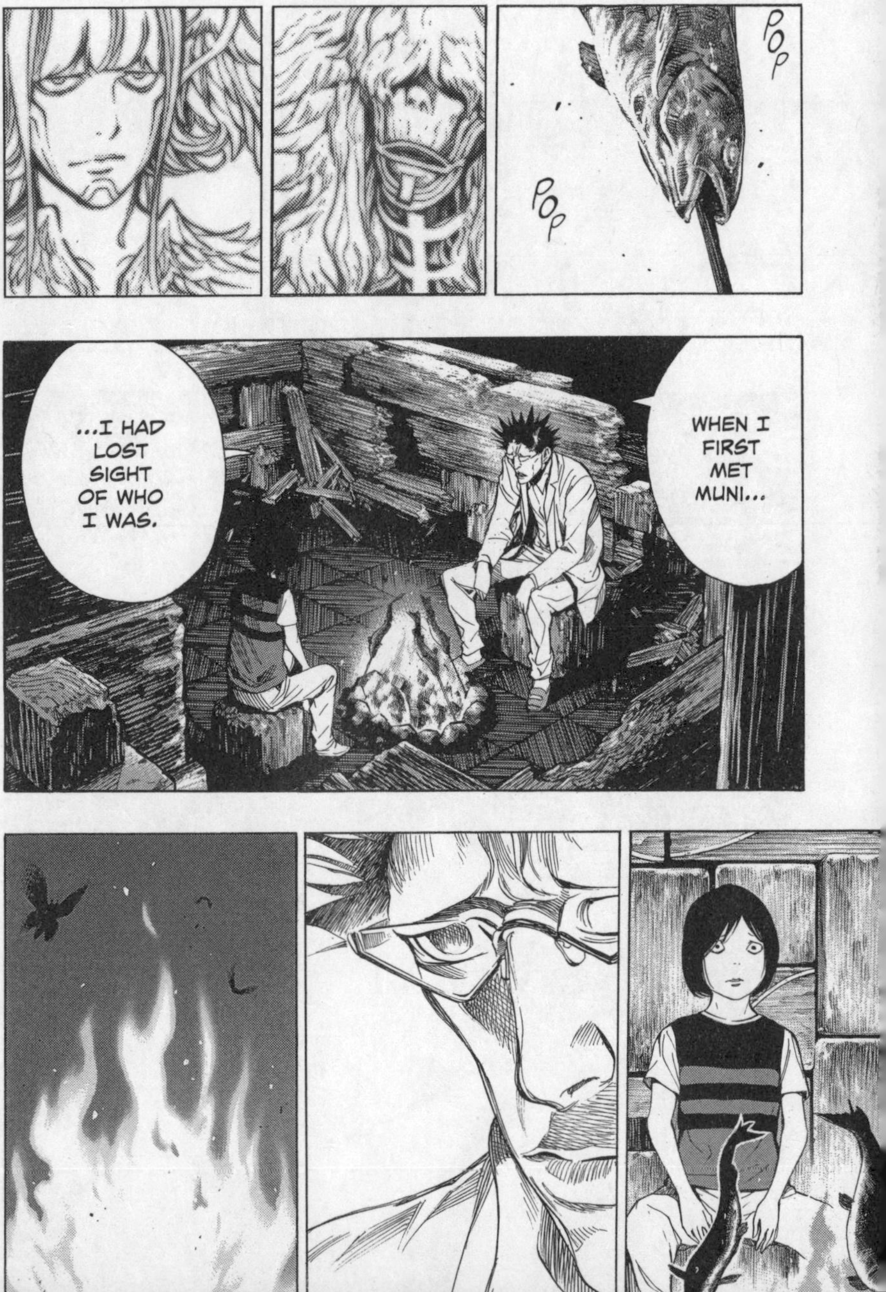
POP
POP
WHEN I FIRST MET MUNI...
...I HAD LOST SIGHT OF WHO I WAS.

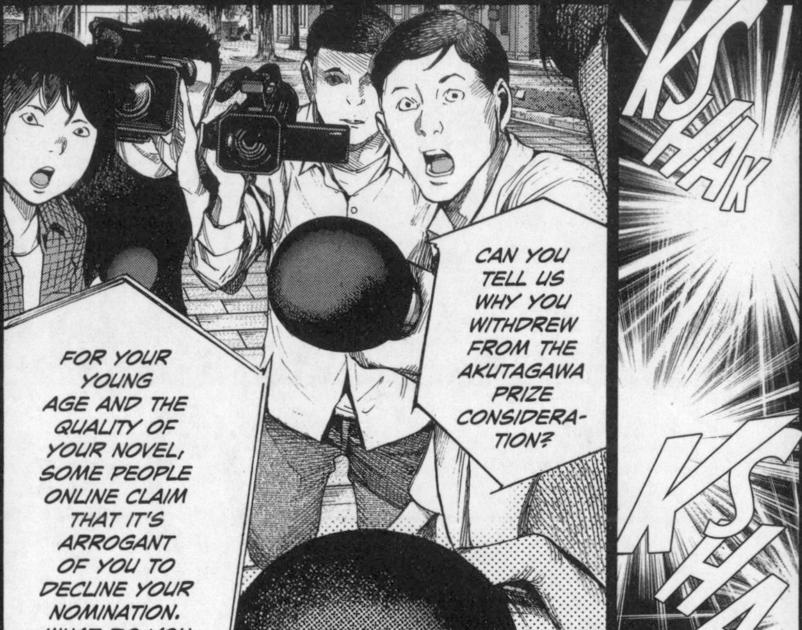
KSHAK
CAN YOU TELL US WHY YOU WITHDREW FROM THE AKUTAGAWA PRIZE CONSIDERA-TION?
KSHAK
FOR YOUR YOUNG AGE AND THE QUALITY OF YOUR NOVEL, SOME PEOPLE ONLINE CLAIM THAT IT'S ARROGANT OF YOU TO DECLINE YOUR NOMINATION. WHAT DO YOU HAVE TO SAY ABOUT THAT?

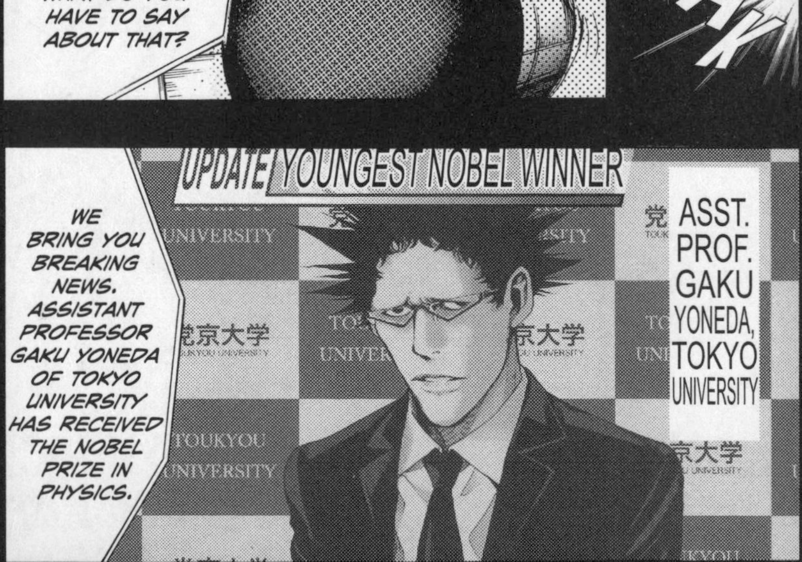
UPDATE! YOUNGEST NOBEL WINNER
ASST. PROF. GAKU YONEDA, TOKYO UNIVERSITY
WE BRING YOU BREAKING NEWS. ASSISTANT PROFESSOR GAKU YONEDA OF TOKYO UNIVERSITY HAS RECEIVED THE NOBEL PRIZE IN PHYSICS.

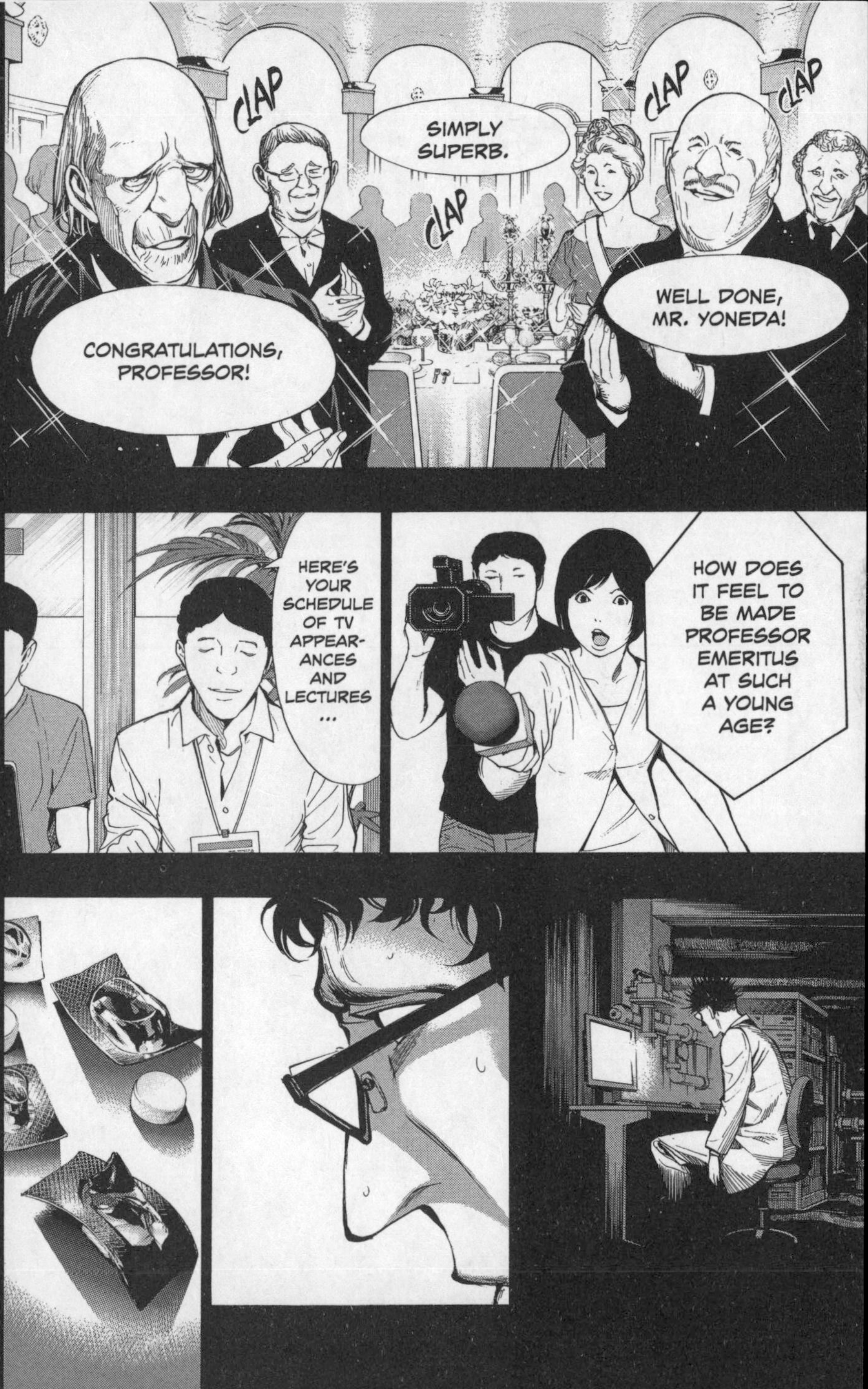
CLAP
CLAP
SIMPLY SUPERB.
CLAP
CLAP
WELL DONE, MR. YONEDA!
CONGRATULATIONS, PROFESSOR!
HOW DOES IT FEEL TO BE MADE PROFESSOR EMERITUS AT SUCH A YOUNG AGE?
HERE'S YOUR SCHEDULE OF TV APPEARANCES AND LECTURES...

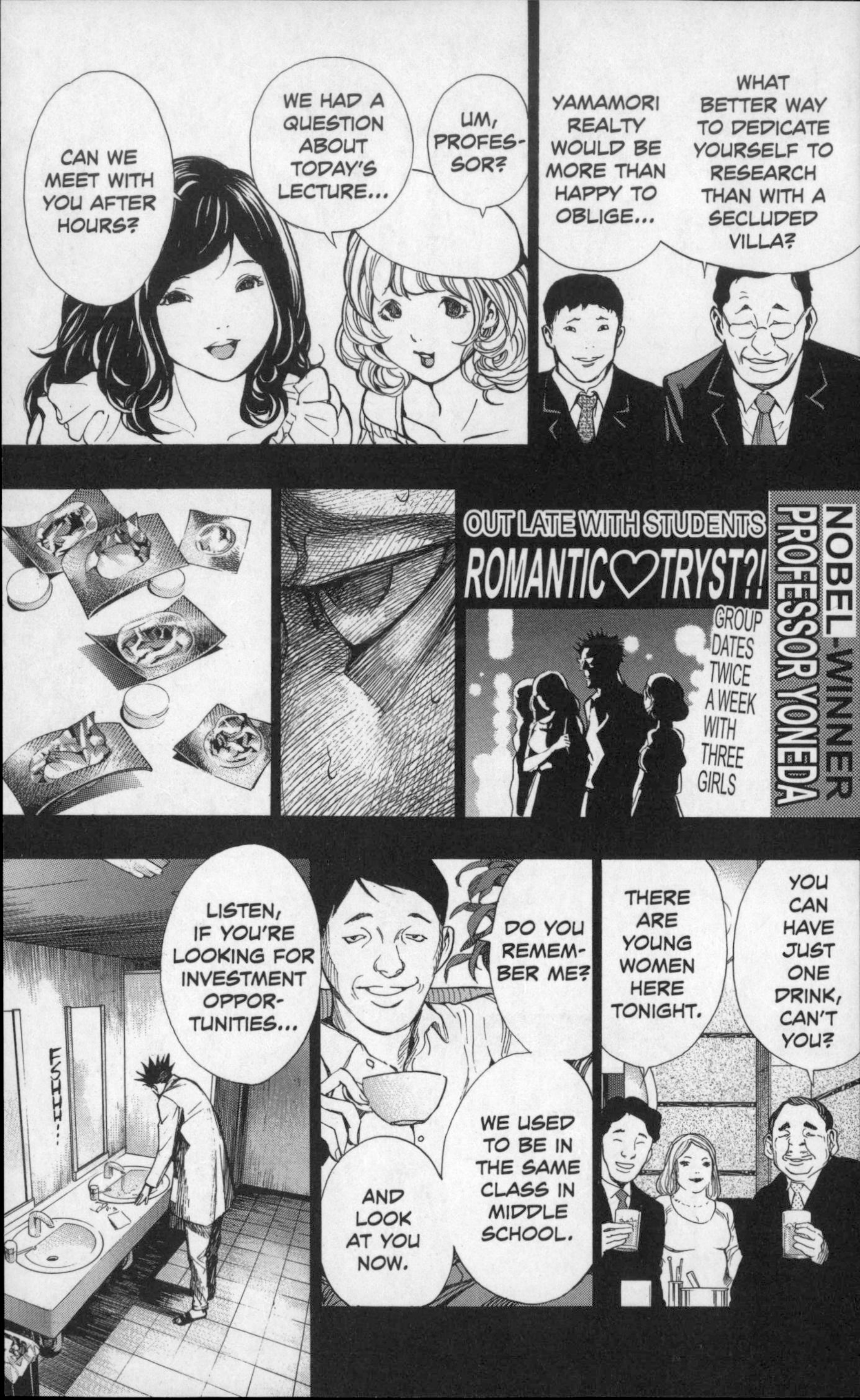
WHAT BETTER WAY TO DEDICATE YOURSELF TO RESEARCH THAN WITH A SECLUDED VILLA?
YAMAMORI REALTY WOULD BE MORE THAN HAPPY TO OBLIGE...
UM, PROFES-SOR?
WE HAD A QUESTION ABOUT TODAY'S LECTURE...
CAN WE MEET WITH YOU AFTER HOURS?
NOBEL-WINNER PROFESSOR YONEDA
OUT LATE WITH STUDENTS
ROMANTIC♡TRYST?!
GROUP DATES TWICE A WEEK WITH THREE GIRLS
YOU CAN HAVE JUST ONE DRINK, CAN'T YOU?
THERE ARE YOUNG WOMEN HERE TONIGHT.
DO YOU REMEM-BER ME?
WE USED TO BE IN THE SAME CLASS IN MIDDLE SCHOOL.
AND LOOK AT YOU NOW.
LISTEN, IF YOU'RE LOOKING FOR INVESTMENT OPPOR-TUNITIES...
FSHHH!!

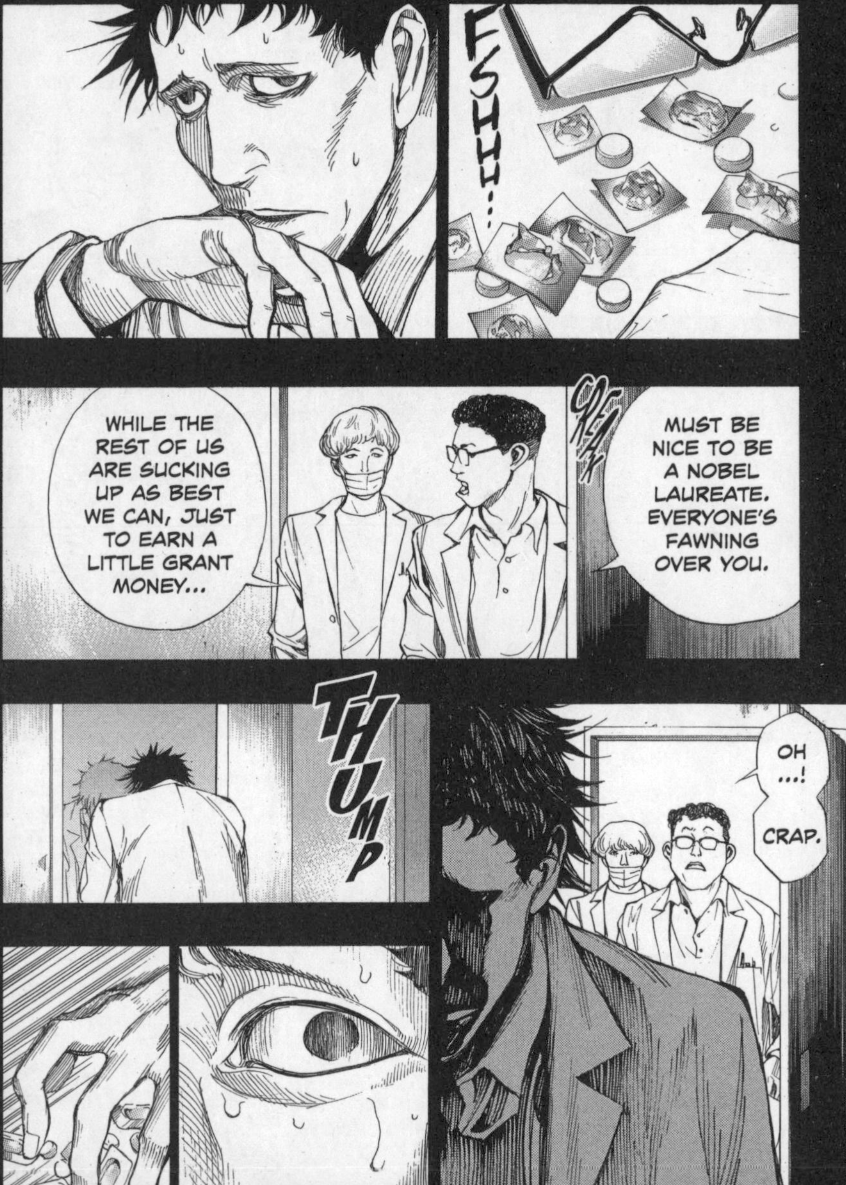
FSHHH...
CREAK
MUST BE NICE TO BE A NOBEL LAUREATE. EVERYONE'S FAWNING OVER YOU.
WHILE THE REST OF US ARE SUCKING UP AS BEST WE CAN, JUST TO EARN A LITTLE GRANT MONEY...
OH ...!
CRAP.
THUMP

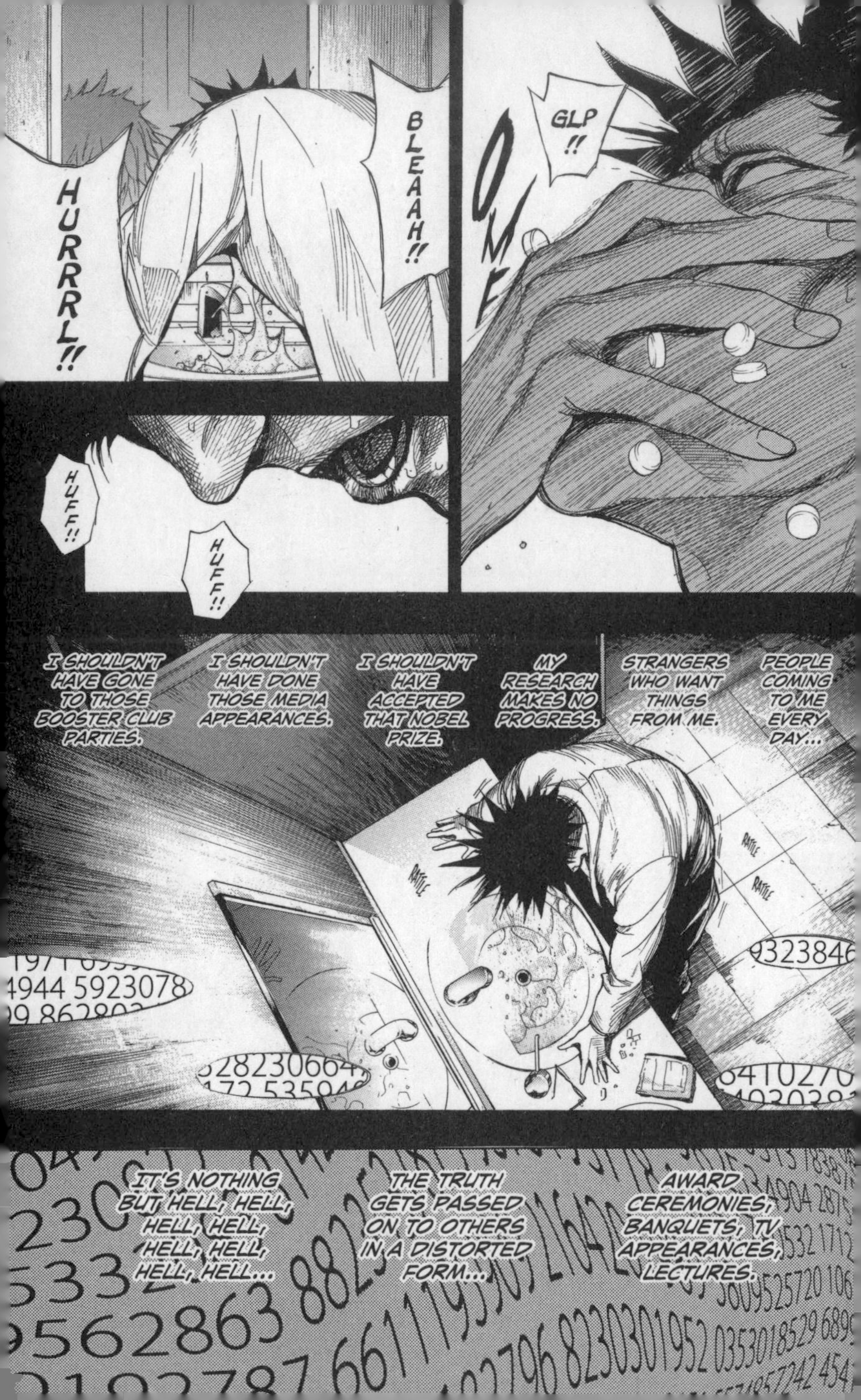
GLP!!
BLEAAAH!!
HURRRL!!
HUFF!!
HUFF!!
PEOPLE COMING TO ME EVERY DAY...
STRANGERS WHO WANT THINGS FROM ME.
MY RESEARCH MAKES NO PROGRESS.
I SHOULDN'T HAVE ACCEPTED THAT NOBEL PRIZE.
I SHOULDN'T HAVE DONE THOSE MEDIA APPEARANCES.
I SHOULDN'T HAVE GONE TO THOSE BOOSTER CLUB PARTIES.
RATTLE
RATTLE
RATTLE
AWARD CEREMONIES, BANQUETS, TV APPEARANCES, LECTURES.
THE TRUTH GETS PASSED ON TO OTHERS IN A DISTORTED FORM...
IT'S NOTHING BUT HELL, HELL, HELL, HELL, HELL, HELL, HELL, HELL...

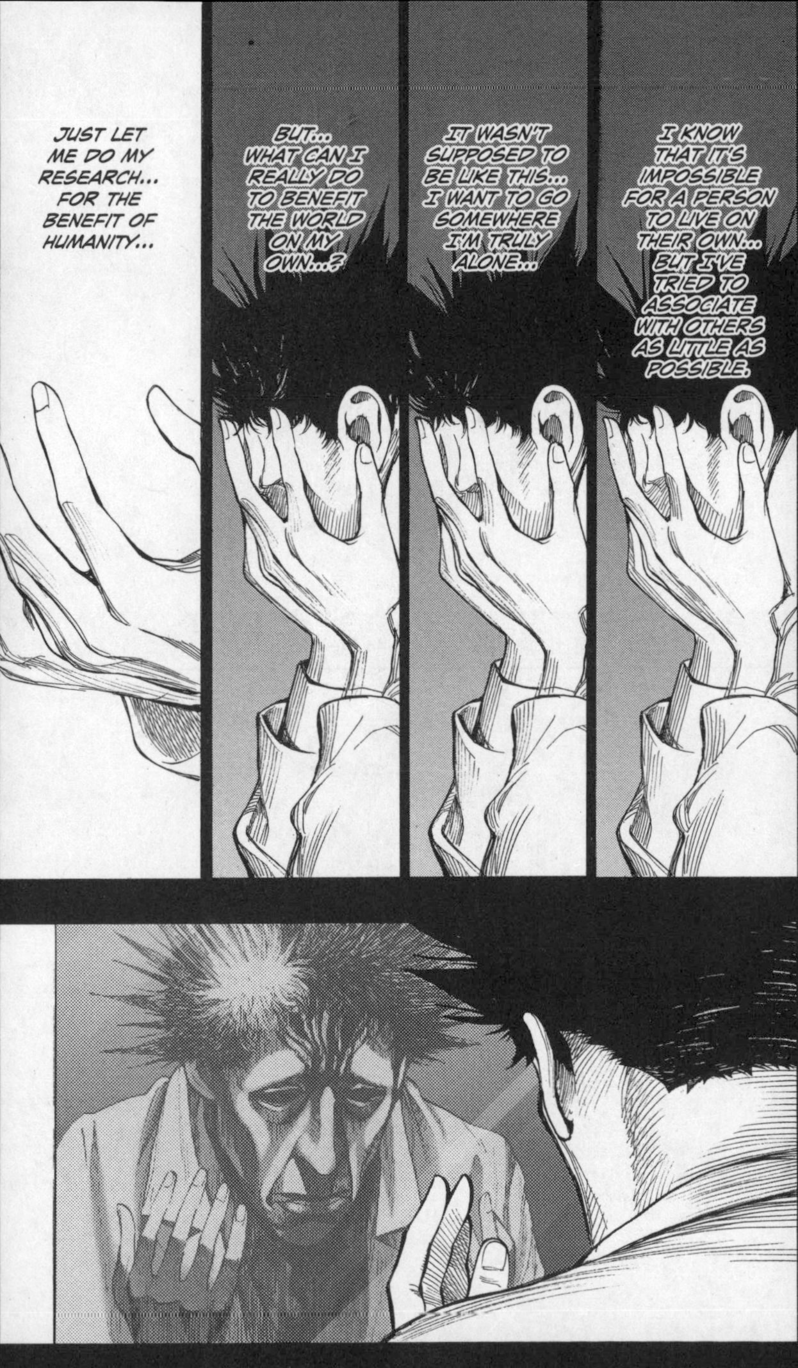
I KNOW THAT IT'S IMPOSSIBLE FOR A PERSON TO LIVE ON THEIR OWN... BUT I'VE TRIED TO ASSOCIATE WITH OTHERS AS LITTLE AS POSSIBLE.
IT WASN'T SUPPOSED TO BE LIKE THIS... I WANT TO GO SOMEWHERE I'M TRULY ALONE...
BUT... WHAT CAN I REALLY DO TO BENEFIT THE WORLD ON MY OWN...?
JUST LET ME DO MY RESEARCH... FOR THE BENEFIT OF HUMANITY...

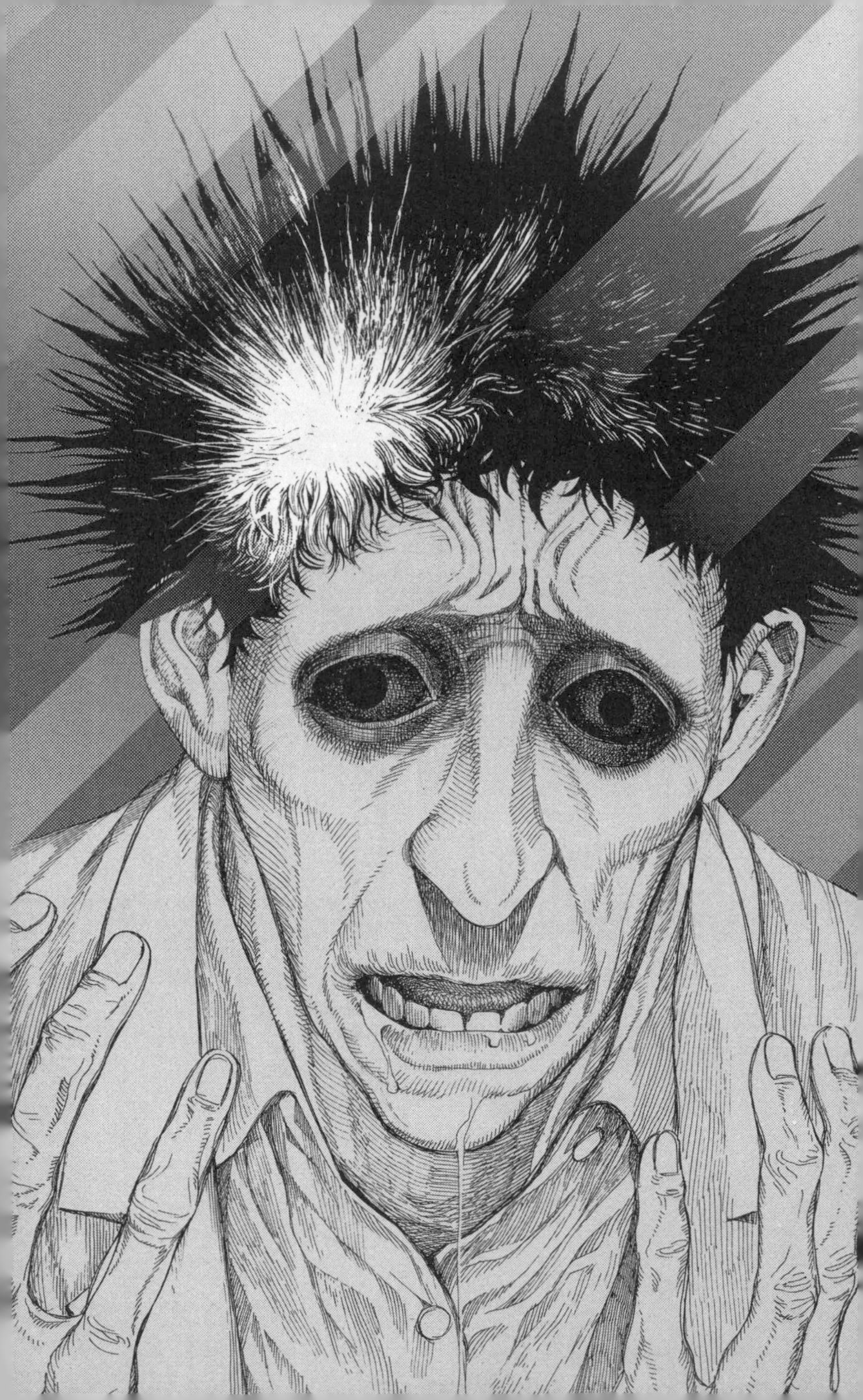

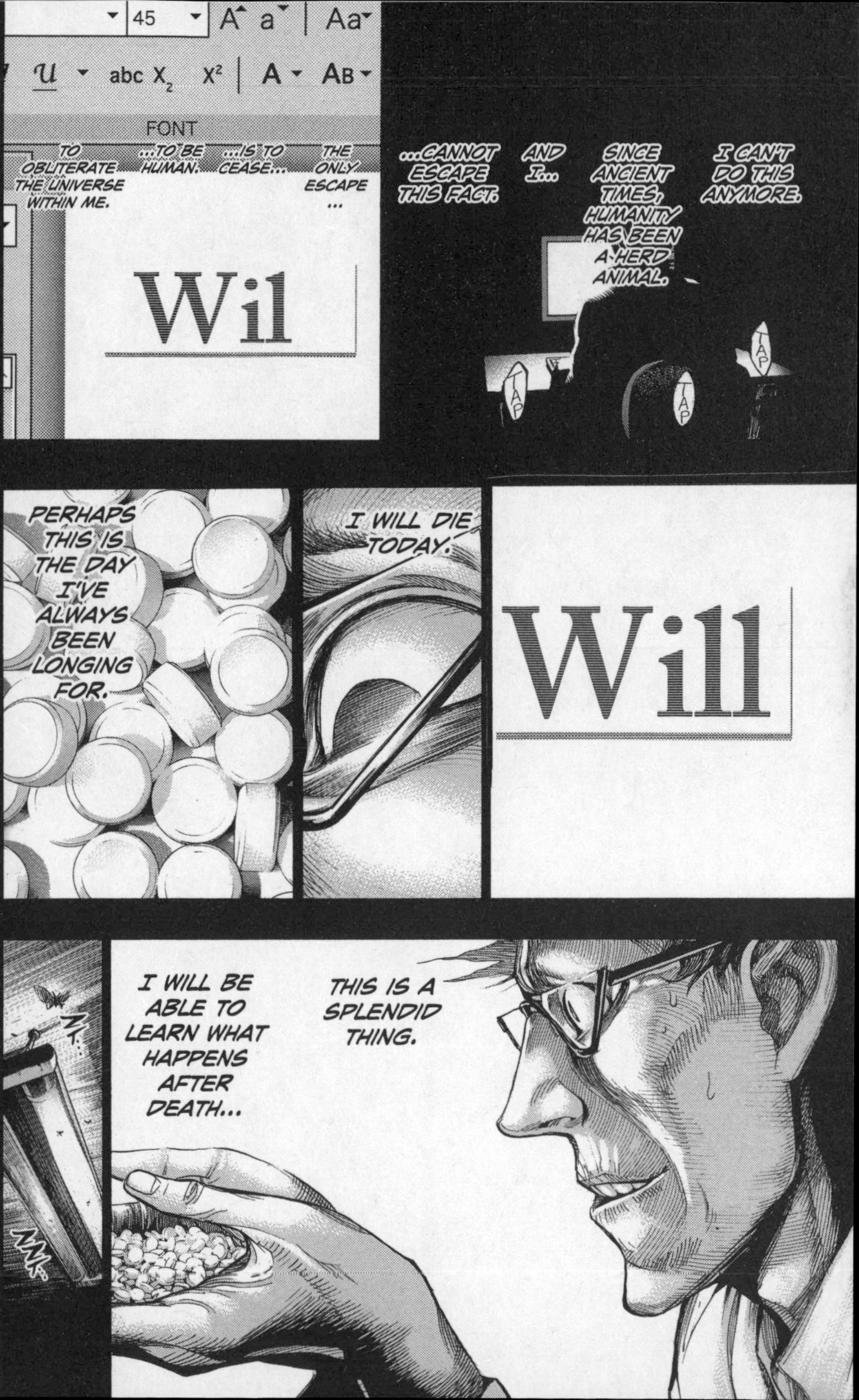
I CAN'T DO THIS ANYMORE.
SINCE ANCIENT TIMES, HUMANITY HAS BEEN A HERD ANIMAL.
AND I...
...CANNOT ESCAPE THIS FACT.
TAP
TAP
TAP
45
FONT
THE ONLY ESCAPE ...
...IS TO CEASE...
...TO BE HUMAN.
TO OBLITERATE THE UNIVERSE WITHIN ME.
Wil
Will
I WILL DIE TODAY.
PERHAPS THIS IS THE DAY I'VE ALWAYS BEEN LONGING FOR.
THIS IS A SPLENDID THING.
I WILL BE ABLE TO LEARN WHAT HAPPENS AFTER DEATH...

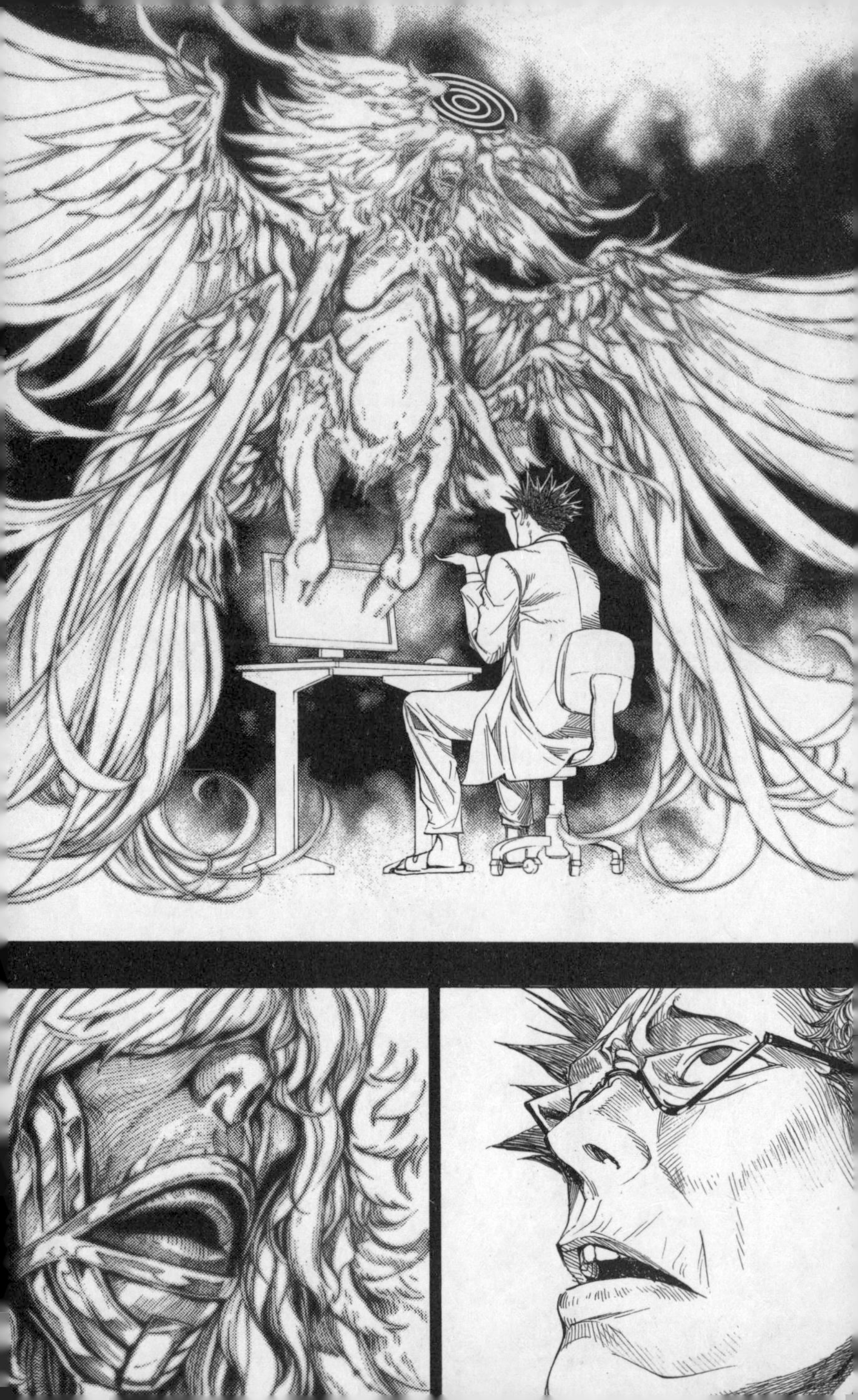

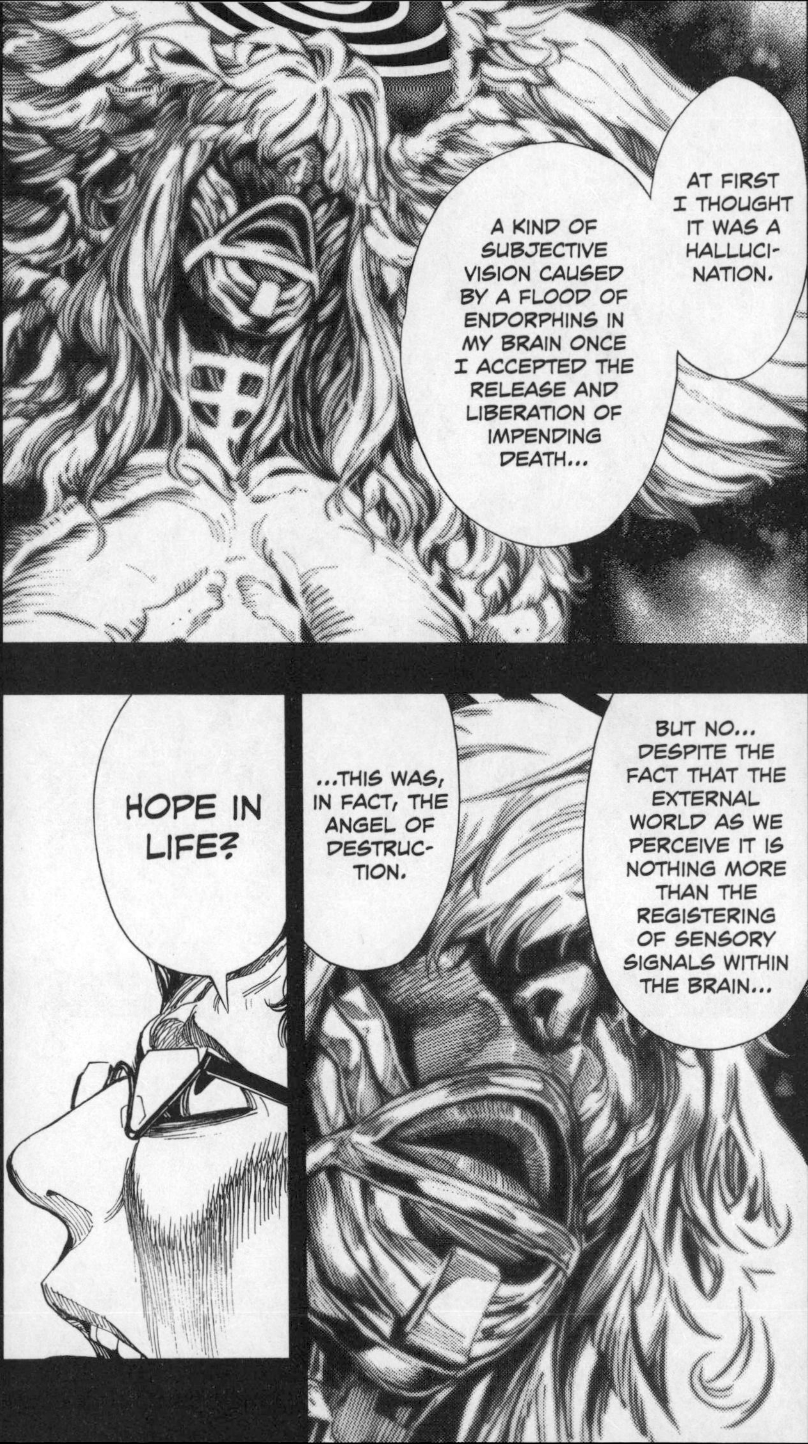
AT FIRST I THOUGHT IT WAS A HALLUCI-NATION.
A KIND OF SUBJECTIVE VISION CAUSED BY A FLOOD OF ENDORPHINS IN MY BRAIN ONCE I ACCEPTED THE RELEASE AND LIBERATION OF IMPENDING DEATH...
BUT NO... DESPITE THE FACT THAT THE EXTERNAL WORLD AS WE PERCEIVE IT IS NOTHING MORE THAN THE REGISTERING OF SENSORY SIGNALS WITHIN THE BRAIN...
...THIS WAS, IN FACT, THE ANGEL OF DESTRUC-TION.
HOPE IN LIFE?

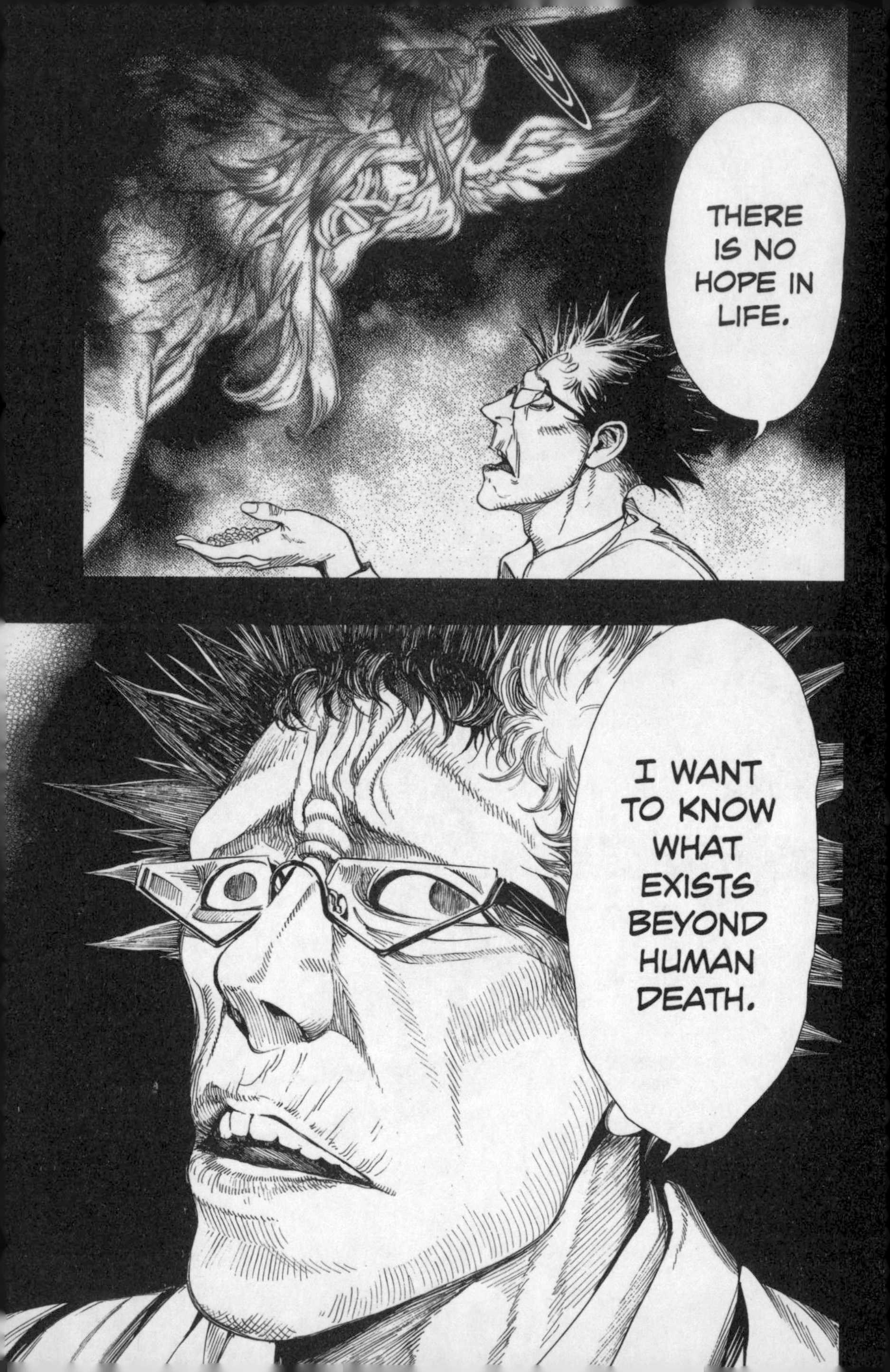
THERE IS NO HOPE IN LIFE.
I WANT TO KNOW WHAT EXISTS BEYOND HUMAN DEATH.

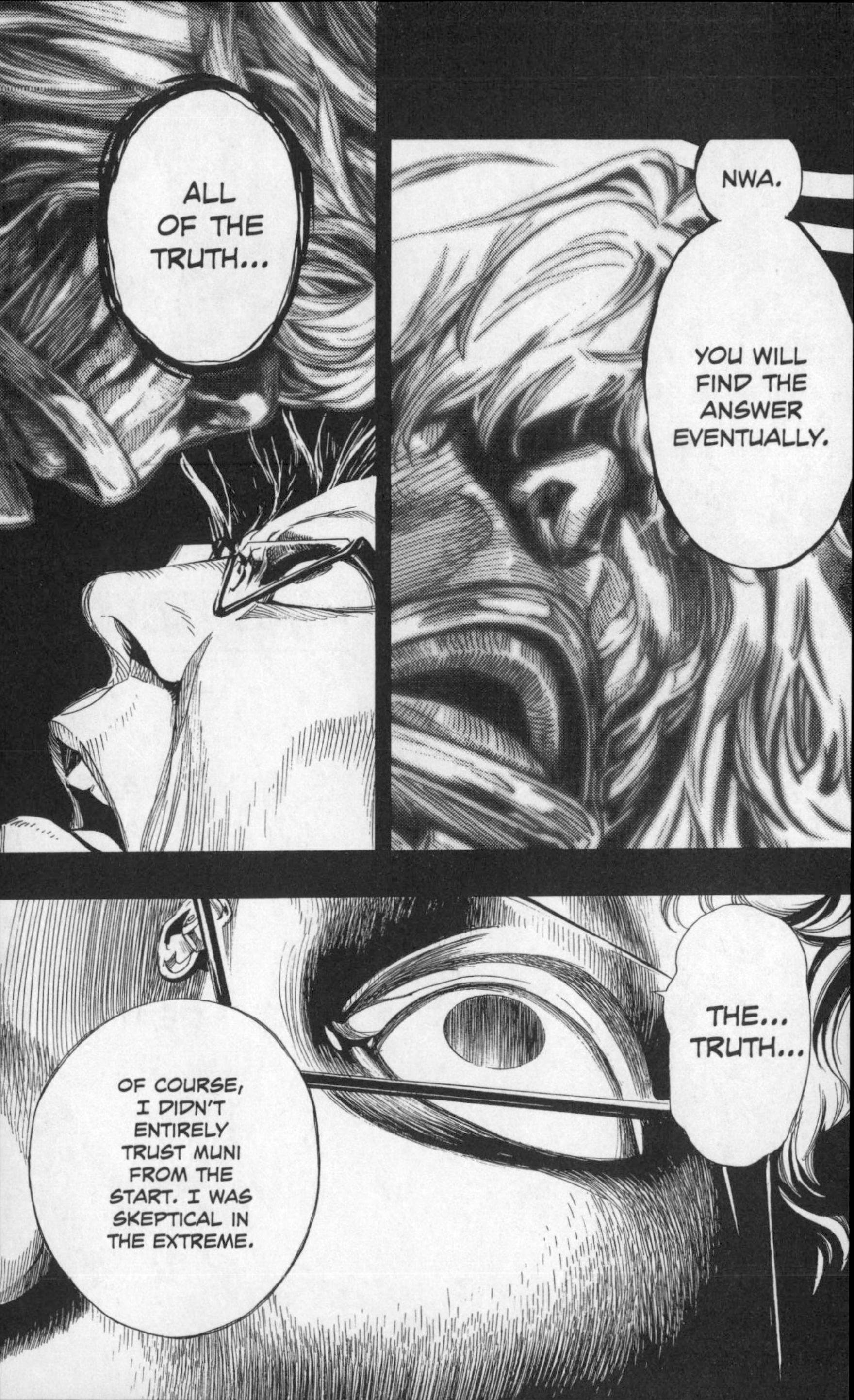
NWA.
YOU WILL FIND THE ANSWER EVENTUALLY.
ALL OF THE TRUTH...
THE... TRUTH...
OF COURSE, I DIDN'T ENTIRELY TRUST MUNI FROM THE START. I WAS SKEPTICAL IN THE EXTREME.

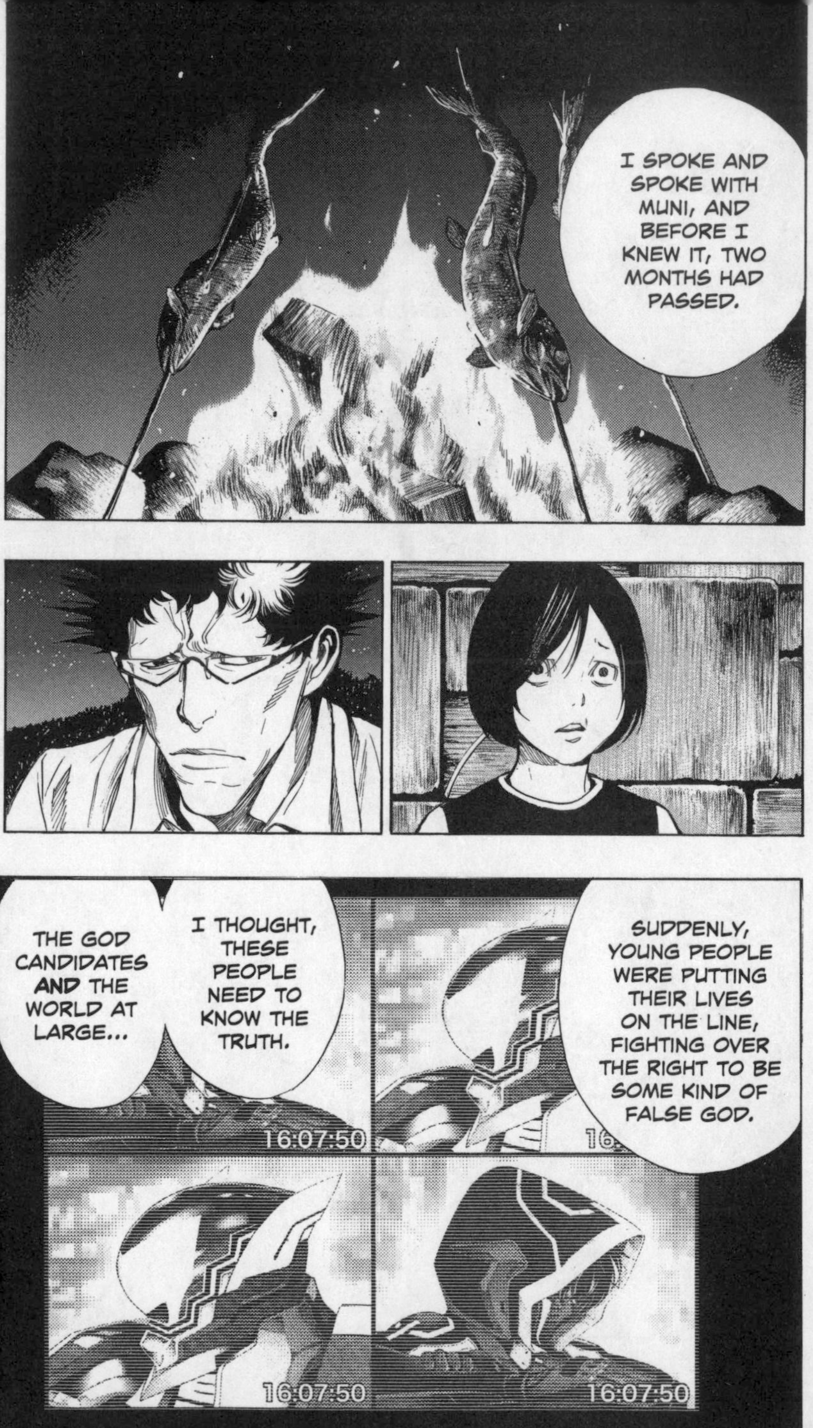
I SPOKE AND SPOKE WITH MUNI, AND BEFORE I KNEW IT, TWO MONTHS HAD PASSED.
SUDDENLY, YOUNG PEOPLE WERE PUTTING THEIR LIVES ON THE LINE, FIGHTING OVER THE RIGHT TO BE SOME KIND OF FALSE GOD.
16:07:50
I THOUGHT, THESE PEOPLE NEED TO KNOW THE TRUTH.
THE GOD CANDIDATES AND THE WORLD AT LARGE...
16:07:50
16:07:50

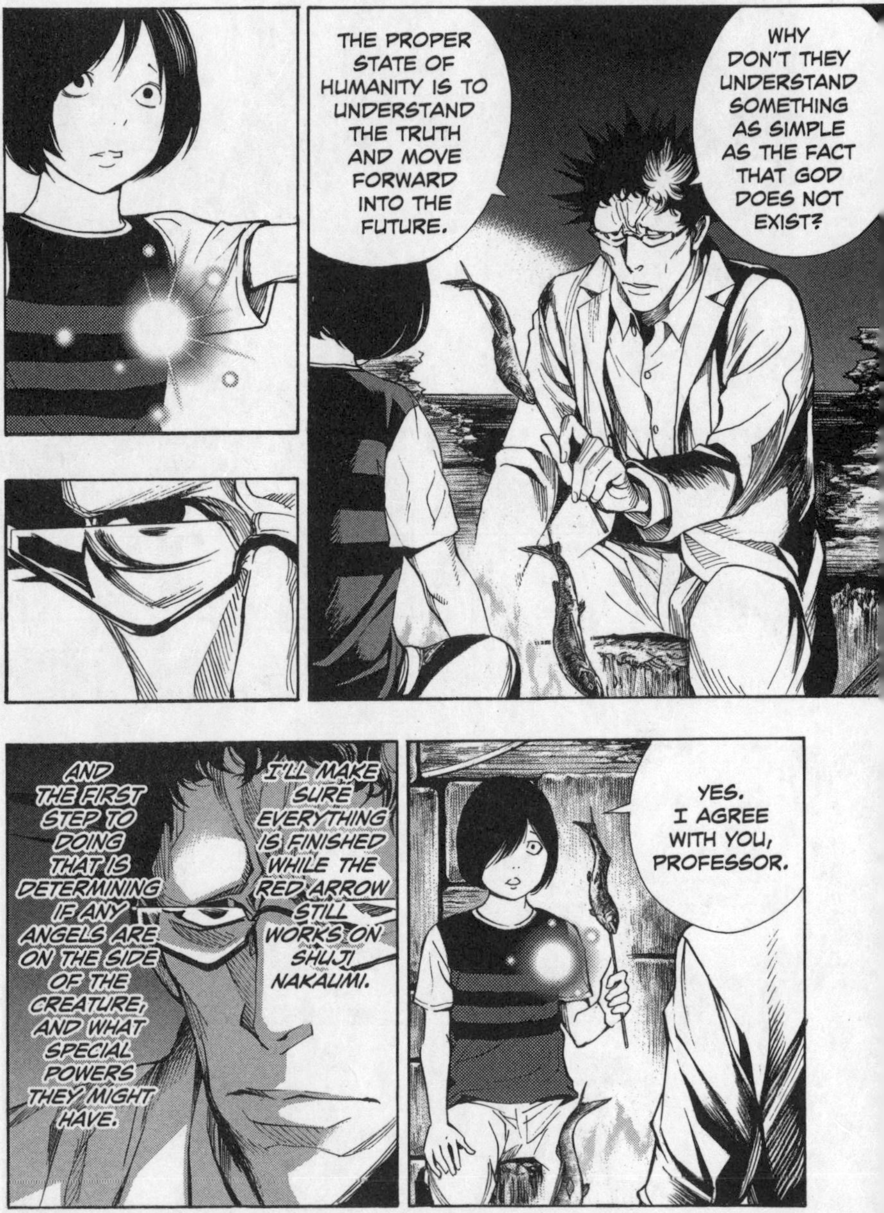
WHY DON'T THEY UNDERSTAND SOMETHING AS SIMPLE AS THE FACT THAT GOD DOES NOT EXIST?
THE PROPER STATE OF HUMANITY IS TO UNDERSTAND THE TRUTH AND MOVE FORWARD INTO THE FUTURE.
YES. I AGREE WITH YOU, PROFESSOR.
I'LL MAKE SURE EVERYTHING IS FINISHED WHILE THE RED ARROW STILL WORKS ON SHUJI NAKAUMI.
AND THE FIRST STEP TO DOING THAT IS DETERMINING IF ANY ANGELS ARE ON THE SIDE OF THE CREATURE, AND WHAT SPECIAL POWERS THEY MIGHT HAVE.

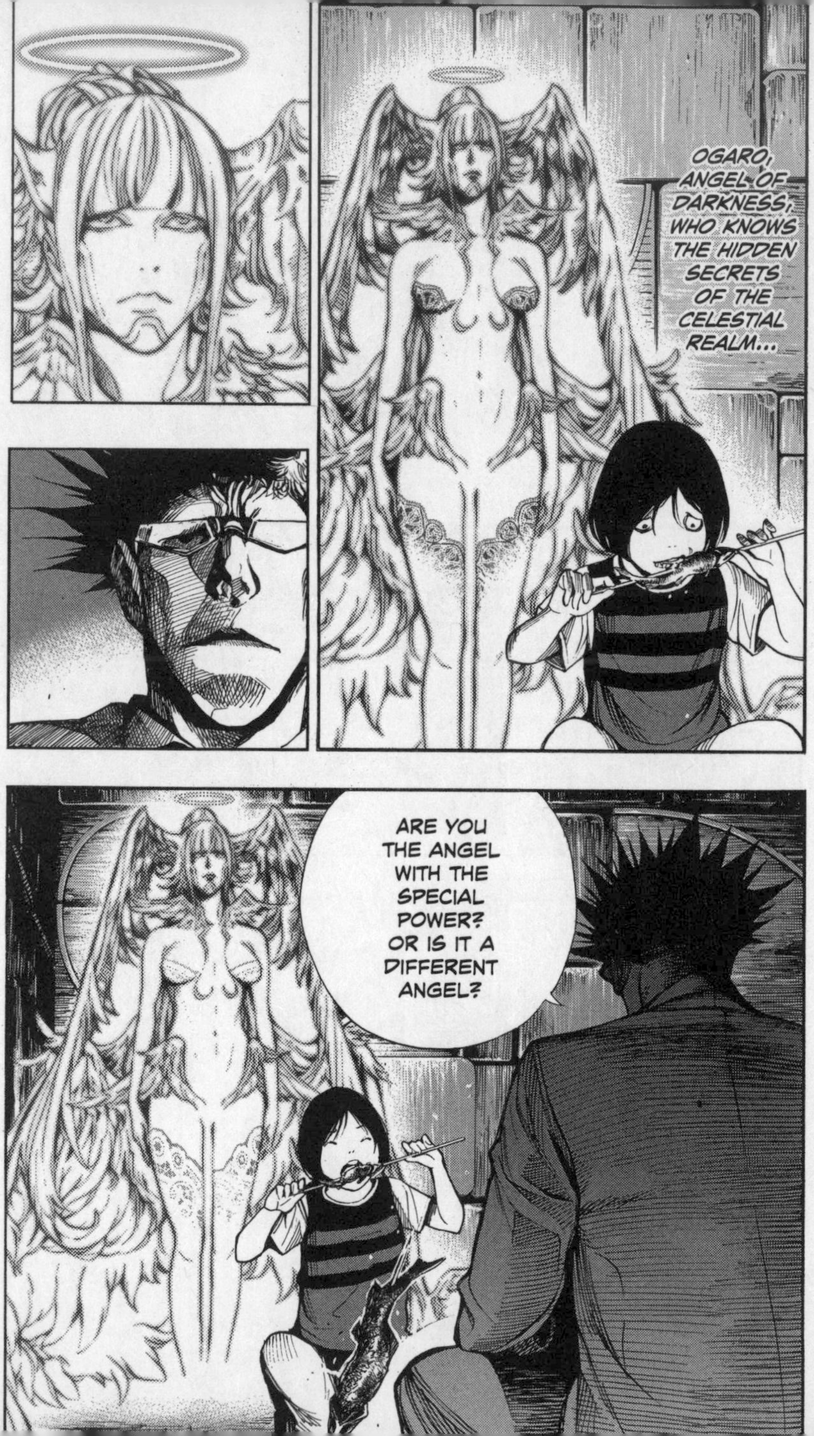
OGARO, ANGEL OF DARKNESS, WHO KNOWS THE HIDDEN SECRETS OF THE CELESTIAL REALM...
ARE YOU THE ANGEL WITH THE SPECIAL POWER? OR IS IT A DIFFERENT ANGEL?

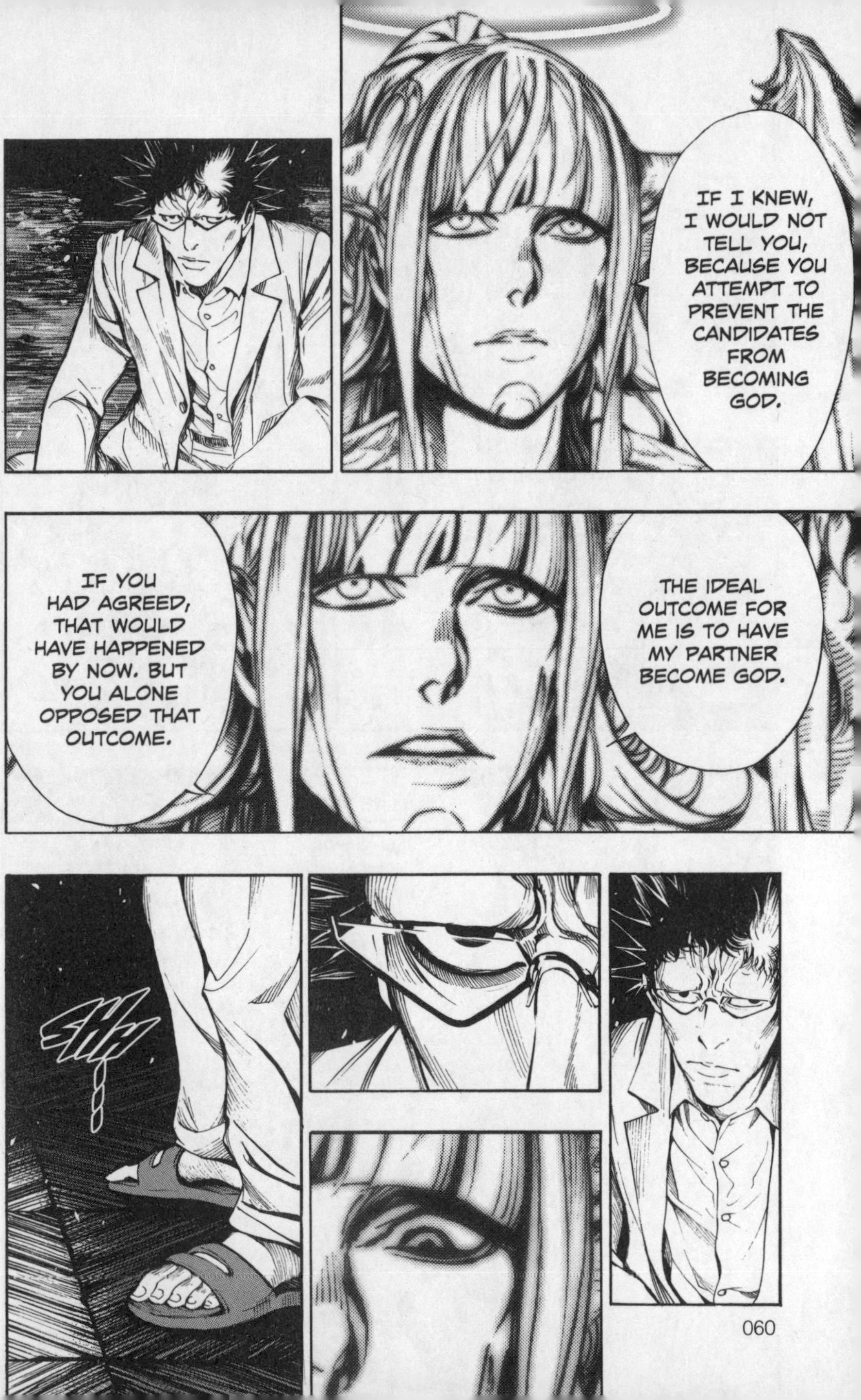
IF I KNEW, I WOULD NOT TELL YOU, BECAUSE YOU ATTEMPT TO PREVENT THE CANDIDATES FROM BECOMING GOD.
THE IDEAL OUTCOME FOR ME IS TO HAVE MY PARTNER BECOME GOD.
IF YOU HAD AGREED, THAT WOULD HAVE HAPPENED BY NOW. BUT YOU ALONE OPPOSED THAT OUTCOME.

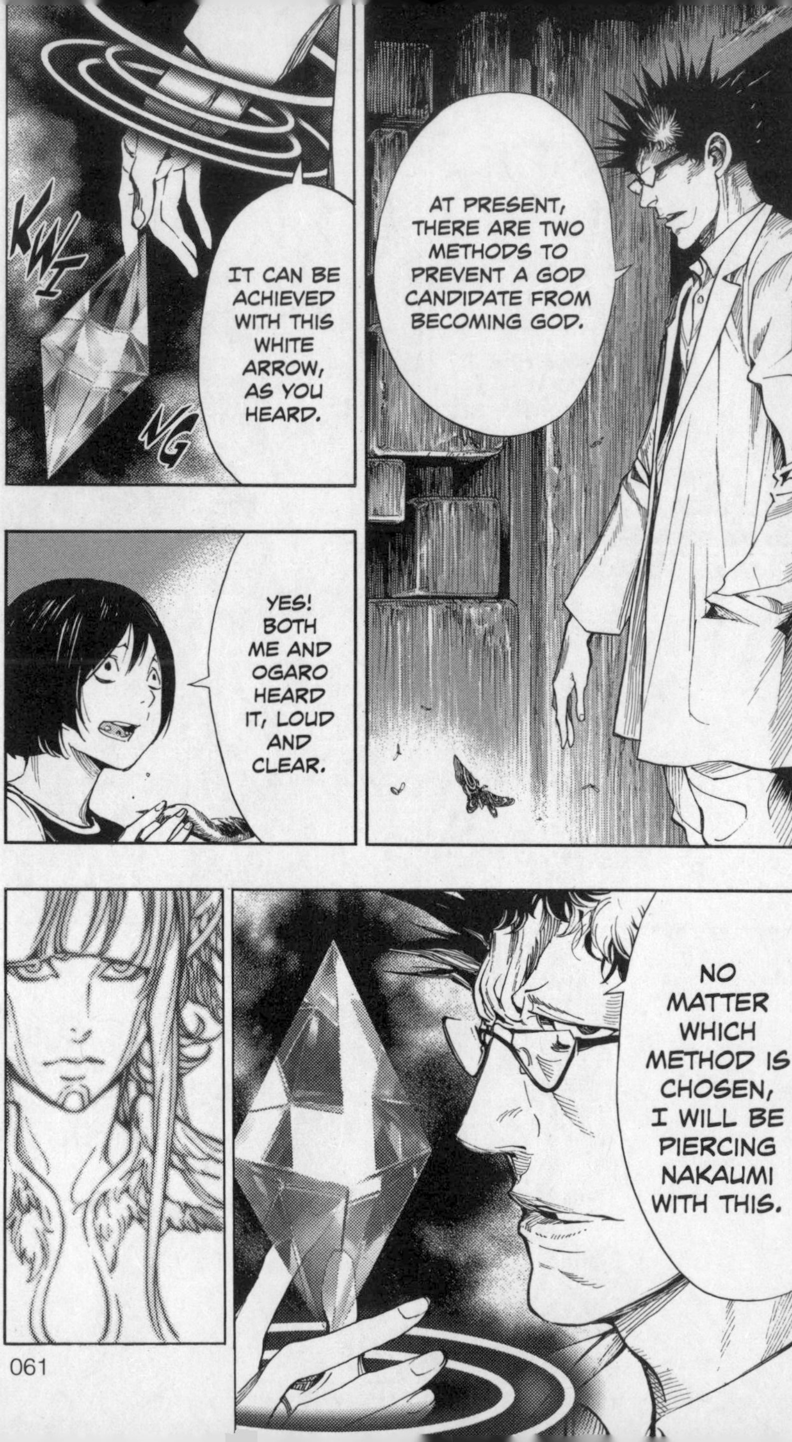
AT PRESENT, THERE ARE TWO METHODS TO PREVENT A GOD CANDIDATE FROM BECOMING GOD.
IT CAN BE ACHIEVED WITH THIS WHITE ARROW, AS YOU HEARD.
KWING
YES! BOTH ME AND OGARO HEARD IT, LOUD AND CLEAR.
NO MATTER WHICH METHOD IS CHOSEN, I WILL BE PIERCING NAKAUMI WITH THIS.

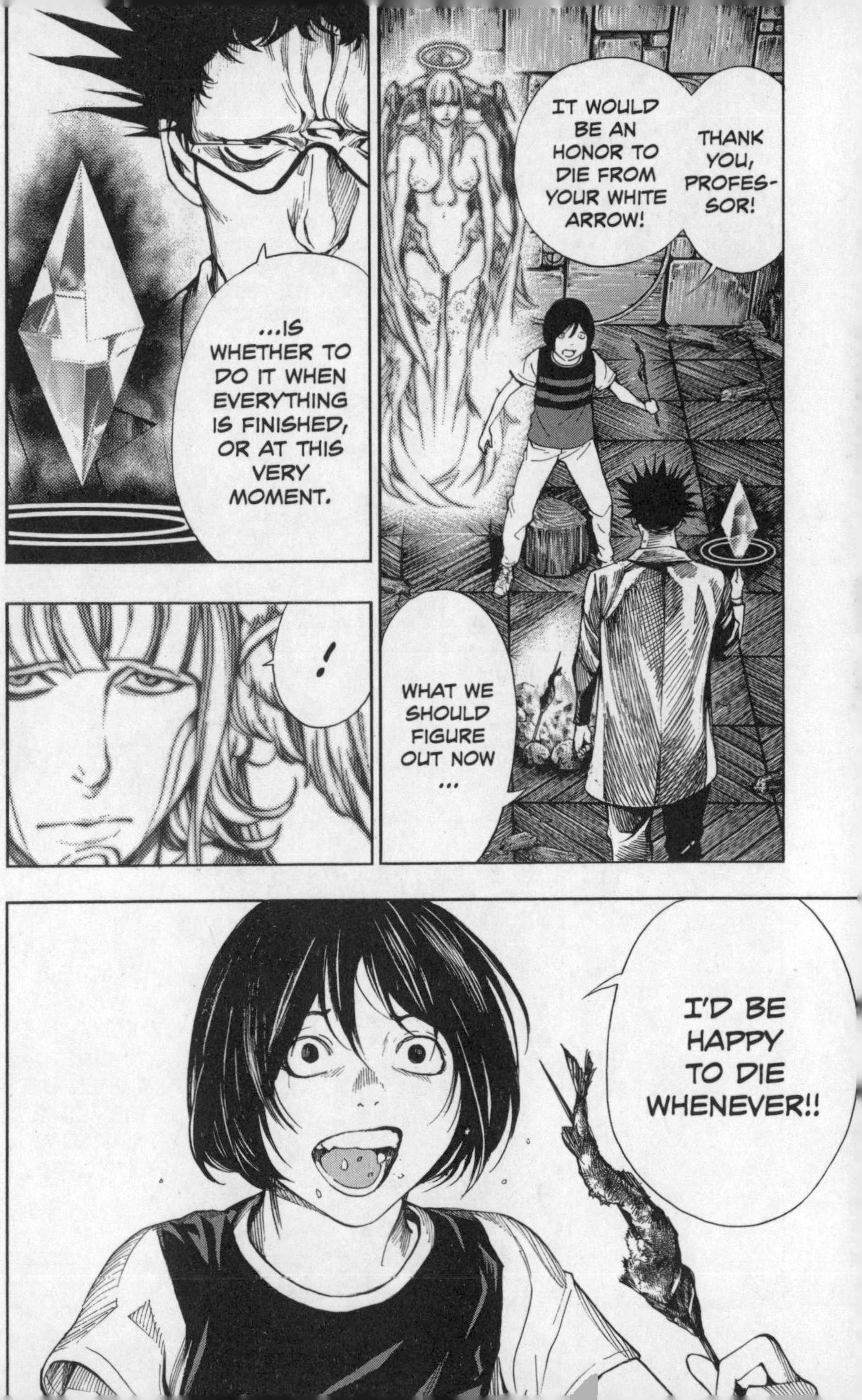
THANK YOU, PROFES-SOR!
IT WOULD BE AN HONOR TO DIE FROM YOUR WHITE ARROW!
WHAT WE SHOULD FIGURE OUT NOW ...
...IS WHETHER TO DO IT WHEN EVERYTHING IS FINISHED, OR AT THIS VERY MOMENT.
!
I'D BE HAPPY TO DIE WHENEVER!!

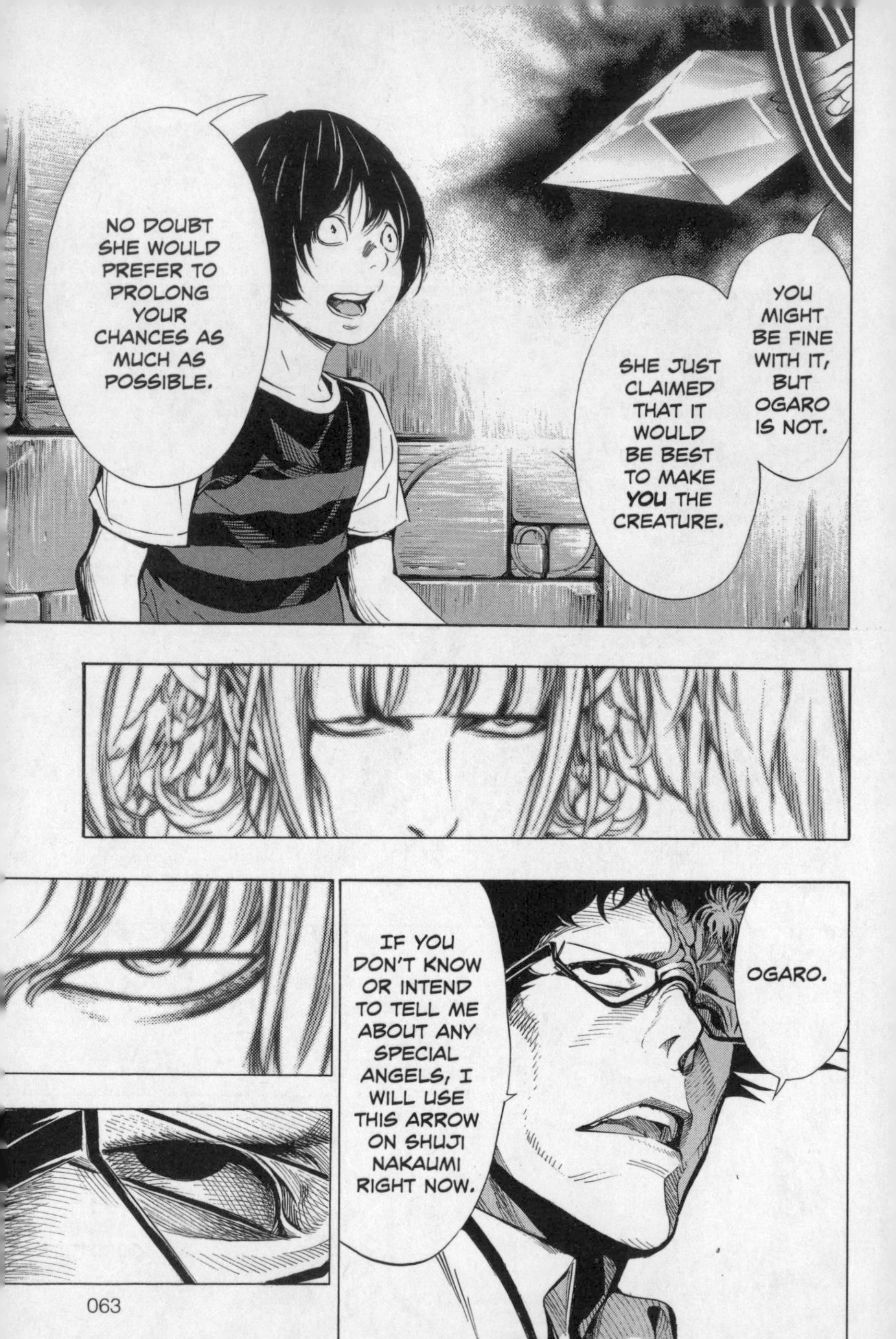
YOU MIGHT BE FINE WITH IT, BUT OGARO IS NOT.
SHE JUST CLAIMED THAT IT WOULD BE BEST TO MAKE **YOU** THE CREATURE.
NO DOUBT SHE WOULD PREFER TO PROLONG YOUR CHANCES AS MUCH AS POSSIBLE.
OGARO.
IF YOU DON'T KNOW OR INTEND TO TELL ME ABOUT ANY SPECIAL ANGELS, I WILL USE THIS ARROW ON SHUJI NAKAUMI RIGHT NOW.

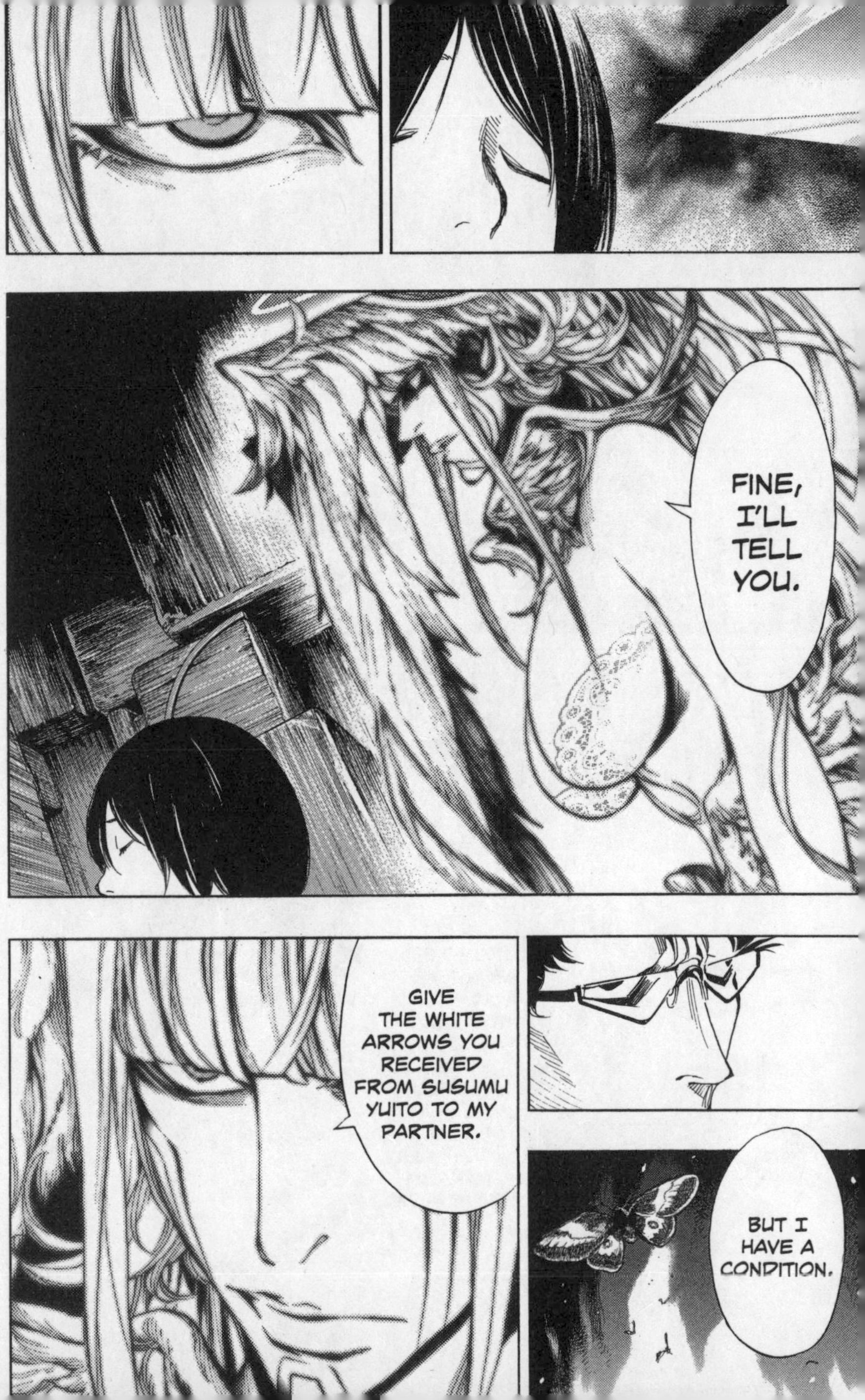
FINE, I'LL TELL YOU.
BUT I HAVE A CONDITION.
GIVE THE WHITE ARROWS YOU RECEIVED FROM SUSUMU YUITO TO MY PARTNER.

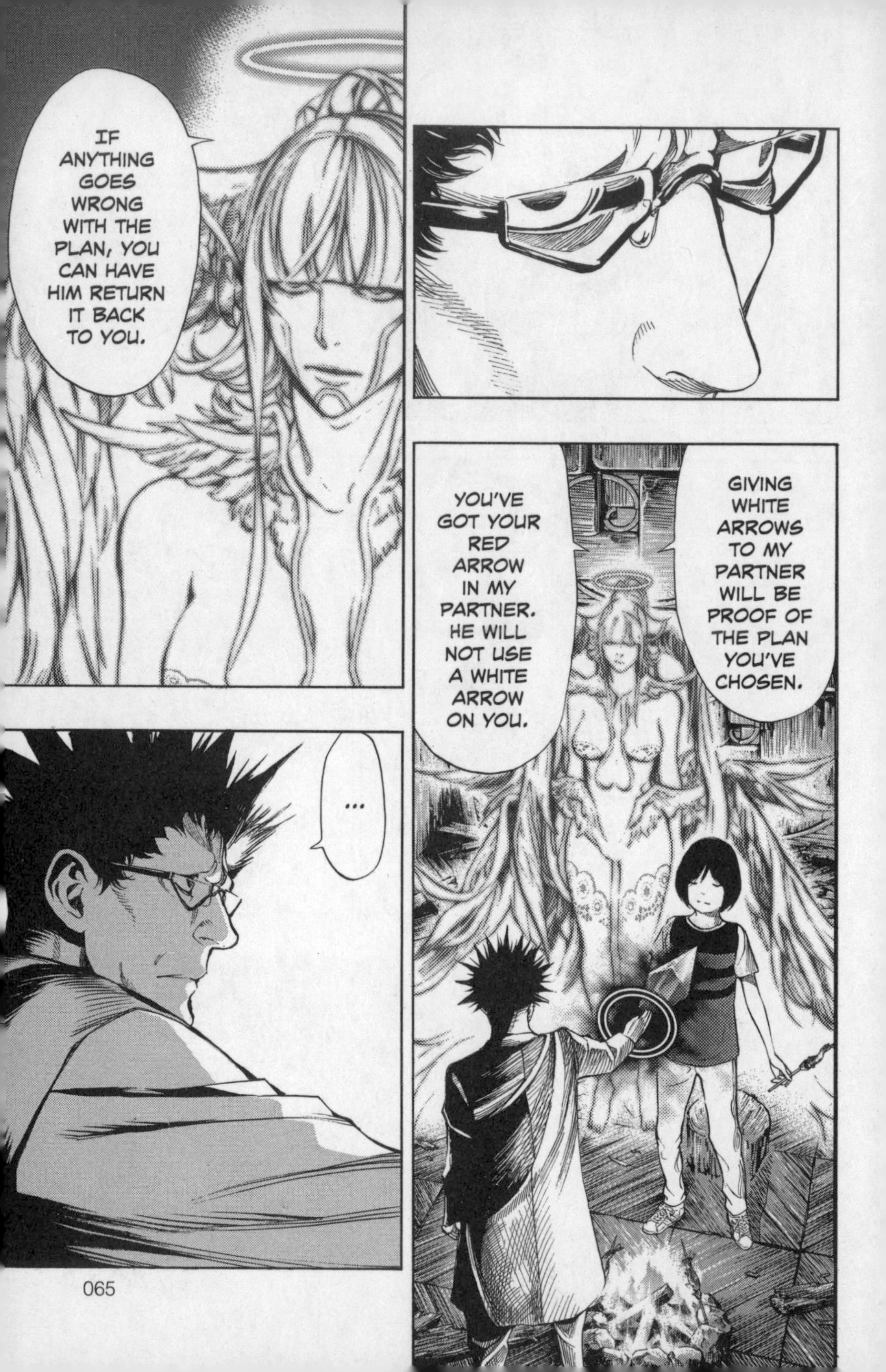
GIVING WHITE ARROWS TO MY PARTNER WILL BE PROOF OF THE PLAN YOU'VE CHOSEN.
YOU'VE GOT YOUR RED ARROW IN MY PARTNER. HE WILL NOT USE A WHITE ARROW ON YOU.
IF ANYTHING GOES WRONG WITH THE PLAN, YOU CAN HAVE HIM RETURN IT BACK TO YOU.
...

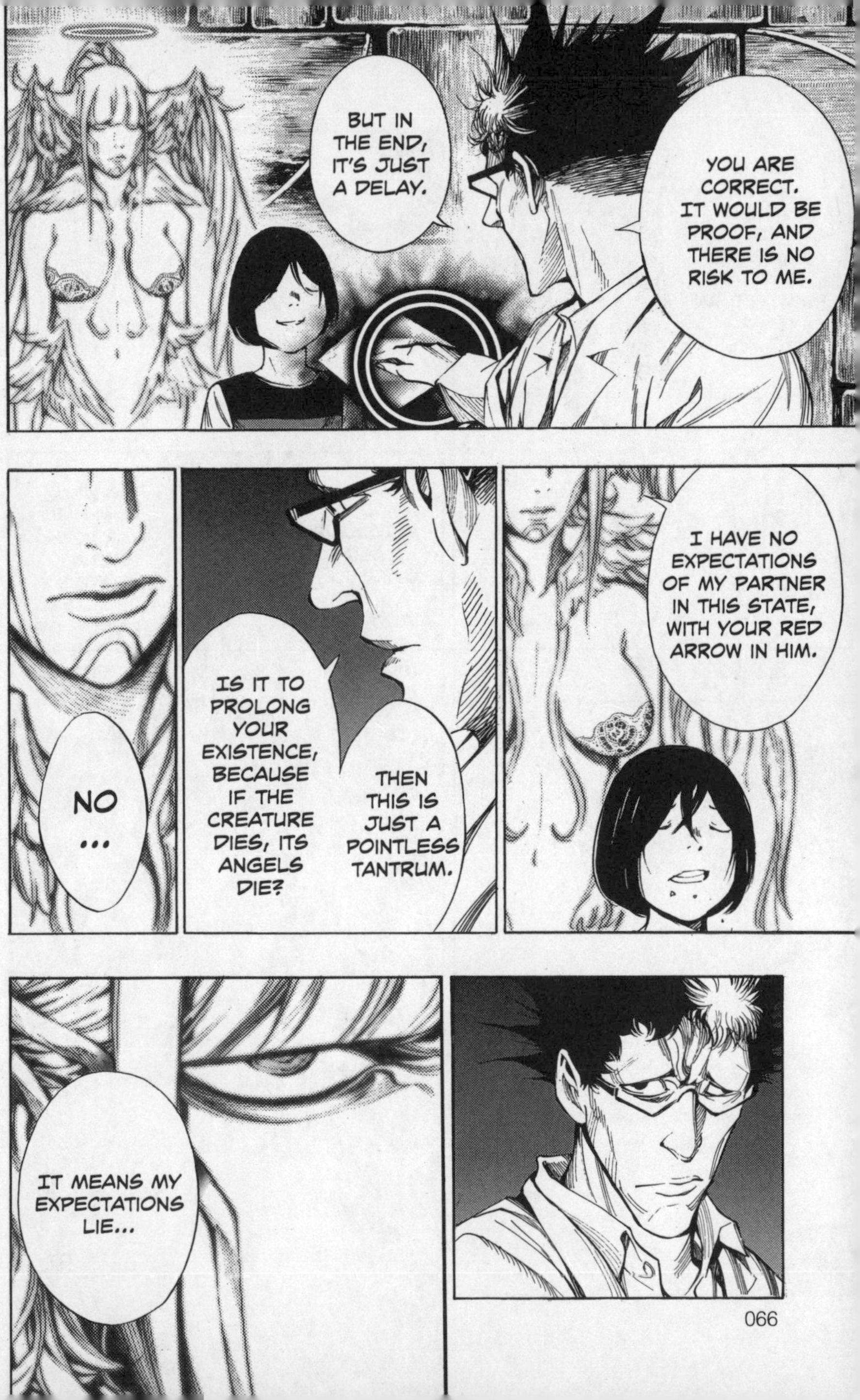
YOU ARE CORRECT. IT WOULD BE PROOF, AND THERE IS NO RISK TO ME.
BUT IN THE END, IT'S JUST A DELAY.
I HAVE NO EXPECTATIONS OF MY PARTNER IN THIS STATE, WITH YOUR RED ARROW IN HIM.
THEN THIS IS JUST A POINTLESS TANTRUM.
IS IT TO PROLONG YOUR EXISTENCE, BECAUSE IF THE CREATURE DIES, ITS ANGELS DIE?
NO ...
IT MEANS MY EXPECTATIONS LIE...

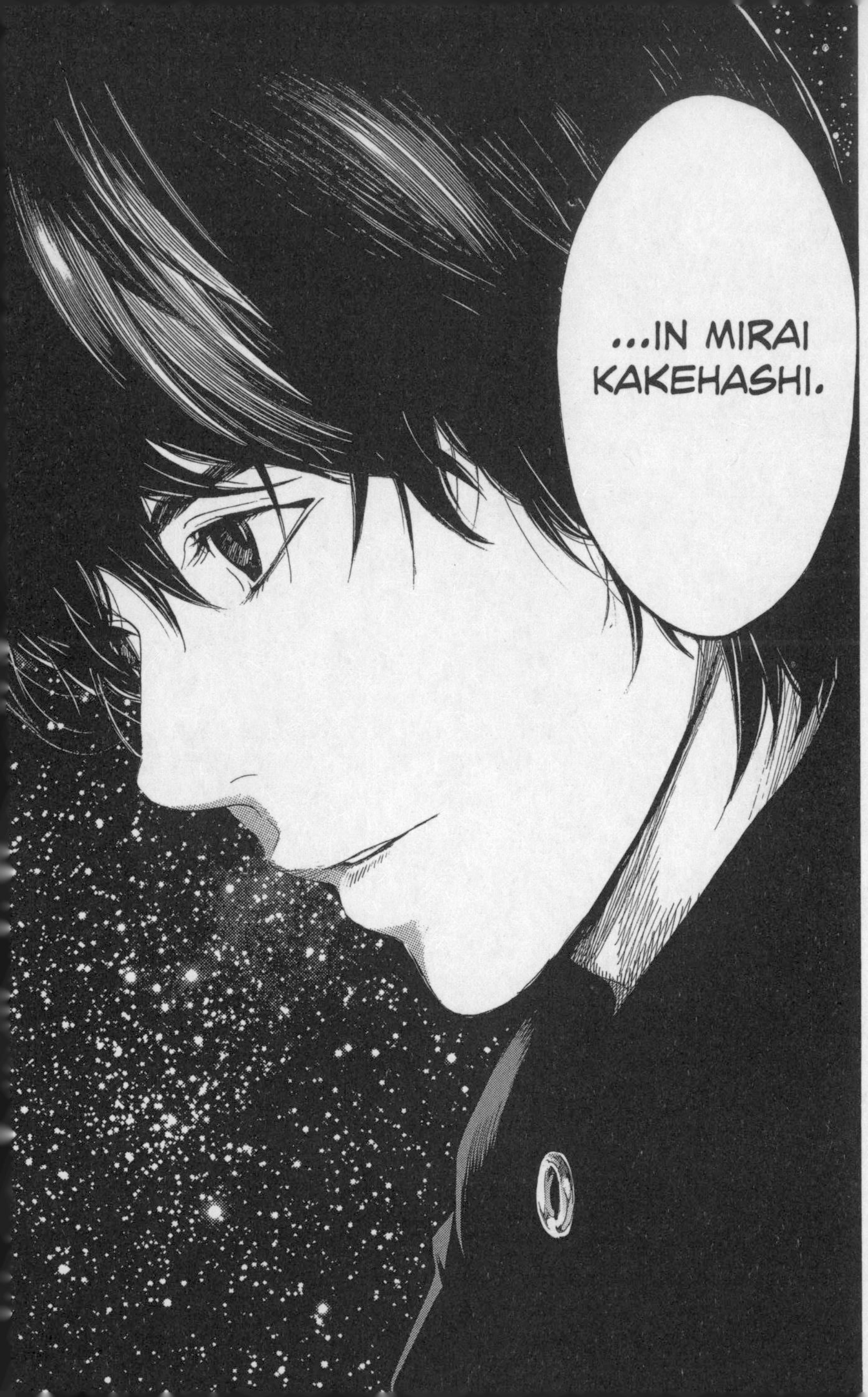
...IN MIRAI KAKEHASHI.

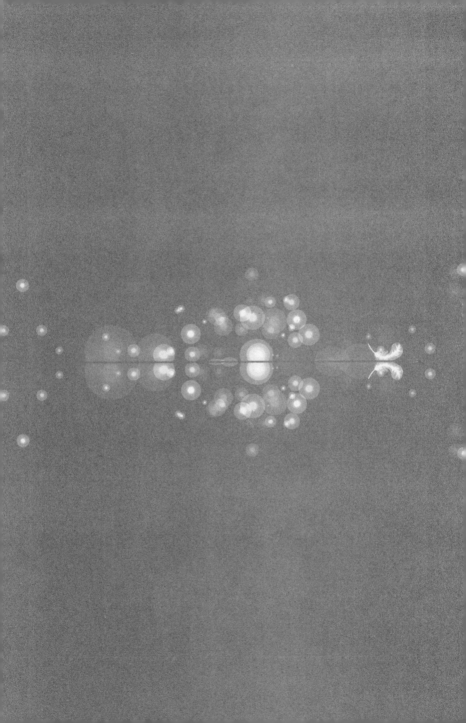

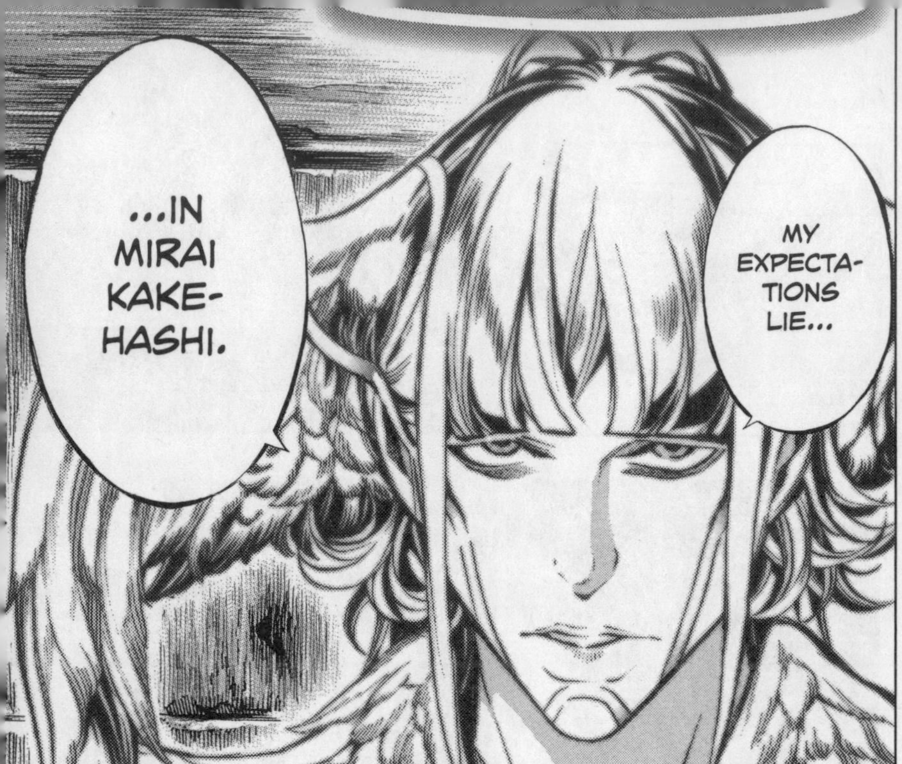
MY EXPECTA-TIONS LIE...
...IN MIRAI KAKE-HASHI.

#44 Stars in the Night Sky

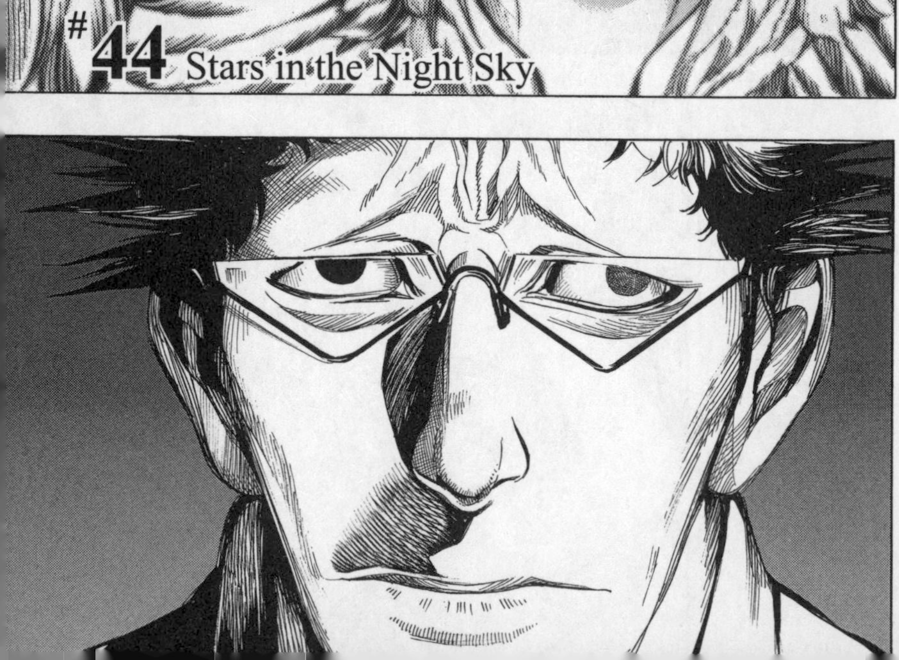

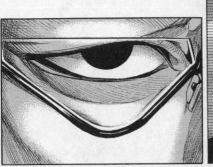

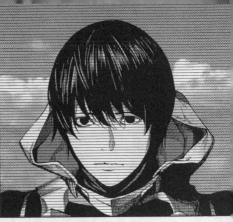

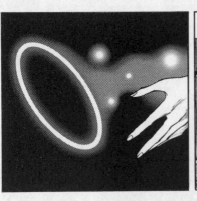

SHWA

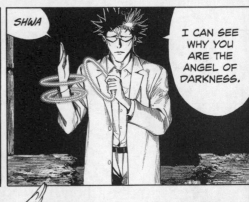

I CAN SEE WHY YOU ARE THE ANGEL OF DARKNESS.

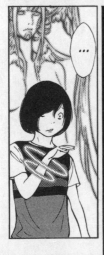

...

SHING...

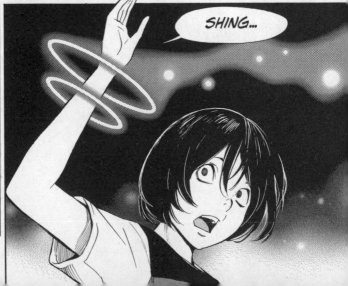

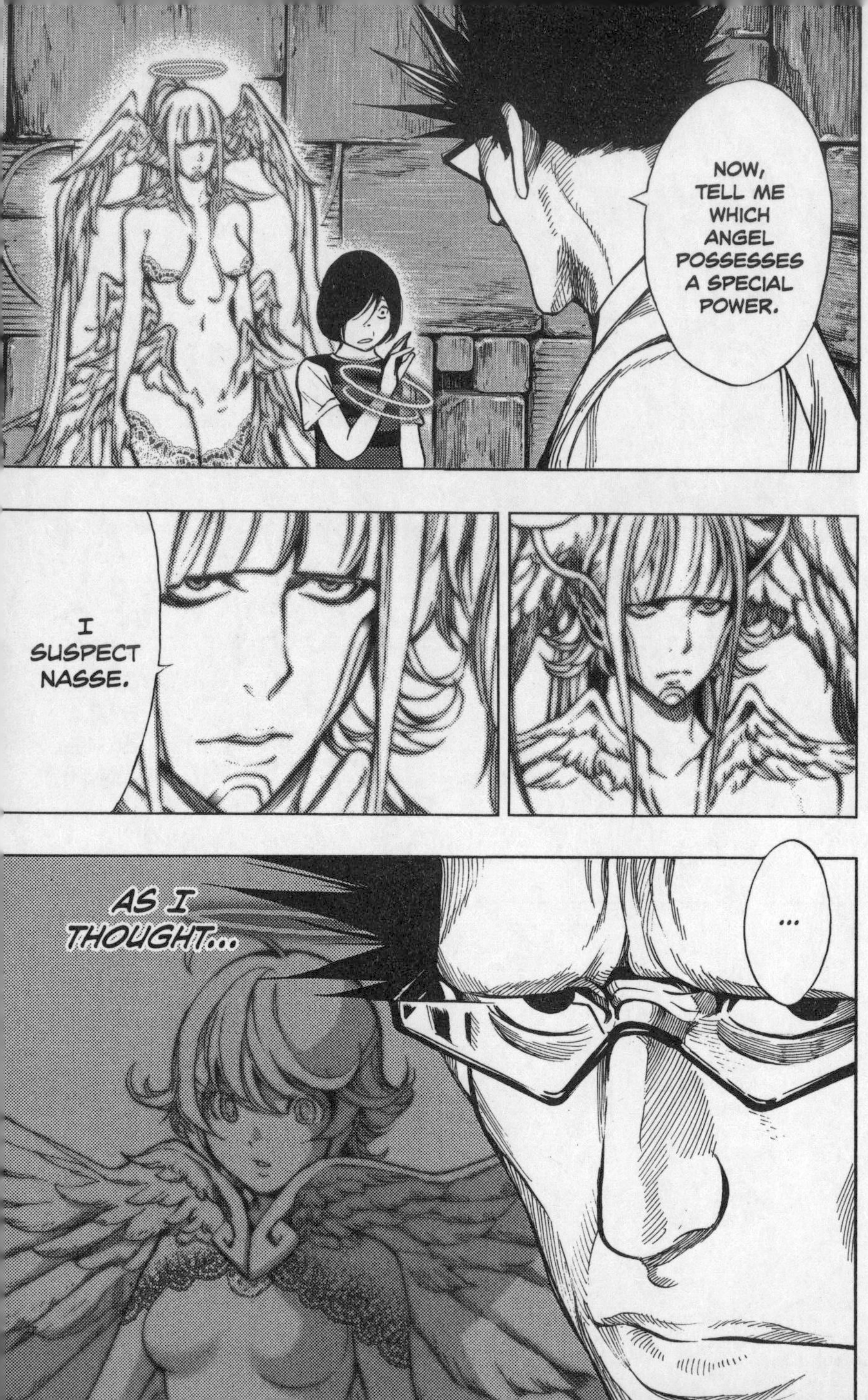
NOW, TELL ME WHICH ANGEL POSSESSES A SPECIAL POWER.
I SUSPECT NASSE.
...
AS I THOUGHT...

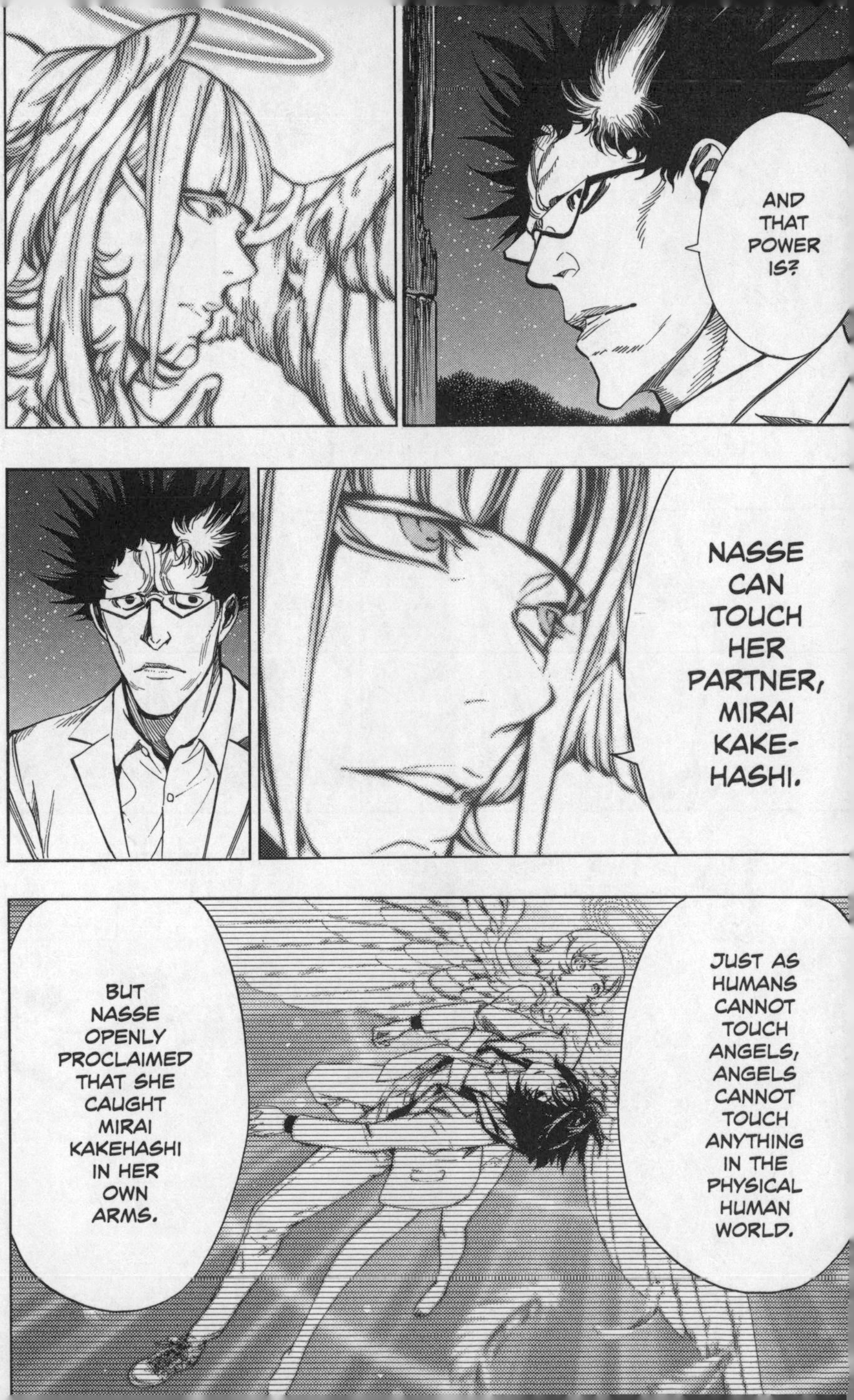
AND THAT POWER IS?
NASSE CAN TOUCH HER PARTNER, MIRAI KAKE-HASHI.
JUST AS HUMANS CANNOT TOUCH ANGELS, ANGELS CANNOT TOUCH ANYTHING IN THE PHYSICAL HUMAN WORLD.
BUT NASSE OPENLY PROCLAIMED THAT SHE CAUGHT MIRAI KAKEHASHI IN HER OWN ARMS.

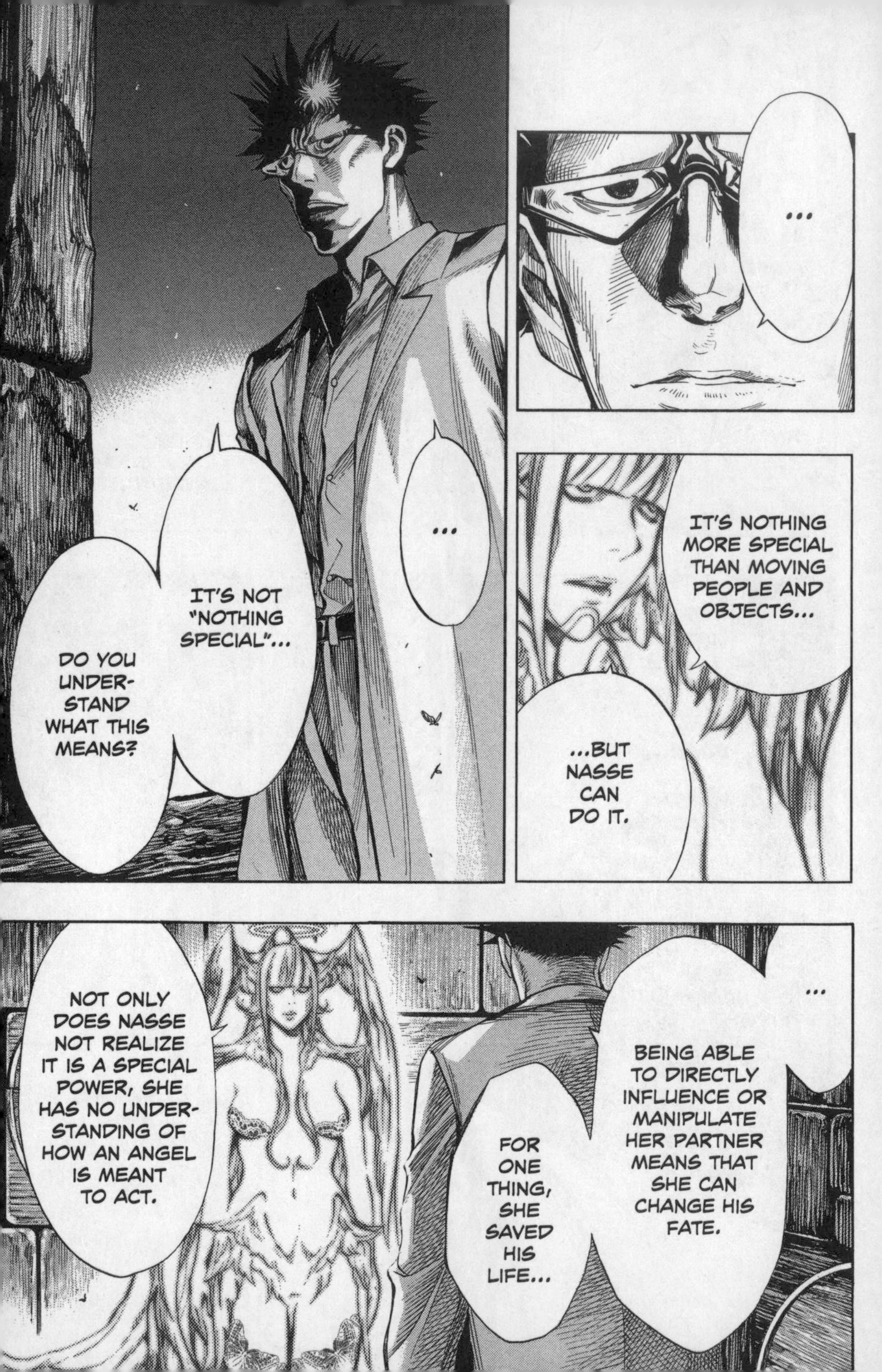
...
IT'S NOTHING MORE SPECIAL THAN MOVING PEOPLE AND OBJECTS...
...BUT NASSE CAN DO IT.
...
IT'S NOT "NOTHING SPECIAL"...
DO YOU UNDERSTAND WHAT THIS MEANS?
...
BEING ABLE TO DIRECTLY INFLUENCE OR MANIPULATE HER PARTNER MEANS THAT SHE CAN CHANGE HIS FATE.
FOR ONE THING, SHE SAVED HIS LIFE...
NOT ONLY DOES NASSE NOT REALIZE IT IS A SPECIAL POWER, SHE HAS NO UNDERSTANDING OF HOW AN ANGEL IS MEANT TO ACT.

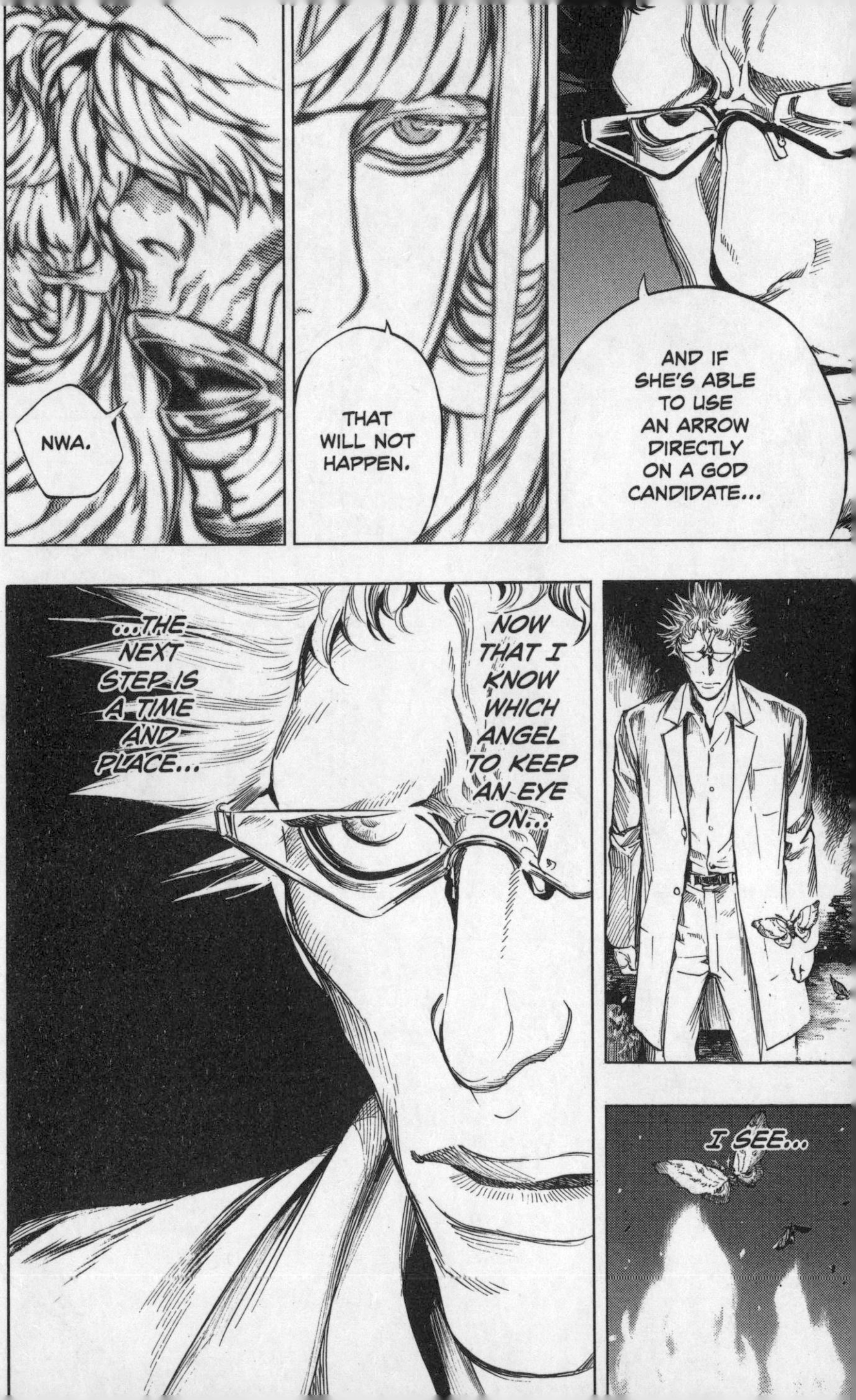
AND IF SHE'S ABLE TO USE AN ARROW DIRECTLY ON A GOD CANDIDATE...
THAT WILL NOT HAPPEN.
NWA.
I SEE...
NOW THAT I KNOW WHICH ANGEL TO KEEP AN EYE ON...
...THE NEXT STEP IS A TIME AND PLACE...

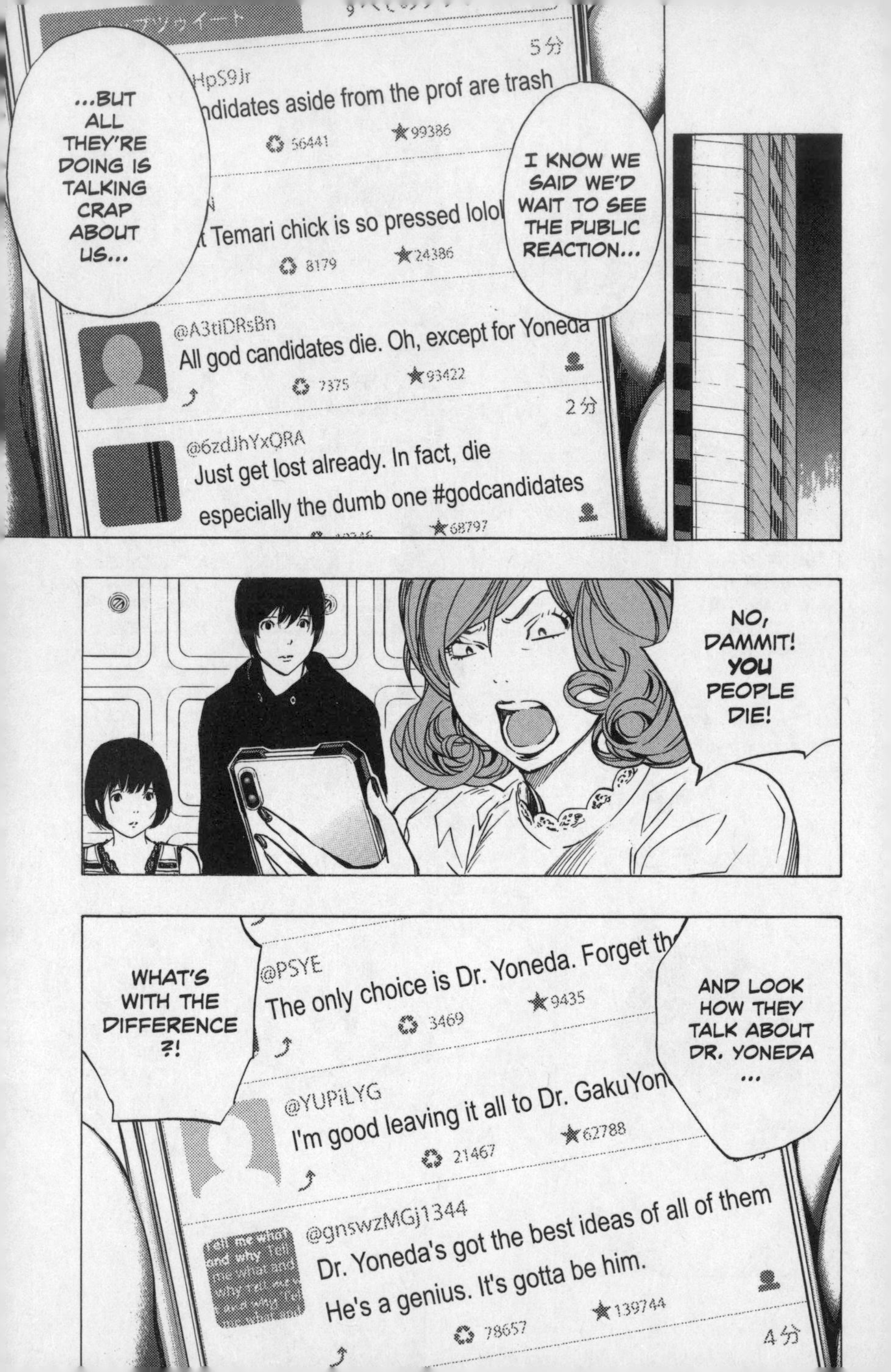
I KNOW WE SAID WE'D WAIT TO SEE THE PUBLIC REACTION...
...BUT ALL THEY'RE DOING IS TALKING CRAP ABOUT US...
5分
HpS9Jr
ndidates aside from the prof are trash
56441 99386
t Temari chick is so pressed lolol
8179 24386
@A3tiDRsBn
All god candidates die. Oh, except for Yoneda
7375 93422
2分
@6zdJhYxQRA
Just get lost already. In fact, die
especially the dumb one #godcandidates
68797
NO, DAMMIT! YOU PEOPLE DIE!
AND LOOK HOW THEY TALK ABOUT DR. YONEDA ...
WHAT'S WITH THE DIFFERENCE ?!
@PSYE
The only choice is Dr. Yoneda. Forget th
3469 9435
@YUPiLYG
I'm good leaving it all to Dr. GakuYon
21467 62788
@gnswzMGj1344
Dr. Yoneda's got the best ideas of all of them
He's a genius. It's gotta be him.
78657 139744
4分

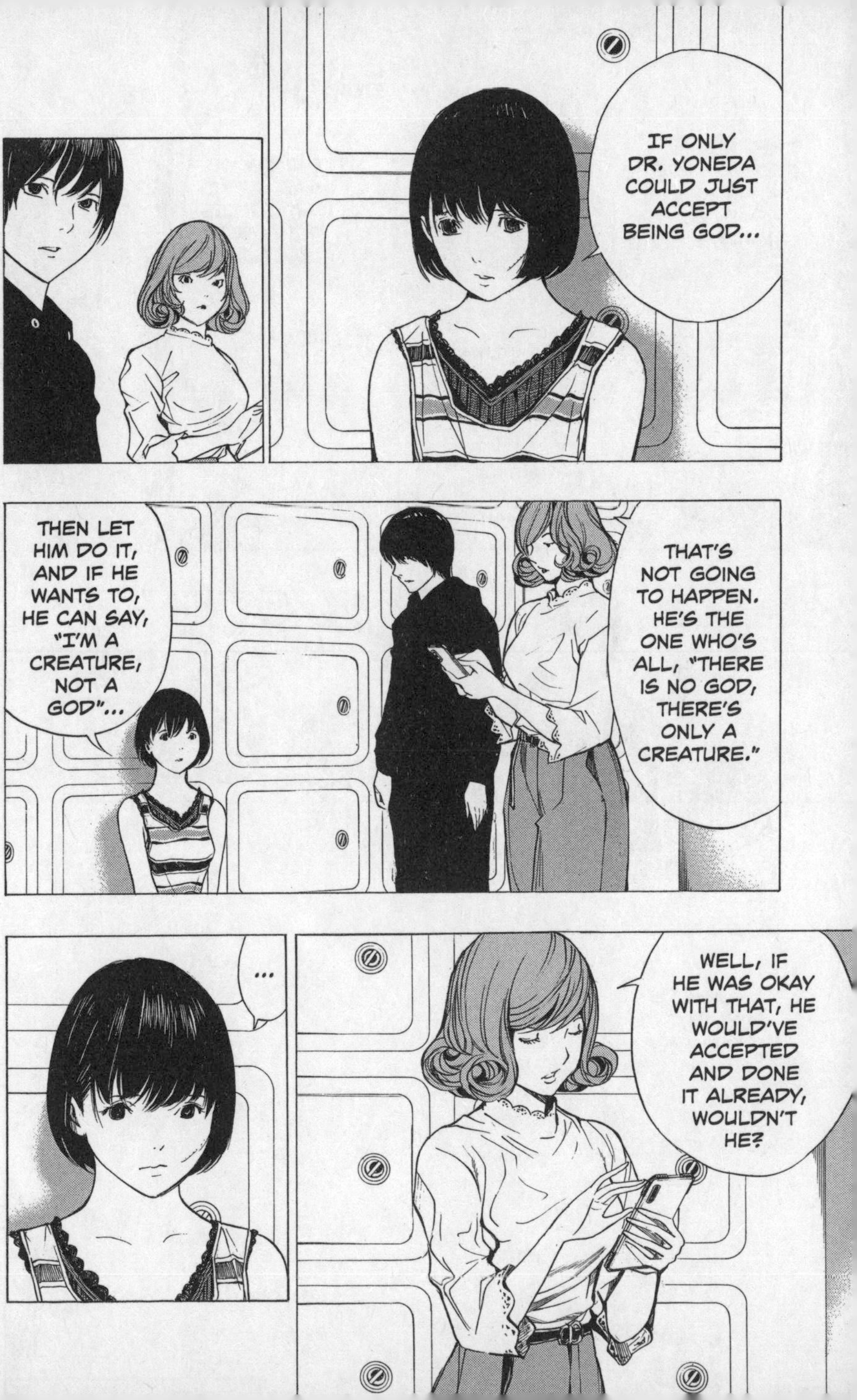
IF ONLY DR. YONEDA COULD JUST ACCEPT BEING GOD...
THAT'S NOT GOING TO HAPPEN. HE'S THE ONE WHO'S ALL, "THERE IS NO GOD, THERE'S ONLY A CREATURE."
THEN LET HIM DO IT, AND IF HE WANTS TO, HE CAN SAY, "I'M A CREATURE, NOT A GOD"...
WELL, IF HE WAS OKAY WITH THAT, HE WOULD'VE ACCEPTED AND DONE IT ALREADY, WOULDN'T HE?
...

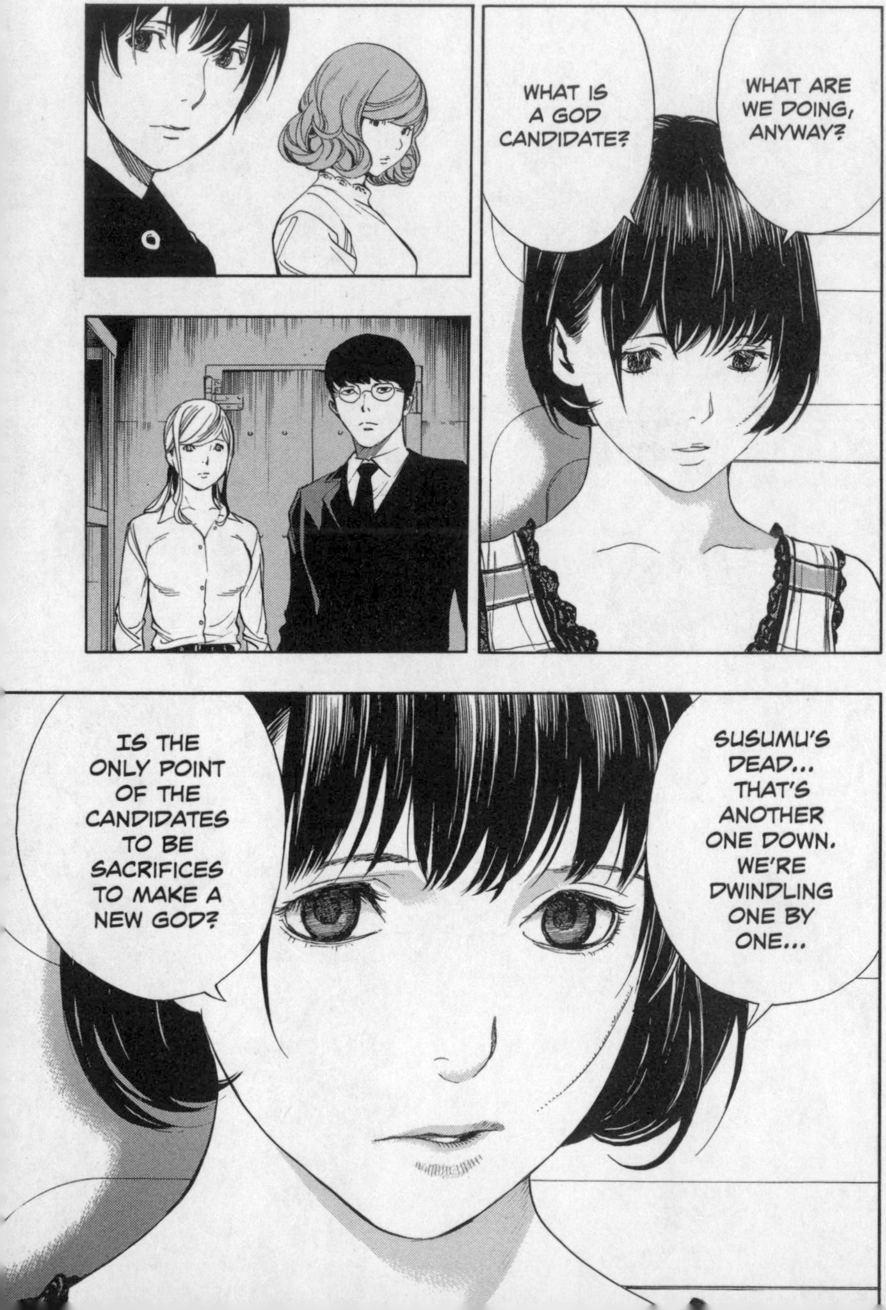
WHAT ARE WE DOING, ANYWAY?
WHAT IS A GOD CANDIDATE?
SUSUMU'S DEAD... THAT'S ANOTHER ONE DOWN. WE'RE DWINDLING ONE BY ONE...
IS THE ONLY POINT OF THE CANDIDATES TO BE SACRIFICES TO MAKE A NEW GOD?

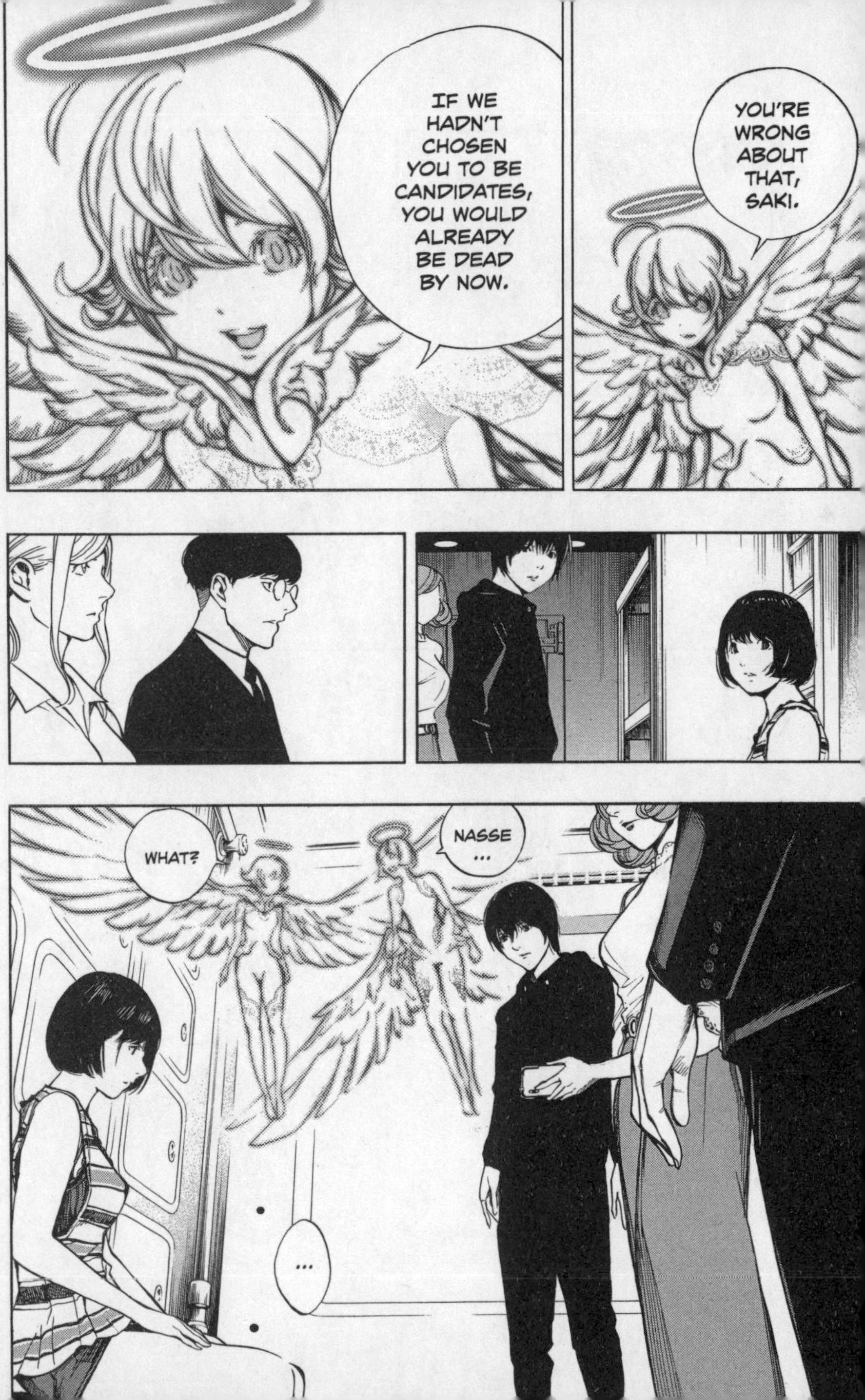
YOU'RE WRONG ABOUT THAT, SAKI.
IF WE HADN'T CHOSEN YOU TO BE CANDIDATES, YOU WOULD ALREADY BE DEAD BY NOW.
NASSE ...
WHAT?
...

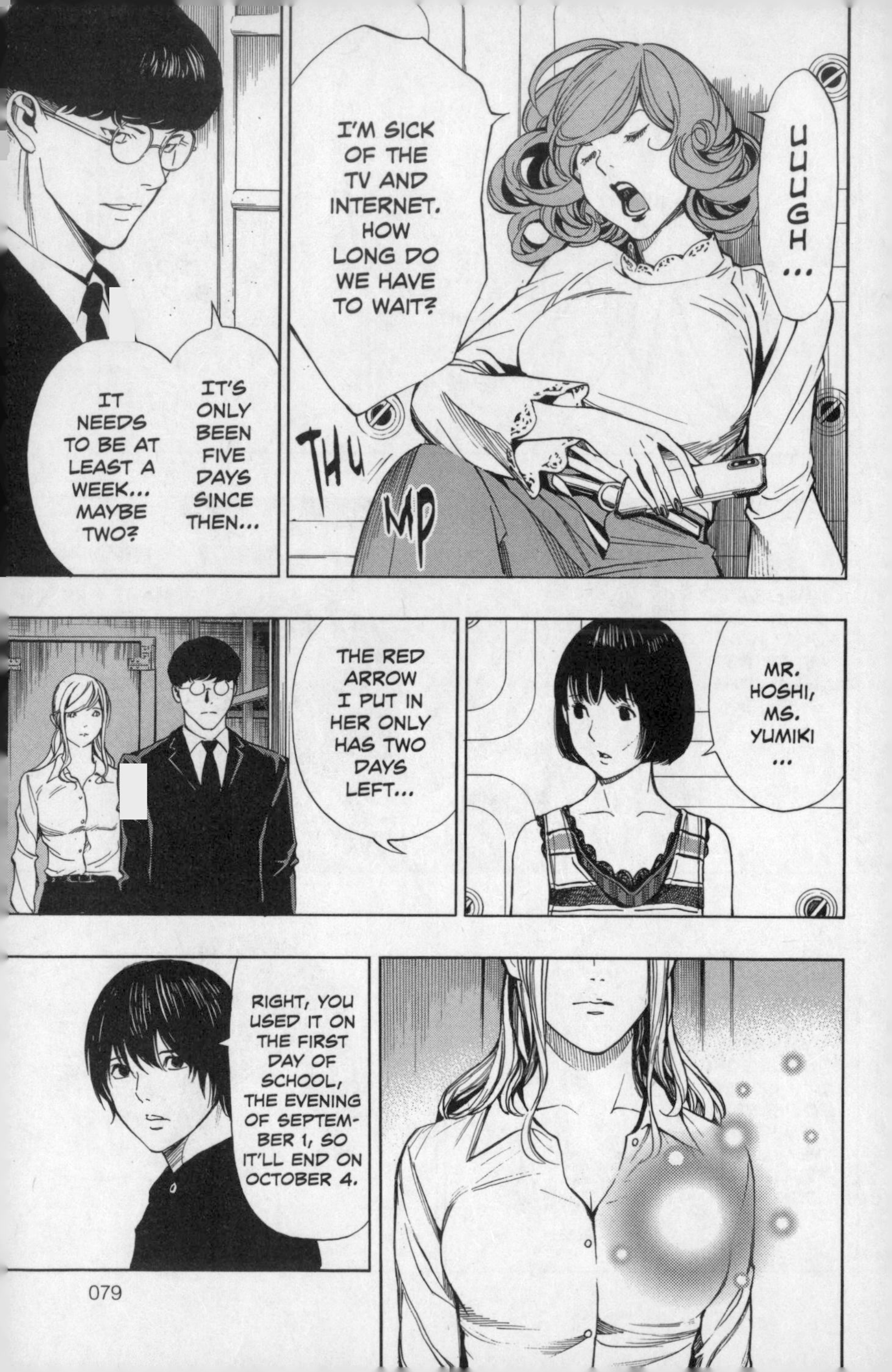
UUUGH...
I'M SICK OF THE TV AND INTERNET. HOW LONG DO WE HAVE TO WAIT?
THUMP
IT'S ONLY BEEN FIVE DAYS SINCE THEN...
IT NEEDS TO BE AT LEAST A WEEK... MAYBE TWO?
MR. HOSHI, MS. YUMIKI...
THE RED ARROW I PUT IN HER ONLY HAS TWO DAYS LEFT...
RIGHT, YOU USED IT ON THE FIRST DAY OF SCHOOL, THE EVENING OF SEPTEMBER 1, SO IT'LL END ON OCTOBER 4.

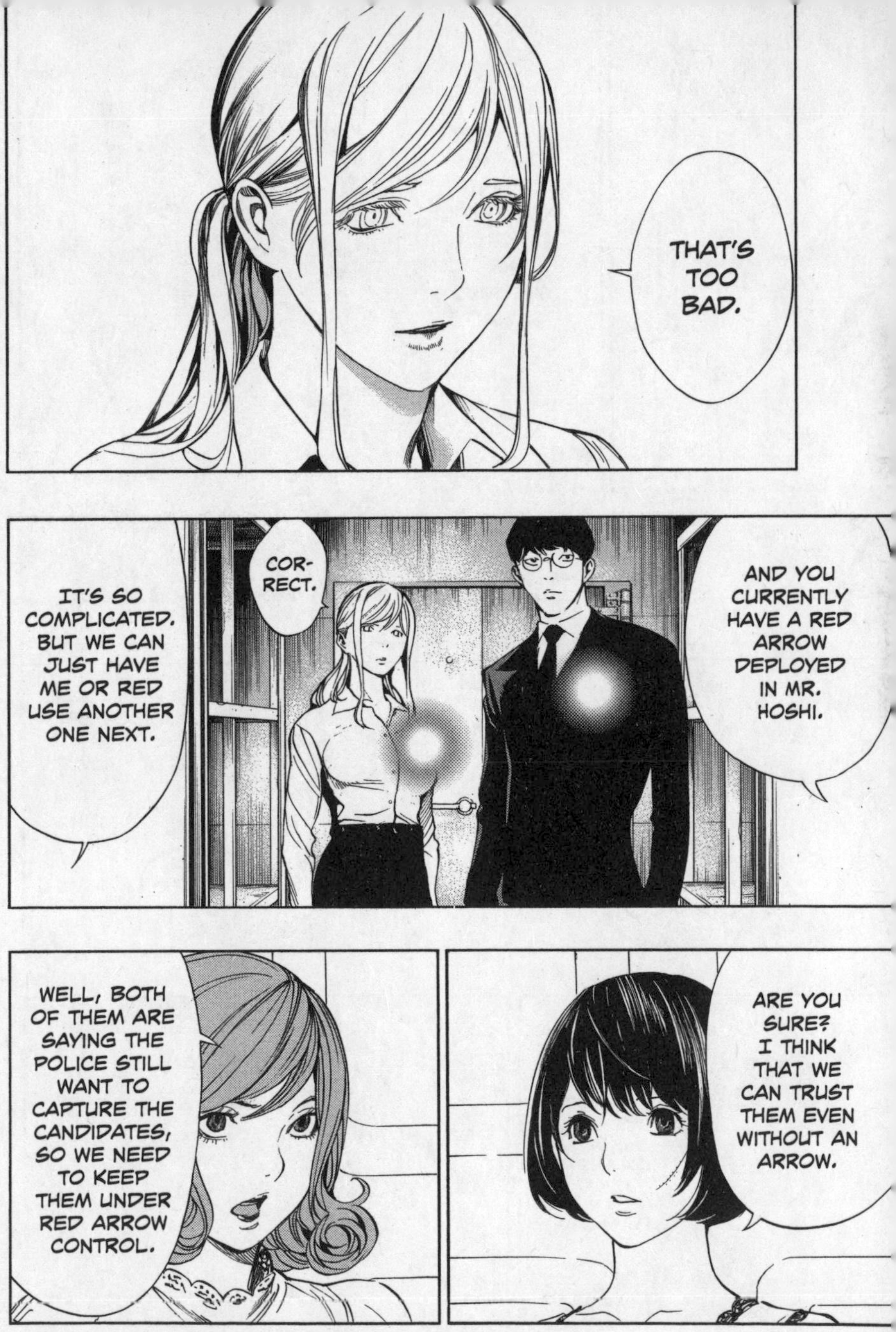
THAT'S TOO BAD.
AND YOU CURRENTLY HAVE A RED ARROW DEPLOYED IN MR. HOSHI.
COR-RECT.
IT'S SO COMPLICATED. BUT WE CAN JUST HAVE ME OR RED USE ANOTHER ONE NEXT.
ARE YOU SURE? I THINK THAT WE CAN TRUST THEM EVEN WITHOUT AN ARROW.
WELL, BOTH OF THEM ARE SAYING THE POLICE STILL WANT TO CAPTURE THE CANDIDATES, SO WE NEED TO KEEP THEM UNDER RED ARROW CONTROL.

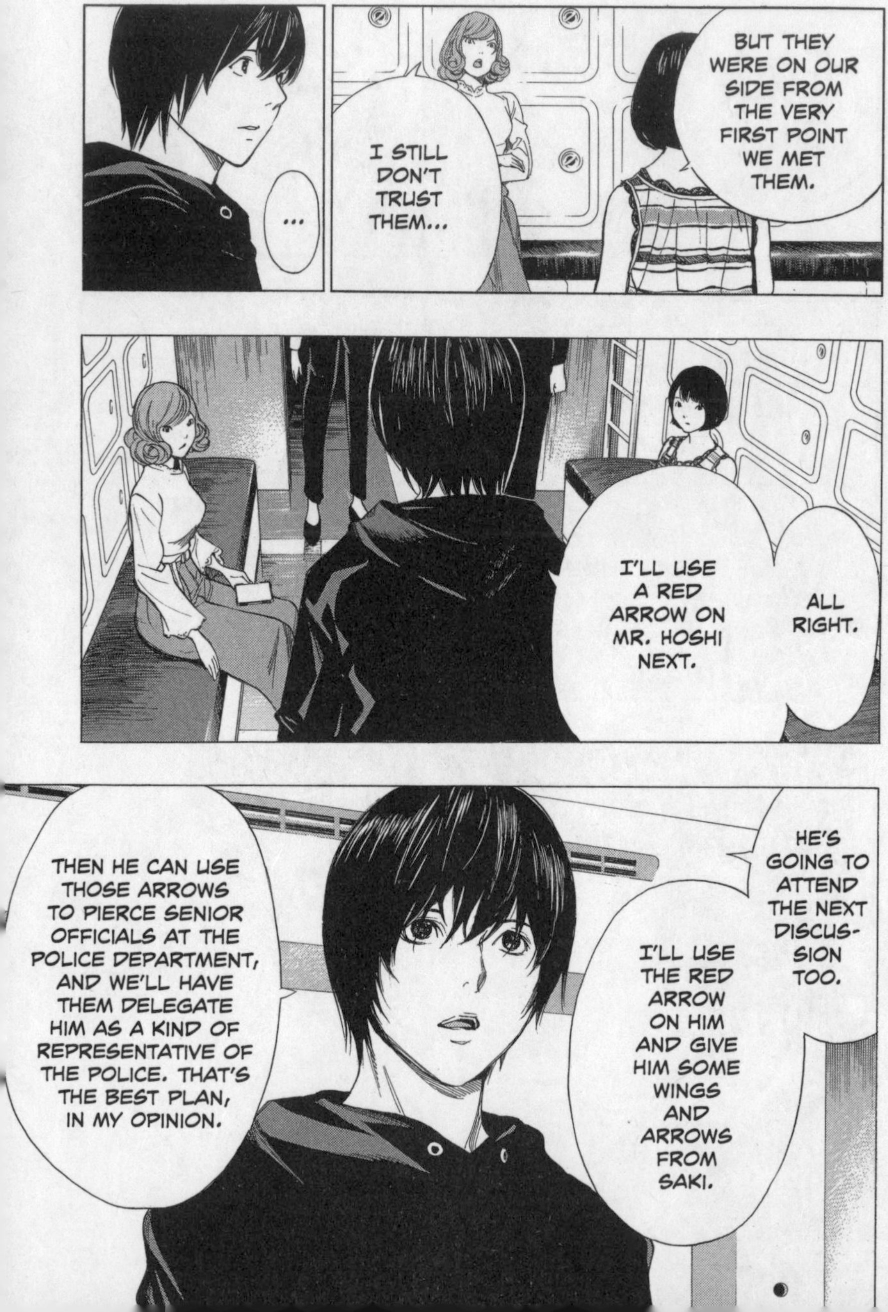
BUT THEY WERE ON OUR SIDE FROM THE VERY FIRST POINT WE MET THEM.
I STILL DON'T TRUST THEM...
...
I'LL USE A RED ARROW ON MR. HOSHI NEXT.
ALL RIGHT.
HE'S GOING TO ATTEND THE NEXT DISCUS-SION TOO.
I'LL USE THE RED ARROW ON HIM AND GIVE HIM SOME WINGS AND ARROWS FROM SAKI.
THEN HE CAN USE THOSE ARROWS TO PIERCE SENIOR OFFICIALS AT THE POLICE DEPARTMENT, AND WE'LL HAVE THEM DELEGATE HIM AS A KIND OF REPRESENTATIVE OF THE POLICE. THAT'S THE BEST PLAN, IN MY OPINION.

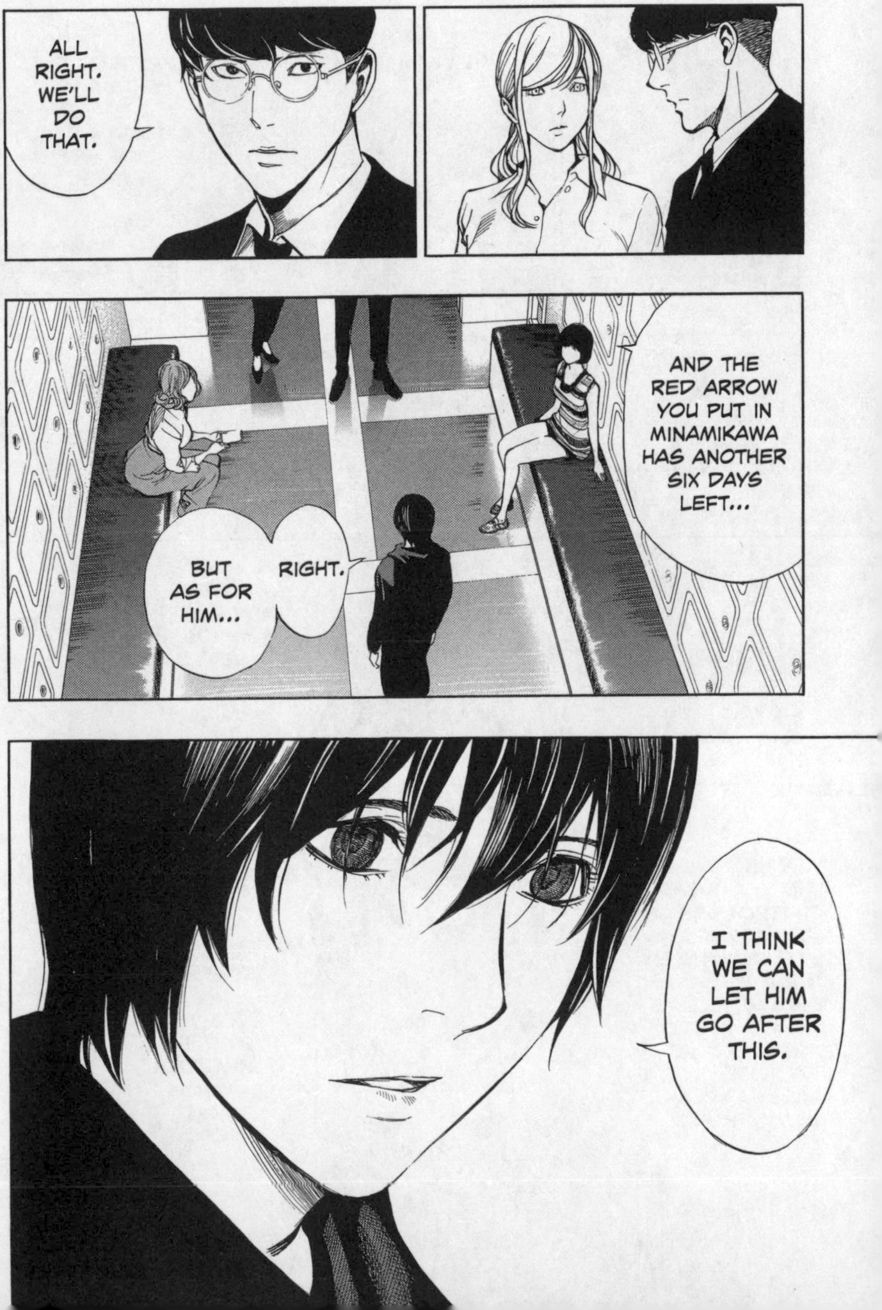
ALL RIGHT. WE'LL DO THAT.
AND THE RED ARROW YOU PUT IN MINAMIKAWA HAS ANOTHER SIX DAYS LEFT...
RIGHT.
BUT AS FOR HIM...
I THINK WE CAN LET HIM GO AFTER THIS.

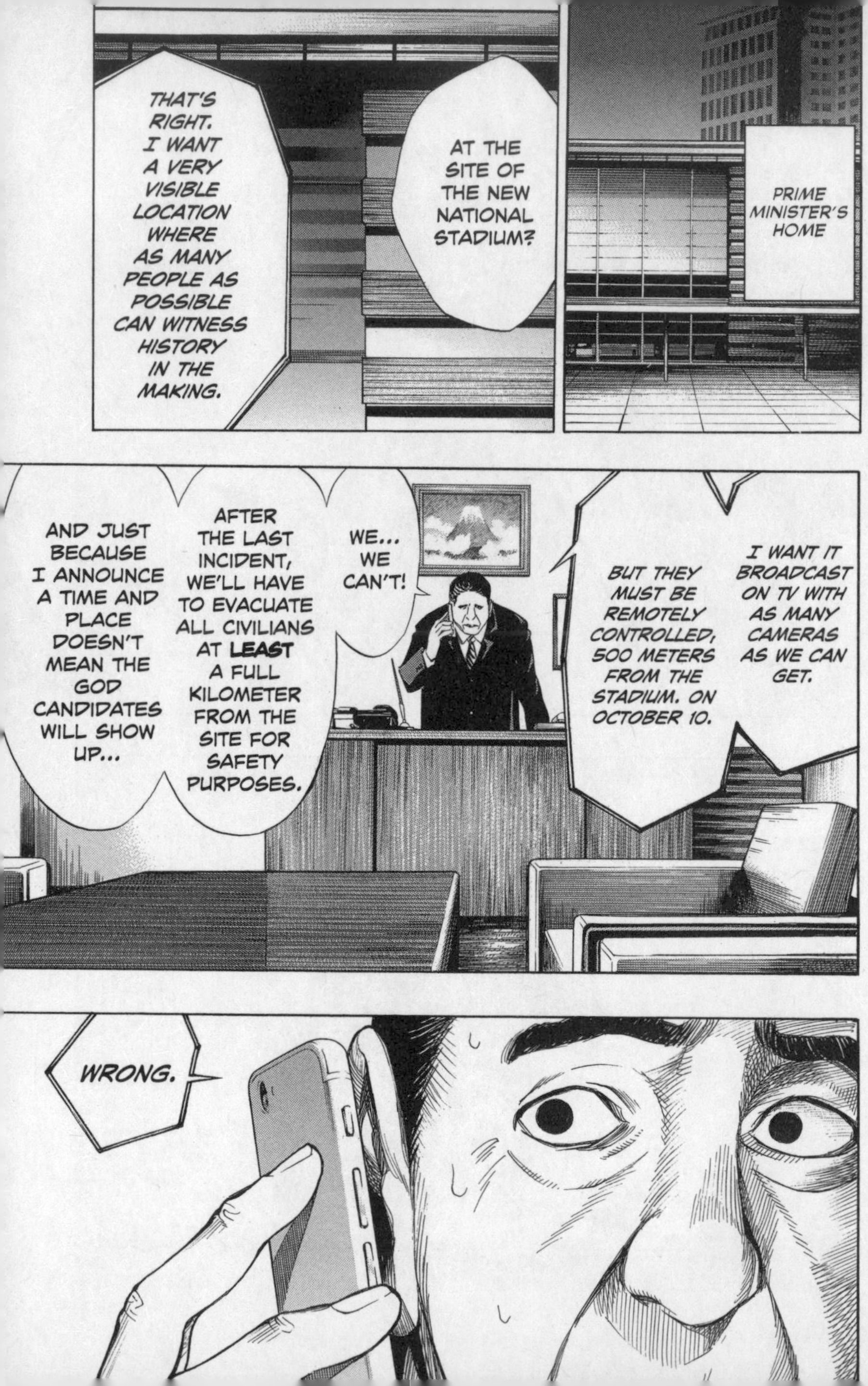
PRIME MINISTER'S HOME
AT THE SITE OF THE NEW NATIONAL STADIUM?
THAT'S RIGHT. I WANT A VERY VISIBLE LOCATION WHERE AS MANY PEOPLE AS POSSIBLE CAN WITNESS HISTORY IN THE MAKING.
I WANT IT BROADCAST ON TV WITH AS MANY CAMERAS AS WE CAN GET.
BUT THEY MUST BE REMOTELY CONTROLLED, 500 METERS FROM THE STADIUM. ON OCTOBER 10.
WE... WE CAN'T!
AFTER THE LAST INCIDENT, WE'LL HAVE TO EVACUATE ALL CIVILIANS AT **LEAST** A FULL KILOMETER FROM THE SITE FOR SAFETY PURPOSES.
AND JUST BECAUSE I ANNOUNCE A TIME AND PLACE DOESN'T MEAN THE GOD CANDIDATES WILL SHOW UP...
WRONG.

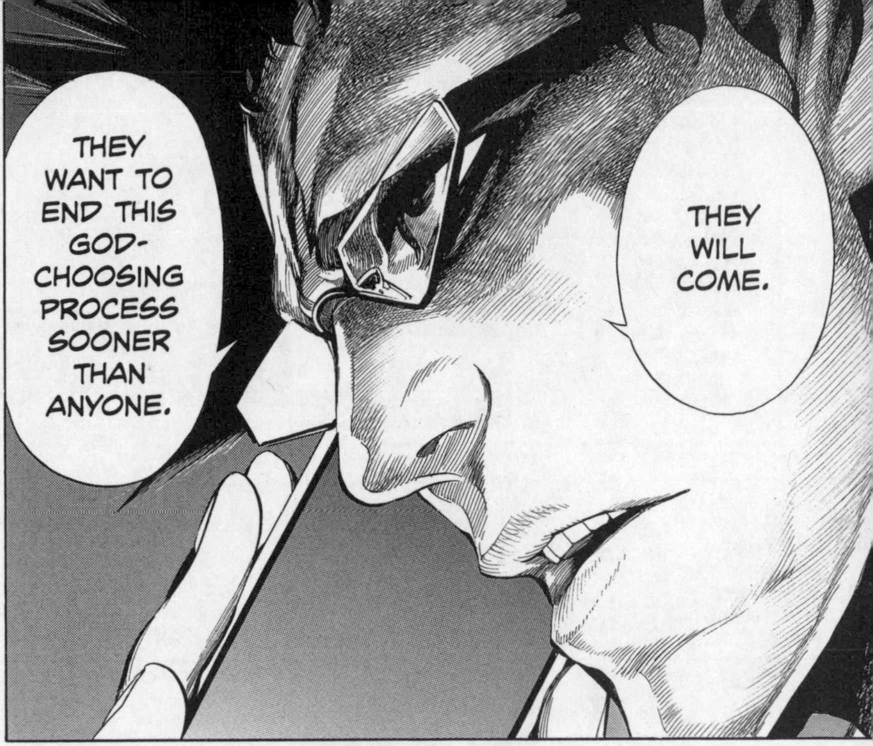
THEY WILL COME.
THEY WANT TO END THIS GOD-CHOOSING PROCESS SOONER THAN ANYONE.

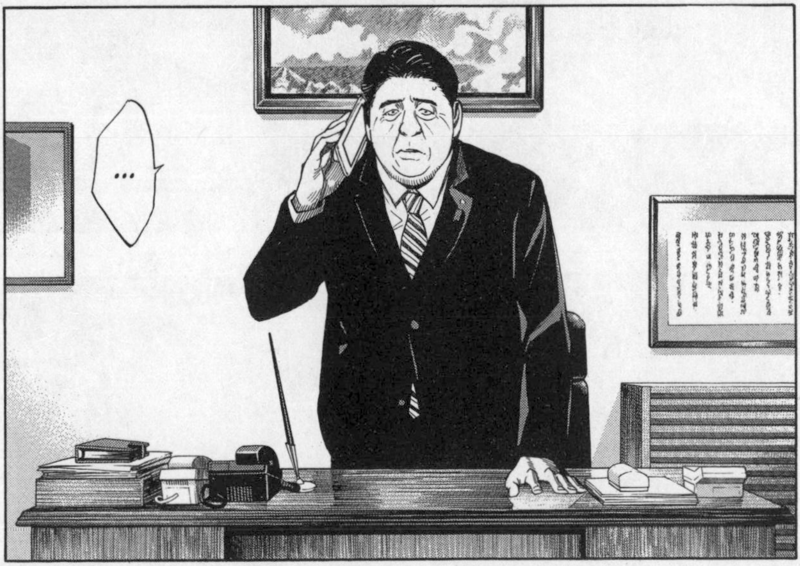
...

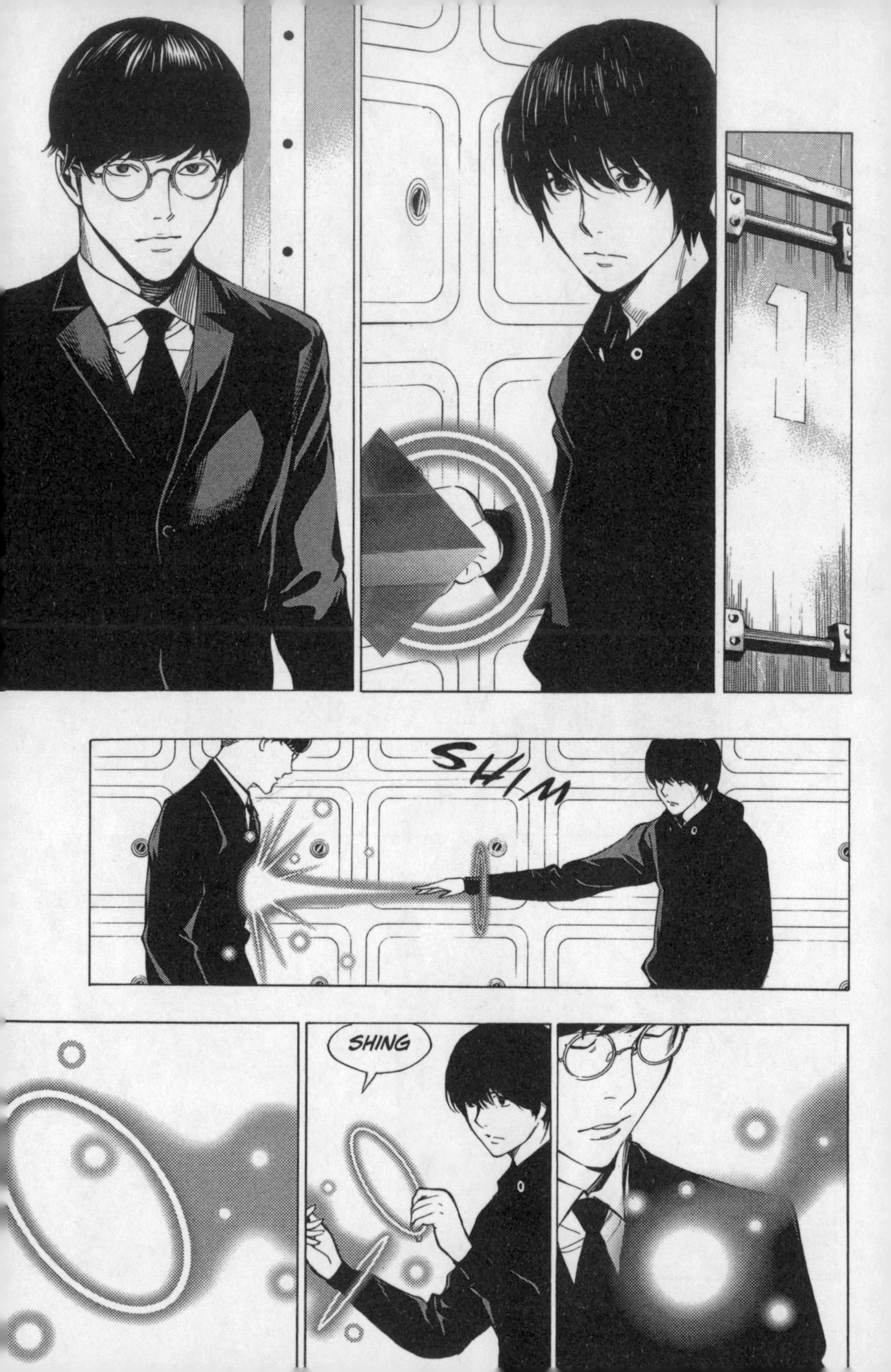
SHIM
SHING

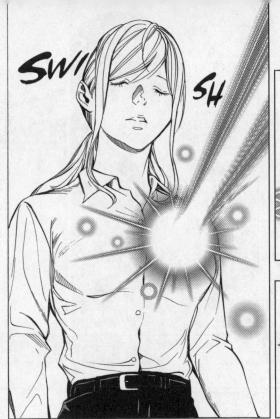

SWI SH

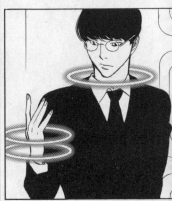

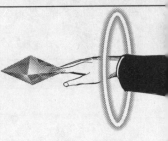

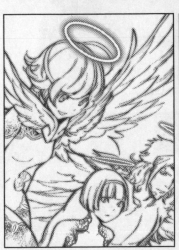

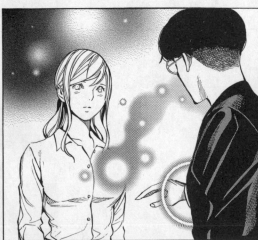

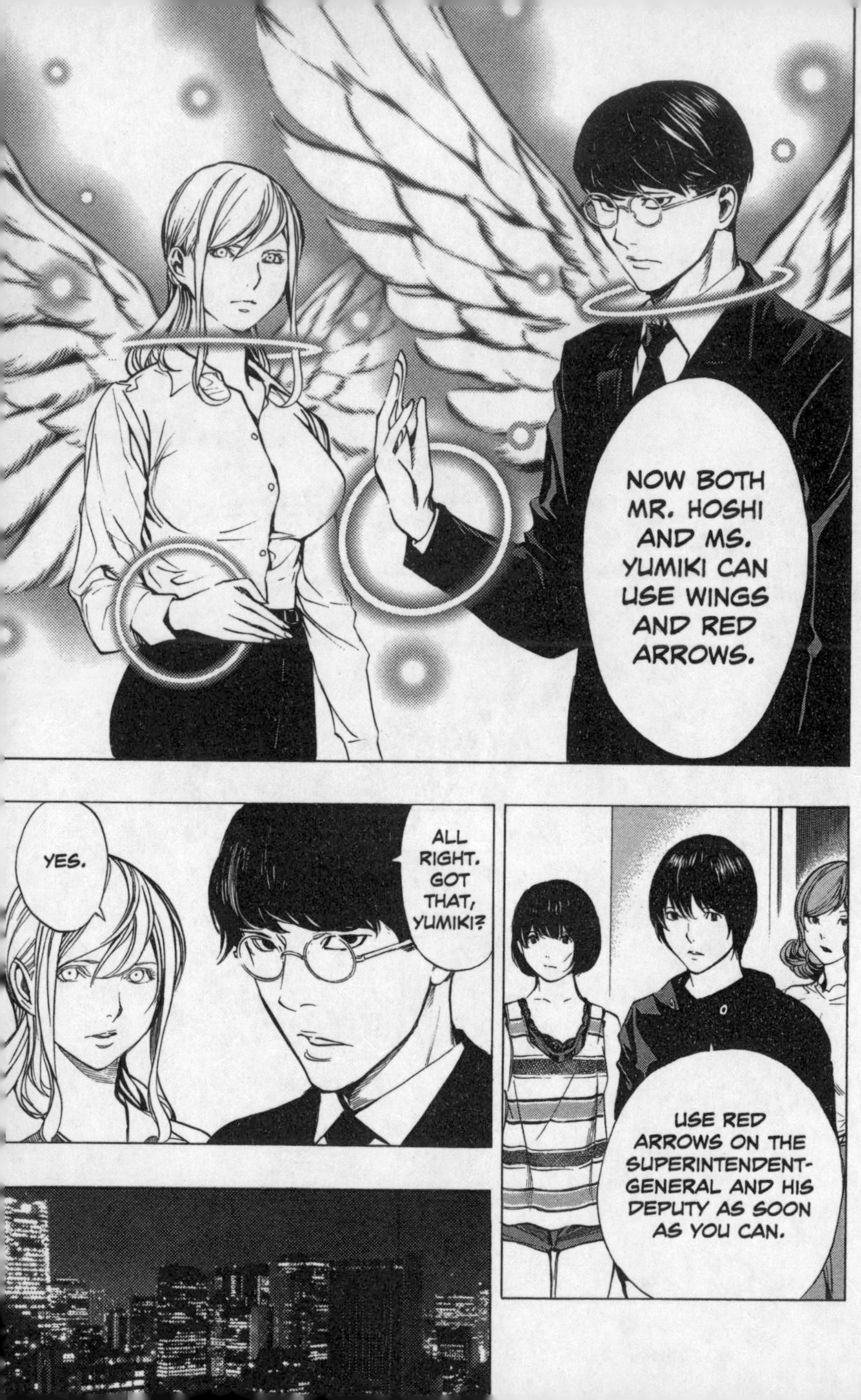
NOW BOTH MR. HOSHI AND MS. YUMIKI CAN USE WINGS AND RED ARROWS.
USE RED ARROWS ON THE SUPERINTENDENT-GENERAL AND HIS DEPUTY AS SOON AS YOU CAN.
ALL RIGHT. GOT THAT, YUMIKI?
YES.

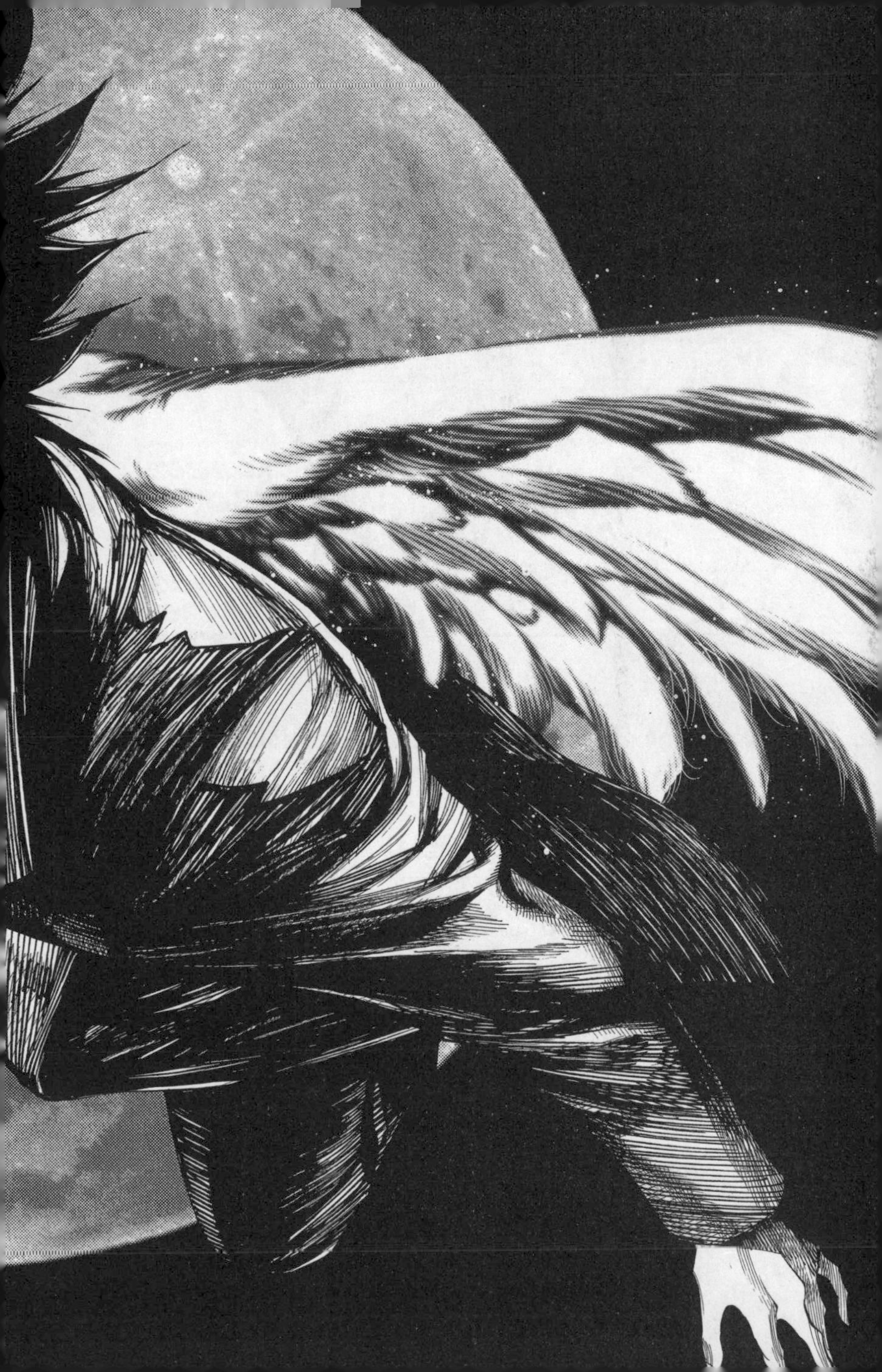

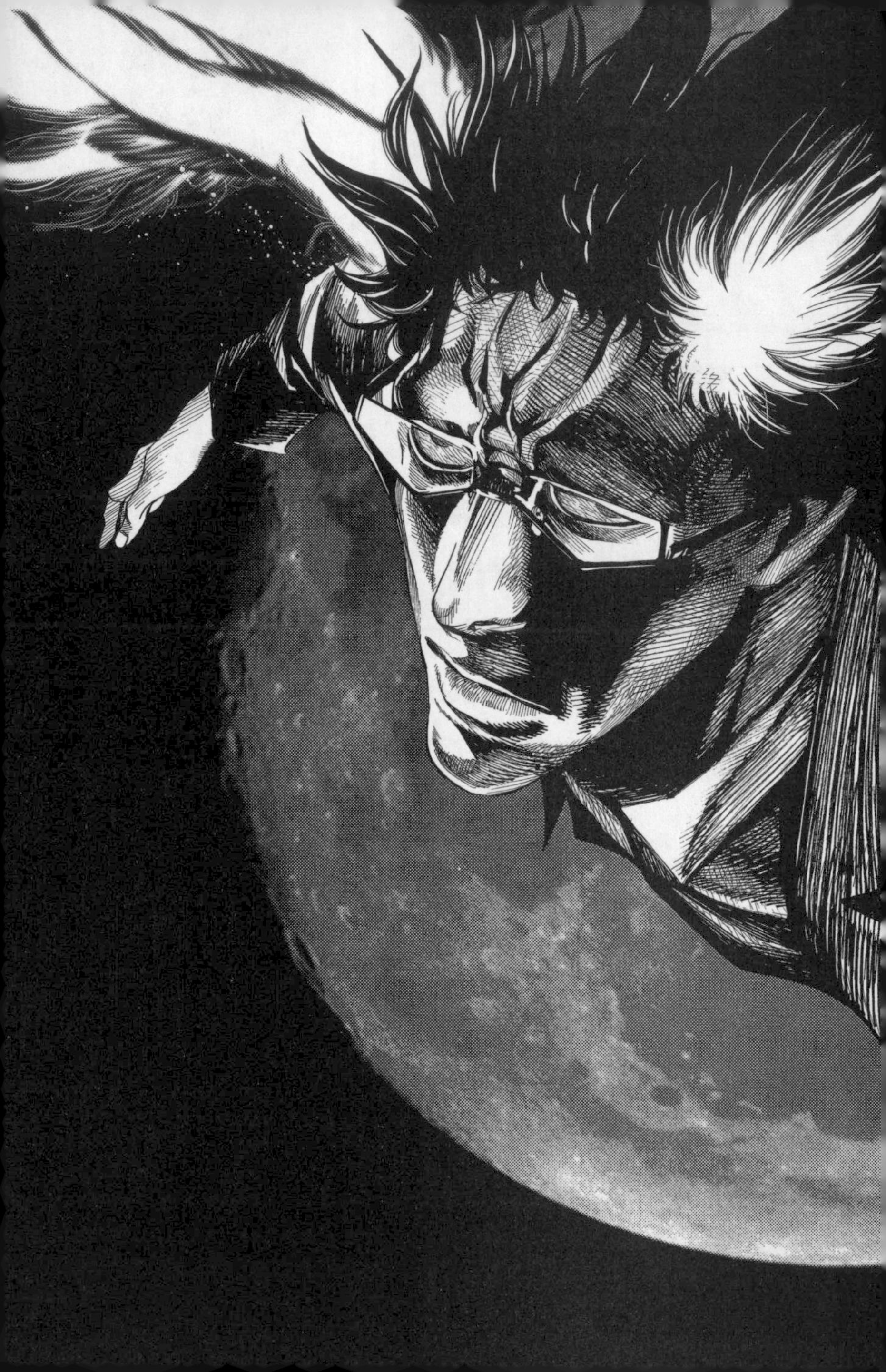

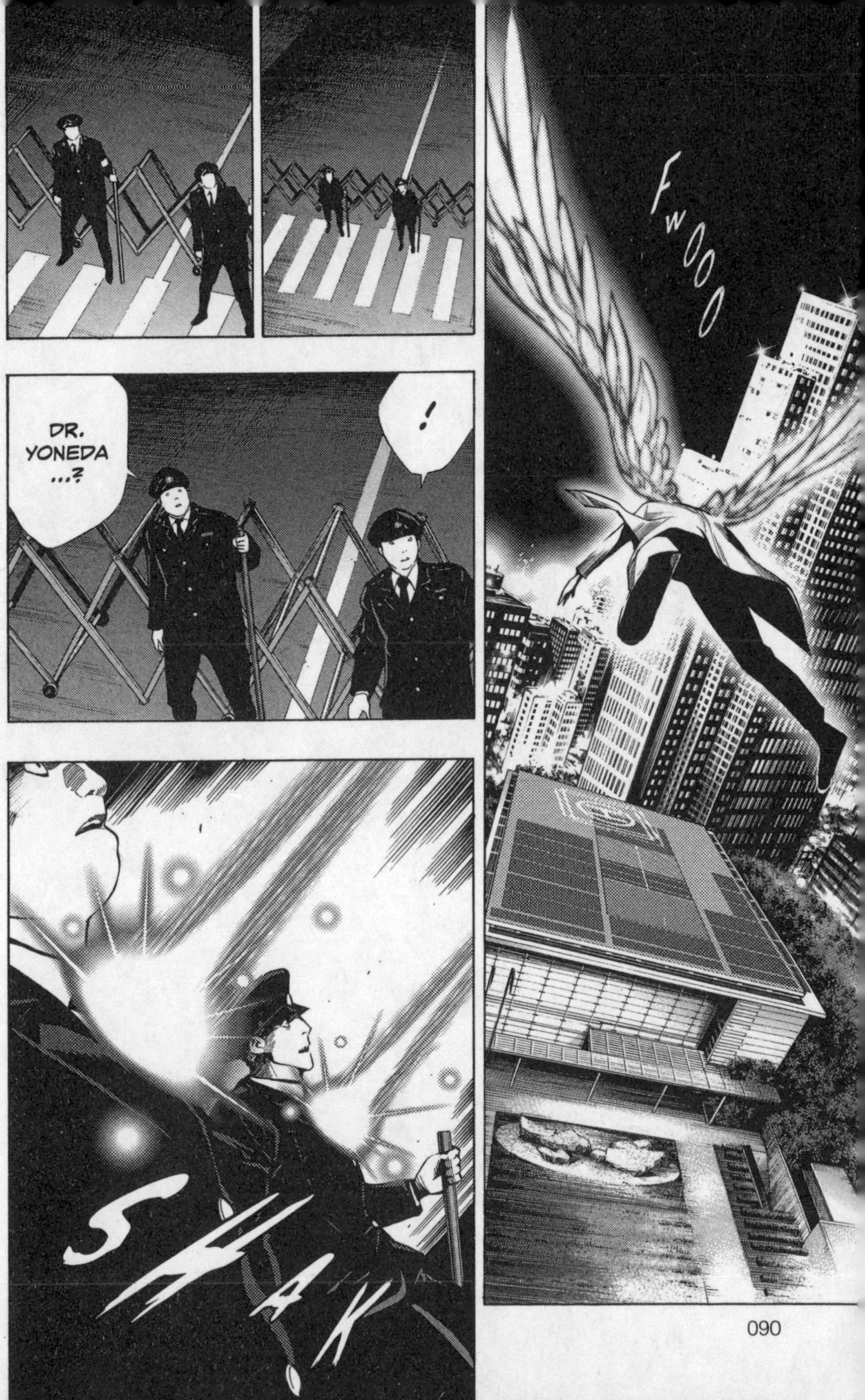
FWOOO
!
DR. YONEDA ...?
SHAK

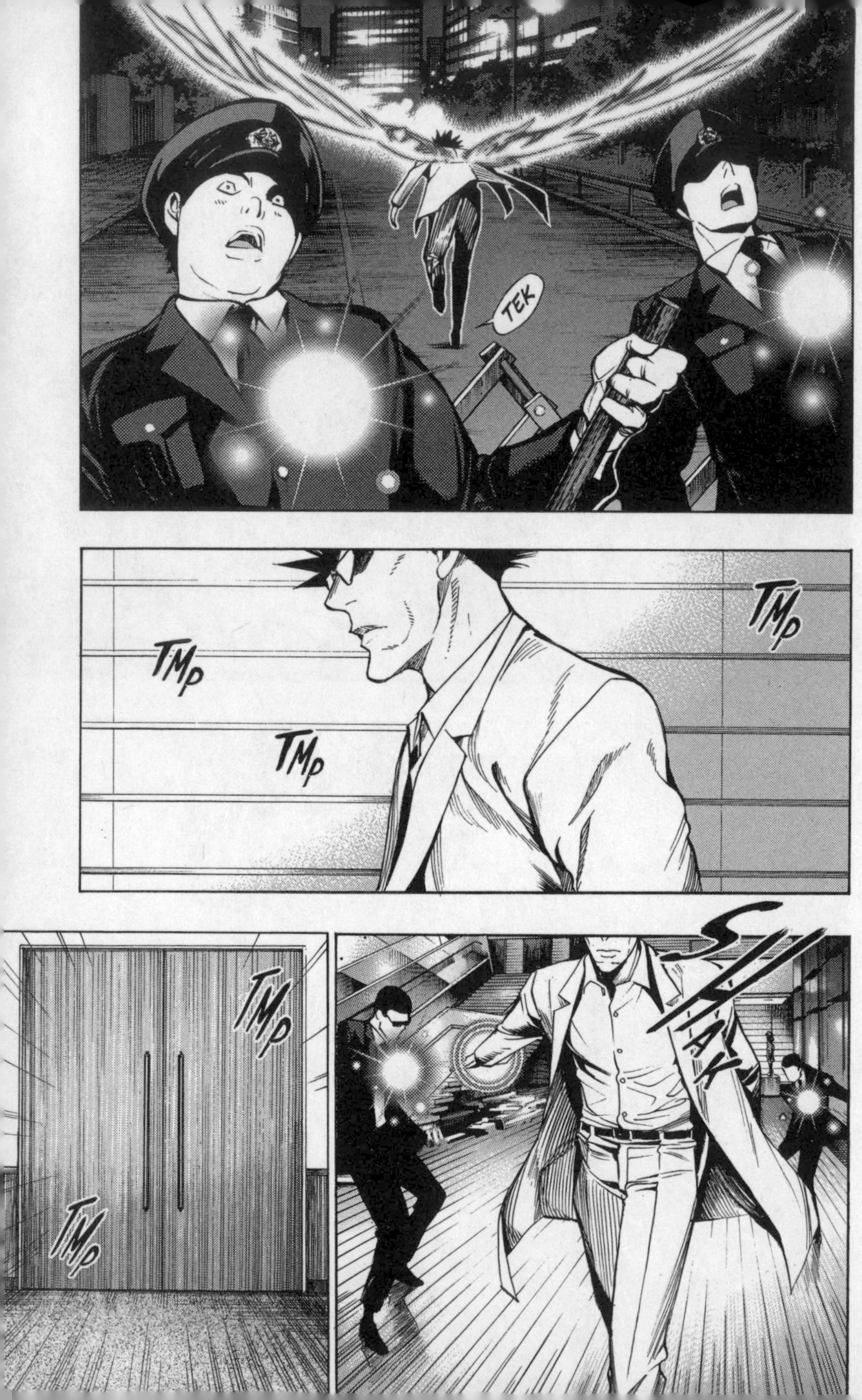
TEK
TMP
TMP
TMP
SHAK
TMP
TMP

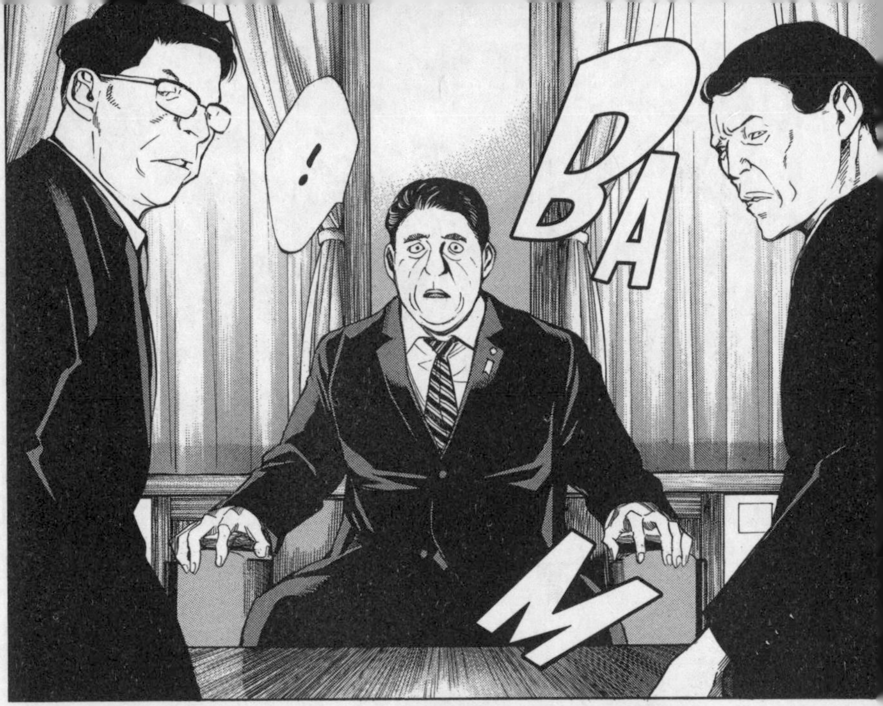
!
BAM

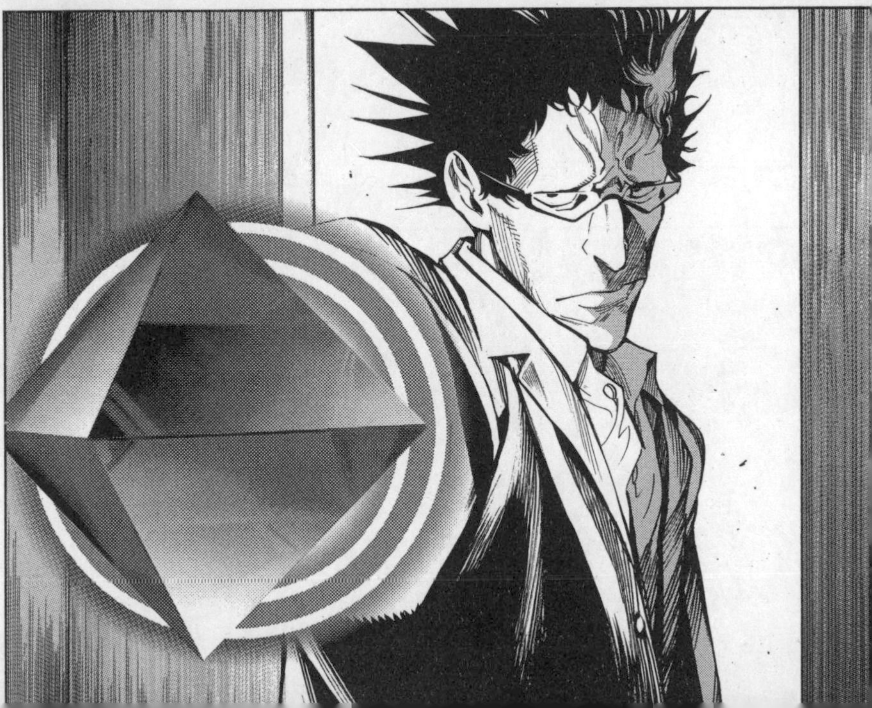

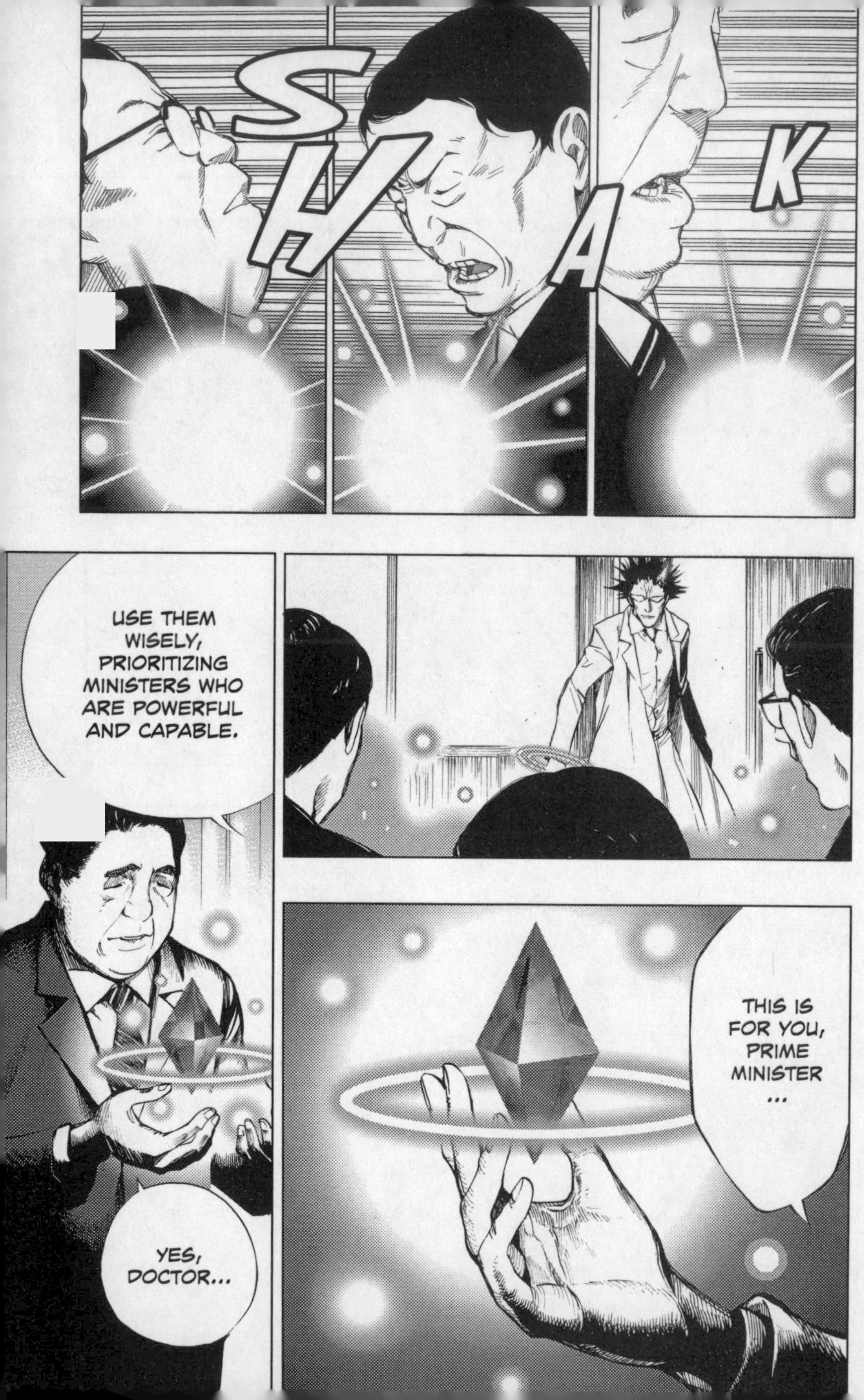
SHAK
THIS IS FOR YOU, PRIME MINISTER ...
USE THEM WISELY, PRIORITIZING MINISTERS WHO ARE POWERFUL AND CAPABLE.
YES, DOCTOR...

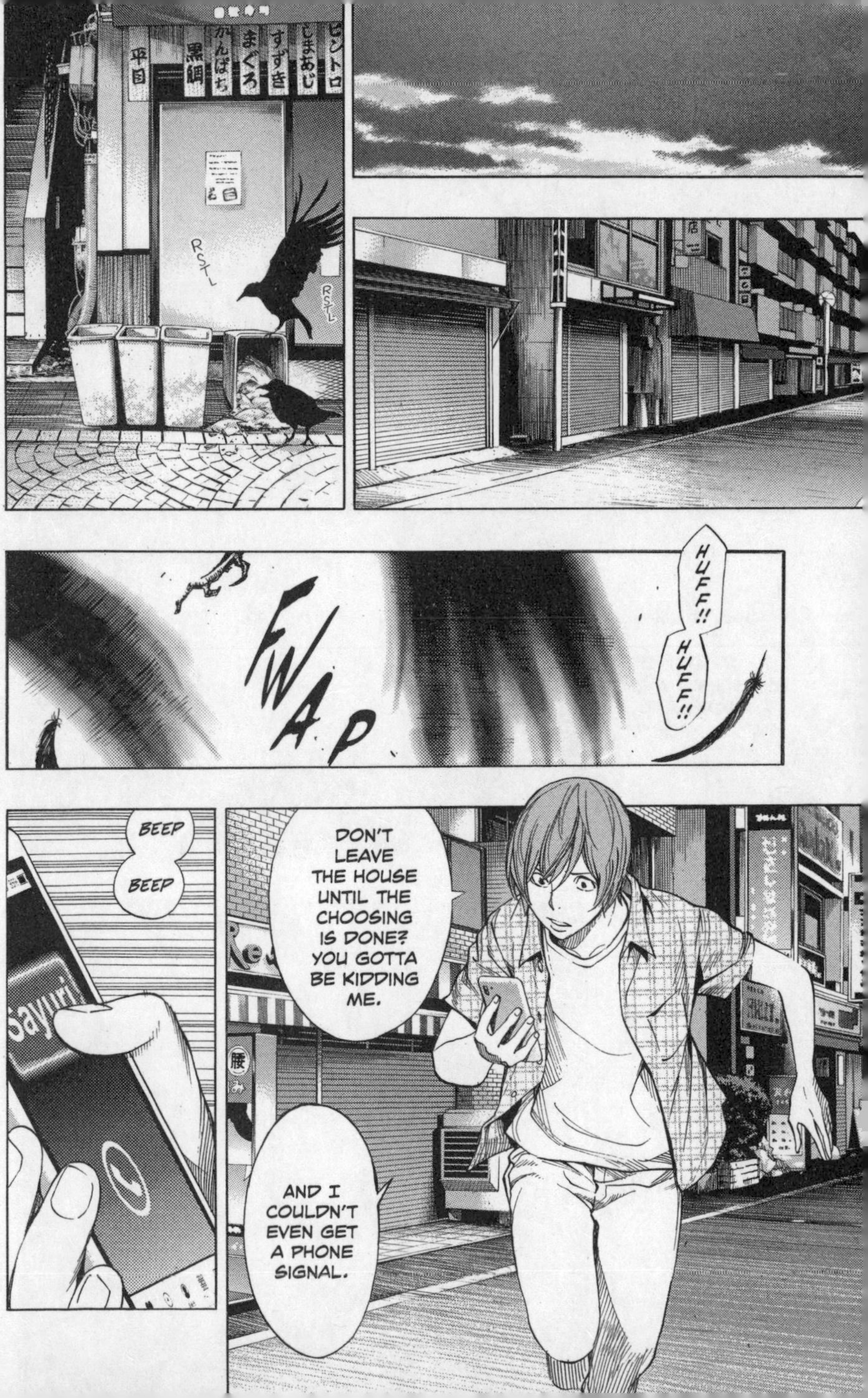

ピントロ
しまあじ
すずき
まぐろ
かんぱち
黒鯛
平目
RSTL
RSTL
HUFF!! HUFF!!
FWAP
DON'T LEAVE THE HOUSE UNTIL THE CHOOSING IS DONE? YOU GOTTA BE KIDDING ME.
AND I COULDN'T EVEN GET A PHONE SIGNAL.
BEEP
BEEP
Sayuri

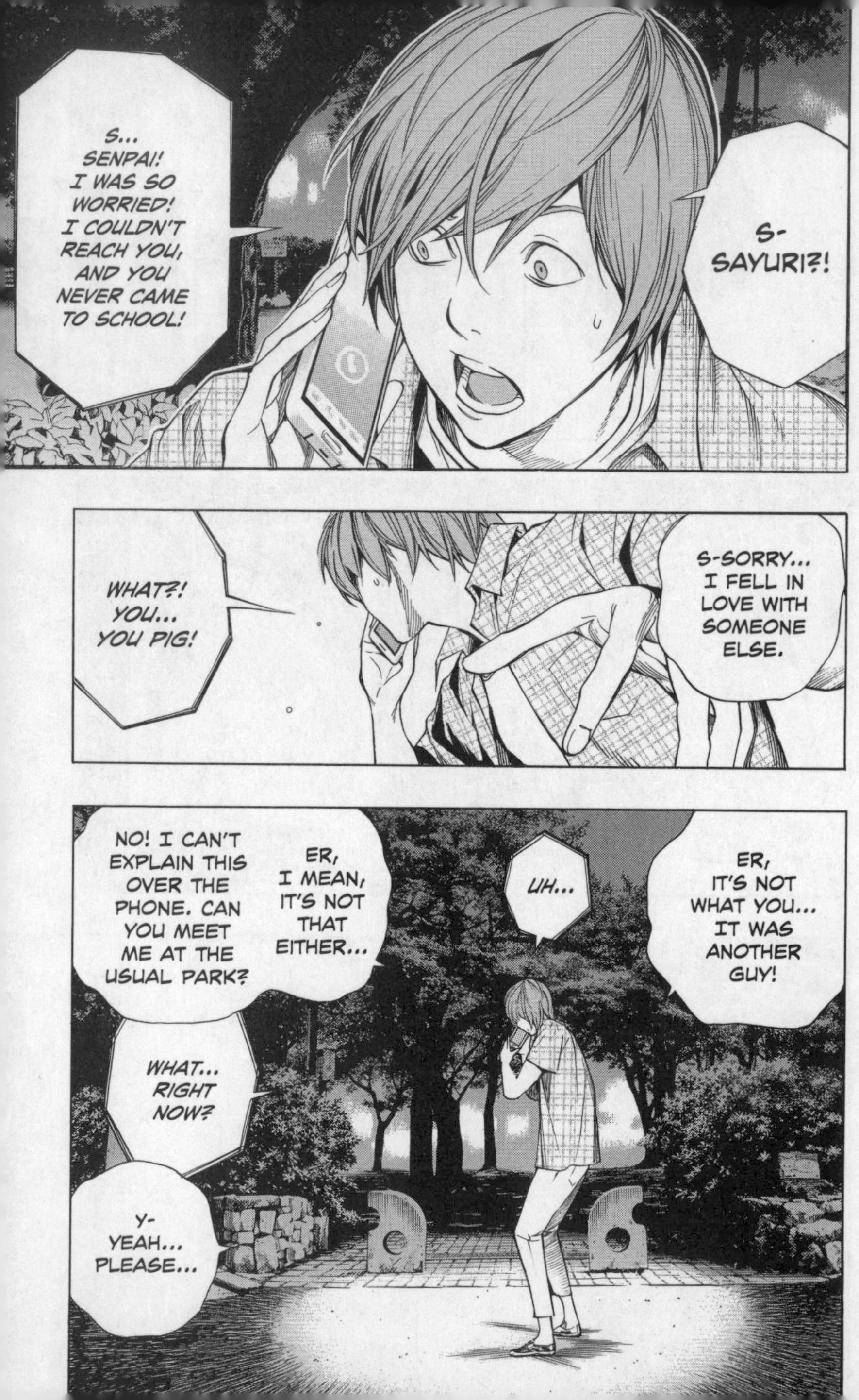
S- SAYURI?!
S... SENPAI! I WAS SO WORRIED! I COULDN'T REACH YOU, AND YOU NEVER CAME TO SCHOOL!
S-SORRY... I FELL IN LOVE WITH SOMEONE ELSE.
WHAT?! YOU... YOU PIG!
ER, IT'S NOT WHAT YOU... IT WAS ANOTHER GUY!
UH...
ER, I MEAN, IT'S NOT THAT EITHER...
NO! I CAN'T EXPLAIN THIS OVER THE PHONE. CAN YOU MEET ME AT THE USUAL PARK?
WHAT... RIGHT NOW?
Y- YEAH... PLEASE...

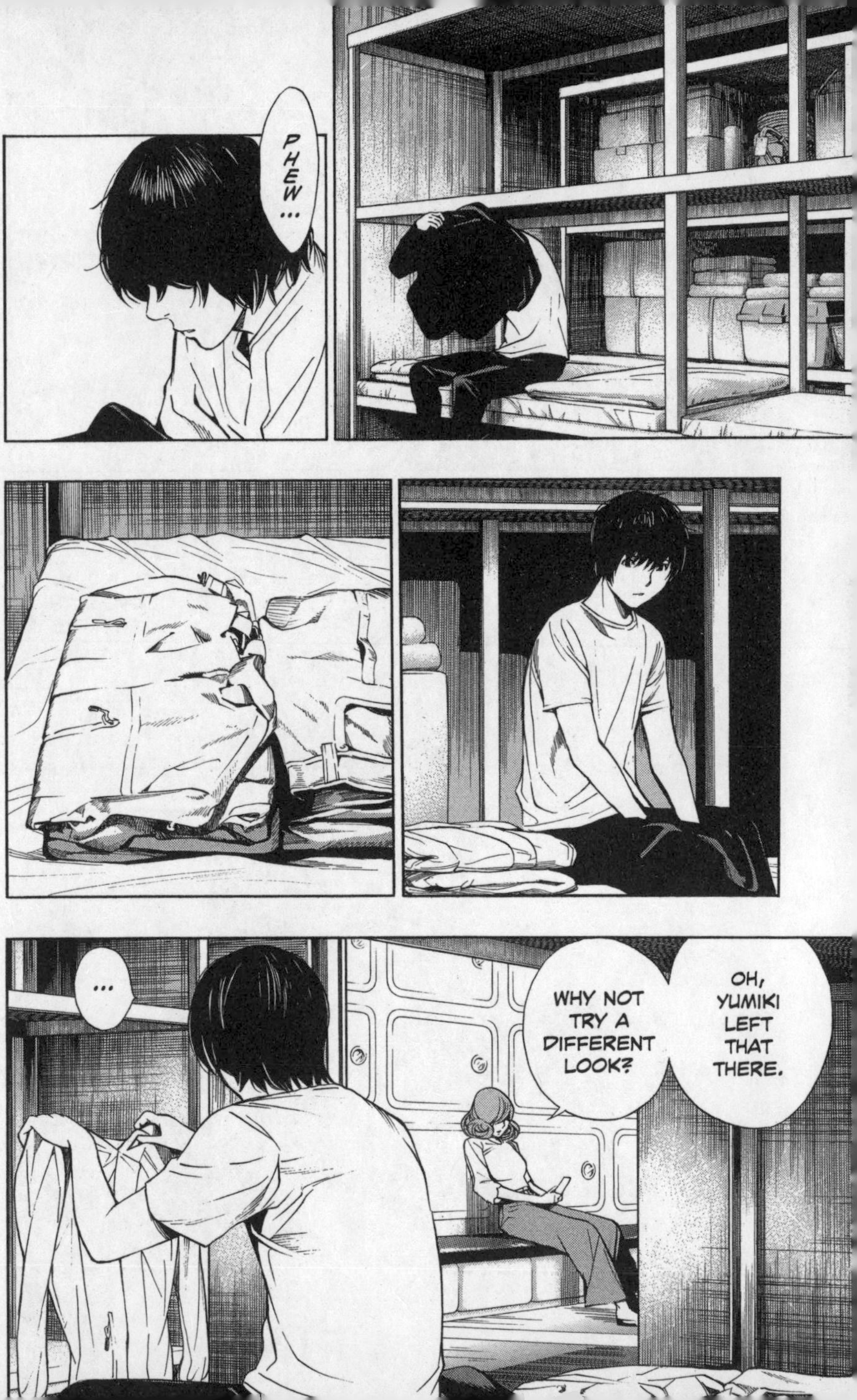
PHEW...
OH, YUMIKI LEFT THAT THERE.
WHY NOT TRY A DIFFERENT LOOK?
...

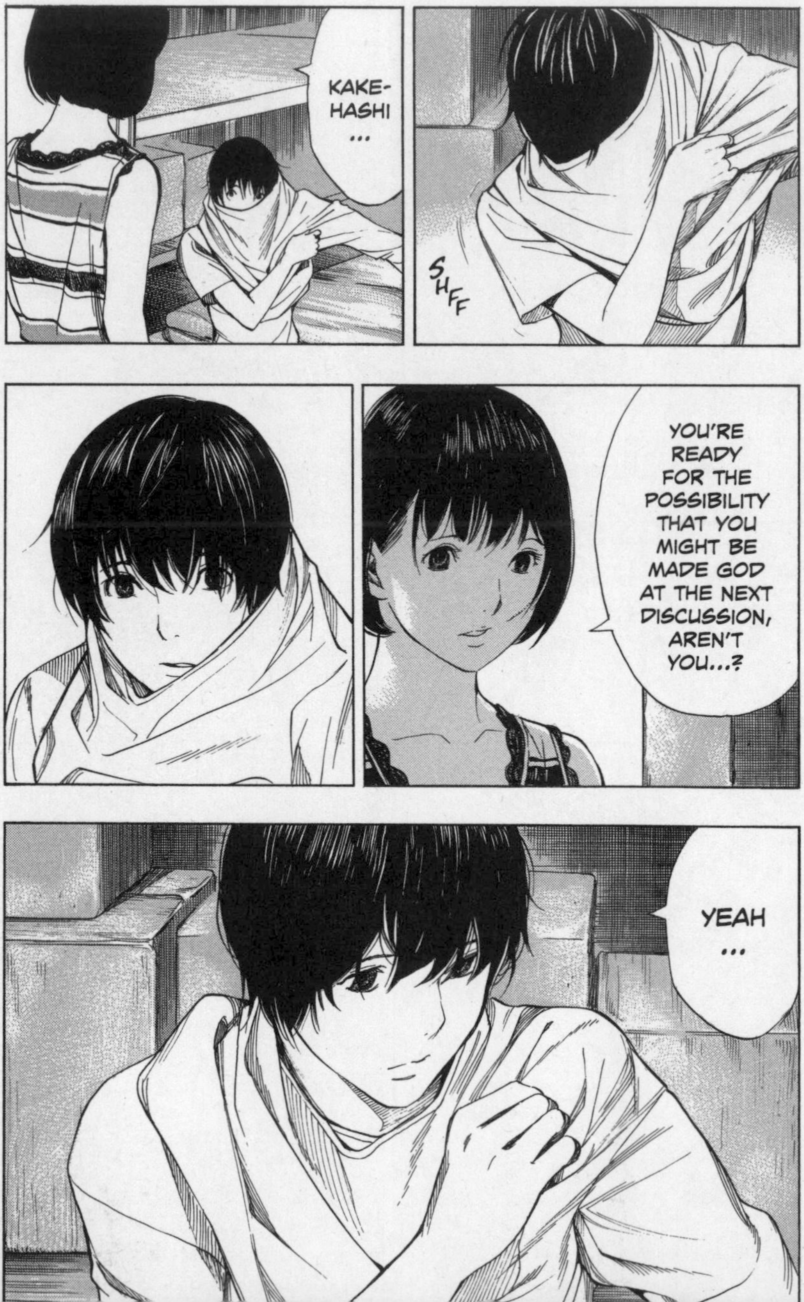
SHFF
KAKE-HASHI ...
YOU'RE READY FOR THE POSSIBILITY THAT YOU MIGHT BE MADE GOD AT THE NEXT DISCUSSION, AREN'T YOU...?
YEAH ...

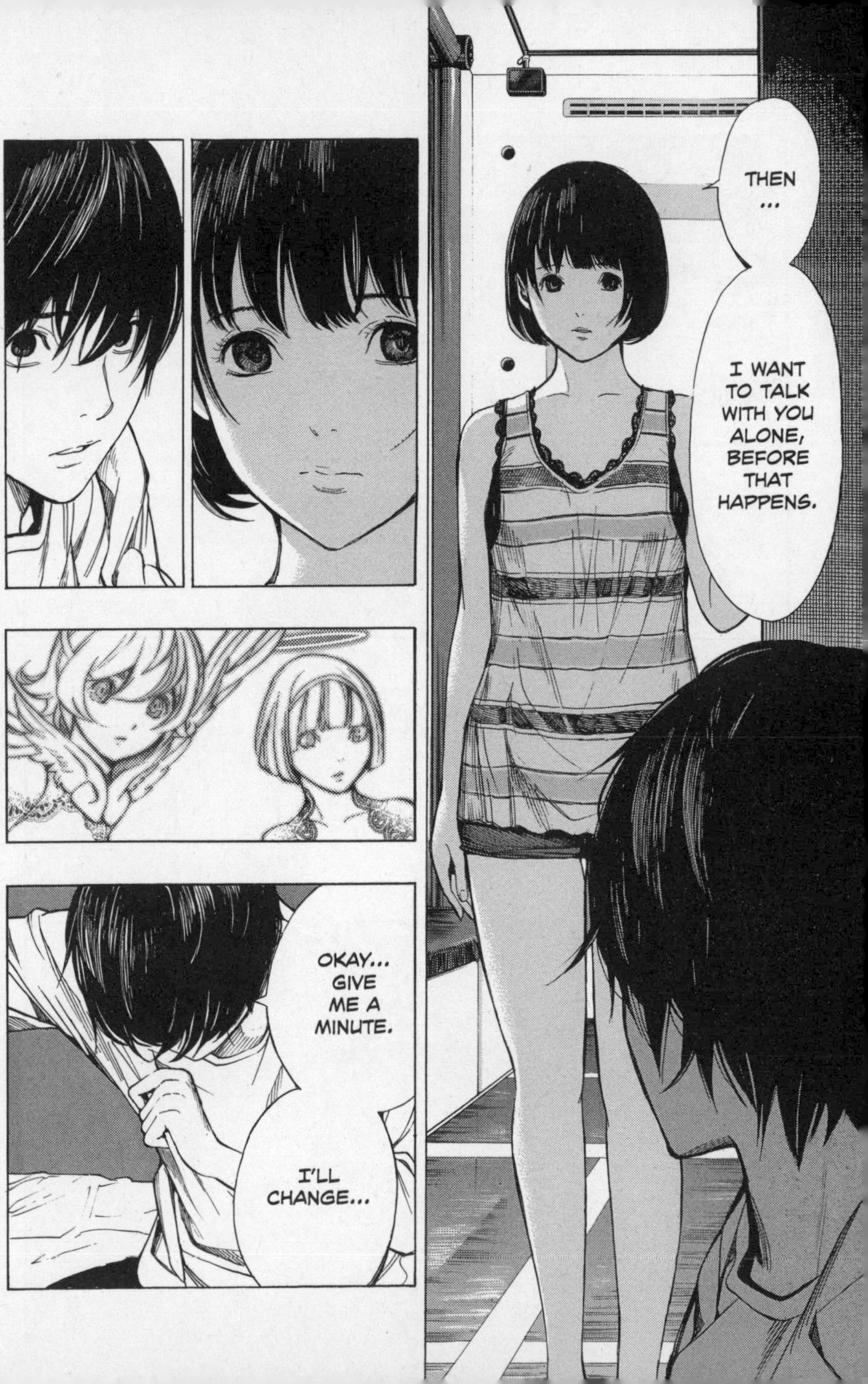
THEN ...
I WANT TO TALK WITH YOU ALONE, BEFORE THAT HAPPENS.
OKAY... GIVE ME A MINUTE.
I'LL CHANGE...

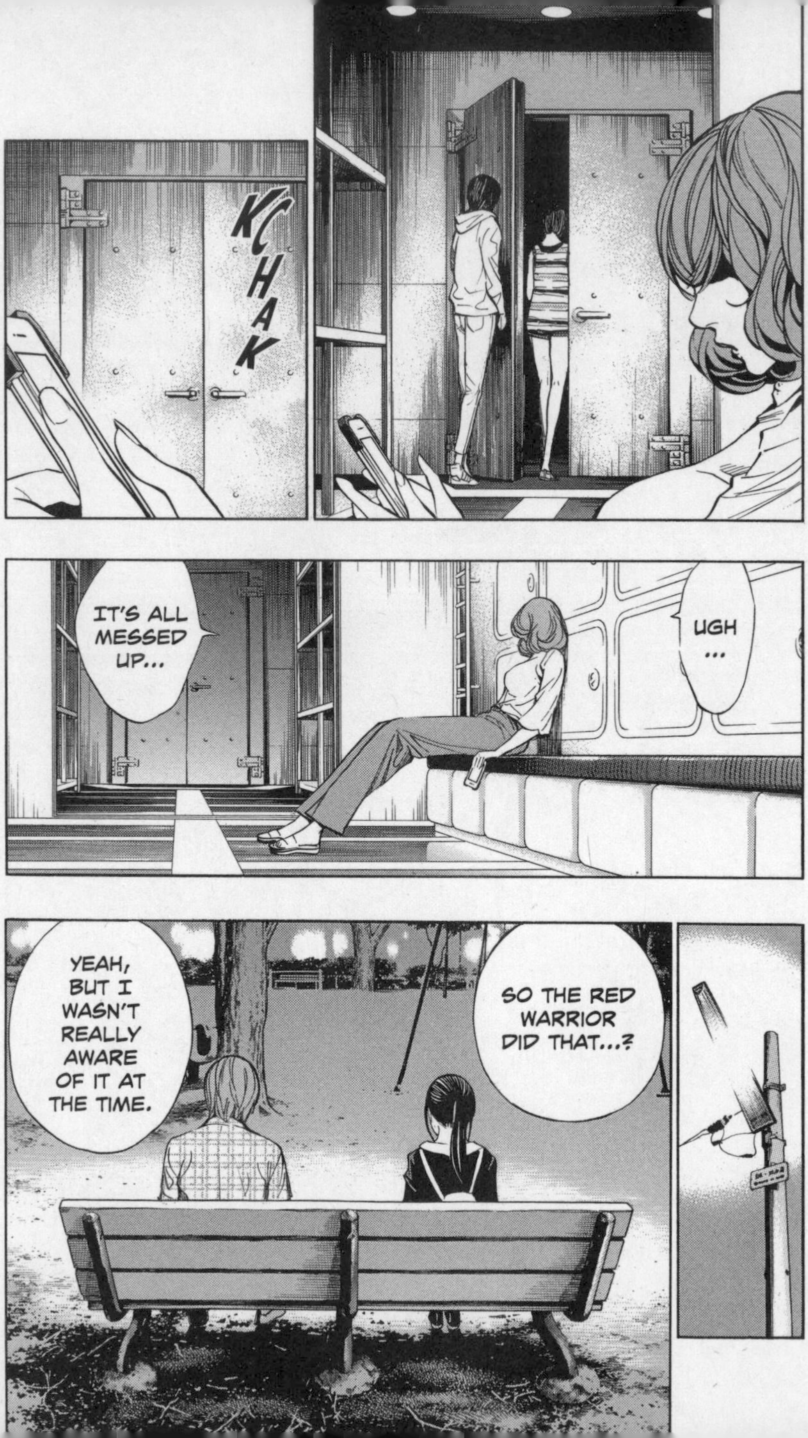
KCHAK
UGH ...
IT'S ALL MESSED UP...
SO THE RED WARRIOR DID THAT...?
YEAH, BUT I WASN'T REALLY AWARE OF IT AT THE TIME.

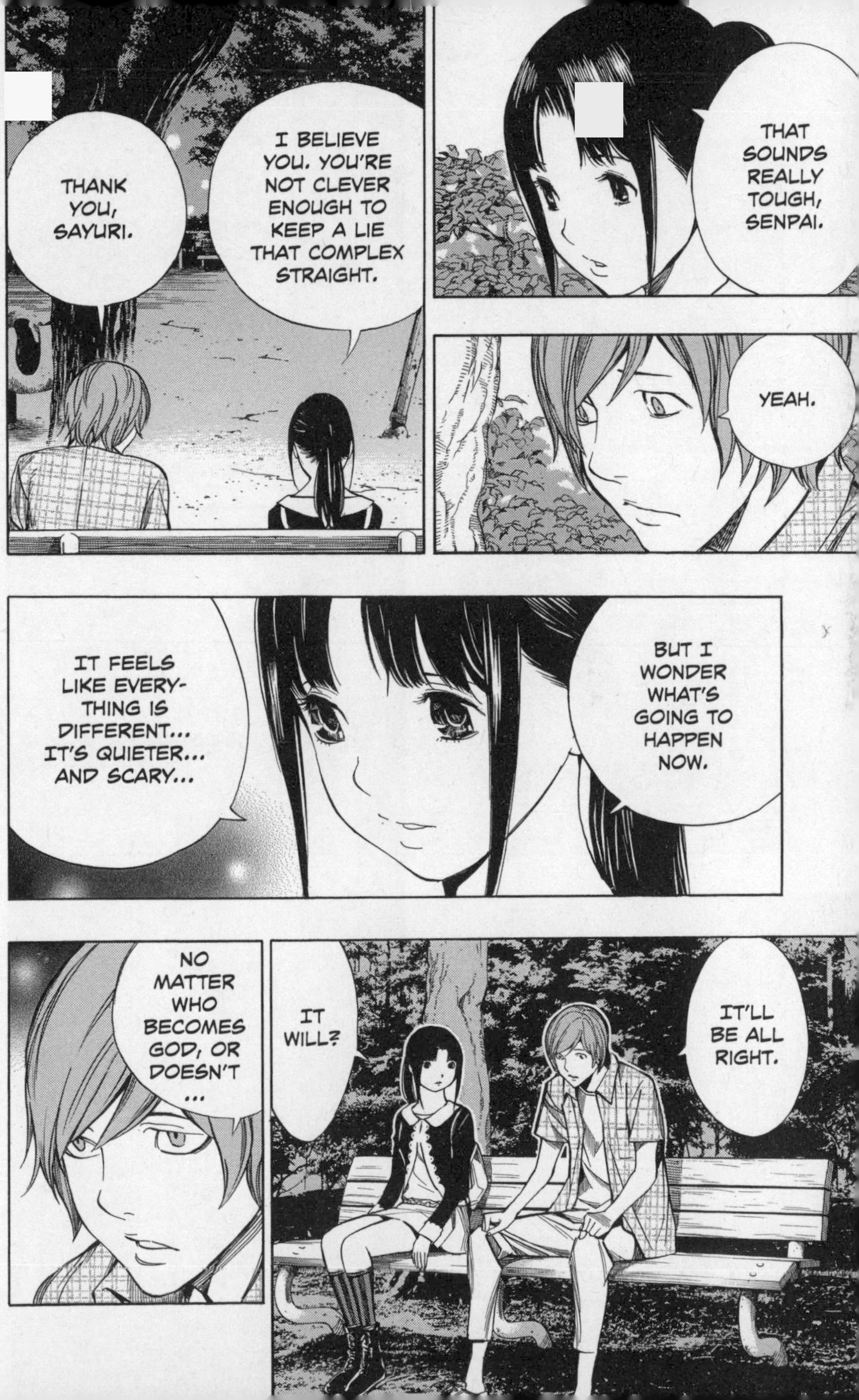
THAT SOUNDS REALLY TOUGH, SENPAI.
YEAH.
I BELIEVE YOU. YOU'RE NOT CLEVER ENOUGH TO KEEP A LIE THAT COMPLEX STRAIGHT.
THANK YOU, SAYURI.
BUT I WONDER WHAT'S GOING TO HAPPEN NOW.
IT FEELS LIKE EVERY-THING IS DIFFERENT... IT'S QUIETER... AND SCARY...
IT'LL BE ALL RIGHT.
IT WILL?
NO MATTER WHO BECOMES GOD, OR DOESN'T ...

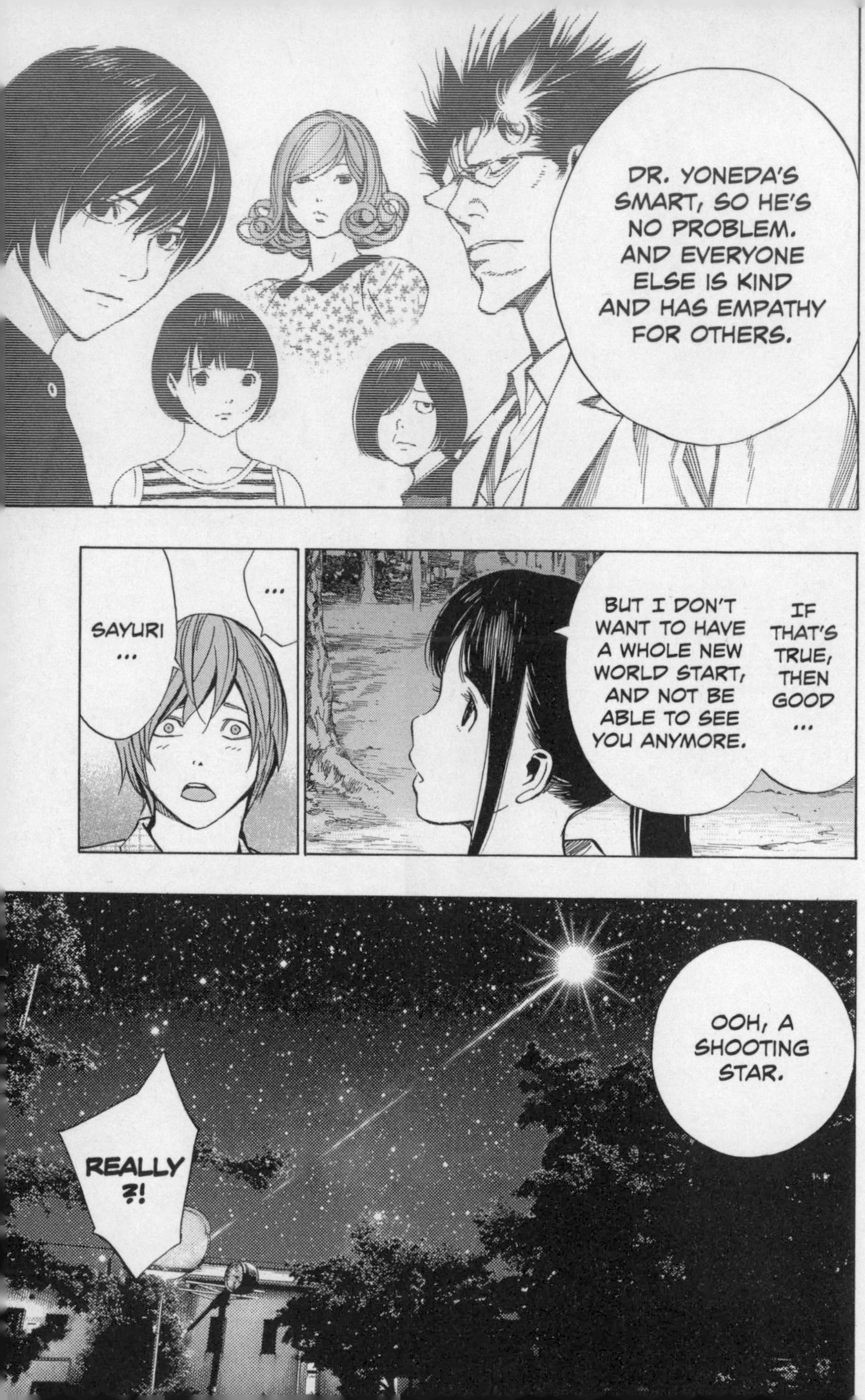
DR. YONEDA'S SMART, SO HE'S NO PROBLEM. AND EVERYONE ELSE IS KIND AND HAS EMPATHY FOR OTHERS.
IF THAT'S TRUE, THEN GOOD...
BUT I DON'T WANT TO HAVE A WHOLE NEW WORLD START, AND NOT BE ABLE TO SEE YOU ANYMORE.
...
SAYURI...
OOH, A SHOOTING STAR.
REALLY?!

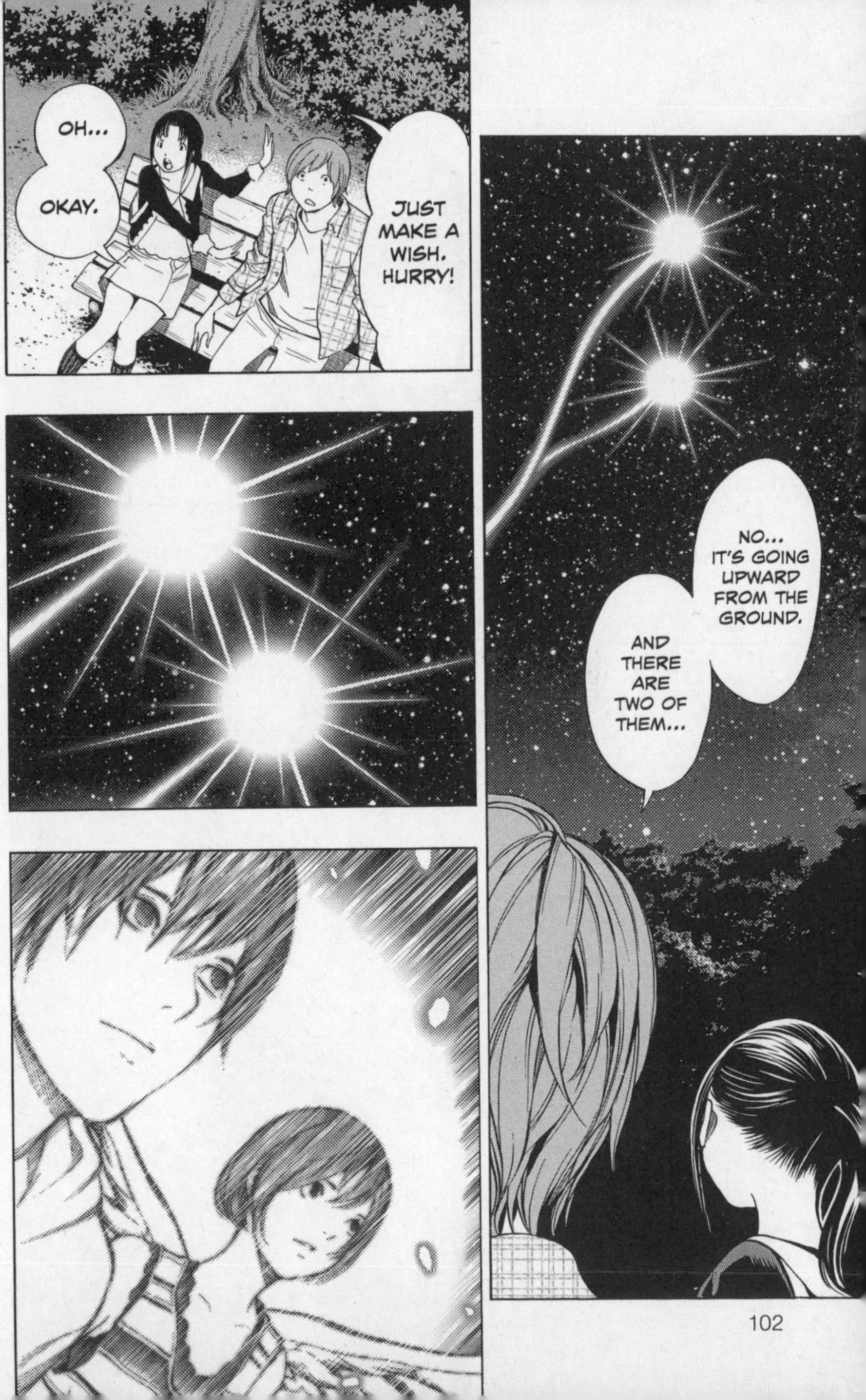
JUST MAKE A WISH. HURRY!
OH...
OKAY.
NO... IT'S GOING UPWARD FROM THE GROUND.
AND THERE ARE TWO OF THEM...

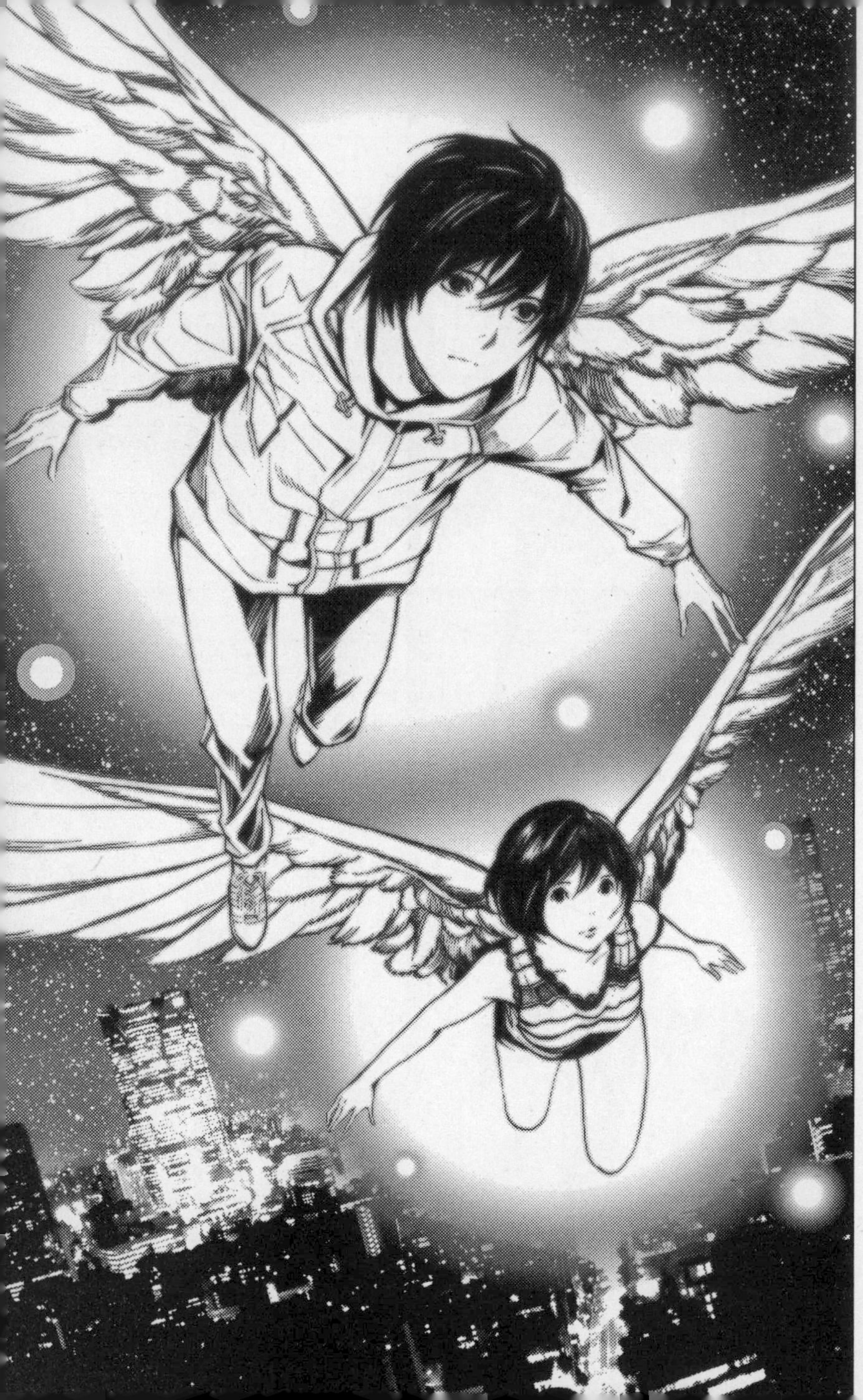

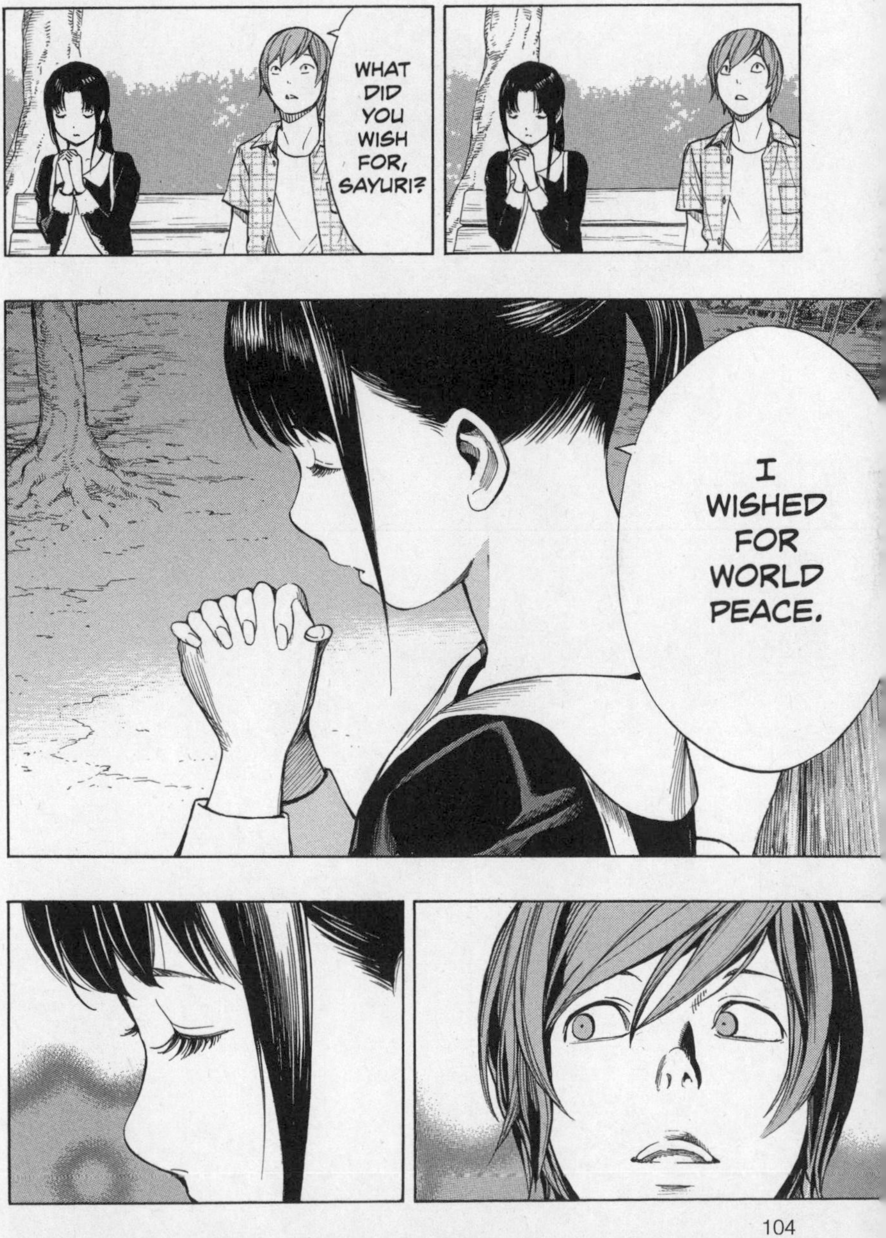
WHAT DID YOU WISH FOR, SAYURI?
I WISHED FOR WORLD PEACE.

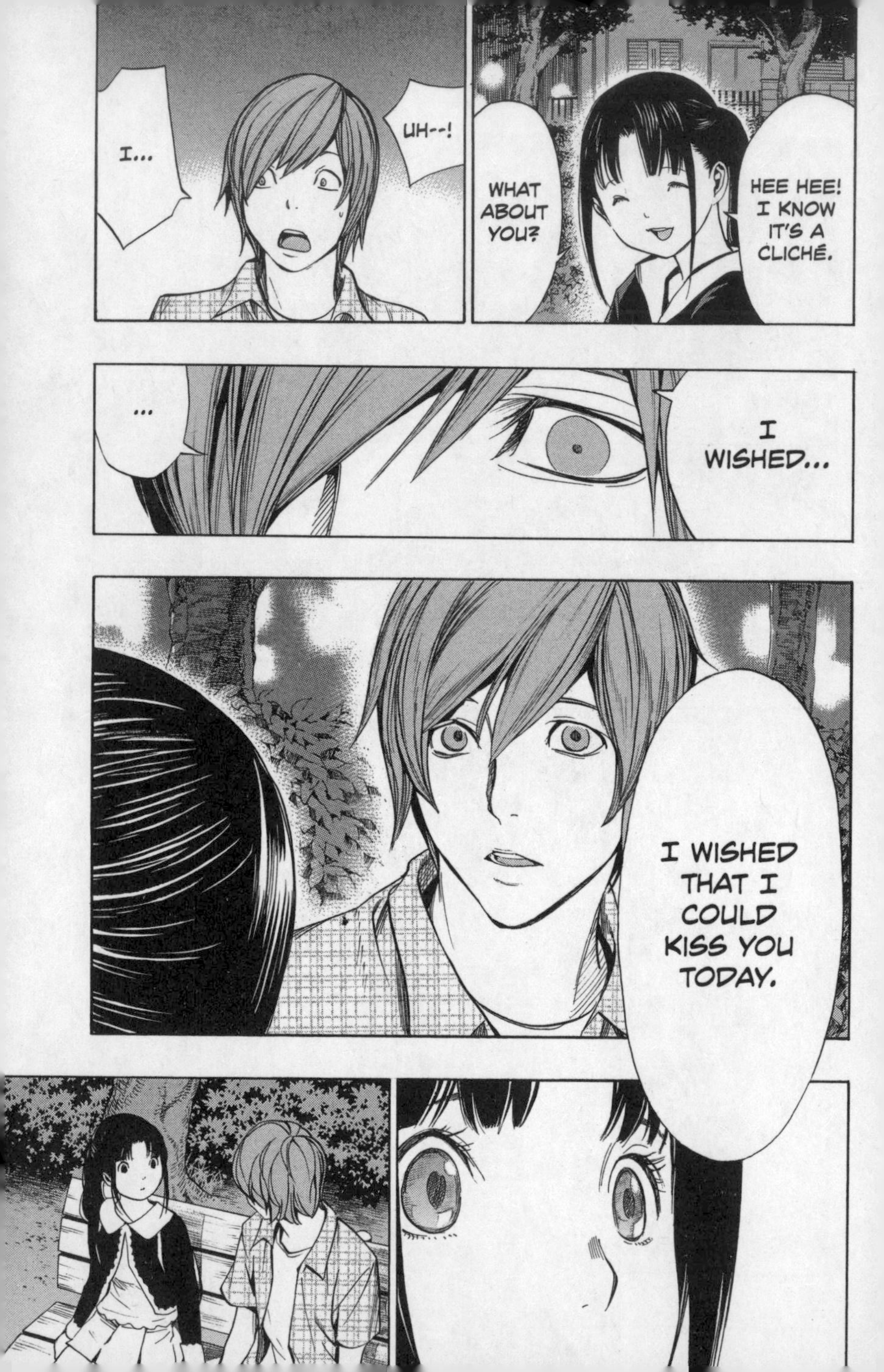
HEE HEE! I KNOW IT'S A CLICHÉ.
WHAT ABOUT YOU?
UH--!
I...
I WISHED...
...
I WISHED THAT I COULD KISS YOU TODAY.

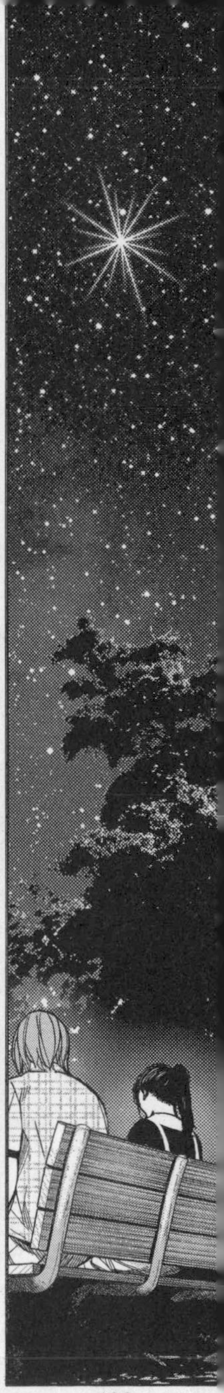

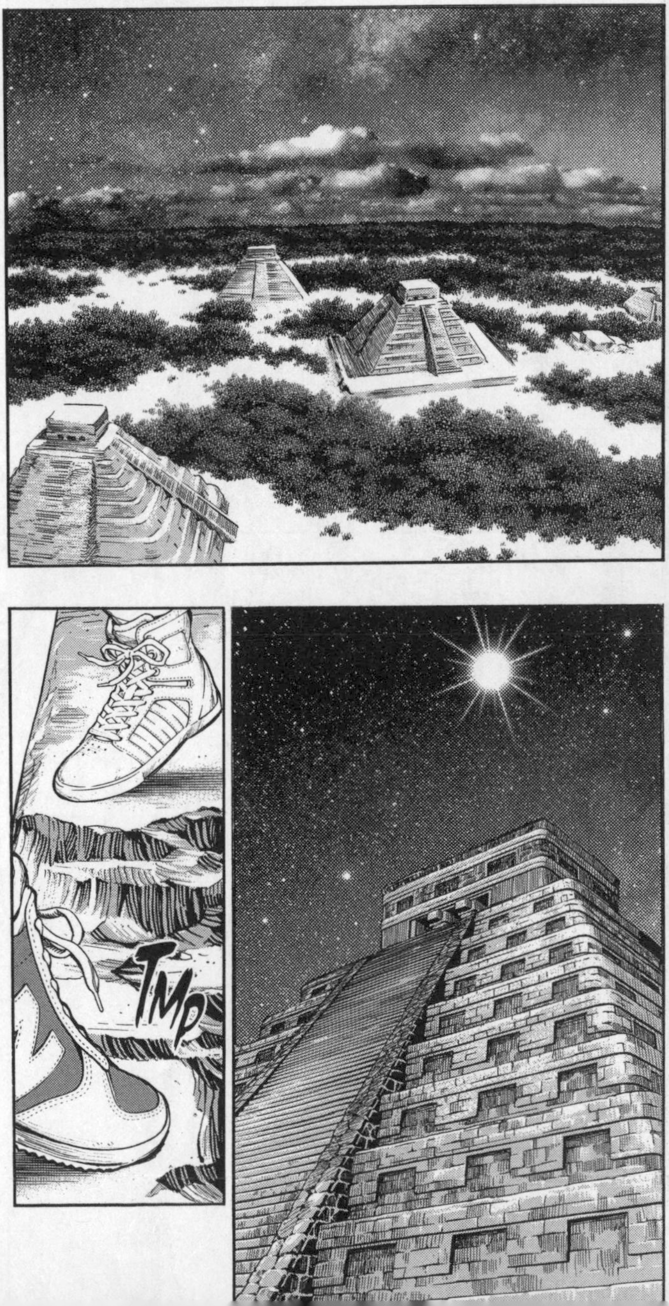
TMP

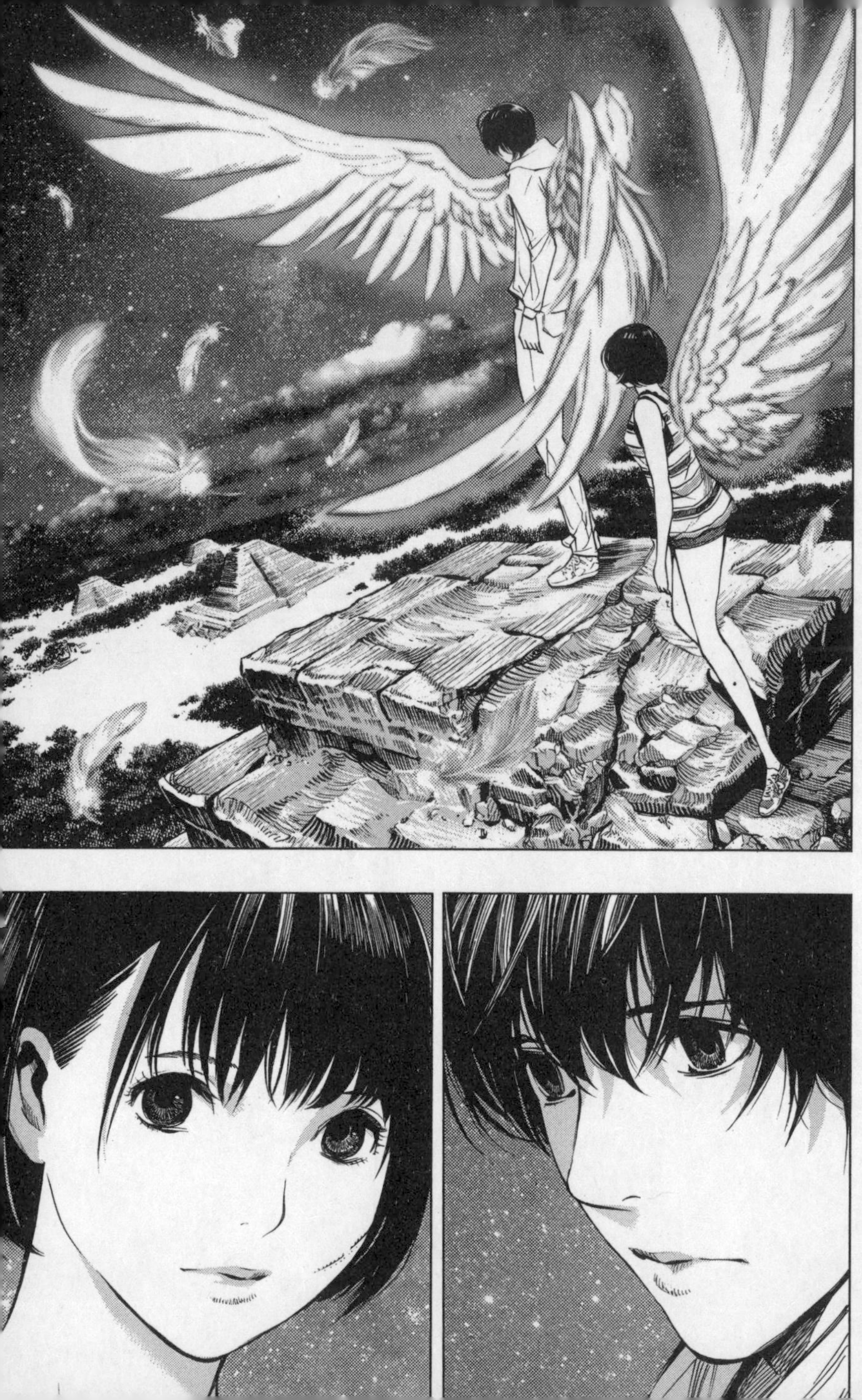

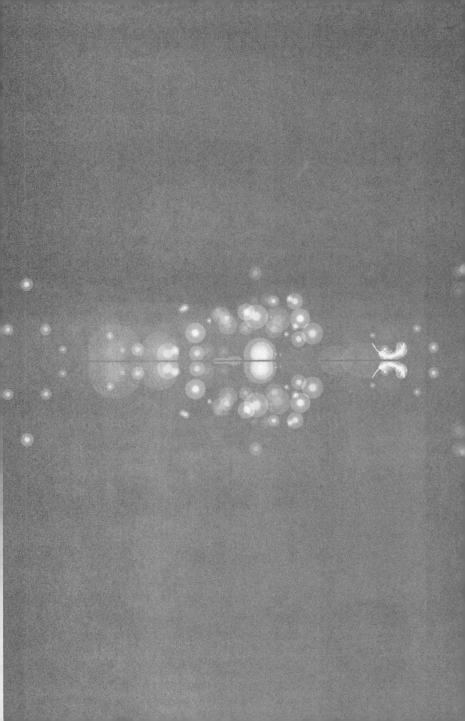

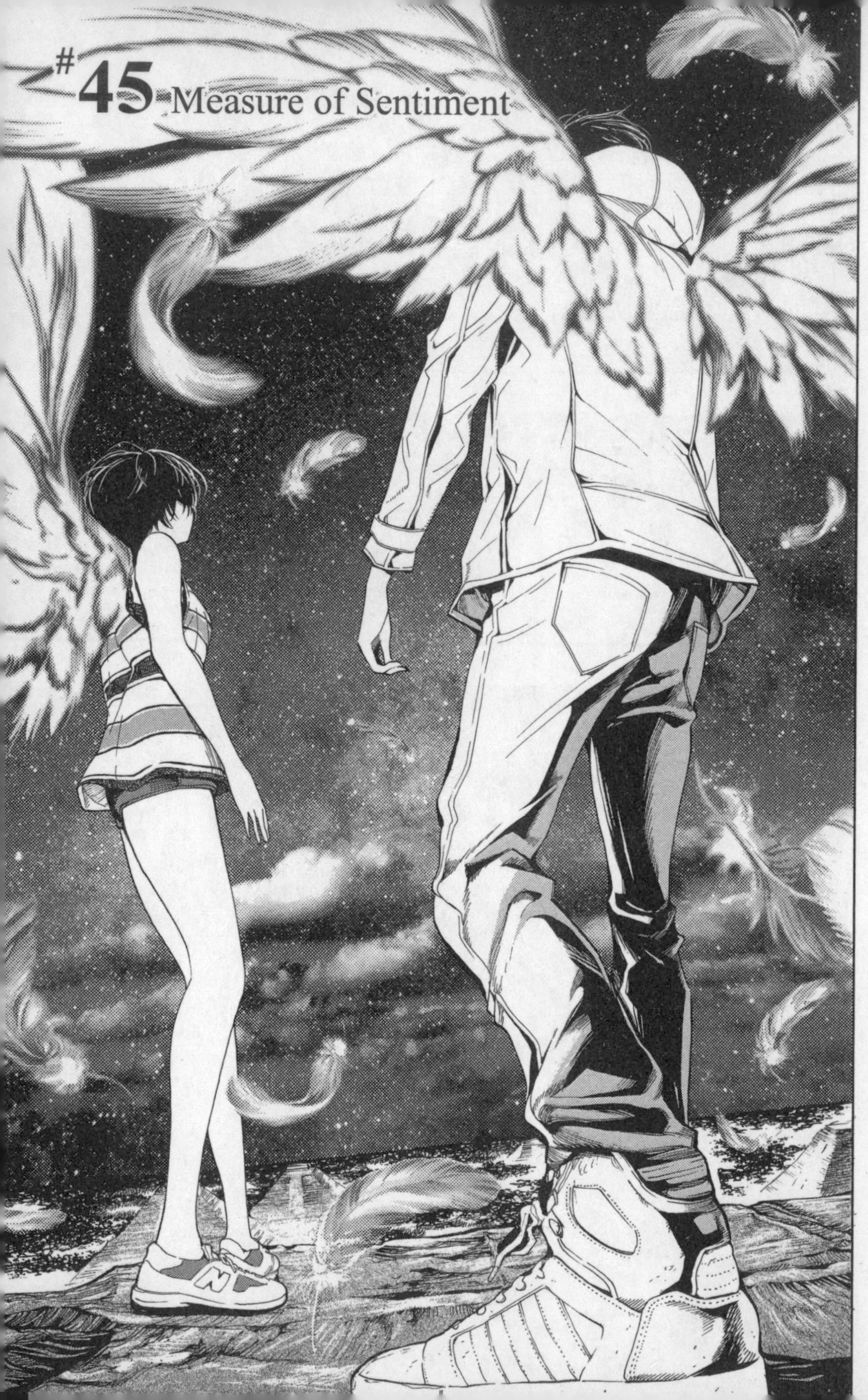
#45 Measure of Sentiment

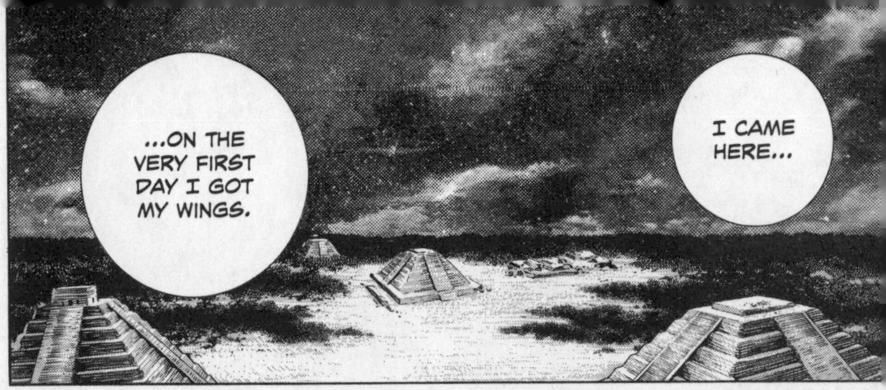
I CAME HERE...
...ON THE VERY FIRST DAY I GOT MY WINGS.

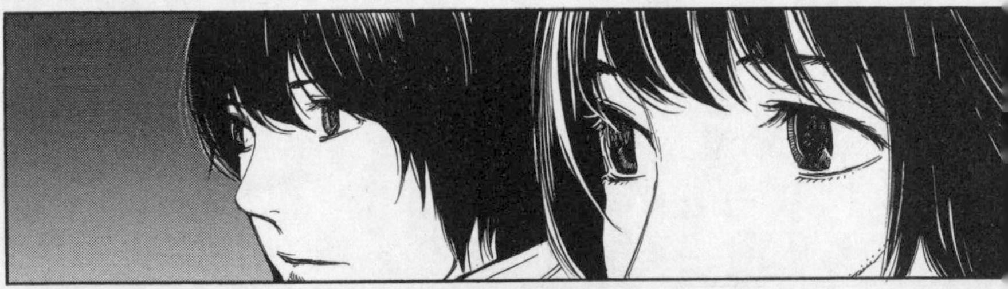

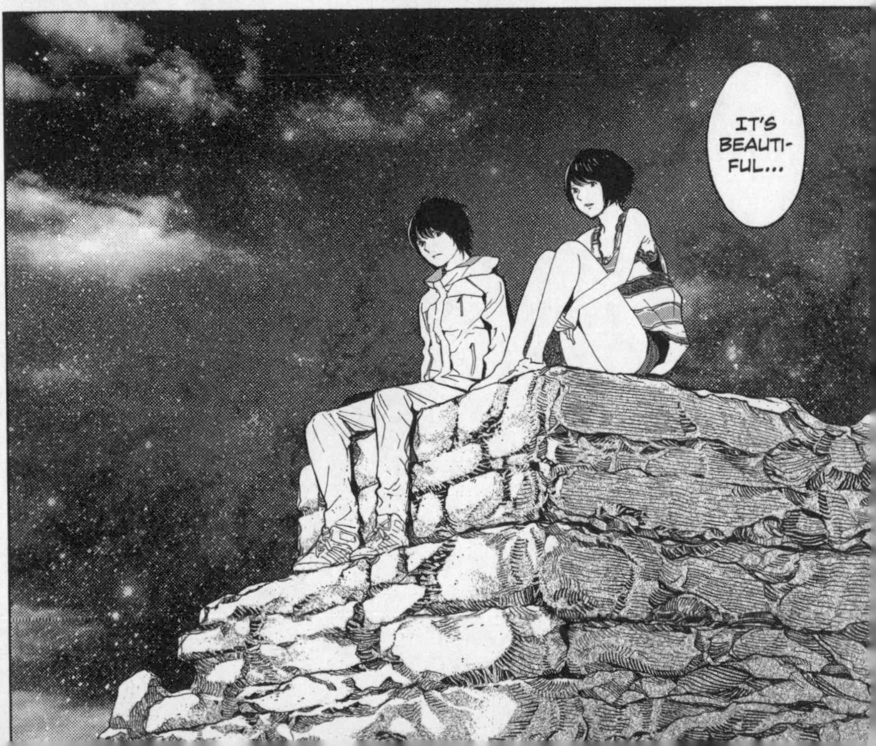
IT'S BEAUTI-FUL...

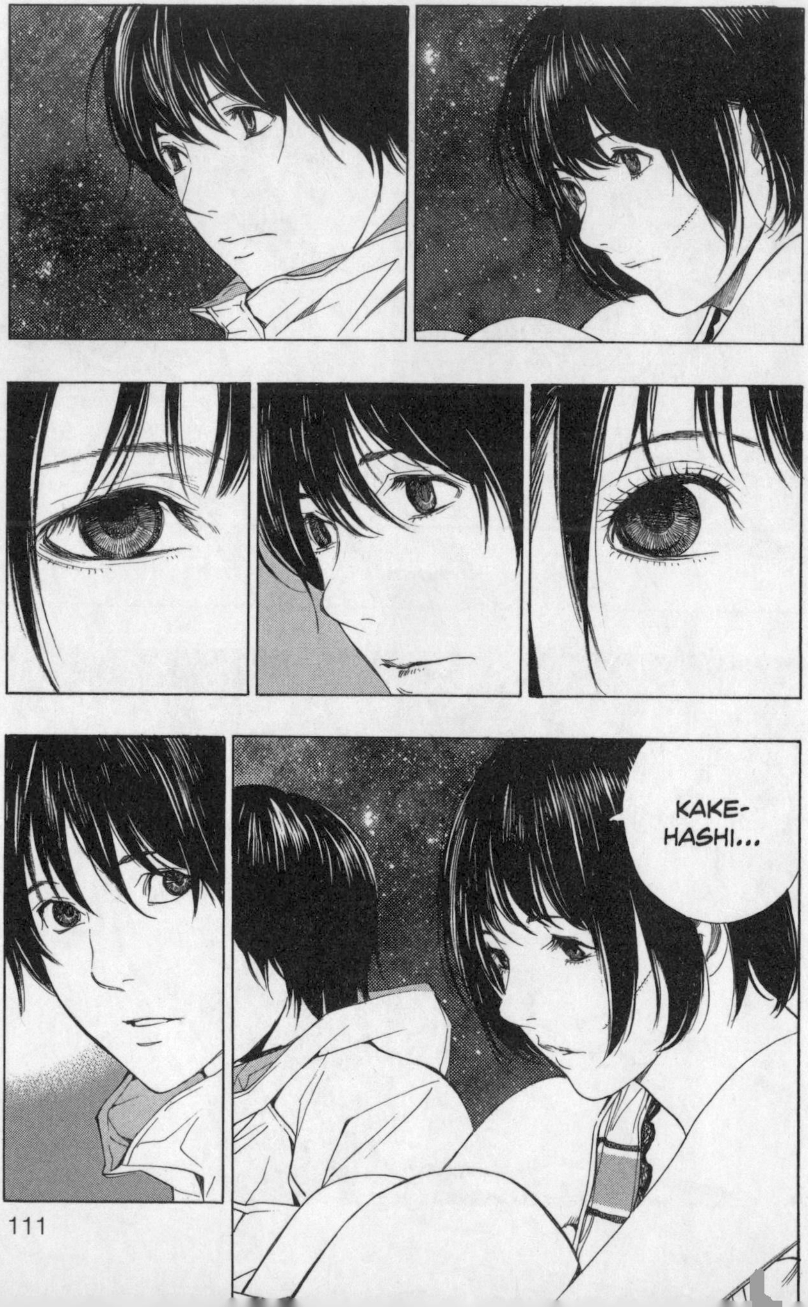
KAKE-HASHI...

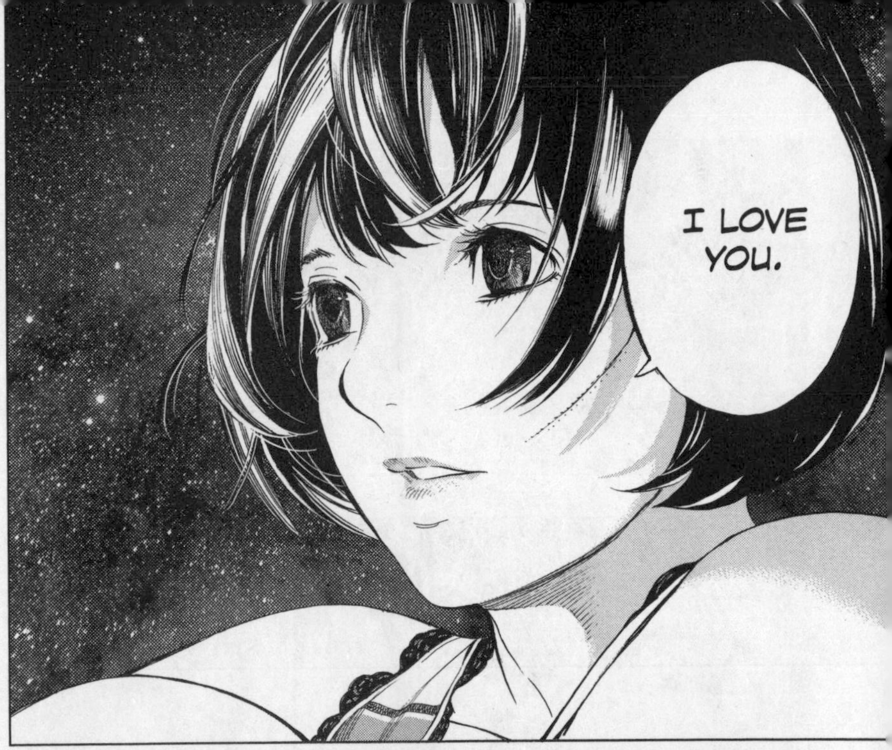
I LOVE YOU.
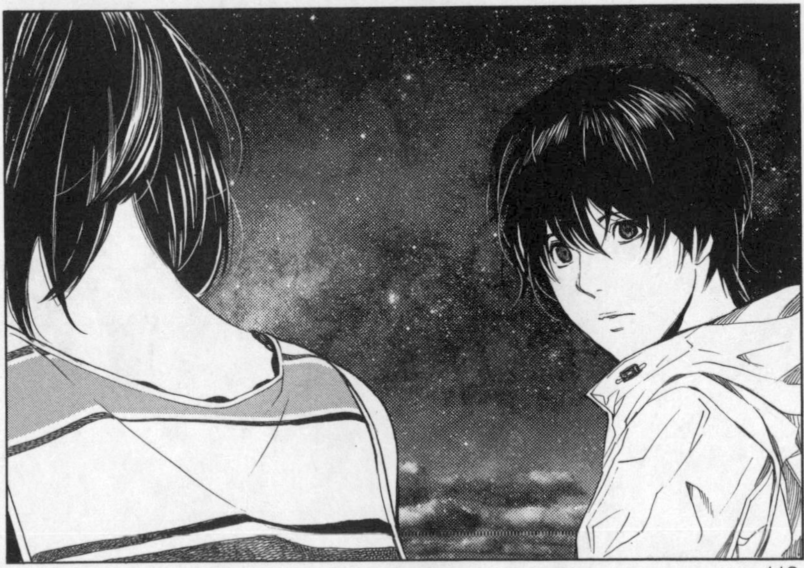

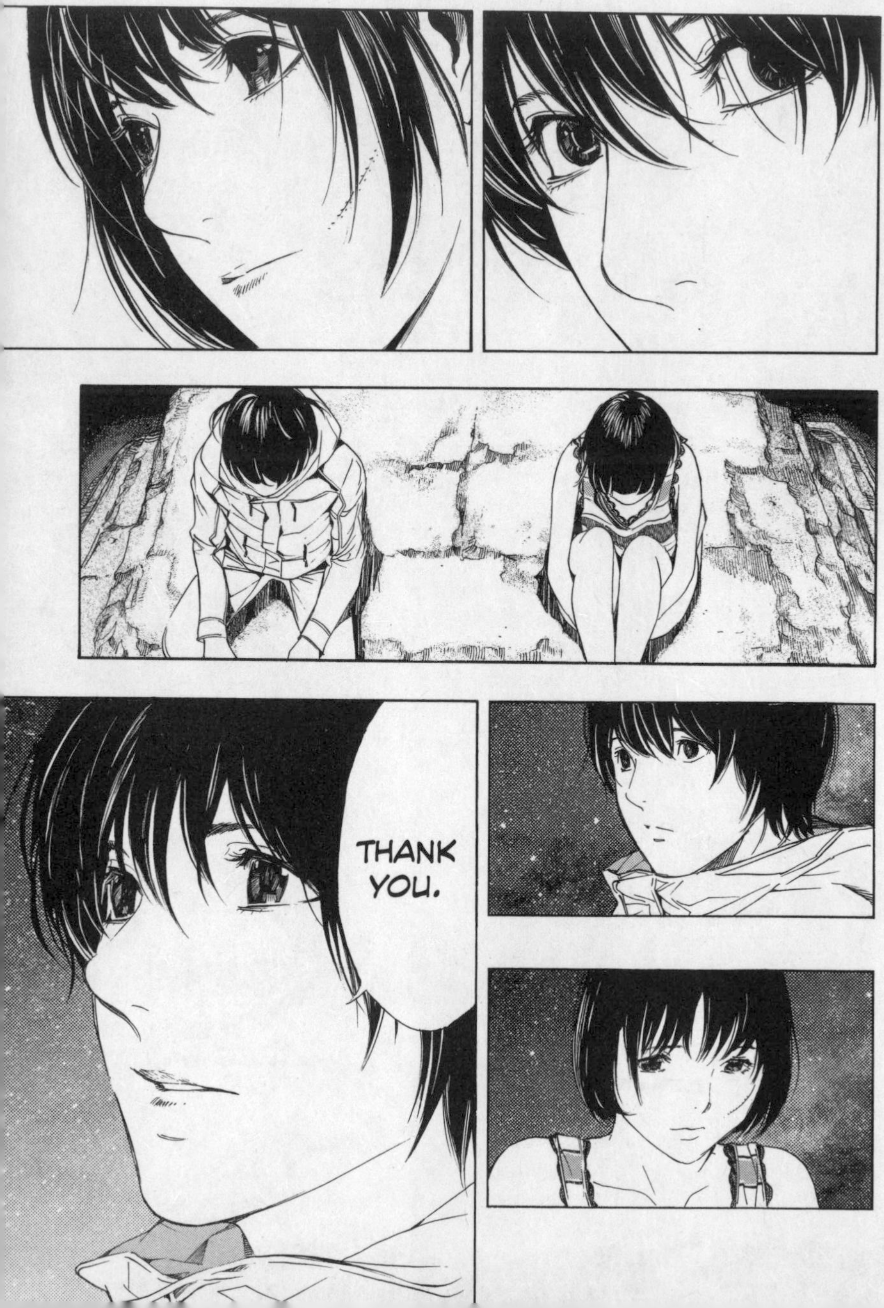
THANK YOU.

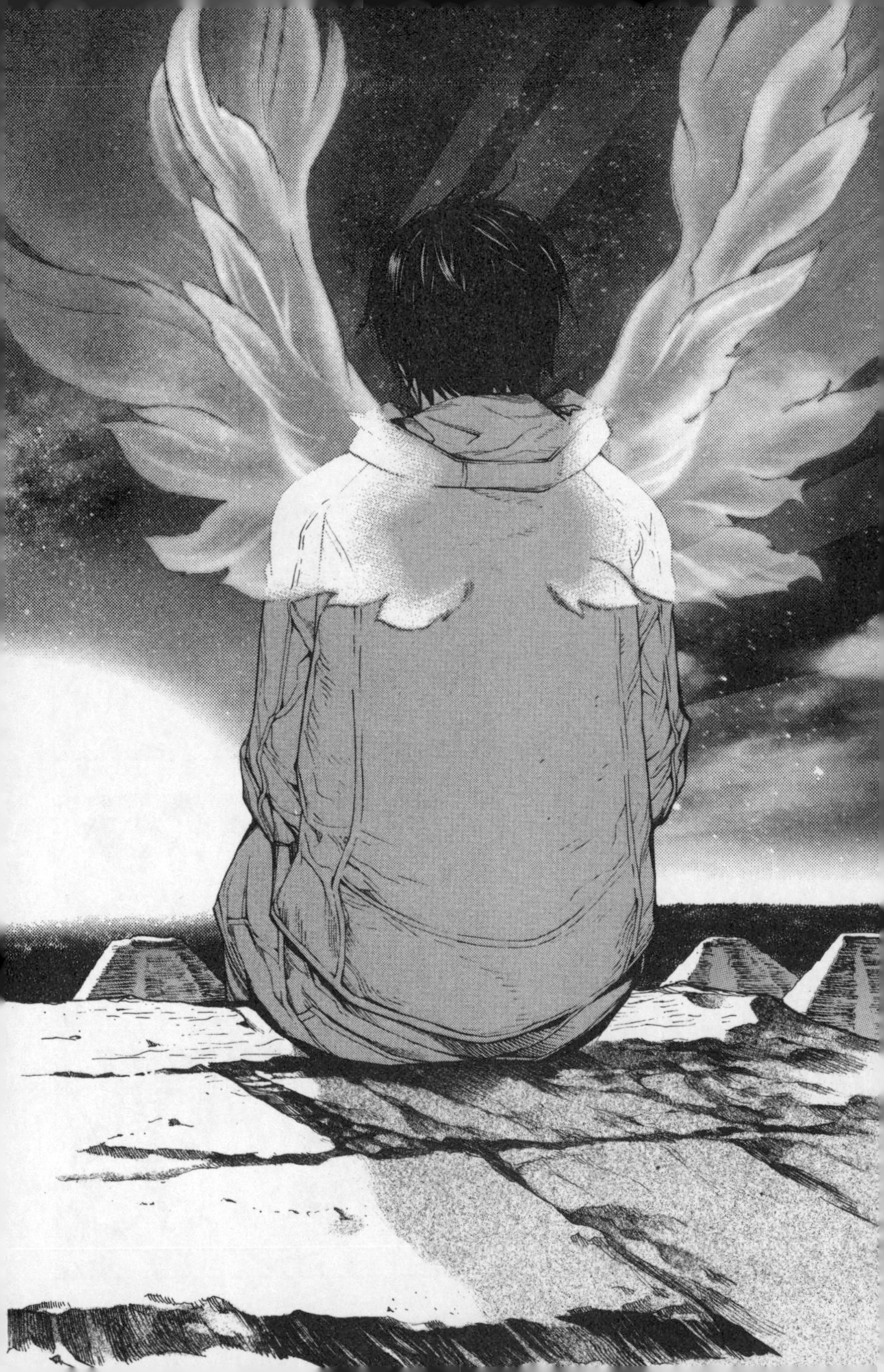

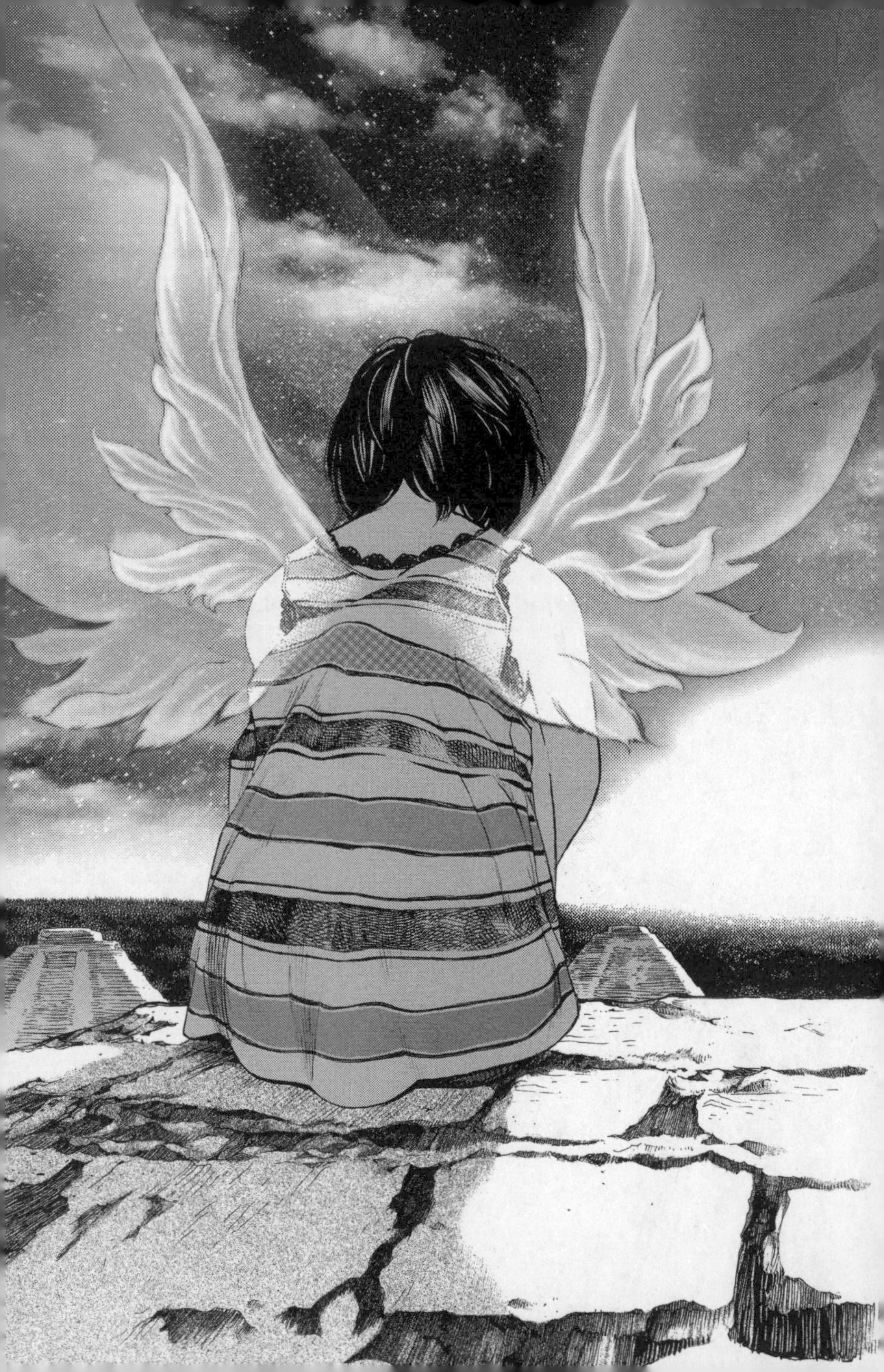

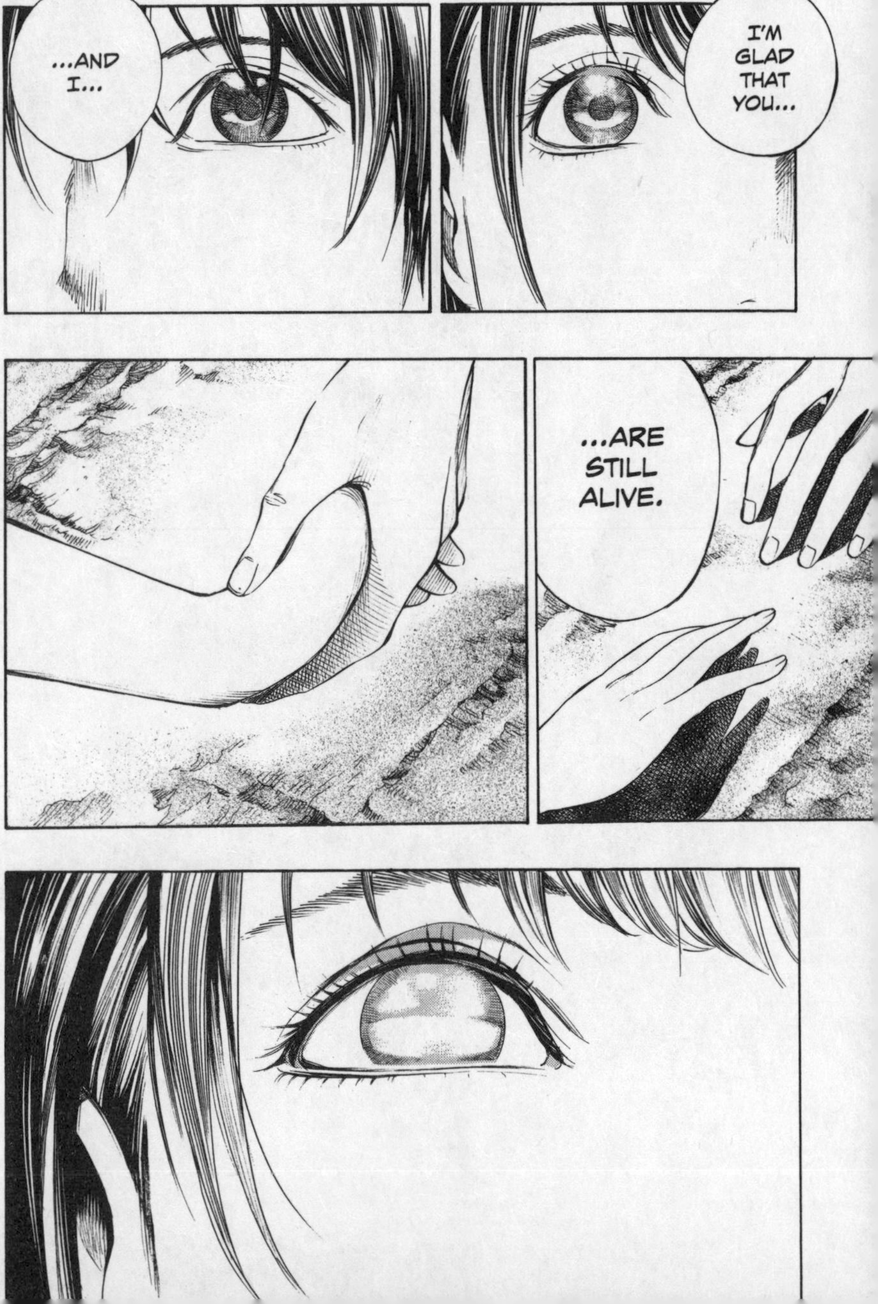
I'M GLAD THAT YOU...
...AND I...
...ARE STILL ALIVE.

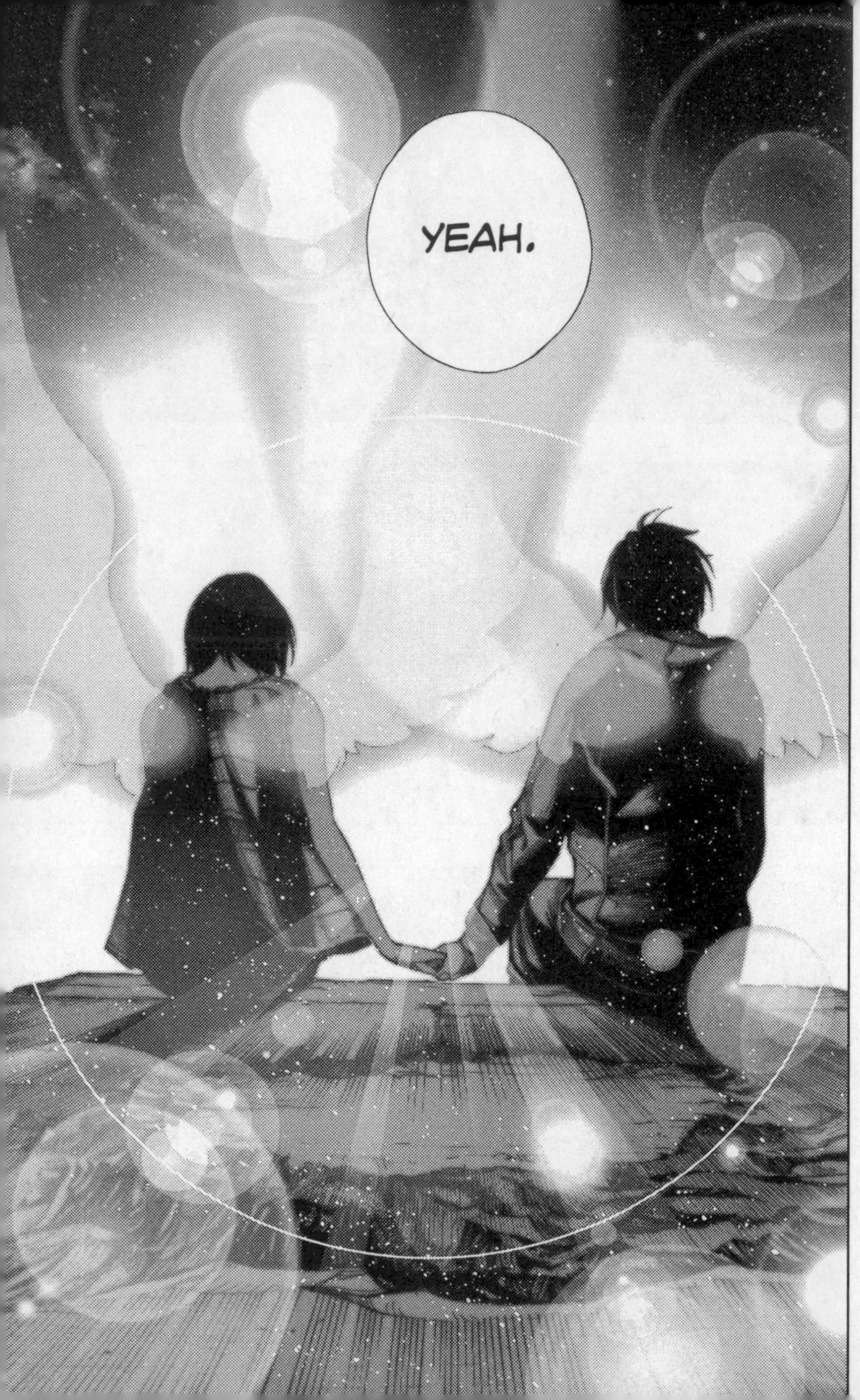
YEAH.

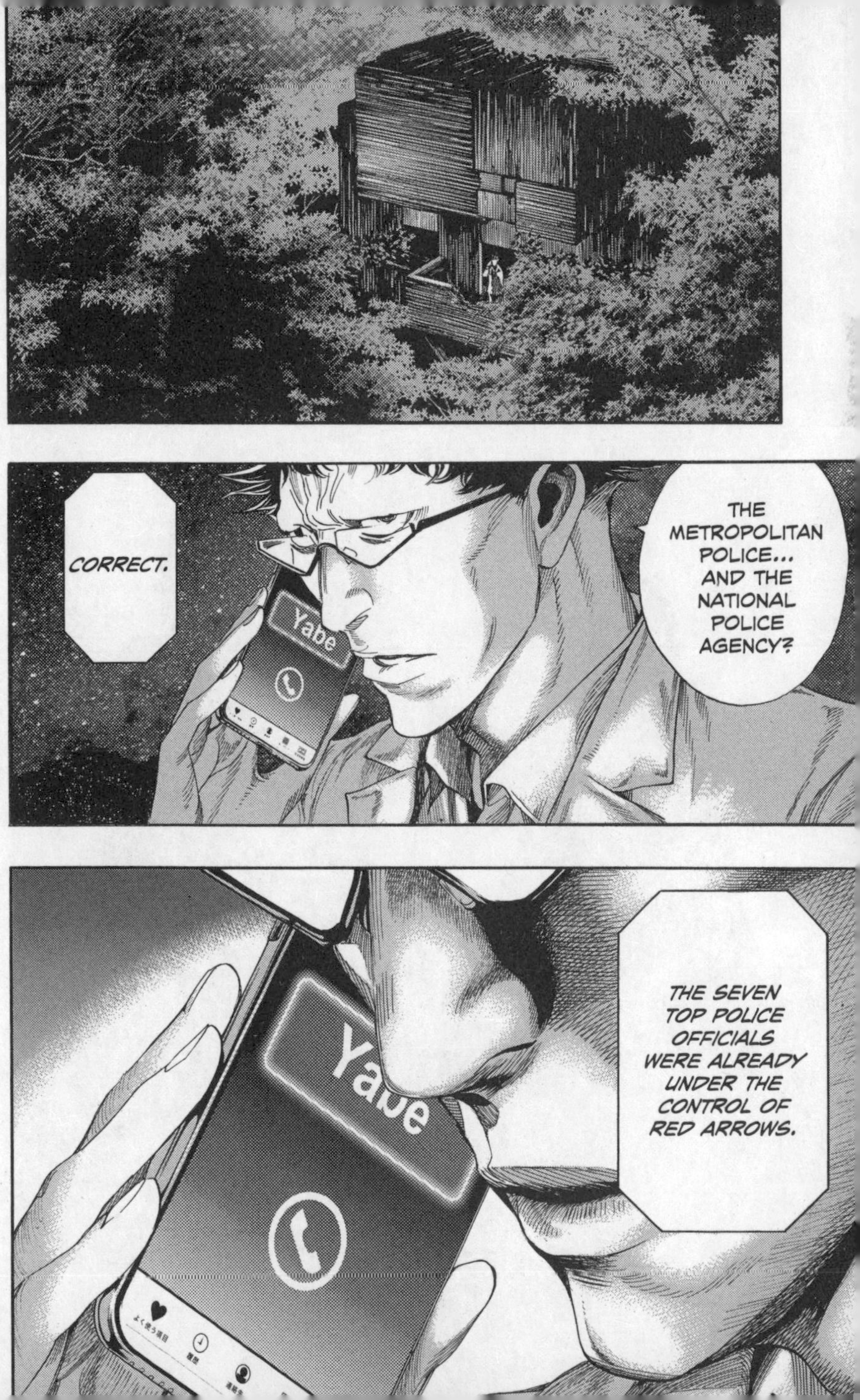
THE METROPOLITAN POLICE... AND THE NATIONAL POLICE AGENCY?
Yabe
CORRECT.
THE SEVEN TOP POLICE OFFICIALS WERE ALREADY UNDER THE CONTROL OF RED ARROWS.
Yabe

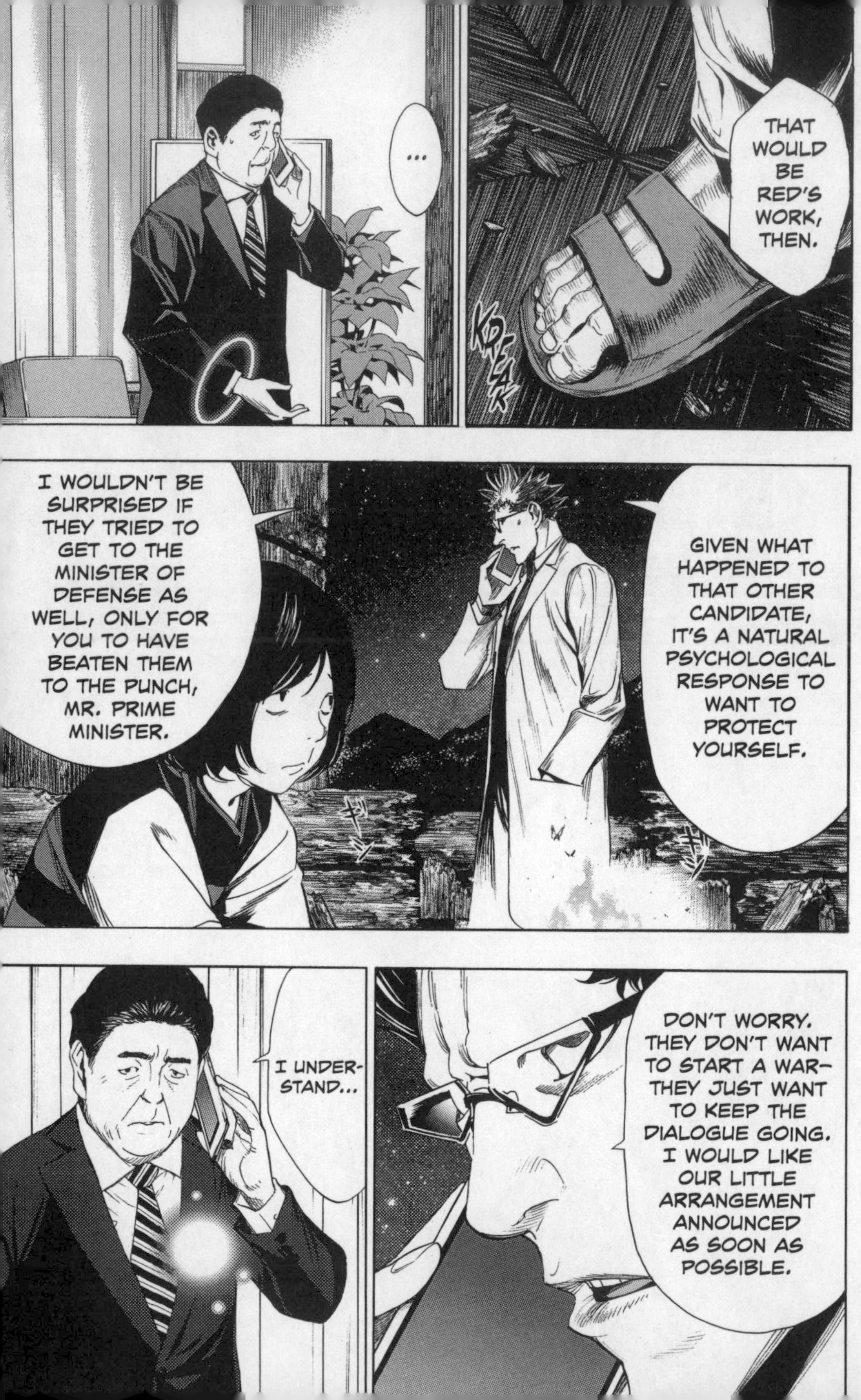
THAT WOULD BE RED'S WORK, THEN.
...
GIVEN WHAT HAPPENED TO THAT OTHER CANDIDATE, IT'S A NATURAL PSYCHOLOGICAL RESPONSE TO WANT TO PROTECT YOURSELF.
I WOULDN'T BE SURPRISED IF THEY TRIED TO GET TO THE MINISTER OF DEFENSE AS WELL, ONLY FOR YOU TO HAVE BEATEN THEM TO THE PUNCH, MR. PRIME MINISTER.
DON'T WORRY. THEY DON'T WANT TO START A WAR–THEY JUST WANT TO KEEP THE DIALOGUE GOING. I WOULD LIKE OUR LITTLE ARRANGEMENT ANNOUNCED AS SOON AS POSSIBLE.
I UNDER-STAND...

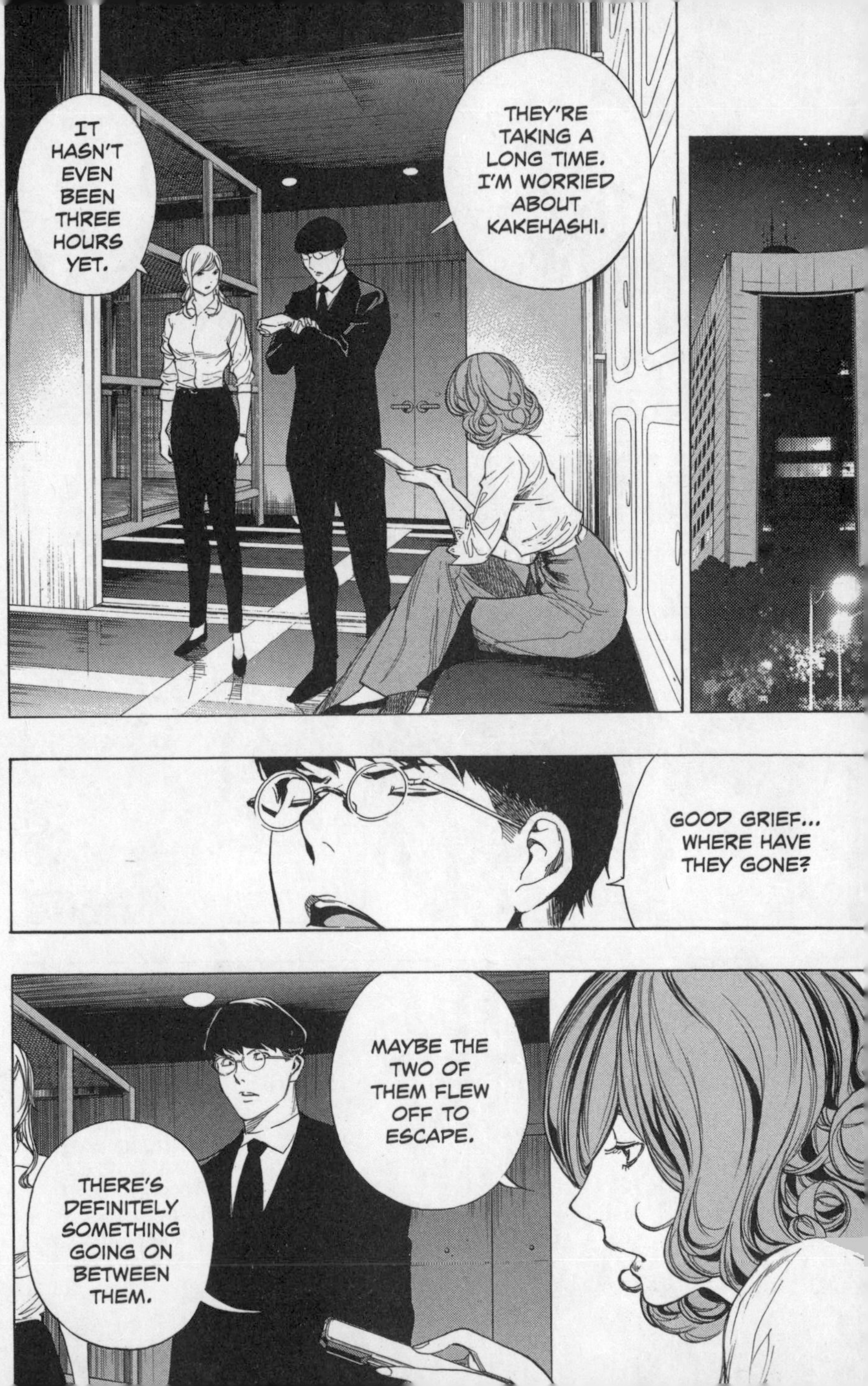
THEY'RE TAKING A LONG TIME. I'M WORRIED ABOUT KAKEHASHI.
IT HASN'T EVEN BEEN THREE HOURS YET.
GOOD GRIEF... WHERE HAVE THEY GONE?
MAYBE THE TWO OF THEM FLEW OFF TO ESCAPE.
THERE'S DEFINITELY SOMETHING GOING ON BETWEEN THEM.

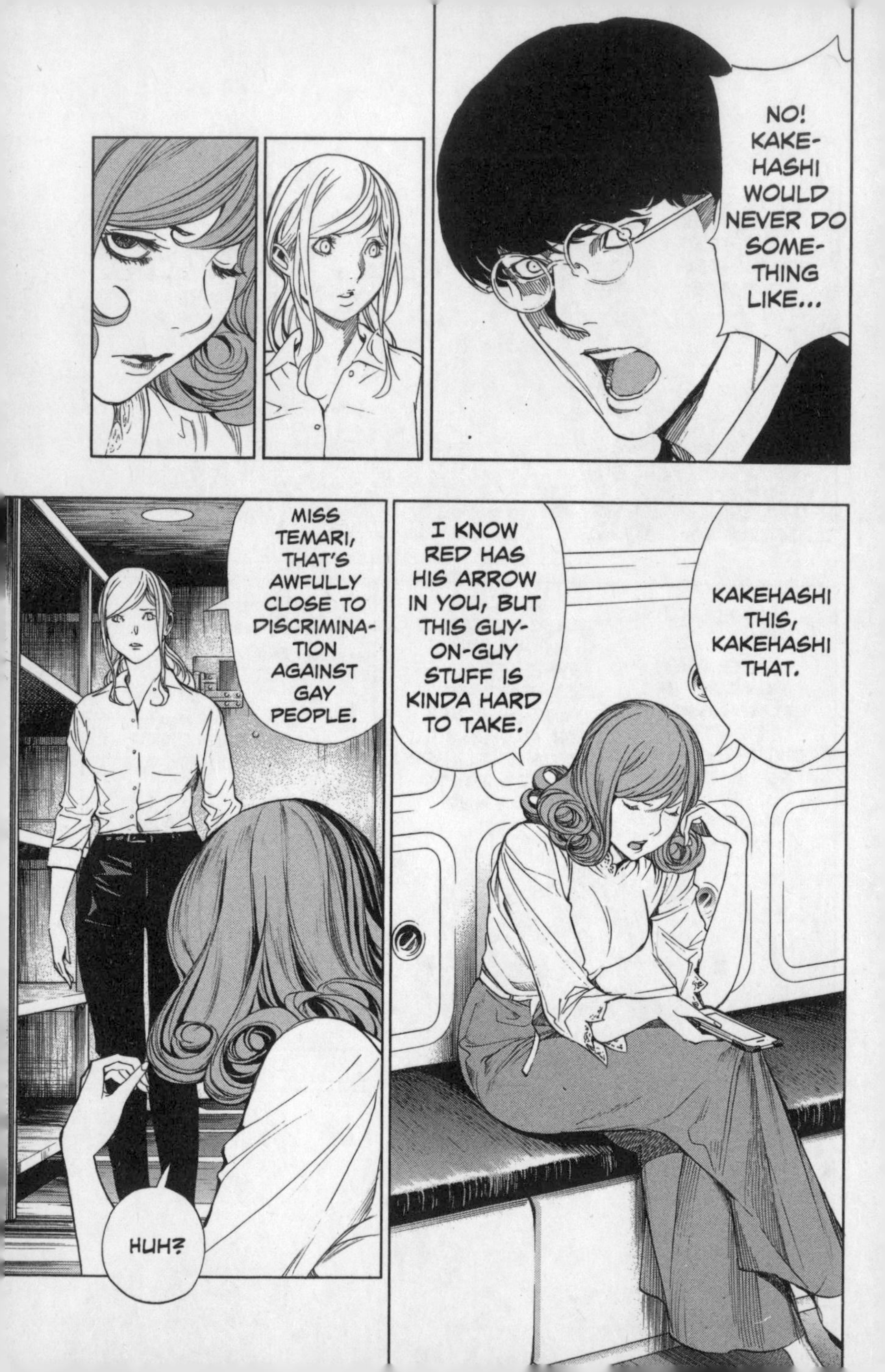
NO! KAKE-HASHI WOULD NEVER DO SOME-THING LIKE...
KAKEHASHI THIS, KAKEHASHI THAT.
I KNOW RED HAS HIS ARROW IN YOU, BUT THIS GUY-ON-GUY STUFF IS KINDA HARD TO TAKE.
MISS TEMARI, THAT'S AWFULLY CLOSE TO DISCRIMINA-TION AGAINST GAY PEOPLE.
HUH?

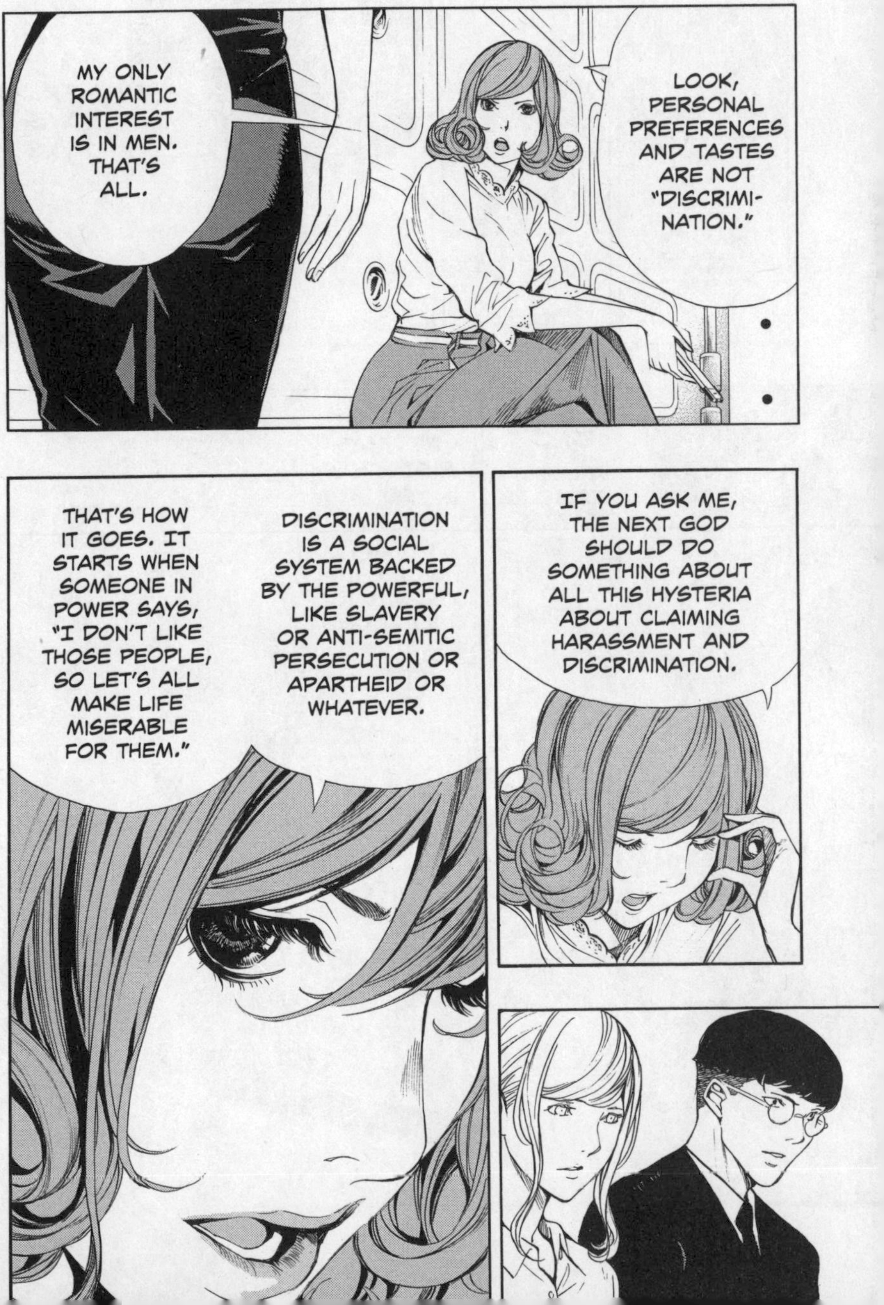
LOOK, PERSONAL PREFERENCES AND TASTES ARE NOT "DISCRIMINATION."
MY ONLY ROMANTIC INTEREST IS IN MEN. THAT'S ALL.
IF YOU ASK ME, THE NEXT GOD SHOULD DO SOMETHING ABOUT ALL THIS HYSTERIA ABOUT CLAIMING HARASSMENT AND DISCRIMINATION.
DISCRIMINATION IS A SOCIAL SYSTEM BACKED BY THE POWERFUL, LIKE SLAVERY OR ANTI-SEMITIC PERSECUTION OR APARTHEID OR WHATEVER.
THAT'S HOW IT GOES. IT STARTS WHEN SOMEONE IN POWER SAYS, "I DON'T LIKE THOSE PEOPLE, SO LET'S ALL MAKE LIFE MISERABLE FOR THEM."

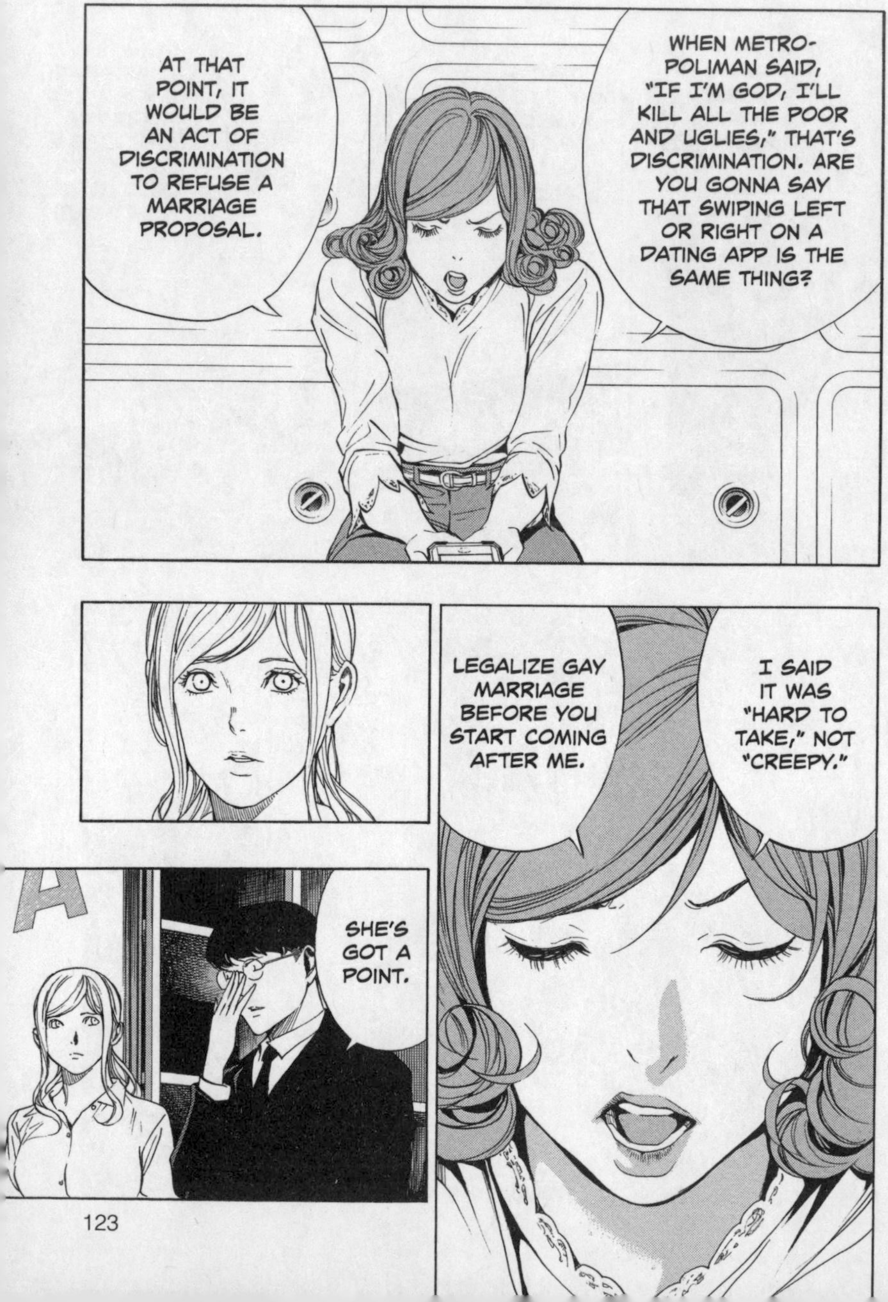
WHEN METRO-POLIMAN SAID, "IF I'M GOD, I'LL KILL ALL THE POOR AND UGLIES," THAT'S DISCRIMINATION. ARE YOU GONNA SAY THAT SWIPING LEFT OR RIGHT ON A DATING APP IS THE SAME THING?
AT THAT POINT, IT WOULD BE AN ACT OF DISCRIMINATION TO REFUSE A MARRIAGE PROPOSAL.
I SAID IT WAS "HARD TO TAKE," NOT "CREEPY."
LEGALIZE GAY MARRIAGE BEFORE YOU START COMING AFTER ME.
SHE'S GOT A POINT.

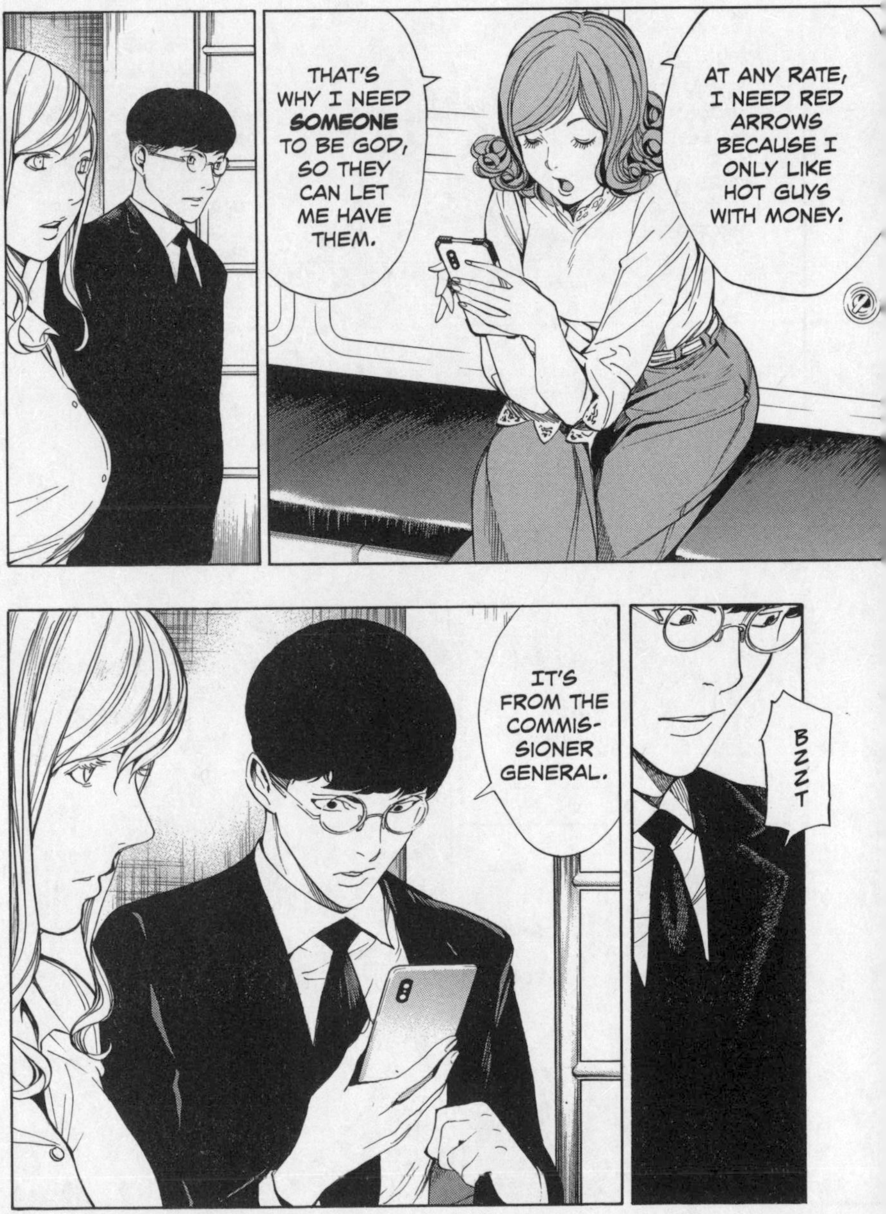
AT ANY RATE, I NEED RED ARROWS BECAUSE I ONLY LIKE HOT GUYS WITH MONEY.
THAT'S WHY I NEED **SOMEONE** TO BE GOD, SO THEY CAN LET ME HAVE THEM.
BZZT
IT'S FROM THE COMMIS-SIONER GENERAL.

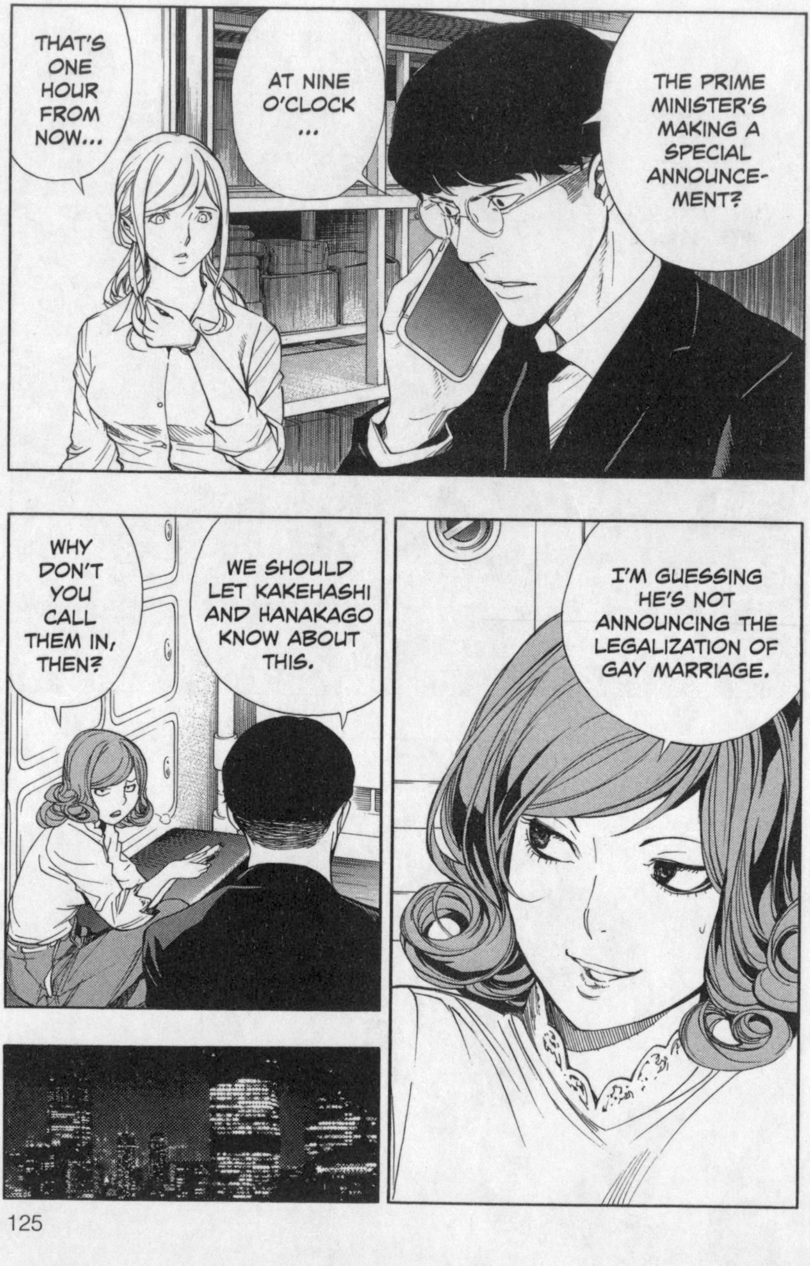
THE PRIME MINISTER'S MAKING A SPECIAL ANNOUNCE-MENT?
AT NINE O'CLOCK ...
THAT'S ONE HOUR FROM NOW...
I'M GUESSING HE'S NOT ANNOUNCING THE LEGALIZATION OF GAY MARRIAGE.
WE SHOULD LET KAKEHASHI AND HANAKAGO KNOW ABOUT THIS.
WHY DON'T YOU CALL THEM IN, THEN?

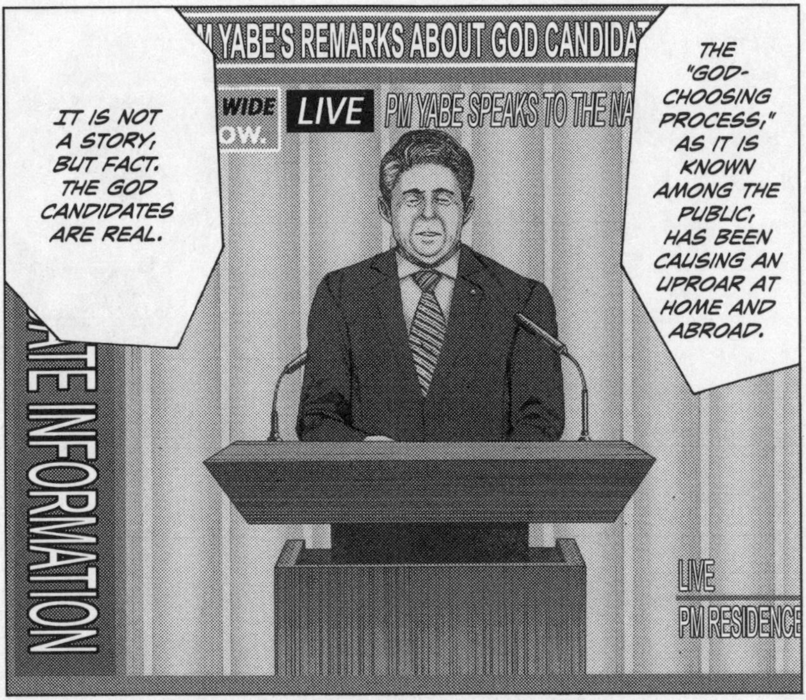
YABE'S REMARKS ABOUT GOD
LIVE
PM YABE SPEAKS TO THE
THE "GOD-CHOOSING PROCESS," AS IT IS KNOWN AMONG THE PUBLIC, HAS BEEN CAUSING AN UPROAR AT HOME AND ABROAD.
IT IS NOT A STORY, BUT FACT. THE GOD CANDIDATES ARE REAL.
INFORMATION
LIVE
PM RESIDENCE
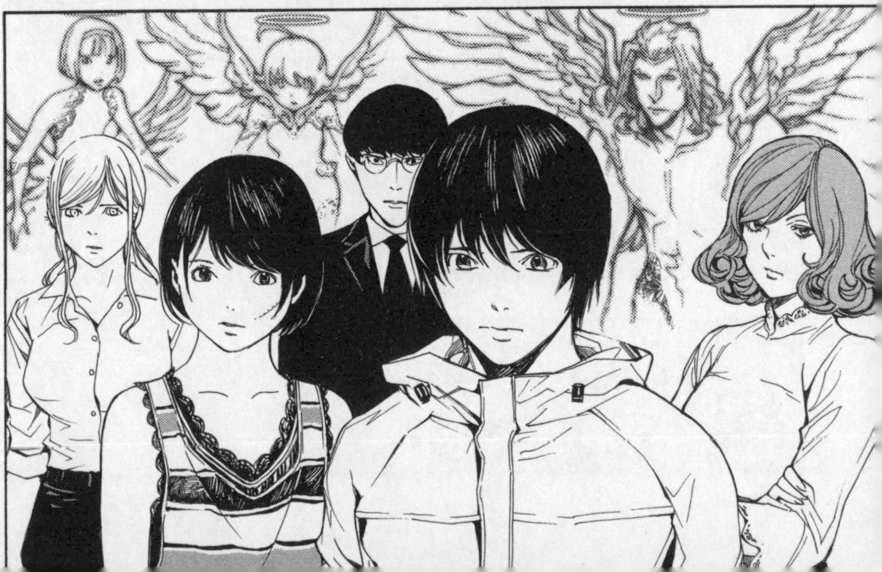

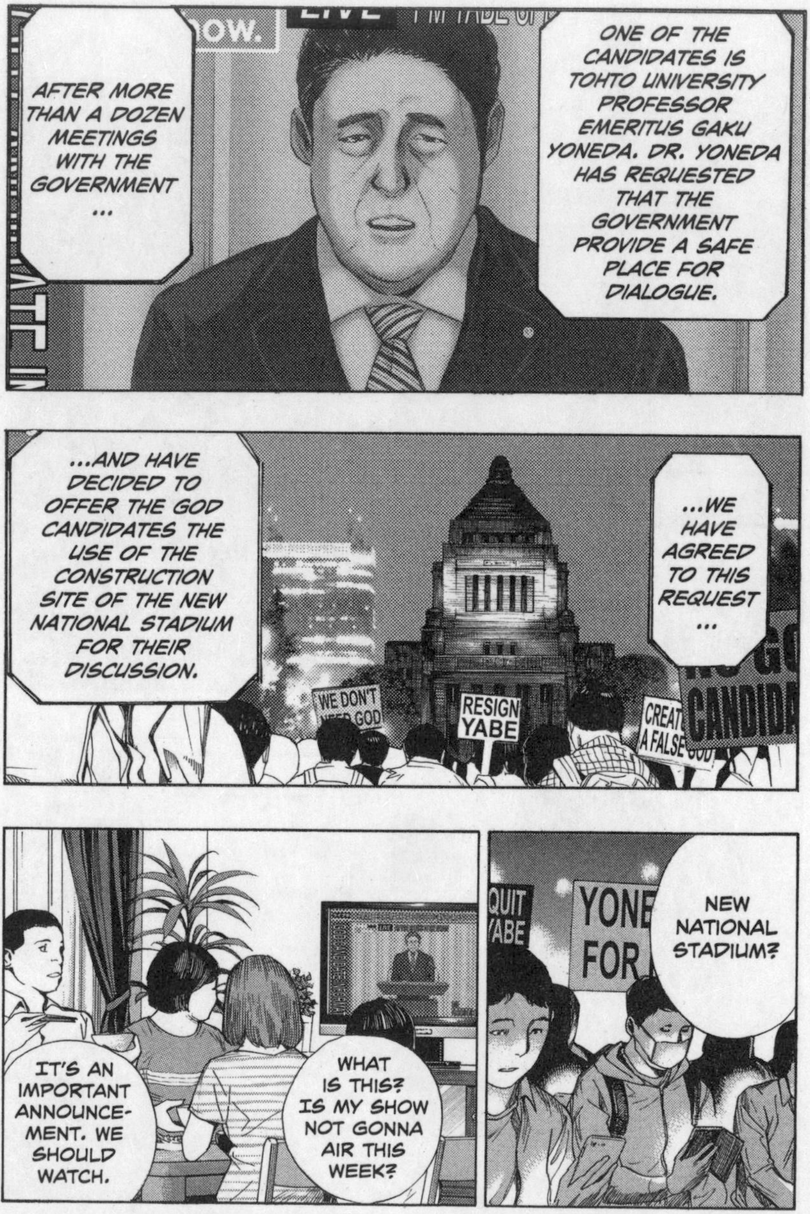
ONE OF THE CANDIDATES IS TOHTO UNIVERSITY PROFESSOR EMERITUS GAKU YONEDA. DR. YONEDA HAS REQUESTED THAT THE GOVERNMENT PROVIDE A SAFE PLACE FOR DIALOGUE.
AFTER MORE THAN A DOZEN MEETINGS WITH THE GOVERNMENT ...
...WE HAVE AGREED TO THIS REQUEST ...
...AND HAVE DECIDED TO OFFER THE GOD CANDIDATES THE USE OF THE CONSTRUCTION SITE OF THE NEW NATIONAL STADIUM FOR THEIR DISCUSSION.
RESIGN YABE
WE DON'T
NEW NATIONAL STADIUM?
QUIT YABE
WHAT IS THIS? IS MY SHOW NOT GONNA AIR THIS WEEK?
IT'S AN IMPORTANT ANNOUNCE-MENT. WE SHOULD WATCH.

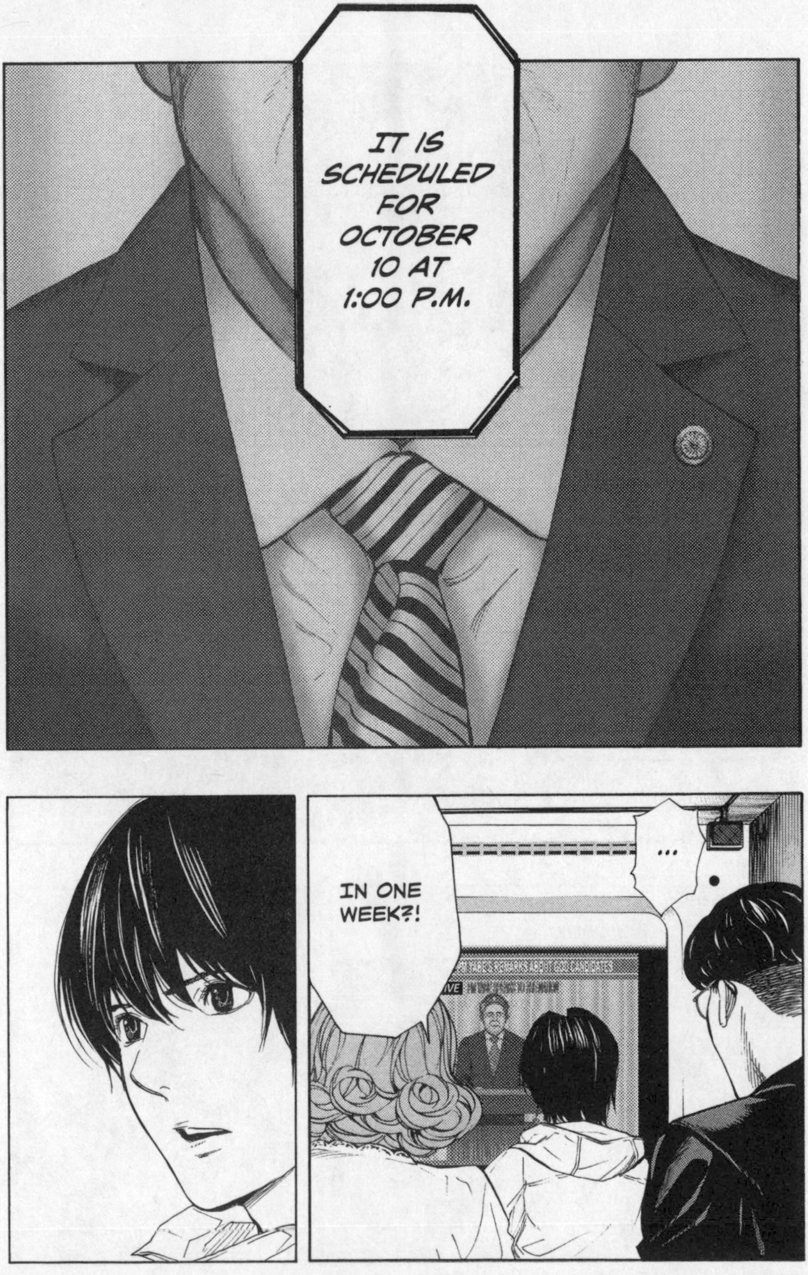
IT IS SCHEDULED FOR OCTOBER 10 AT 1:00 P.M.
IN ONE WEEK?!
...

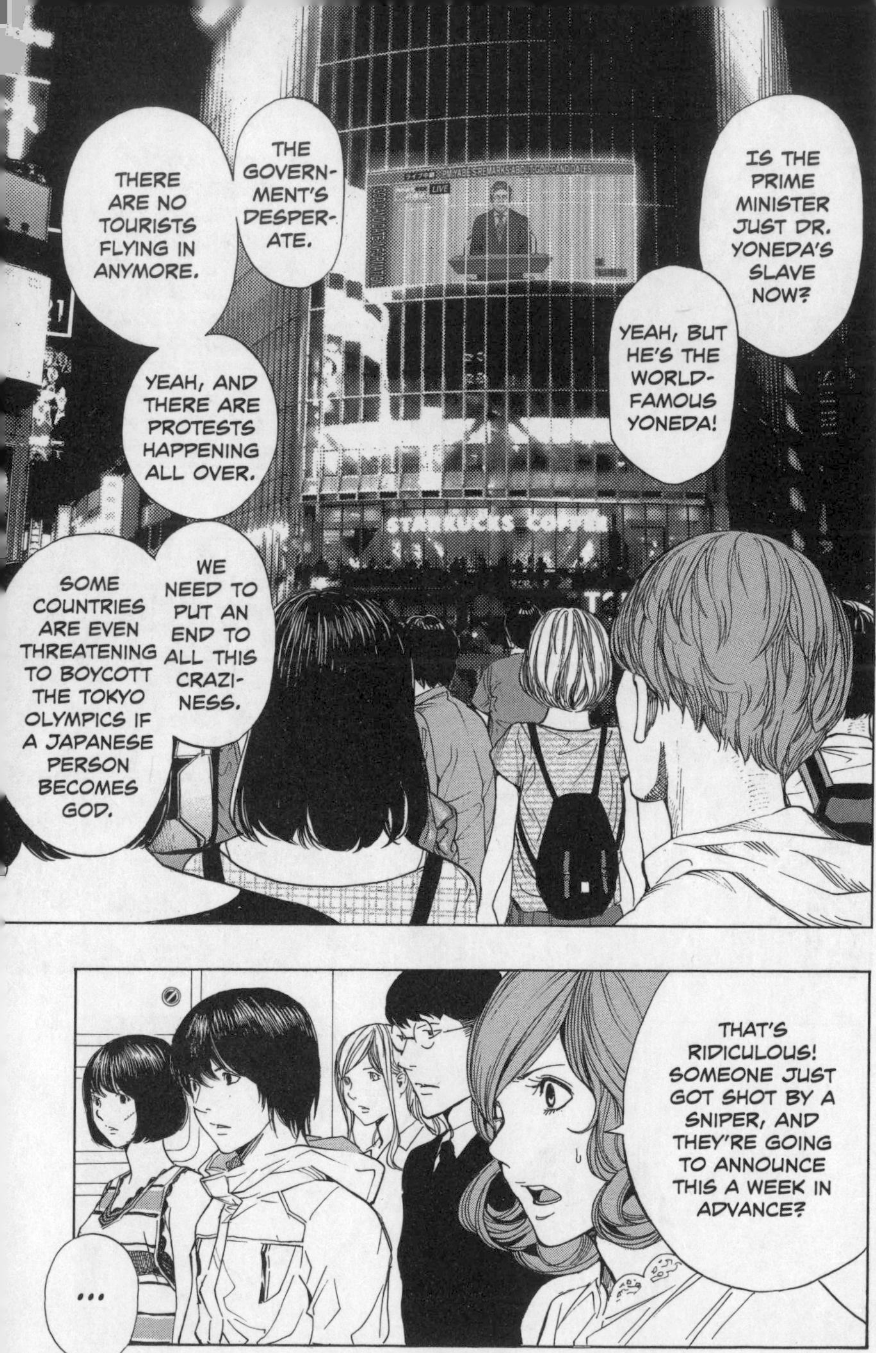
IS THE PRIME MINISTER JUST DR. YONEDA'S SLAVE NOW?
YEAH, BUT HE'S THE WORLD-FAMOUS YONEDA!
THE GOVERNMENT'S DESPERATE.
THERE ARE NO TOURISTS FLYING IN ANYMORE.
YEAH, AND THERE ARE PROTESTS HAPPENING ALL OVER.
WE NEED TO PUT AN END TO ALL THIS CRAZINESS.
SOME COUNTRIES ARE EVEN THREATENING TO BOYCOTT THE TOKYO OLYMPICS IF A JAPANESE PERSON BECOMES GOD.
THAT'S RIDICULOUS! SOMEONE JUST GOT SHOT BY A SNIPER, AND THEY'RE GOING TO ANNOUNCE THIS A WEEK IN ADVANCE?
...

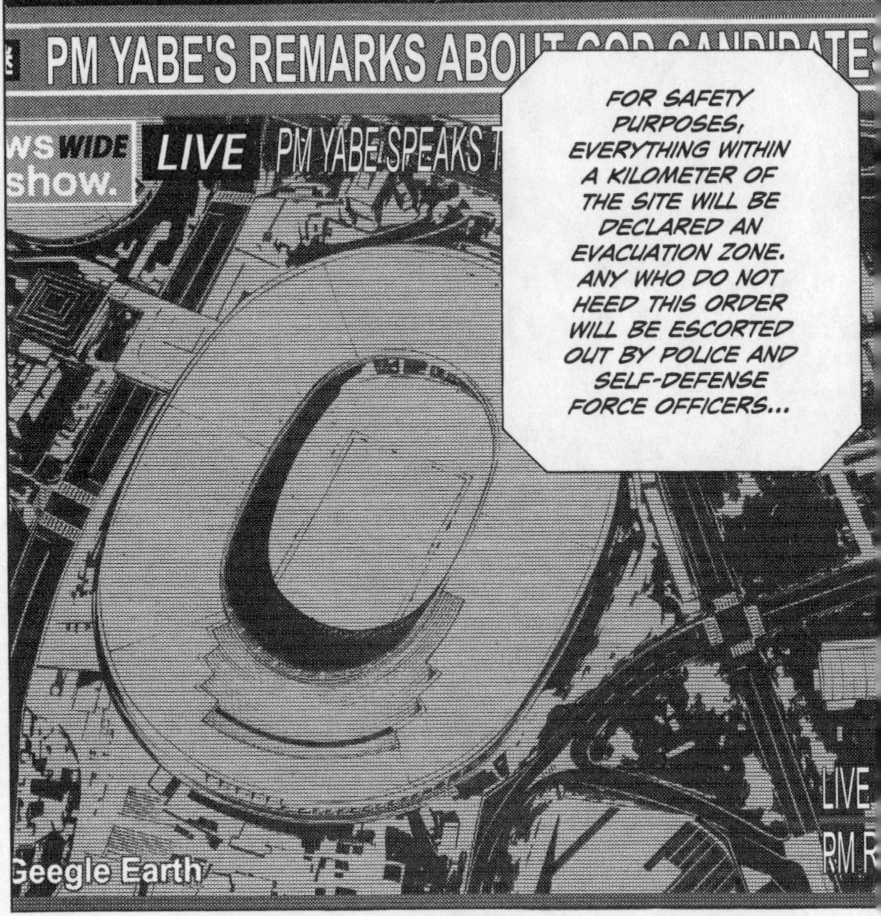
PM YABE'S REMARKS ABOU
WS WIDE show.
LIVE
PM YABE SPEAKS T
FOR SAFETY PURPOSES, EVERYTHING WITHIN A KILOMETER OF THE SITE WILL BE DECLARED AN EVACUATION ZONE. ANY WHO DO NOT HEED THIS ORDER WILL BE ESCORTED OUT BY POLICE AND SELF-DEFENSE FORCE OFFICERS...
LIVE
PM R
Geegle Earth

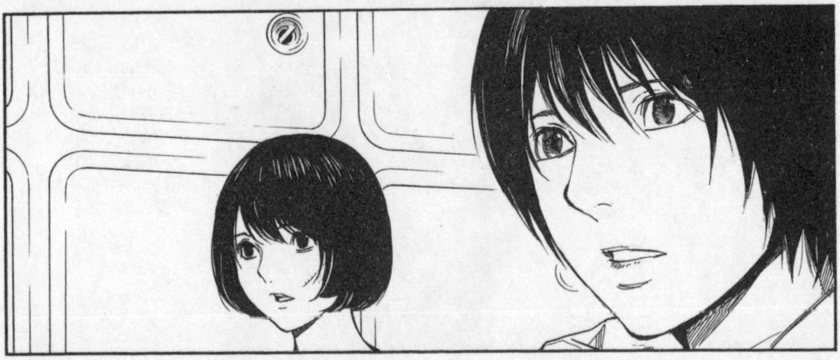

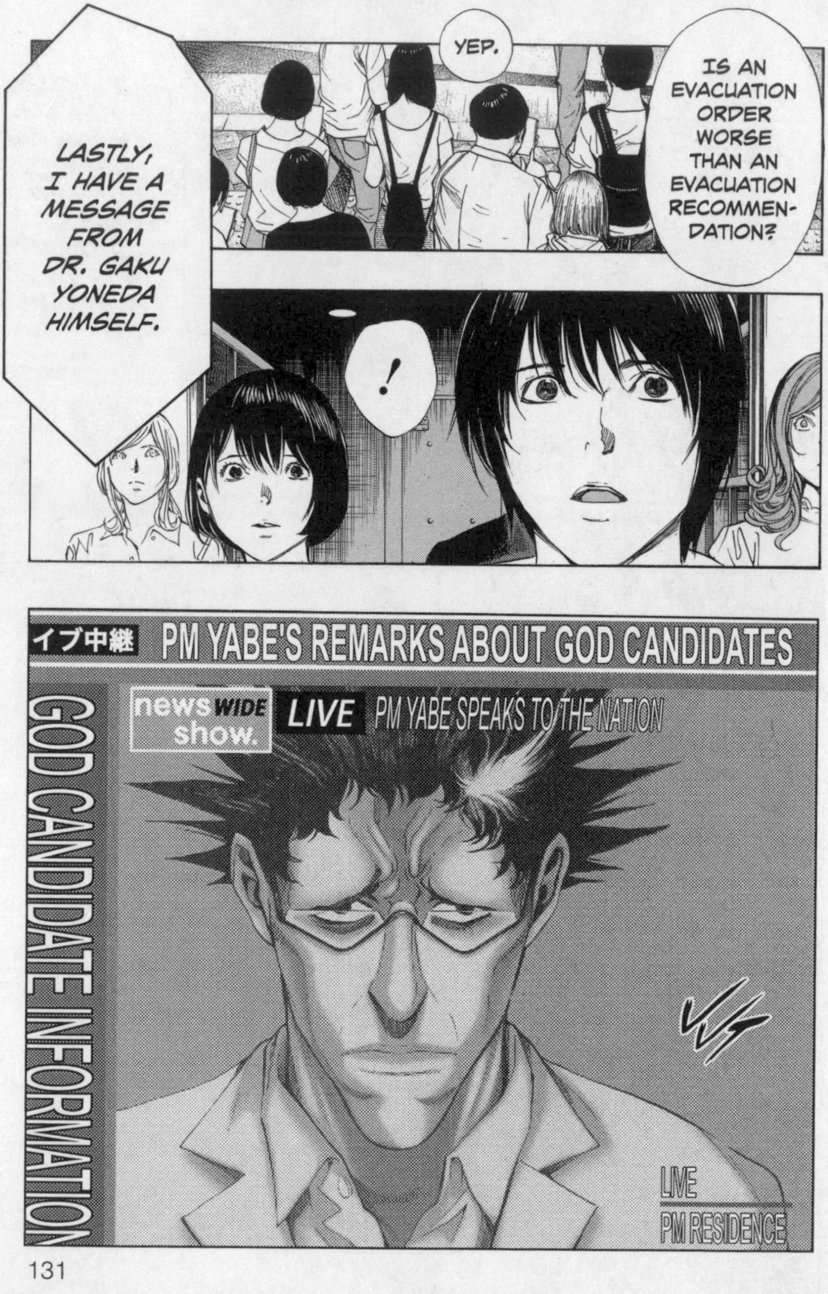
IS AN EVACUATION ORDER WORSE THAN AN EVACUATION RECOMMEN-DATION?
YEP.
LASTLY, I HAVE A MESSAGE FROM DR. GAKU YONEDA HIMSELF.
!
イブ中継
PM YABE'S REMARKS ABOUT GOD CANDIDATES
GOD CANDIDATE INFORMATION
news WIDE show.
LIVE
PM YABE SPEAKS TO THE NATION
LIVE
PM RESIDENCE

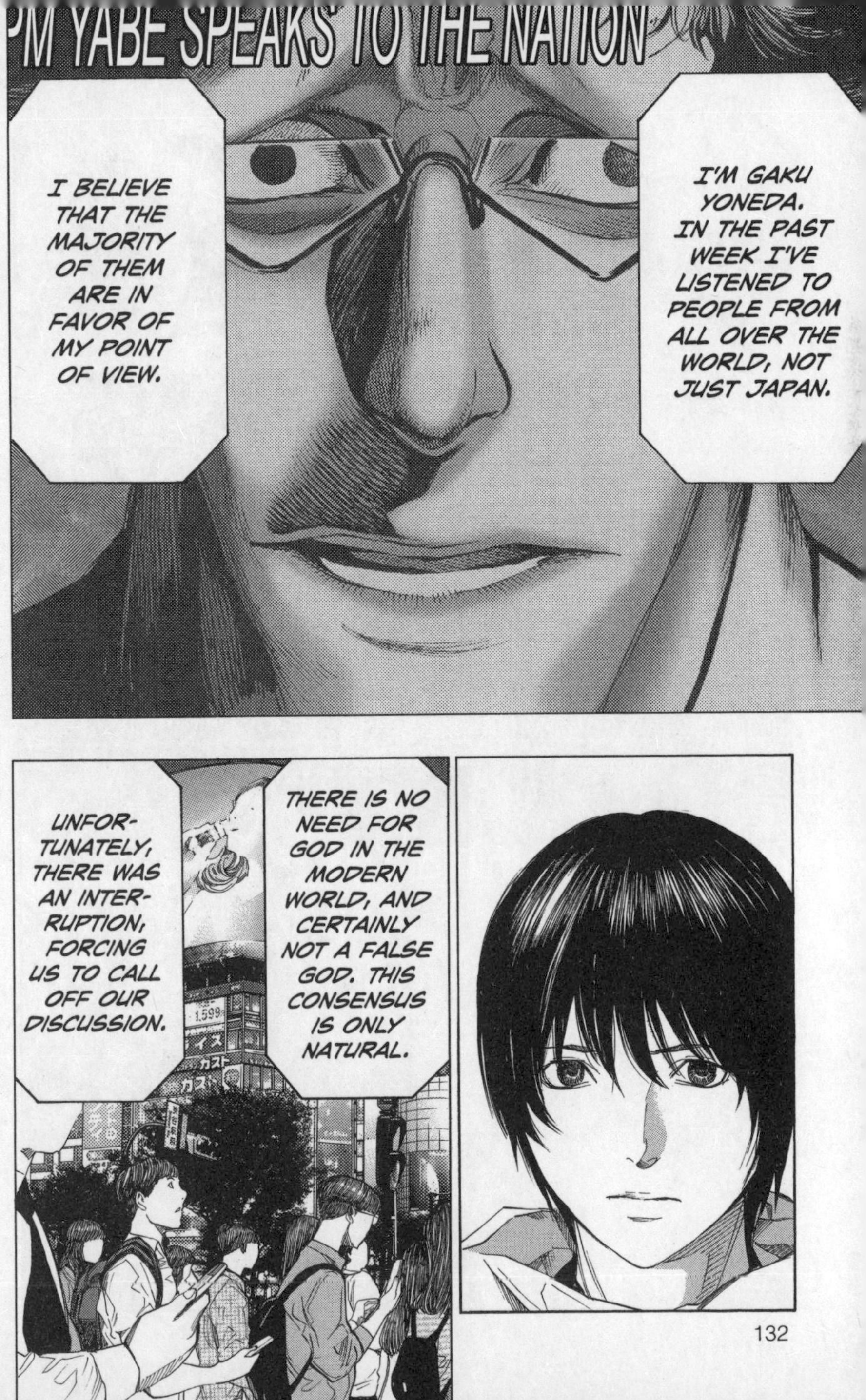
PM YABE SPEAKS TO THE NATION
I'M GAKU YONEDA. IN THE PAST WEEK I'VE LISTENED TO PEOPLE FROM ALL OVER THE WORLD, NOT JUST JAPAN.
I BELIEVE THAT THE MAJORITY OF THEM ARE IN FAVOR OF MY POINT OF VIEW.
THERE IS NO NEED FOR GOD IN THE MODERN WORLD, AND CERTAINLY NOT A FALSE GOD. THIS CONSENSUS IS ONLY NATURAL.
UNFORTUNATELY, THERE WAS AN INTERRUPTION, FORCING US TO CALL OFF OUR DISCUSSION.

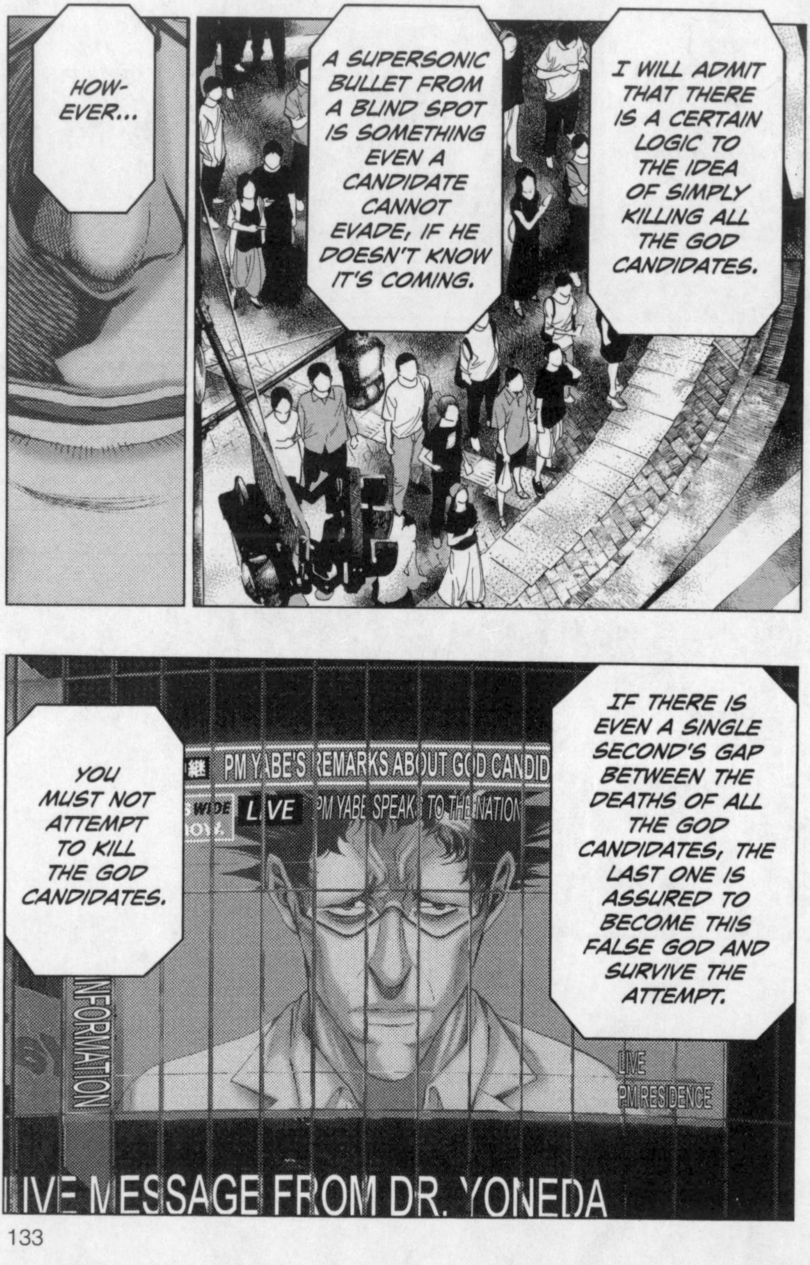
I WILL ADMIT THAT THERE IS A CERTAIN LOGIC TO THE IDEA OF SIMPLY KILLING ALL THE GOD CANDIDATES.
A SUPERSONIC BULLET FROM A BLIND SPOT IS SOMETHING EVEN A CANDIDATE CANNOT EVADE, IF HE DOESN'T KNOW IT'S COMING.
HOW-EVER...
IF THERE IS EVEN A SINGLE SECOND'S GAP BETWEEN THE DEATHS OF ALL THE GOD CANDIDATES, THE LAST ONE IS ASSURED TO BECOME THIS FALSE GOD AND SURVIVE THE ATTEMPT.
YOU MUST NOT ATTEMPT TO KILL THE GOD CANDIDATES.
PM YABE'S REMARKS ABOUT GOD CANDID
LIVE
PM YABE SPEAKS TO THE NATION
INFORMATION
LIVE
PM RESIDENCE
LIVE MESSAGE FROM DR. YONEDA

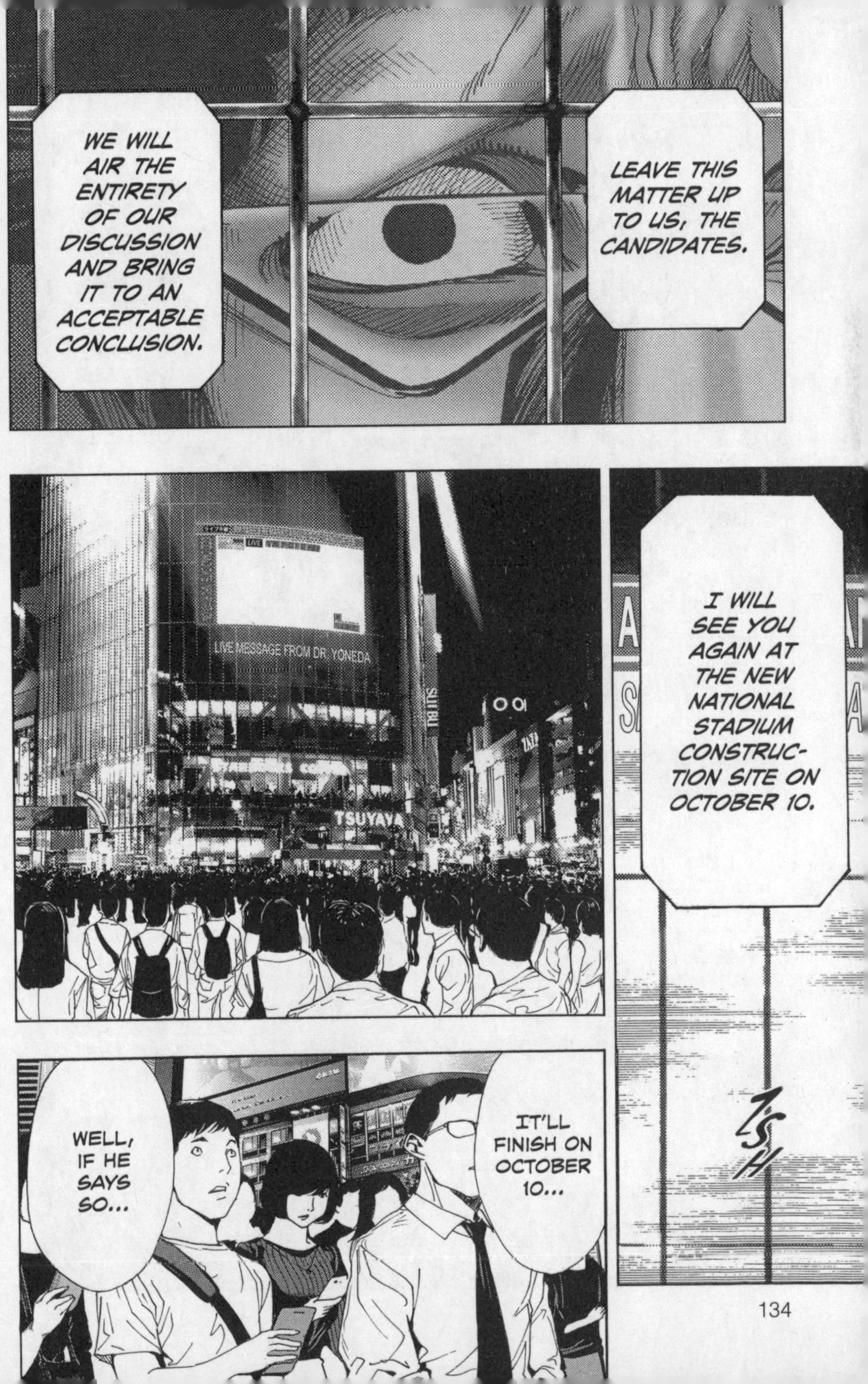
LEAVE THIS MATTER UP TO US, THE CANDIDATES.
WE WILL AIR THE ENTIRETY OF OUR DISCUSSION AND BRING IT TO AN ACCEPTABLE CONCLUSION.
I WILL SEE YOU AGAIN AT THE NEW NATIONAL STADIUM CONSTRUCTION SITE ON OCTOBER 10.
ZSH
LIVE MESSAGE FROM DR. YONEDA
TSUYAYA
IT'LL FINISH ON OCTOBER 10...
WELL, IF HE SAYS SO...

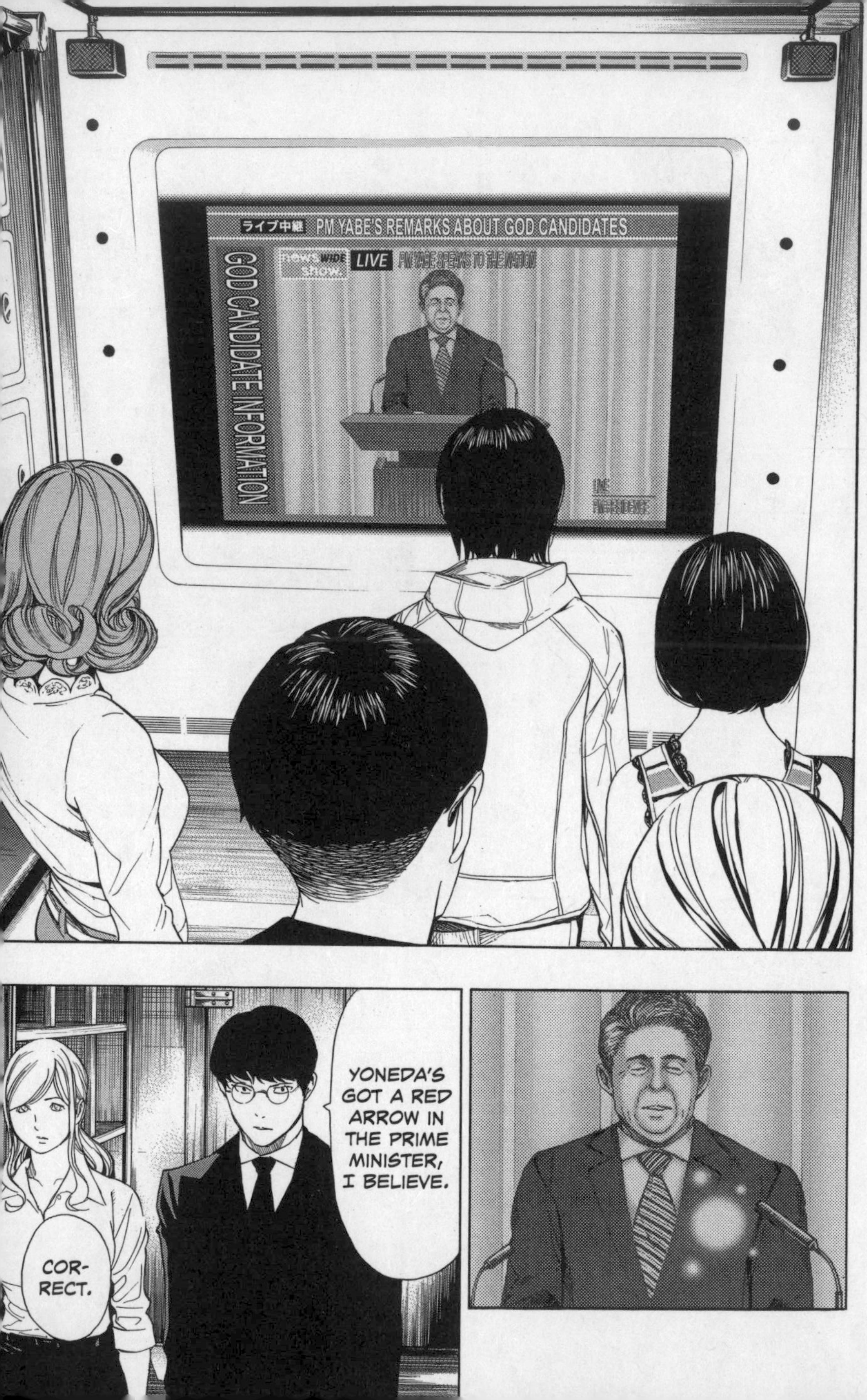
ライブ中継
PM YABE'S REMARKS ABOUT GOD CANDIDATES
news WIDE show.
LIVE
PM YABE SPEAKS TO THE NATION
GOD CANDIDATE INFORMATION
YONEDA'S GOT A RED ARROW IN THE PRIME MINISTER, I BELIEVE.
COR-RECT.

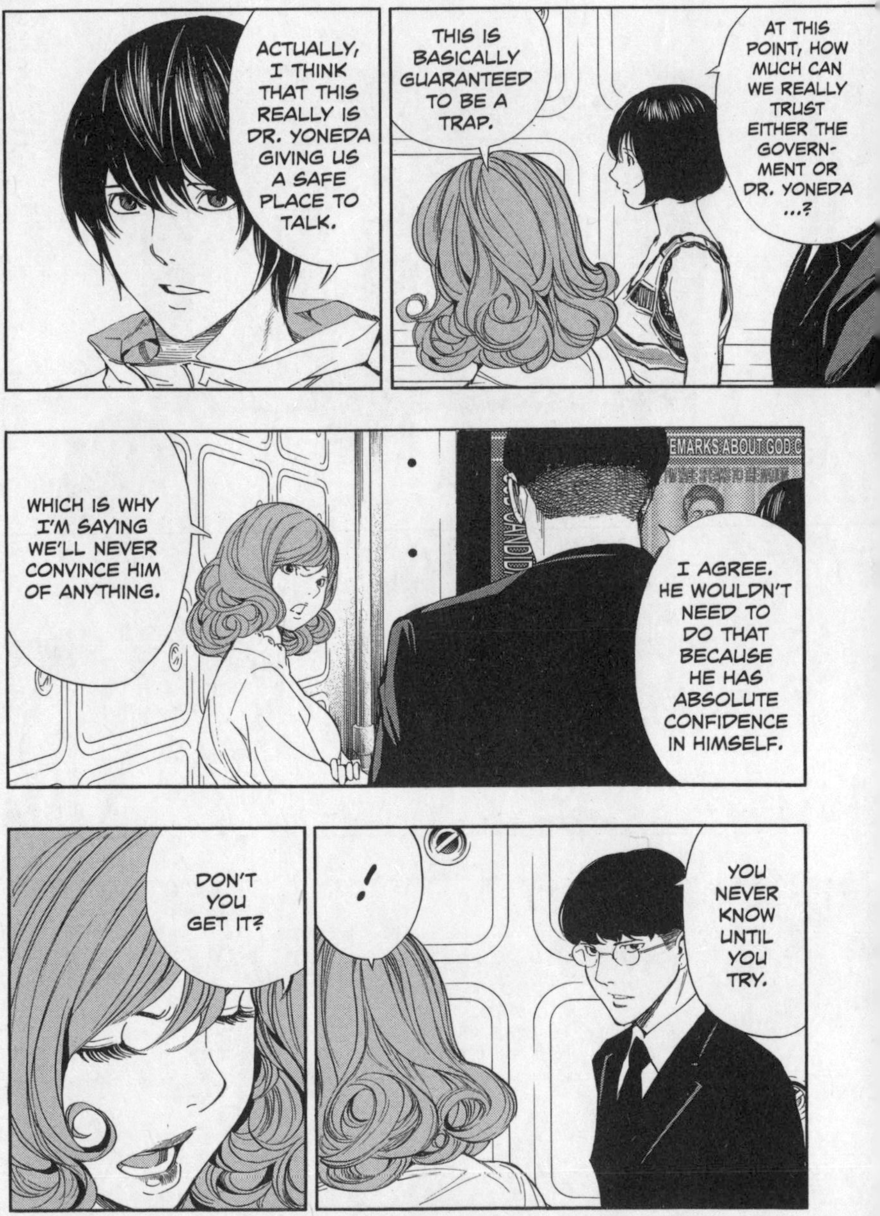
AT THIS POINT, HOW MUCH CAN WE REALLY TRUST EITHER THE GOVERN-MENT OR DR. YONEDA ...?
THIS IS BASICALLY GUARANTEED TO BE A TRAP.
ACTUALLY, I THINK THAT THIS REALLY IS DR. YONEDA GIVING US A SAFE PLACE TO TALK.
EMARKS ABOUT GOD C
I AGREE. HE WOULDN'T NEED TO DO THAT BECAUSE HE HAS ABSOLUTE CONFIDENCE IN HIMSELF.
WHICH IS WHY I'M SAYING WE'LL NEVER CONVINCE HIM OF ANYTHING.
YOU NEVER KNOW UNTIL YOU TRY.
!
DON'T YOU GET IT?

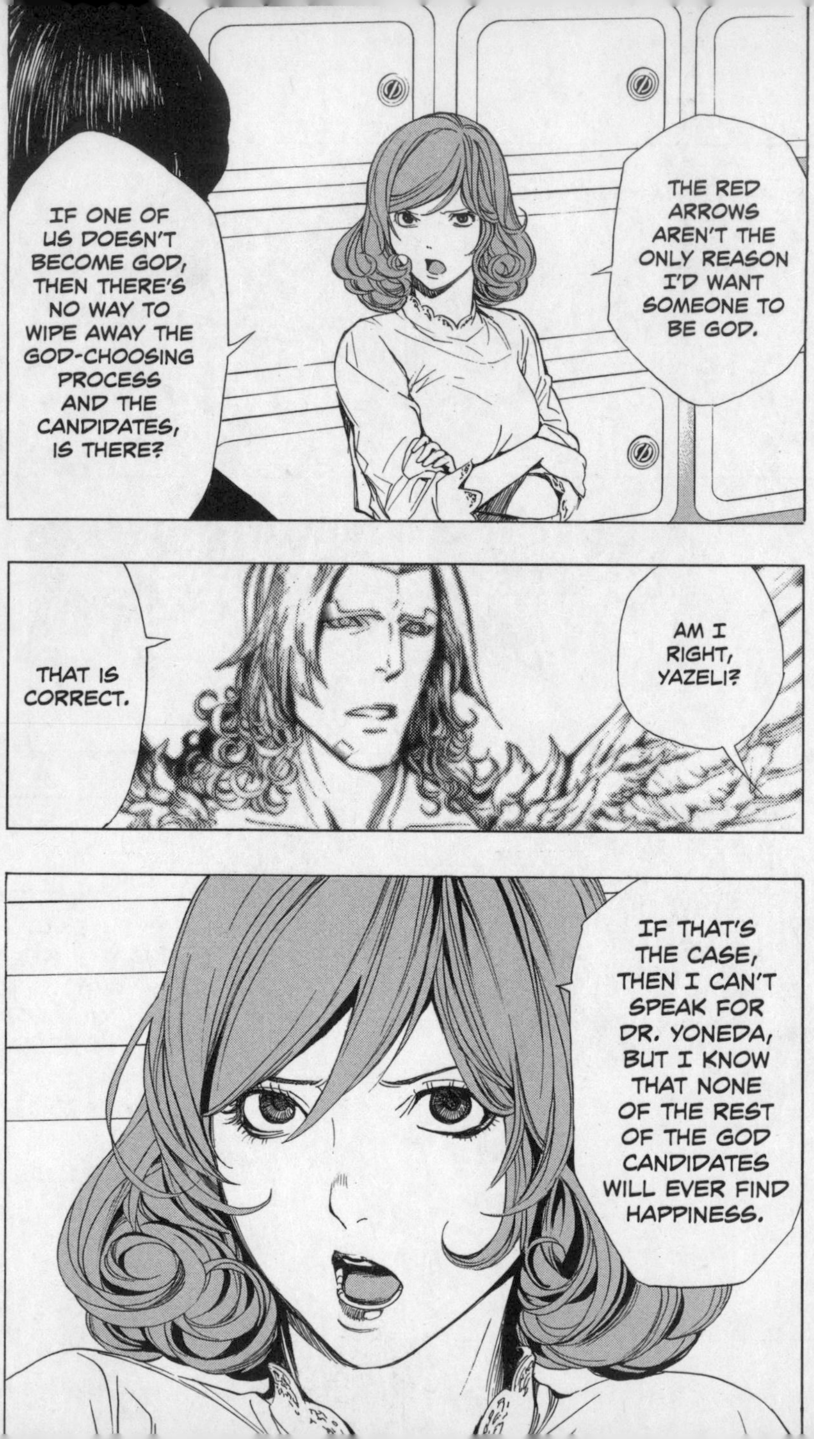
THE RED ARROWS AREN'T THE ONLY REASON I'D WANT SOMEONE TO BE GOD.
IF ONE OF US DOESN'T BECOME GOD, THEN THERE'S NO WAY TO WIPE AWAY THE GOD-CHOOSING PROCESS AND THE CANDIDATES, IS THERE?
AM I RIGHT, YAZELI?
THAT IS CORRECT.
IF THAT'S THE CASE, THEN I CAN'T SPEAK FOR DR. YONEDA, BUT I KNOW THAT NONE OF THE REST OF THE GOD CANDIDATES WILL EVER FIND HAPPINESS.

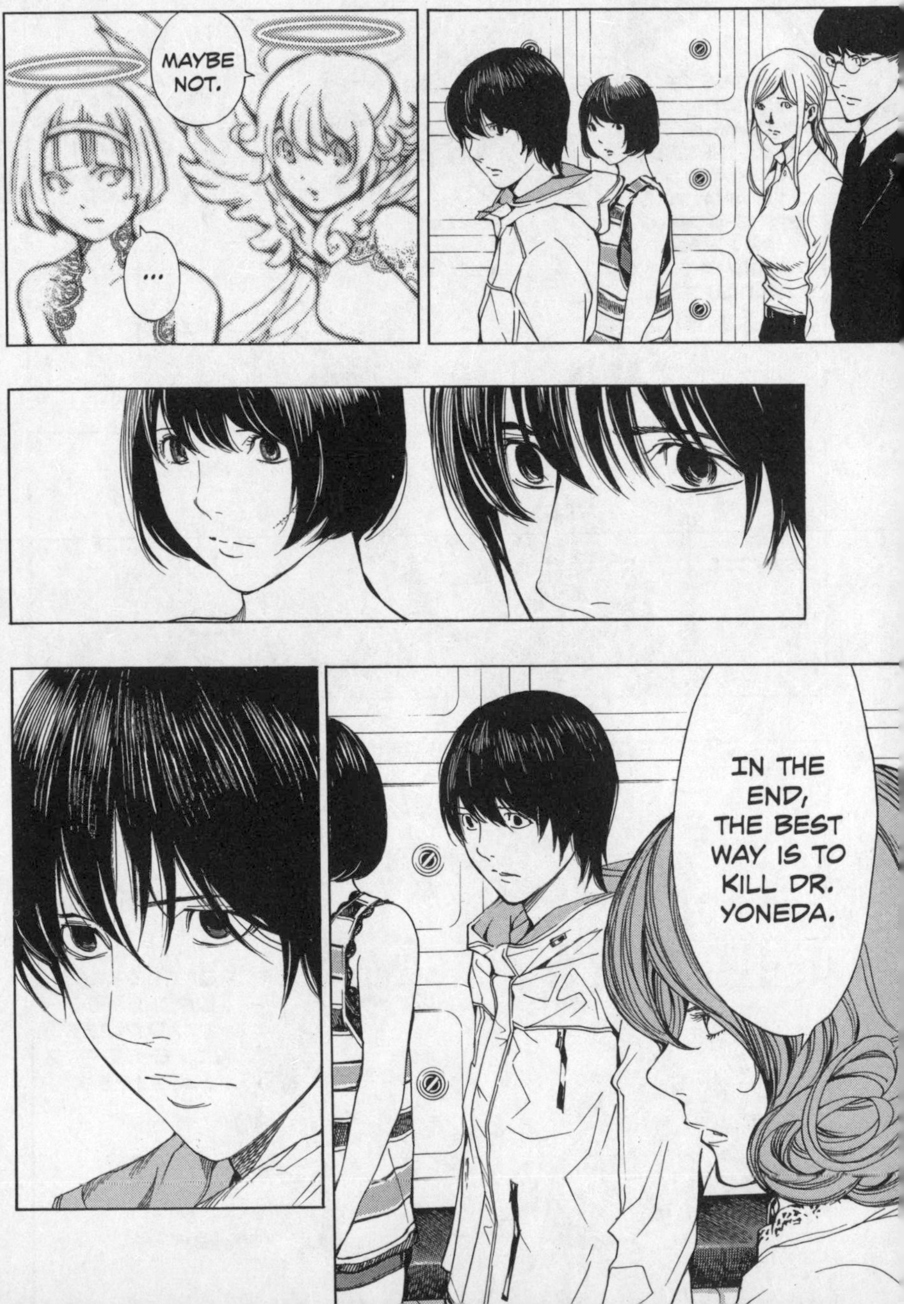
MAYBE NOT.
...
IN THE END, THE BEST WAY IS TO KILL DR. YONEDA.

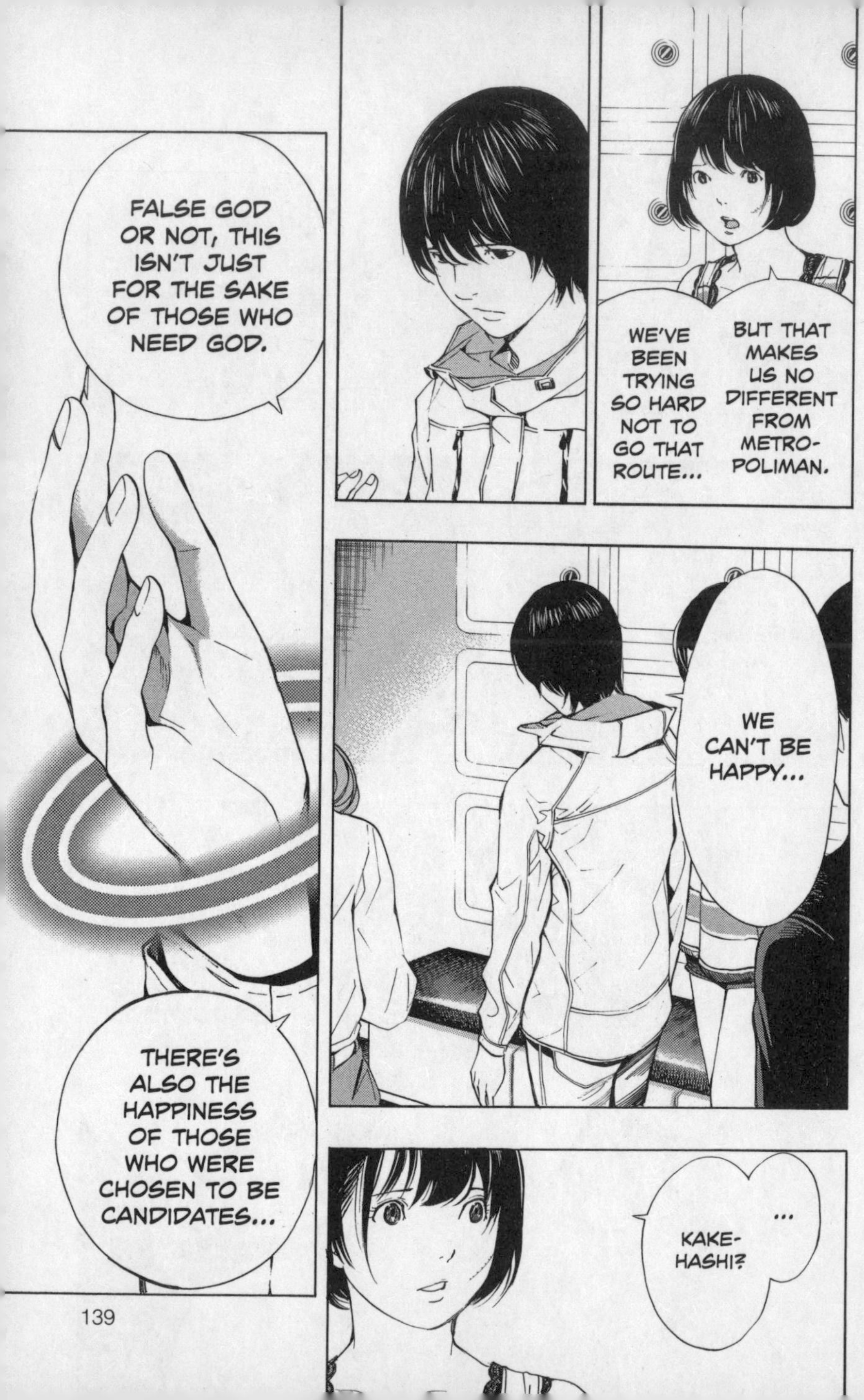
BUT THAT MAKES US NO DIFFERENT FROM METRO-POLIMAN.
WE'VE BEEN TRYING SO HARD NOT TO GO THAT ROUTE...
WE CAN'T BE HAPPY...
...
KAKE-HASHI?
FALSE GOD OR NOT, THIS ISN'T JUST FOR THE SAKE OF THOSE WHO NEED GOD.
THERE'S ALSO THE HAPPINESS OF THOSE WHO WERE CHOSEN TO BE CANDIDATES...

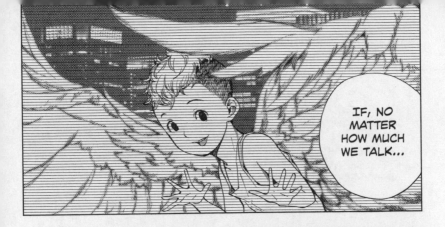

IF, NO MATTER HOW MUCH WE TALK...

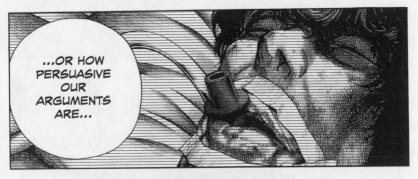

...OR HOW PERSUASIVE OUR ARGUMENTS ARE...

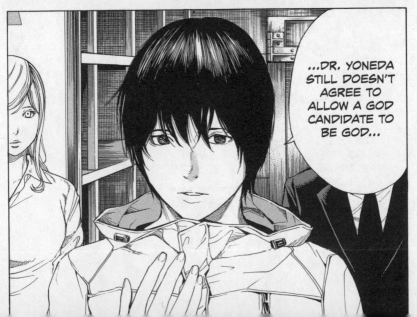

...DR. YONEDA STILL DOESN'T AGREE TO ALLOW A GOD CANDIDATE TO BE GOD...

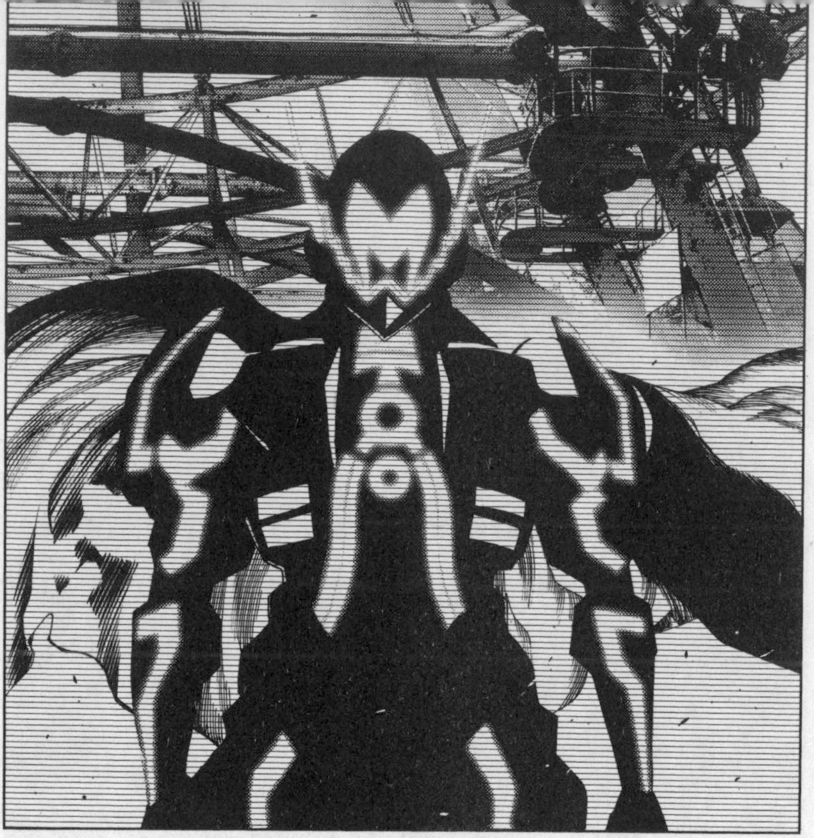
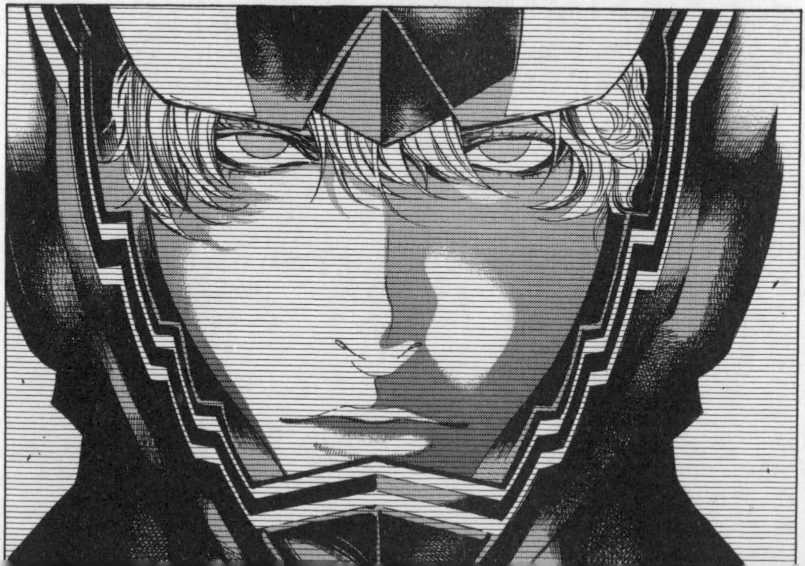

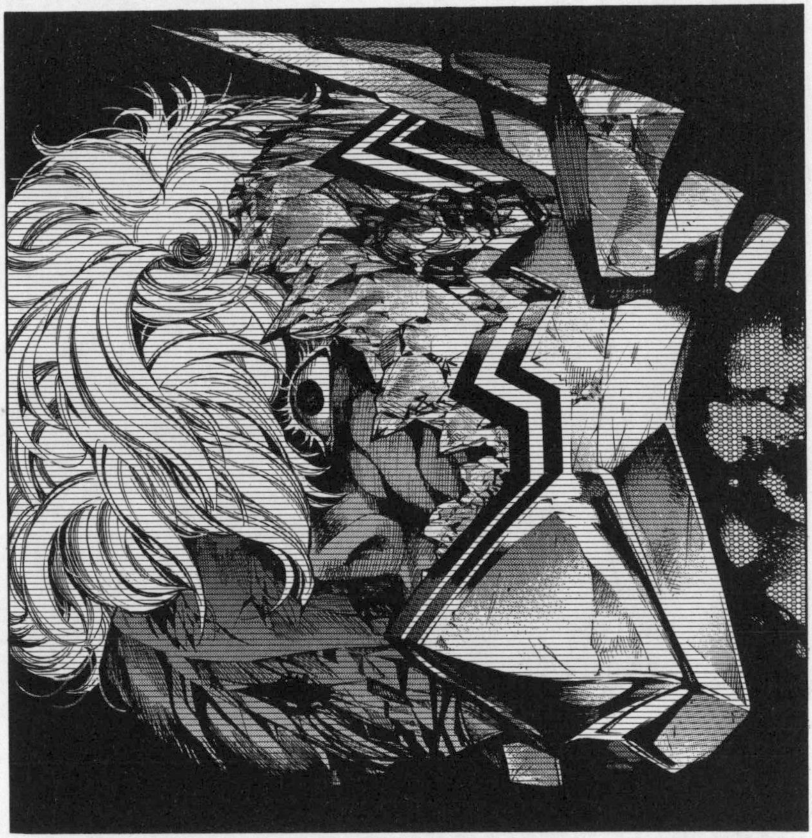

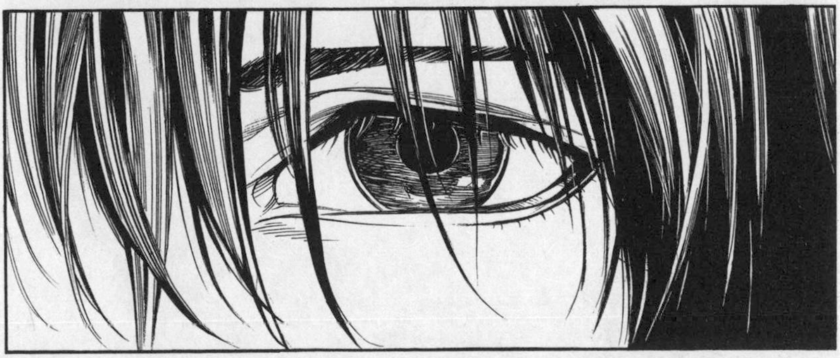

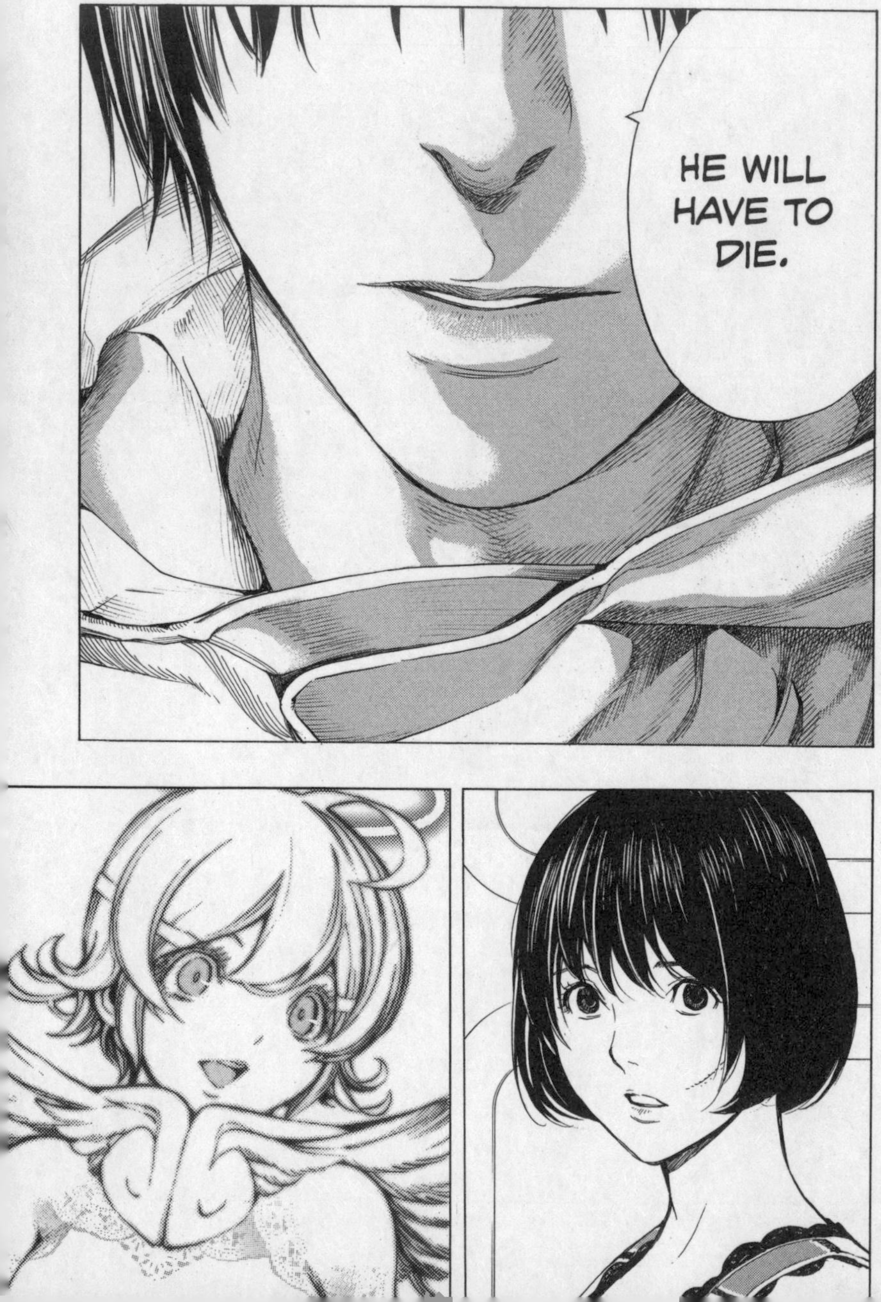
HE WILL HAVE TO DIE.

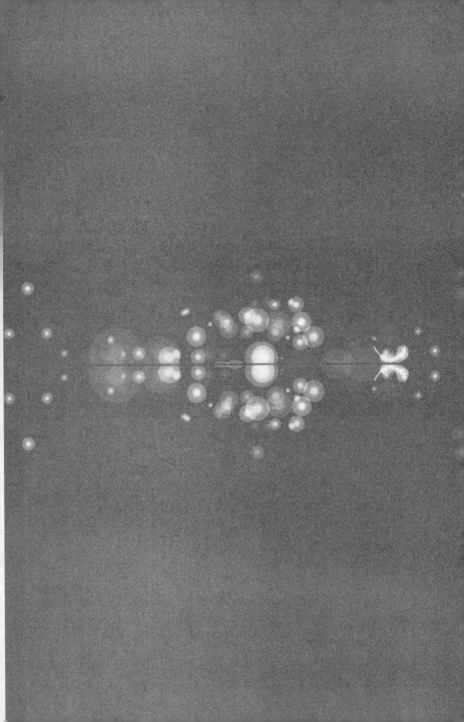

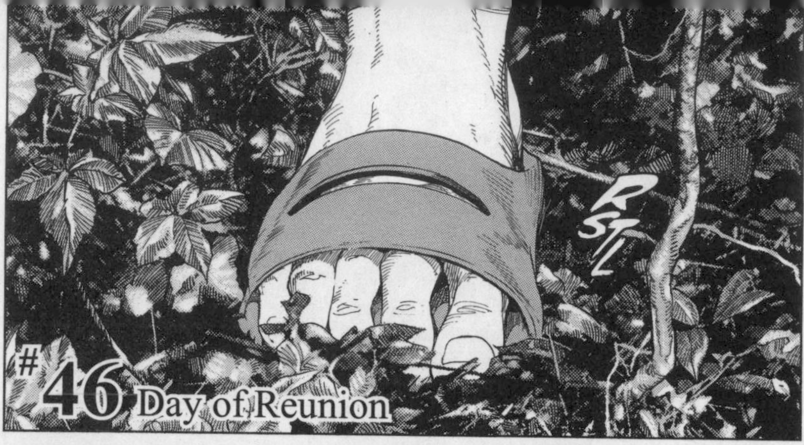
RSTL
#46 Day of Reunion

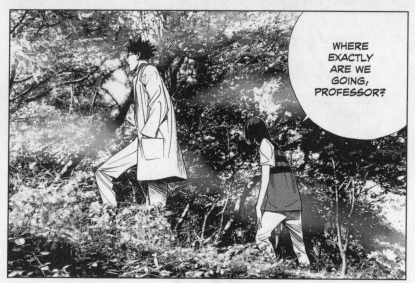

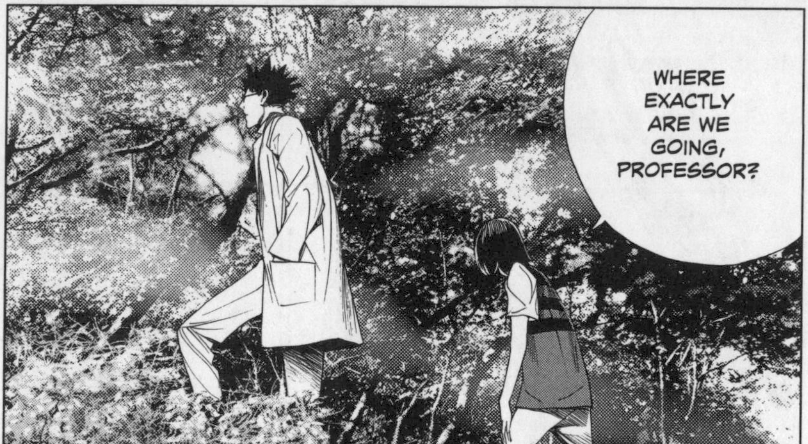
WHERE EXACTLY ARE WE GOING, PROFESSOR?

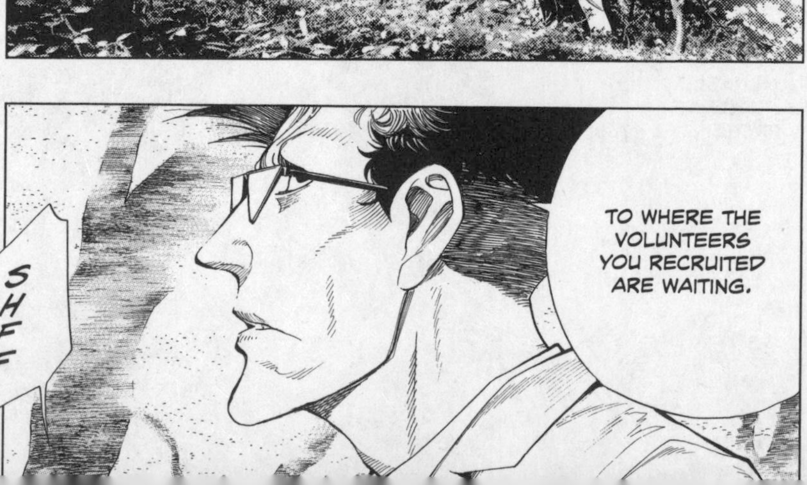
TO WHERE THE VOLUNTEERS YOU RECRUITED ARE WAITING.
SHFF

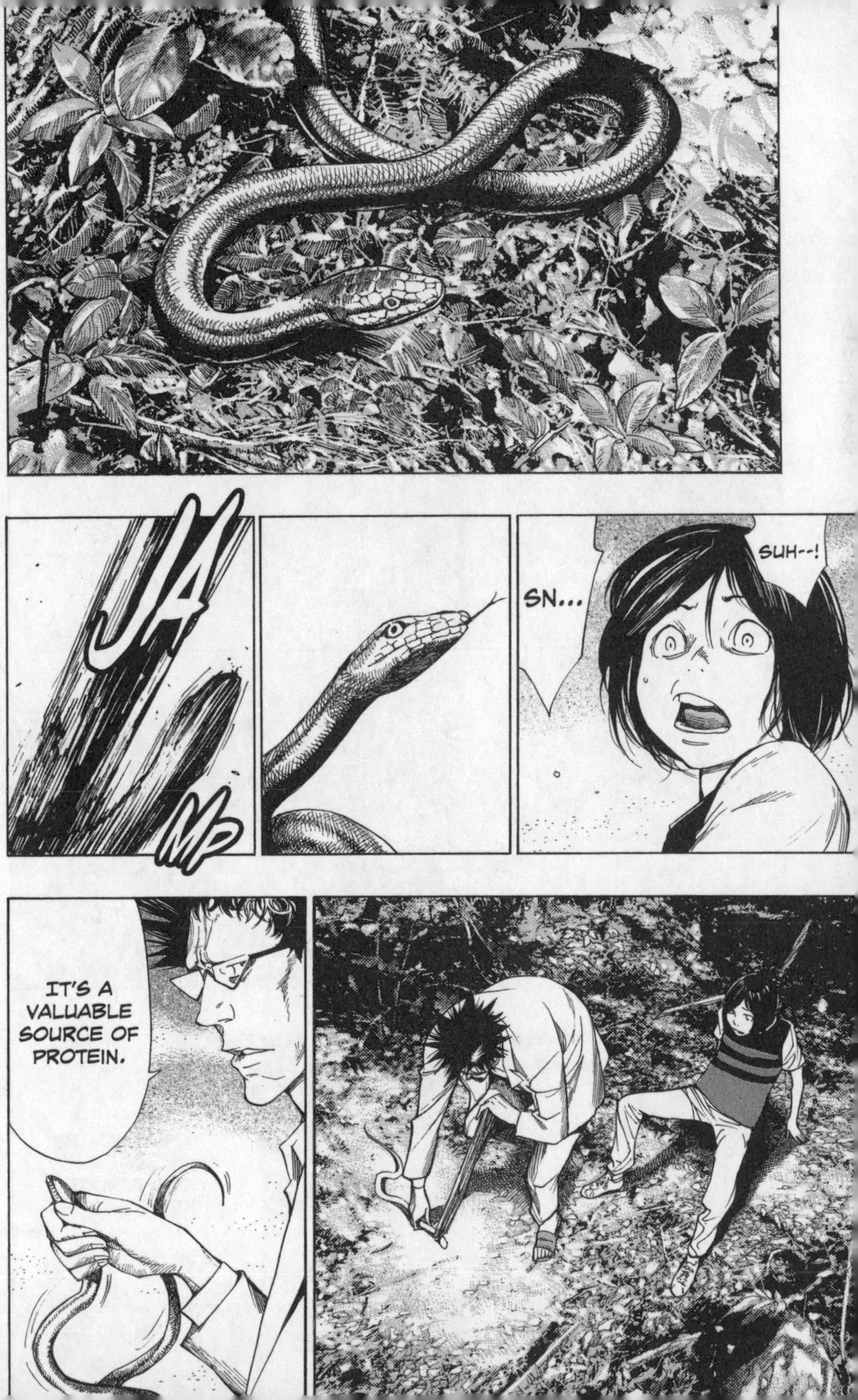
SUH--!
SN...
JA
MP
IT'S A VALUABLE SOURCE OF PROTEIN.

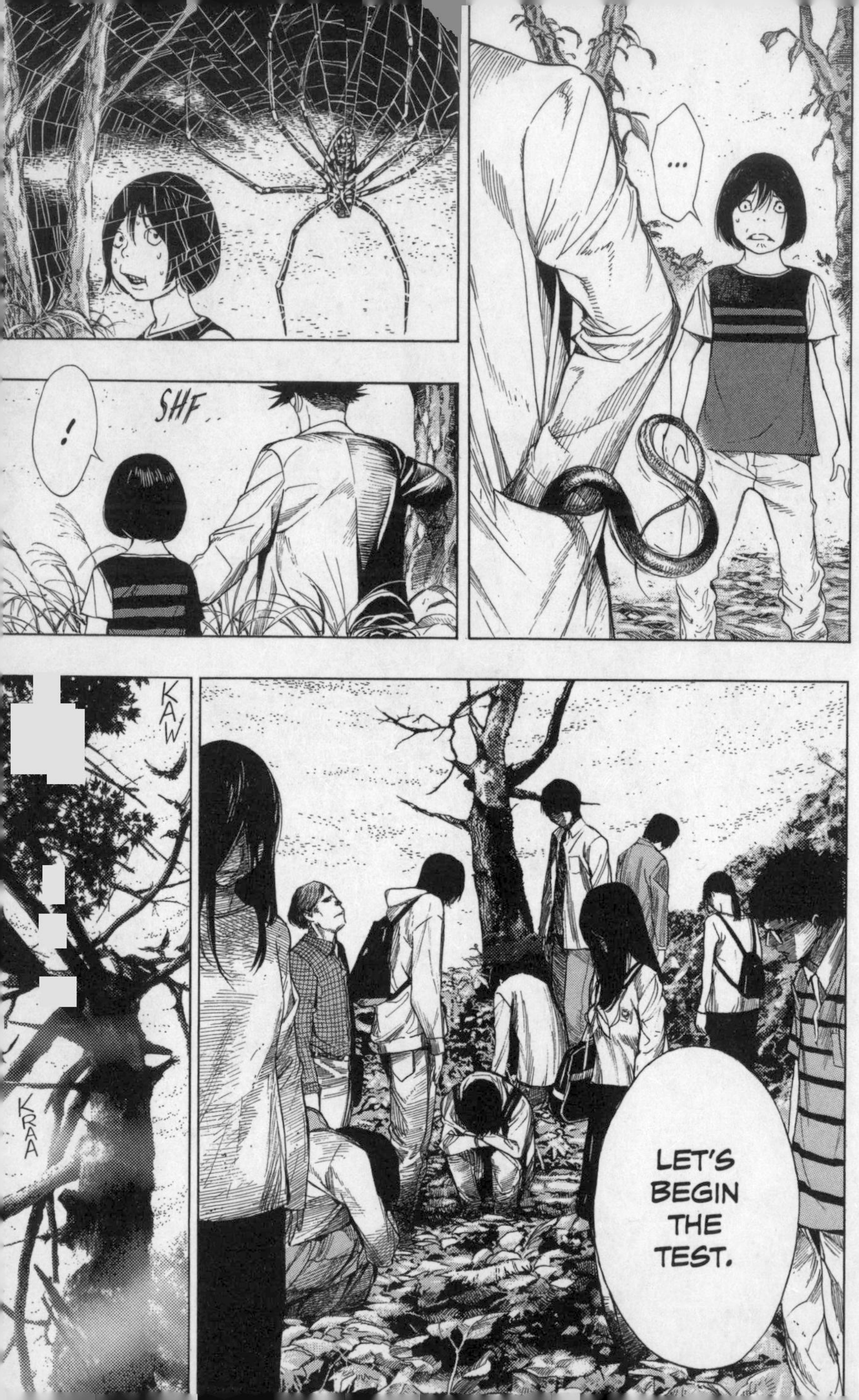
...
SHF..
!
LET'S BEGIN THE TEST.
KAW
KRAA

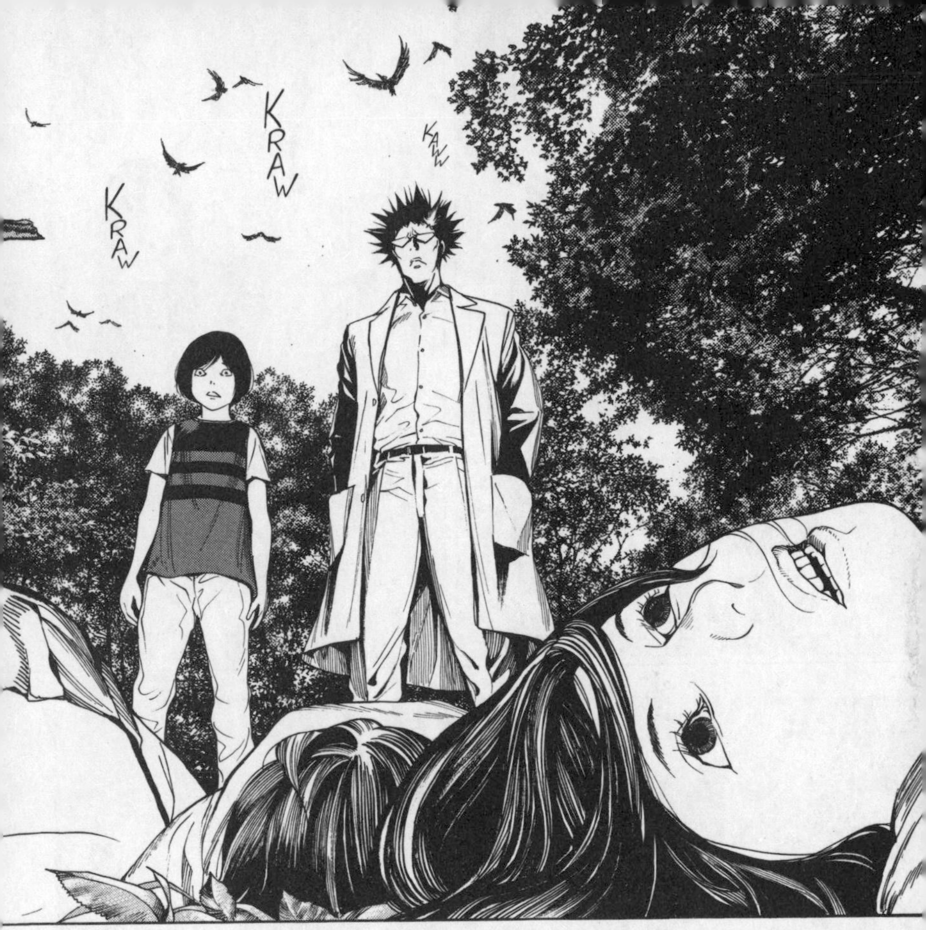
KAW
KRAW
KRAW
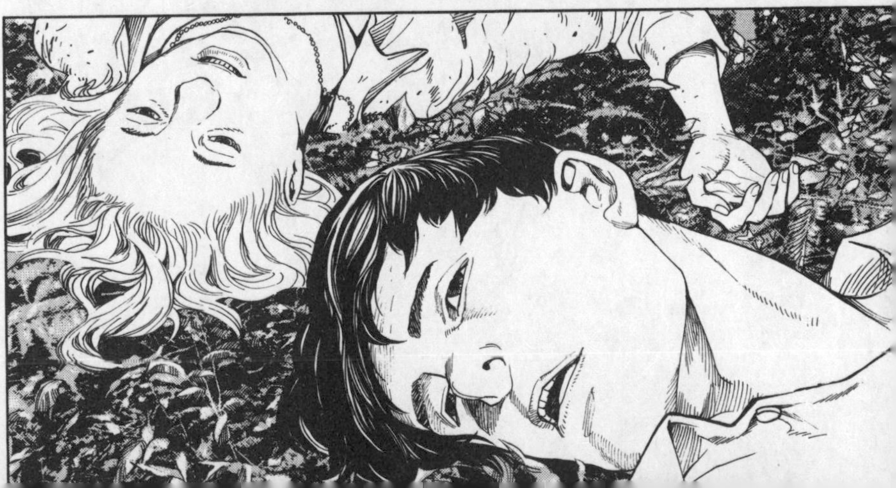

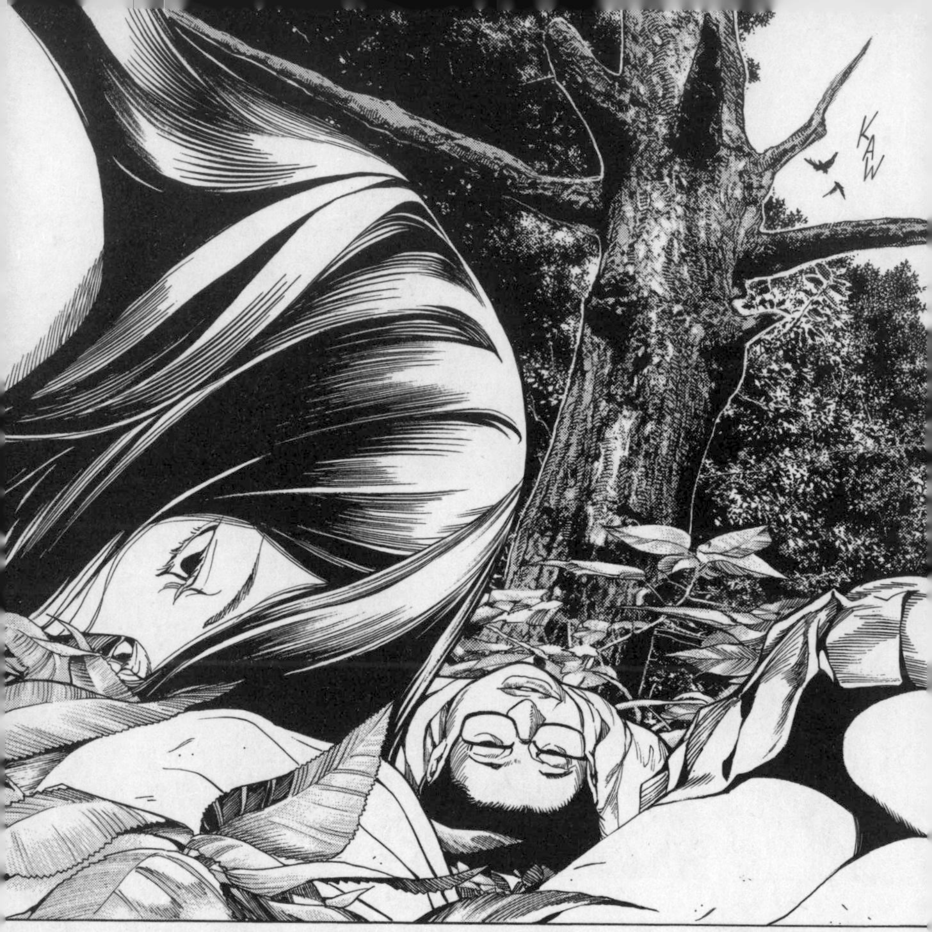
KAW
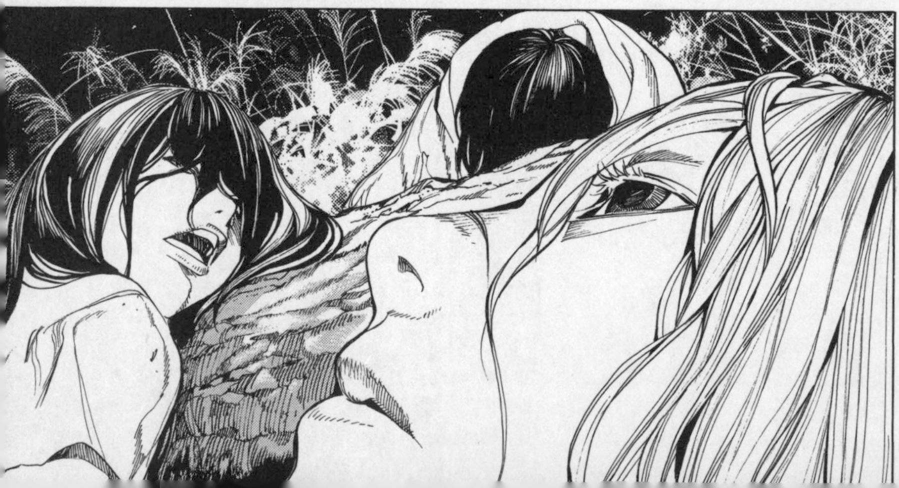

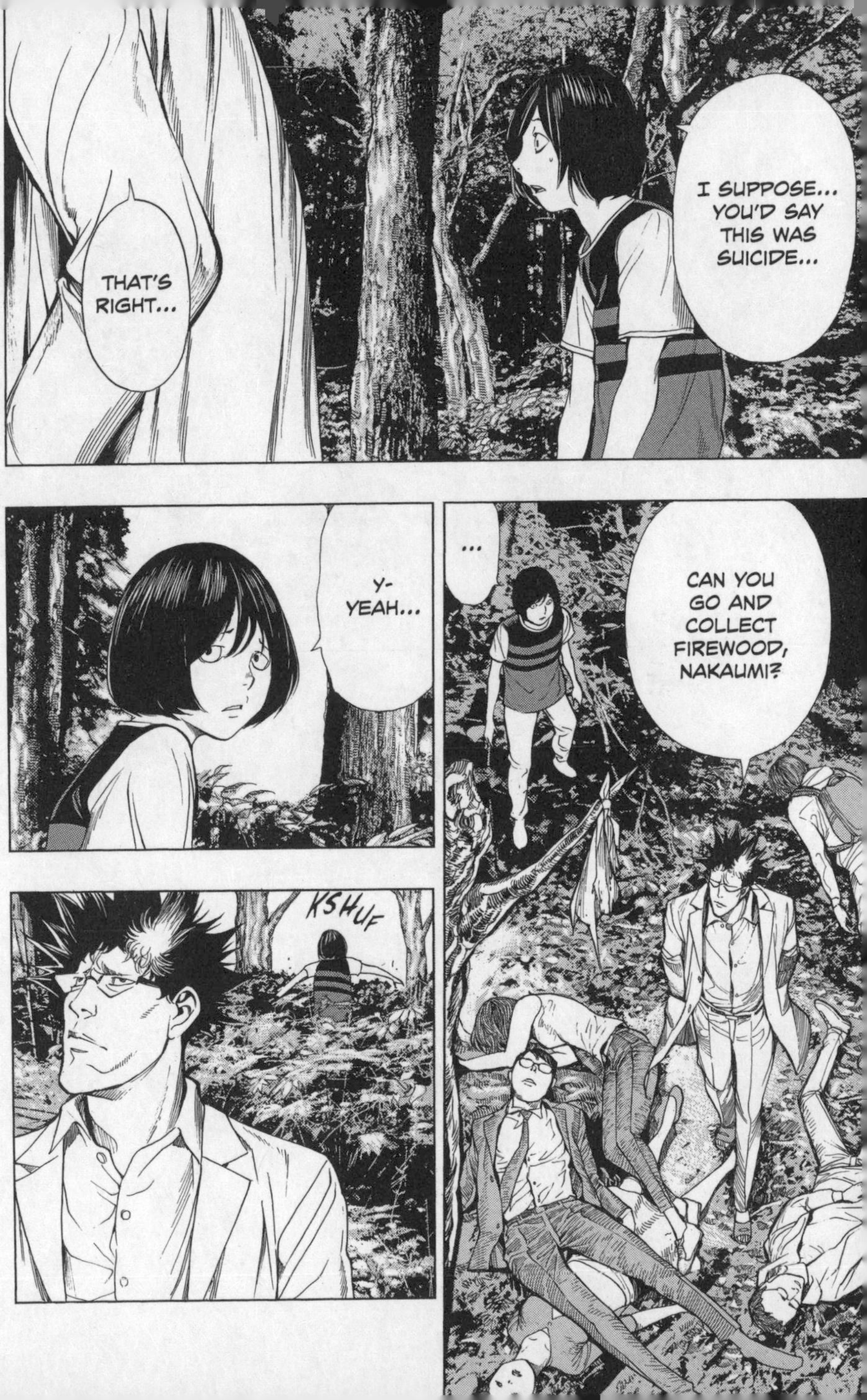
I SUPPOSE... YOU'D SAY THIS WAS SUICIDE...
THAT'S RIGHT...
CAN YOU GO AND COLLECT FIREWOOD, NAKAUMI?
...
Y- YEAH...
KSHUF

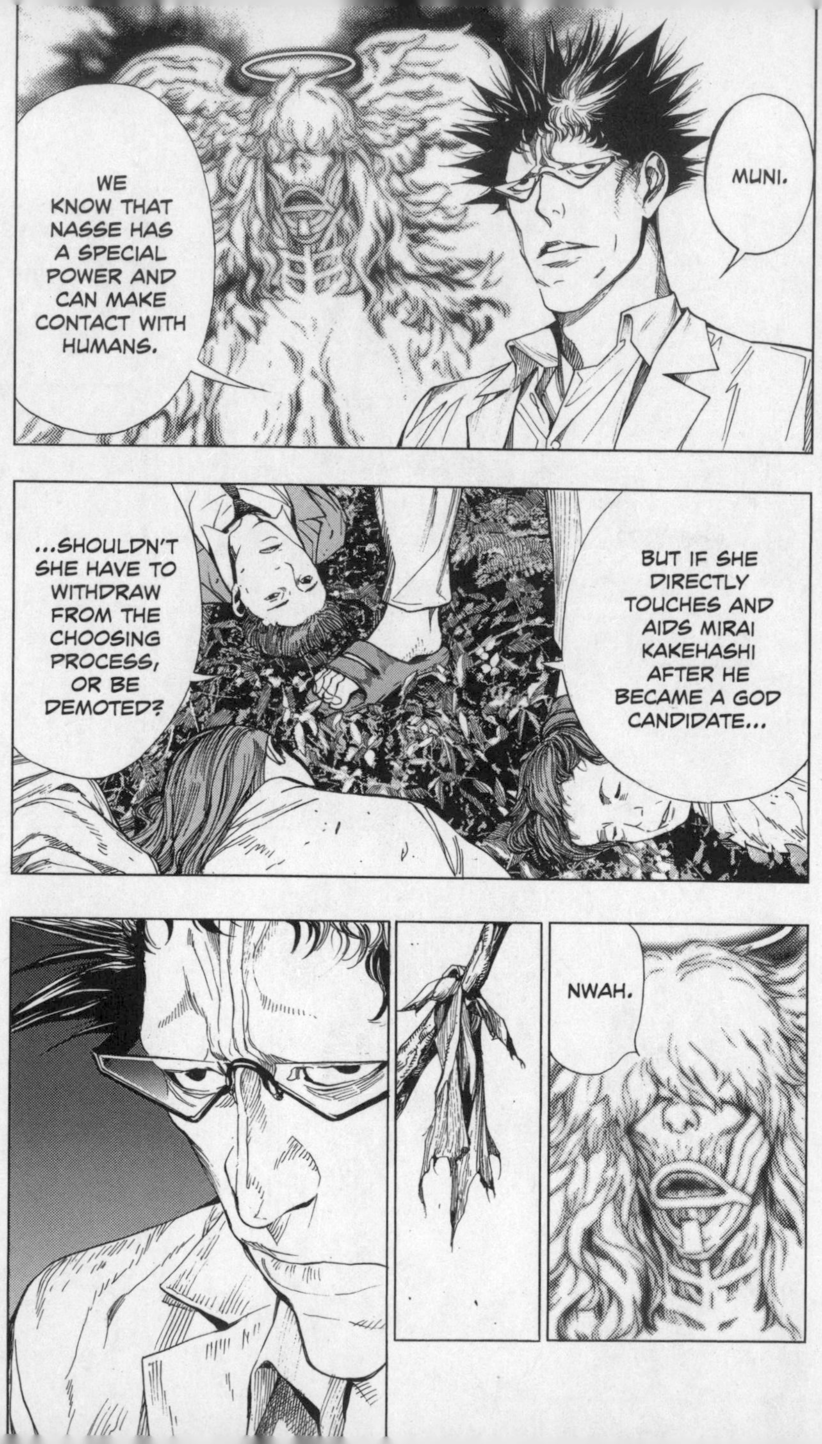
MUNI.
WE KNOW THAT NASSE HAS A SPECIAL POWER AND CAN MAKE CONTACT WITH HUMANS.
BUT IF SHE DIRECTLY TOUCHES AND AIDS MIRAI KAKEHASHI AFTER HE BECAME A GOD CANDIDATE...
...SHOULDN'T SHE HAVE TO WITHDRAW FROM THE CHOOSING PROCESS, OR BE DEMOTED?
NWAH.

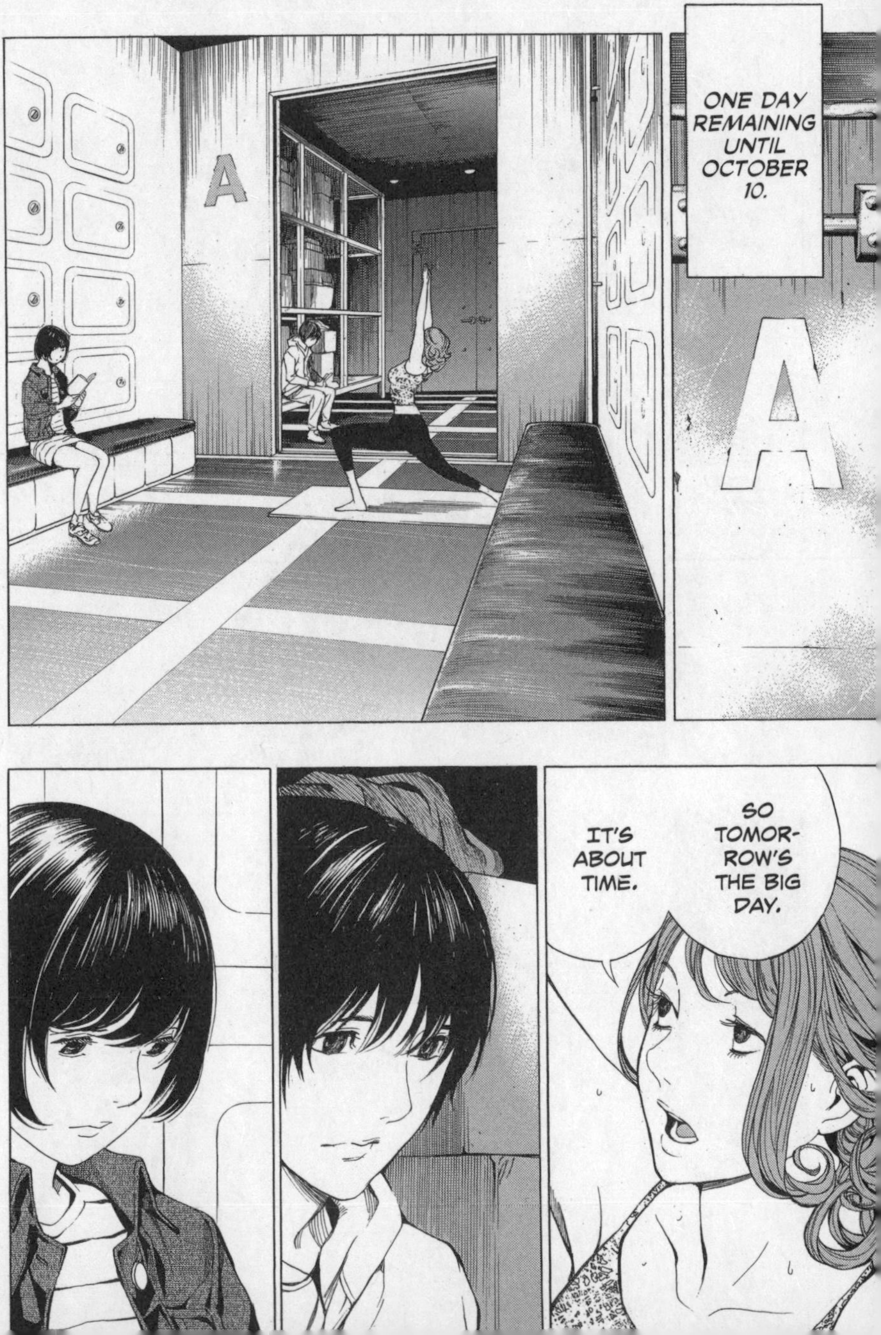
ONE DAY REMAINING UNTIL OCTOBER 10.
SO TOMORROW'S THE BIG DAY.
IT'S ABOUT TIME.

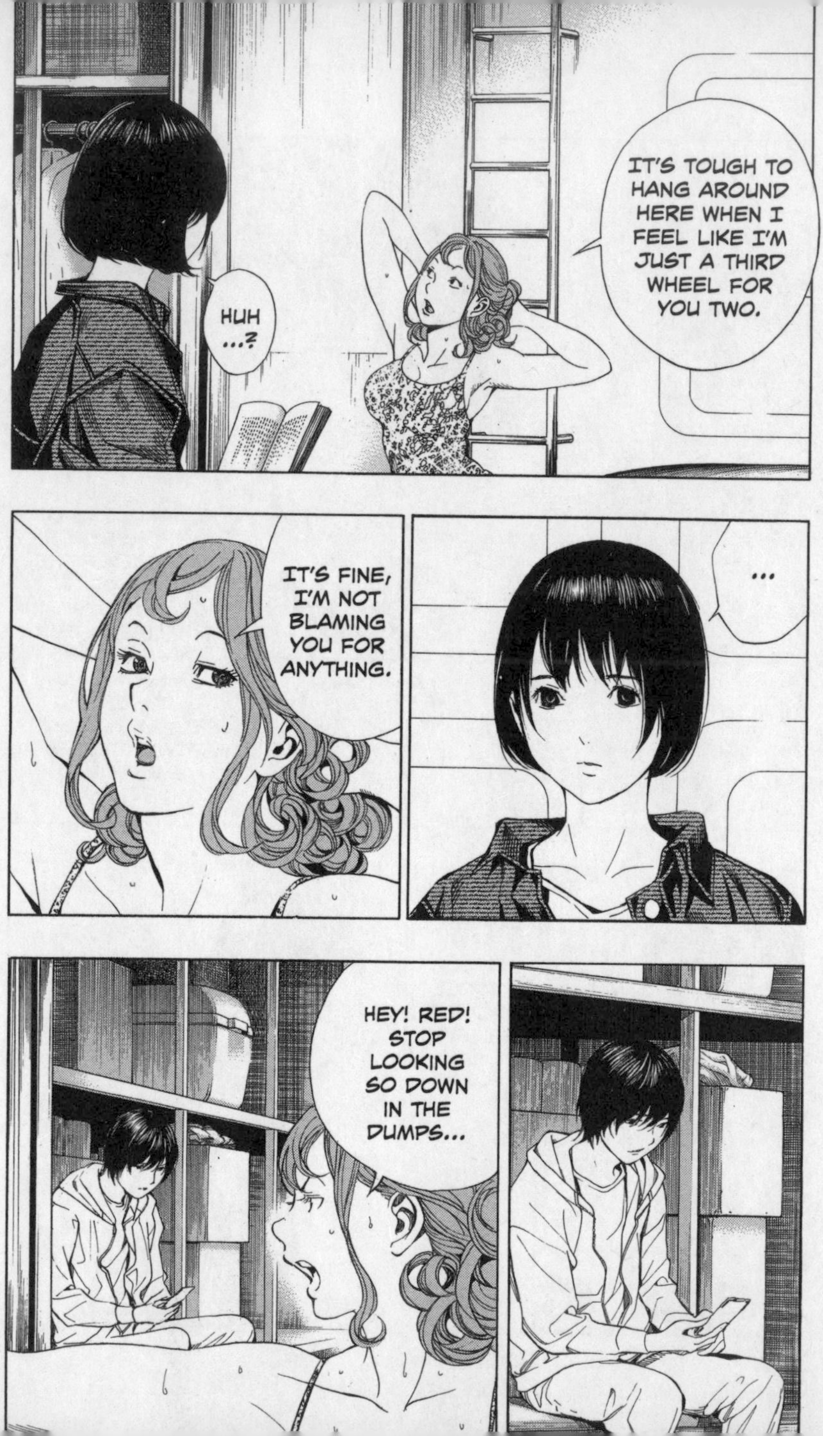
IT'S TOUGH TO HANG AROUND HERE WHEN I FEEL LIKE I'M JUST A THIRD WHEEL FOR YOU TWO.
HUH ...?
...
IT'S FINE, I'M NOT BLAMING YOU FOR ANYTHING.
HEY! RED! STOP LOOKING SO DOWN IN THE DUMPS...

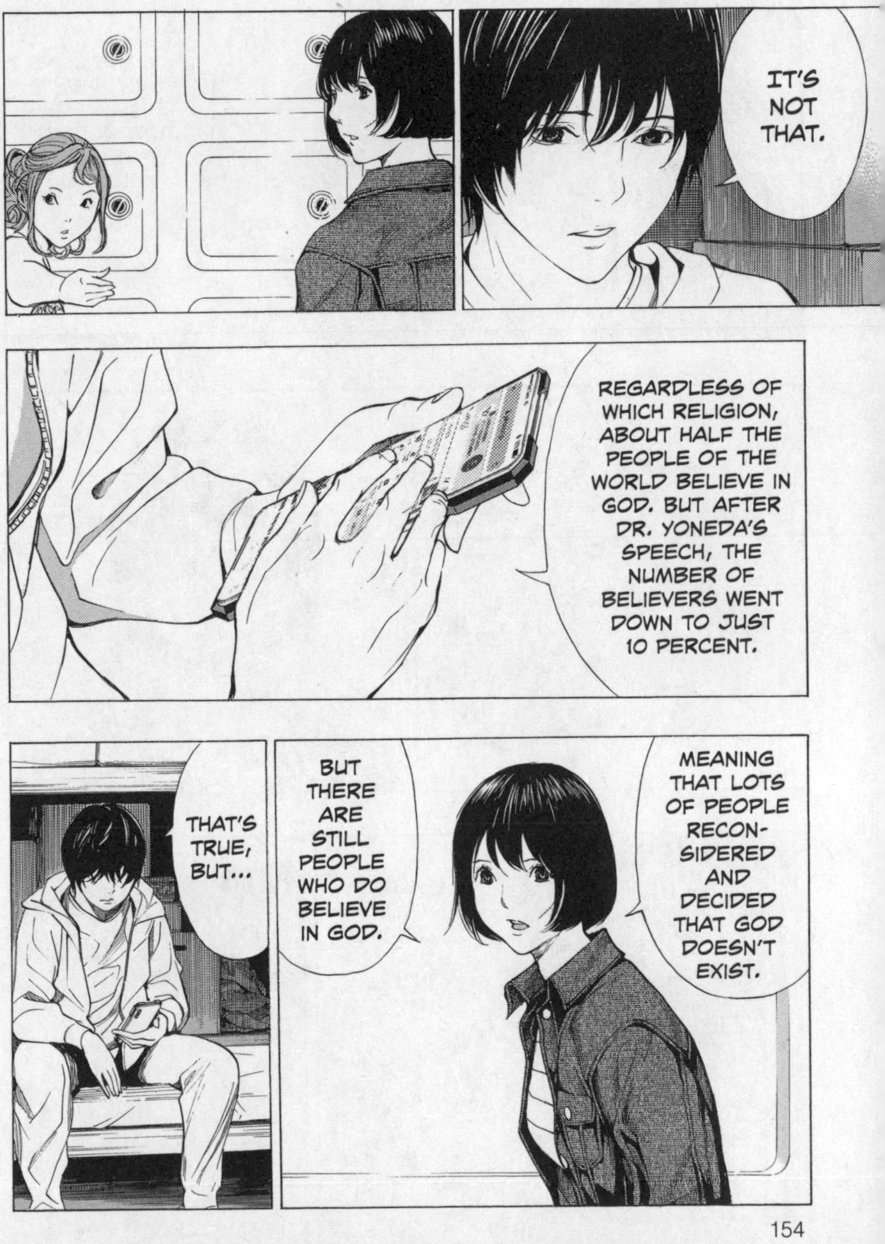
IT'S NOT THAT.
REGARDLESS OF WHICH RELIGION, ABOUT HALF THE PEOPLE OF THE WORLD BELIEVE IN GOD. BUT AFTER DR. YONEDA'S SPEECH, THE NUMBER OF BELIEVERS WENT DOWN TO JUST 10 PERCENT.
MEANING THAT LOTS OF PEOPLE RECON-SIDERED AND DECIDED THAT GOD DOESN'T EXIST.
BUT THERE ARE STILL PEOPLE WHO DO BELIEVE IN GOD.
THAT'S TRUE, BUT...

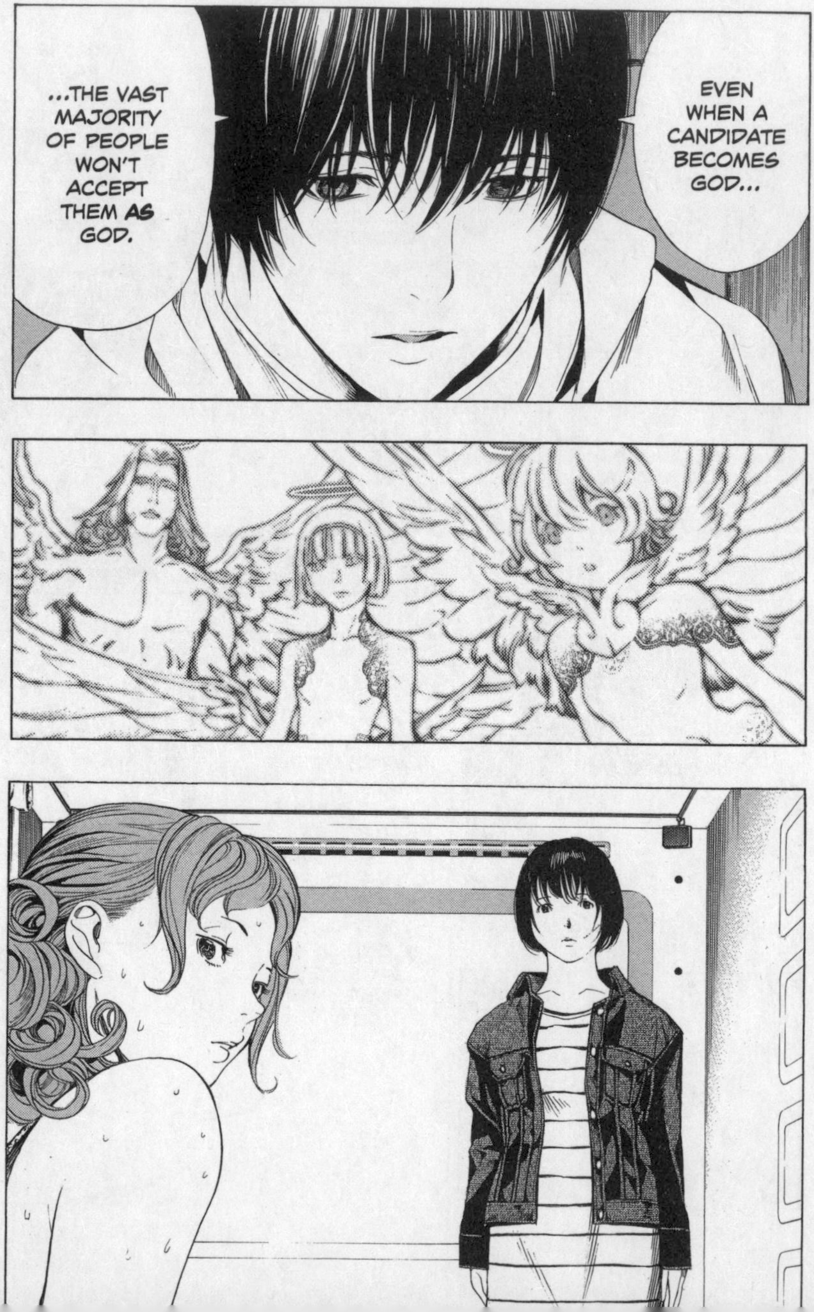
EVEN WHEN A CANDIDATE BECOMES GOD...
...THE VAST MAJORITY OF PEOPLE WON'T ACCEPT THEM AS GOD.

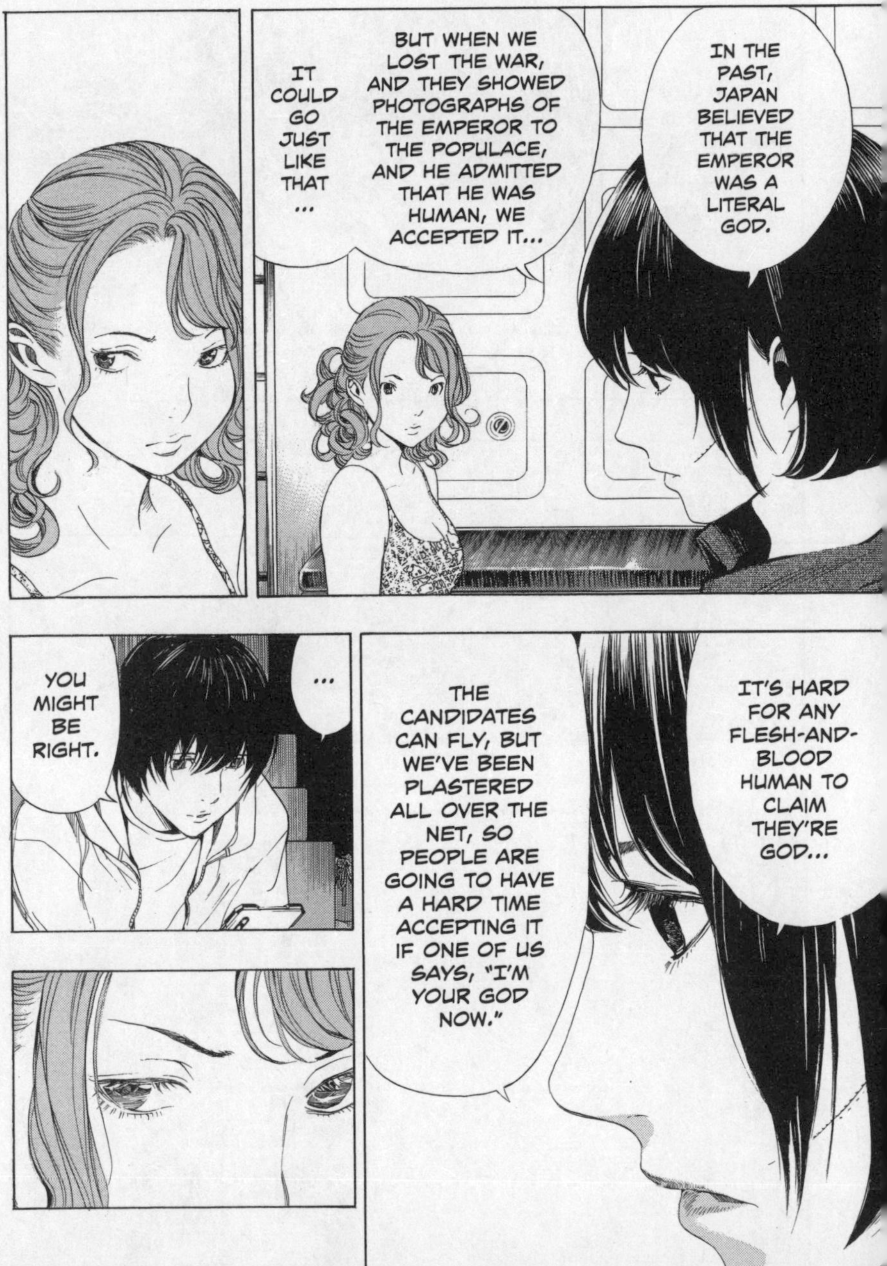
IN THE PAST, JAPAN BELIEVED THAT THE EMPEROR WAS A LITERAL GOD.
BUT WHEN WE LOST THE WAR, AND THEY SHOWED PHOTOGRAPHS OF THE EMPEROR TO THE POPULACE, AND HE ADMITTED THAT HE WAS HUMAN, WE ACCEPTED IT...
IT COULD GO JUST LIKE THAT ...
IT'S HARD FOR ANY FLESH-AND-BLOOD HUMAN TO CLAIM THEY'RE GOD...
THE CANDIDATES CAN FLY, BUT WE'VE BEEN PLASTERED ALL OVER THE NET, SO PEOPLE ARE GOING TO HAVE A HARD TIME ACCEPTING IT IF ONE OF US SAYS, "I'M YOUR GOD NOW."
...
YOU MIGHT BE RIGHT.

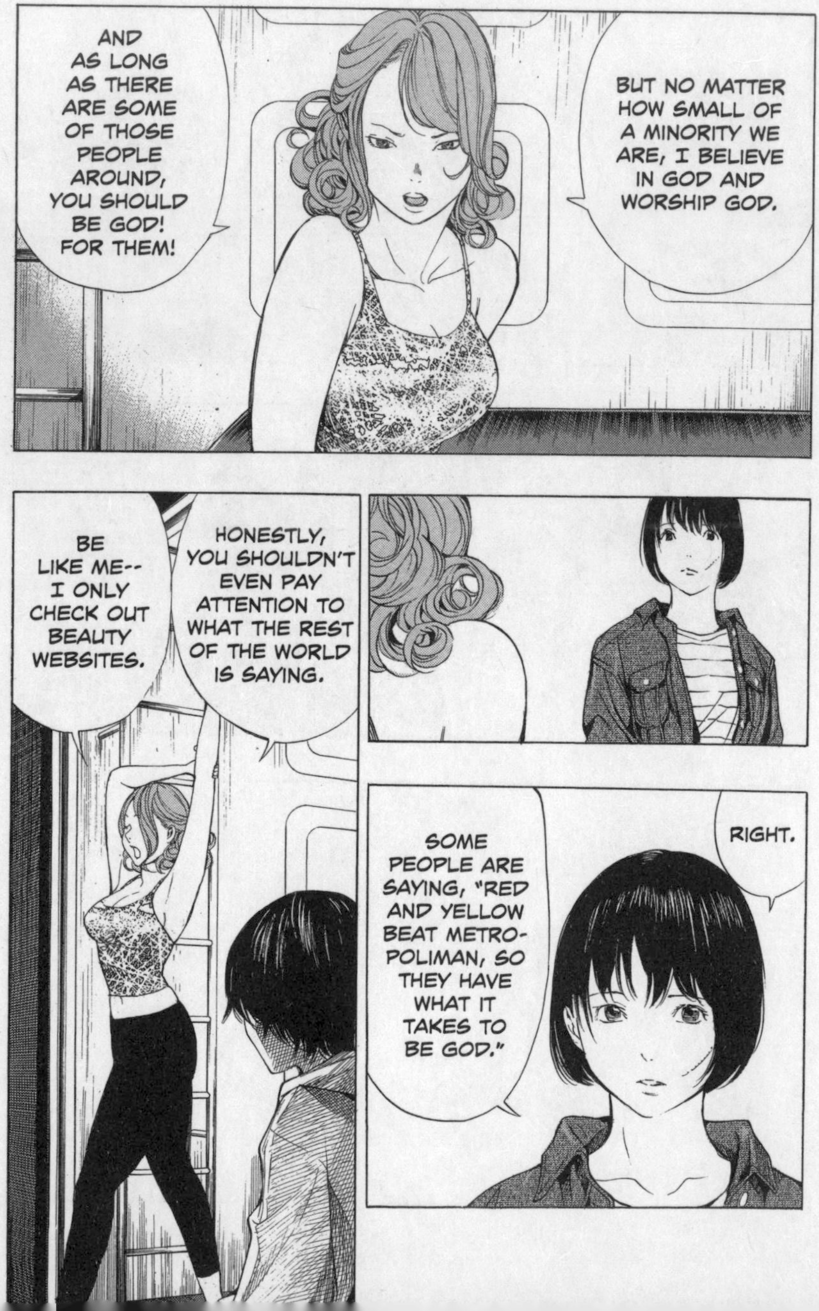
BUT NO MATTER HOW SMALL OF A MINORITY WE ARE, I BELIEVE IN GOD AND WORSHIP GOD.
AND AS LONG AS THERE ARE SOME OF THOSE PEOPLE AROUND, YOU SHOULD BE GOD! FOR THEM!
RIGHT.
SOME PEOPLE ARE SAYING, "RED AND YELLOW BEAT METRO-POLIMAN, SO THEY HAVE WHAT IT TAKES TO BE GOD."
HONESTLY, YOU SHOULDN'T EVEN PAY ATTENTION TO WHAT THE REST OF THE WORLD IS SAYING.
BE LIKE ME-- I ONLY CHECK OUT BEAUTY WEBSITES.

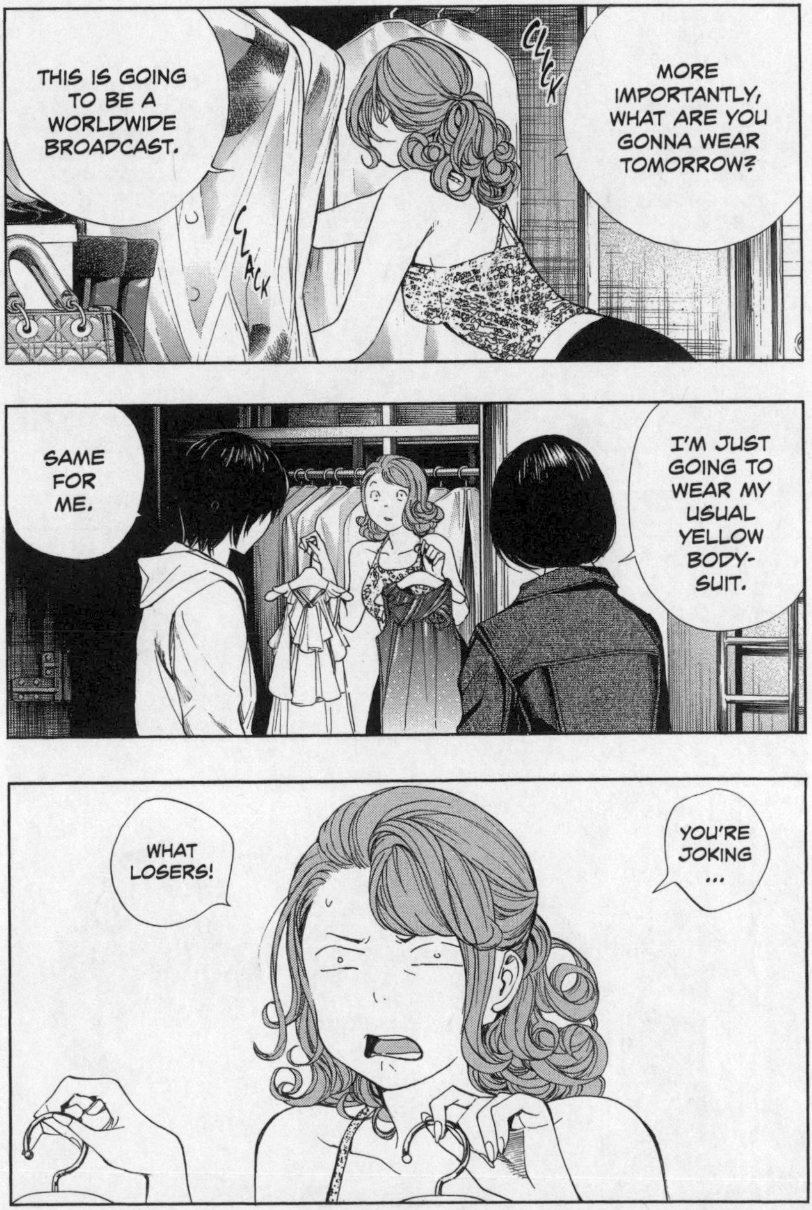
MORE IMPORTANTLY, WHAT ARE YOU GONNA WEAR TOMORROW?
CLICK
THIS IS GOING TO BE A WORLDWIDE BROADCAST.
CLACK
I'M JUST GOING TO WEAR MY USUAL YELLOW BODY-SUIT.
SAME FOR ME.
YOU'RE JOKING ...
WHAT LOSERS!

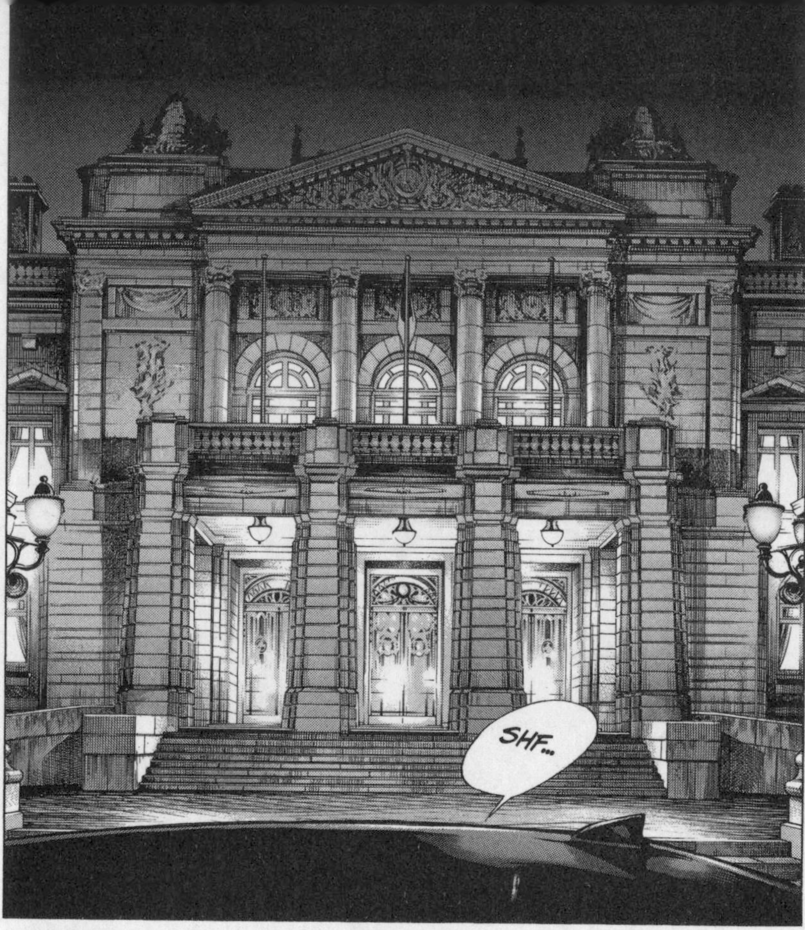
SHF...
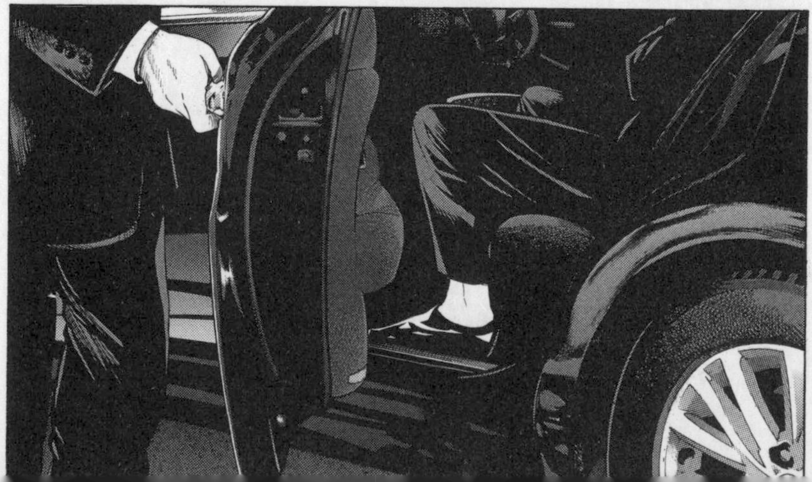

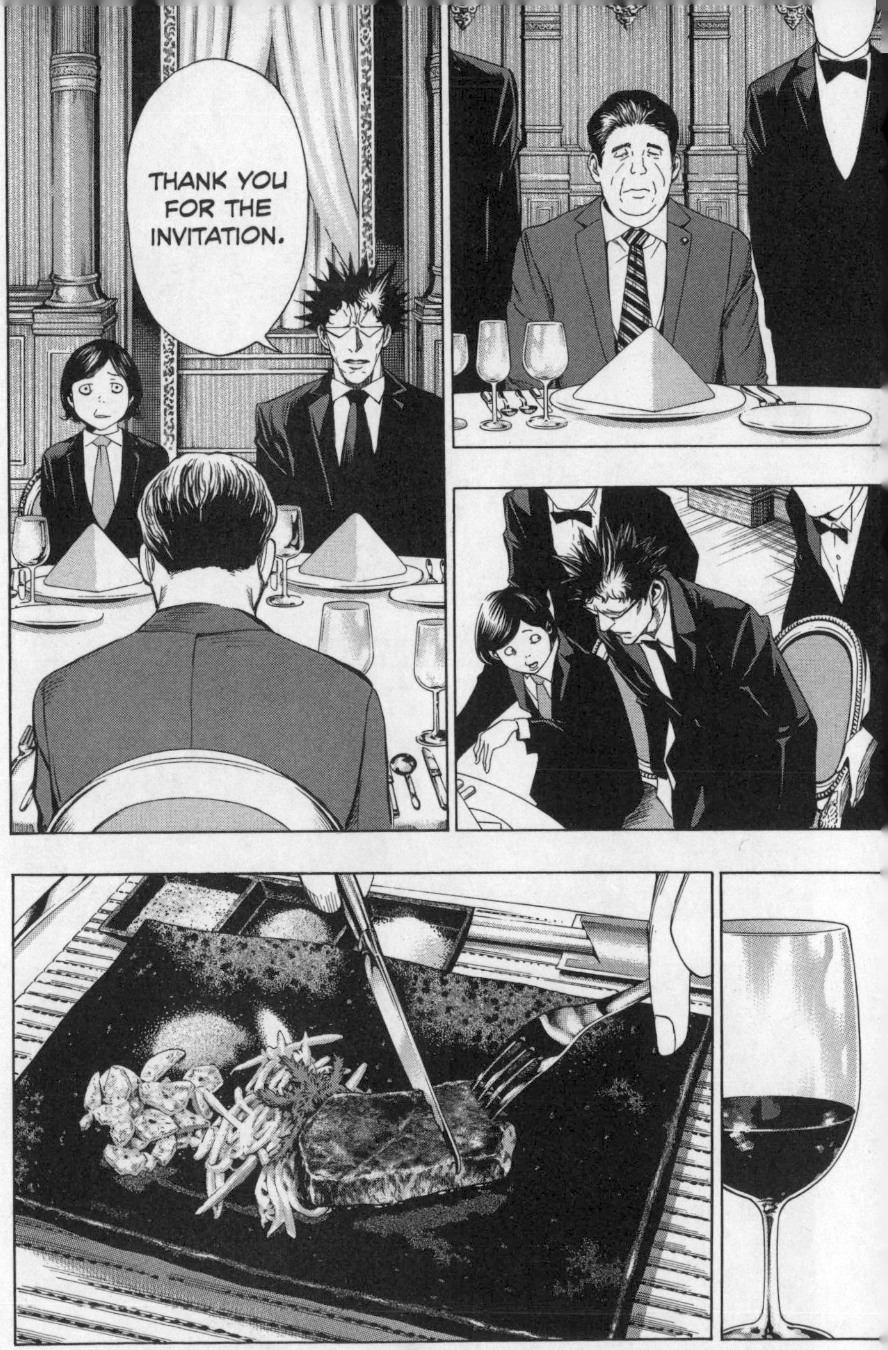
THANK YOU FOR THE INVITATION.

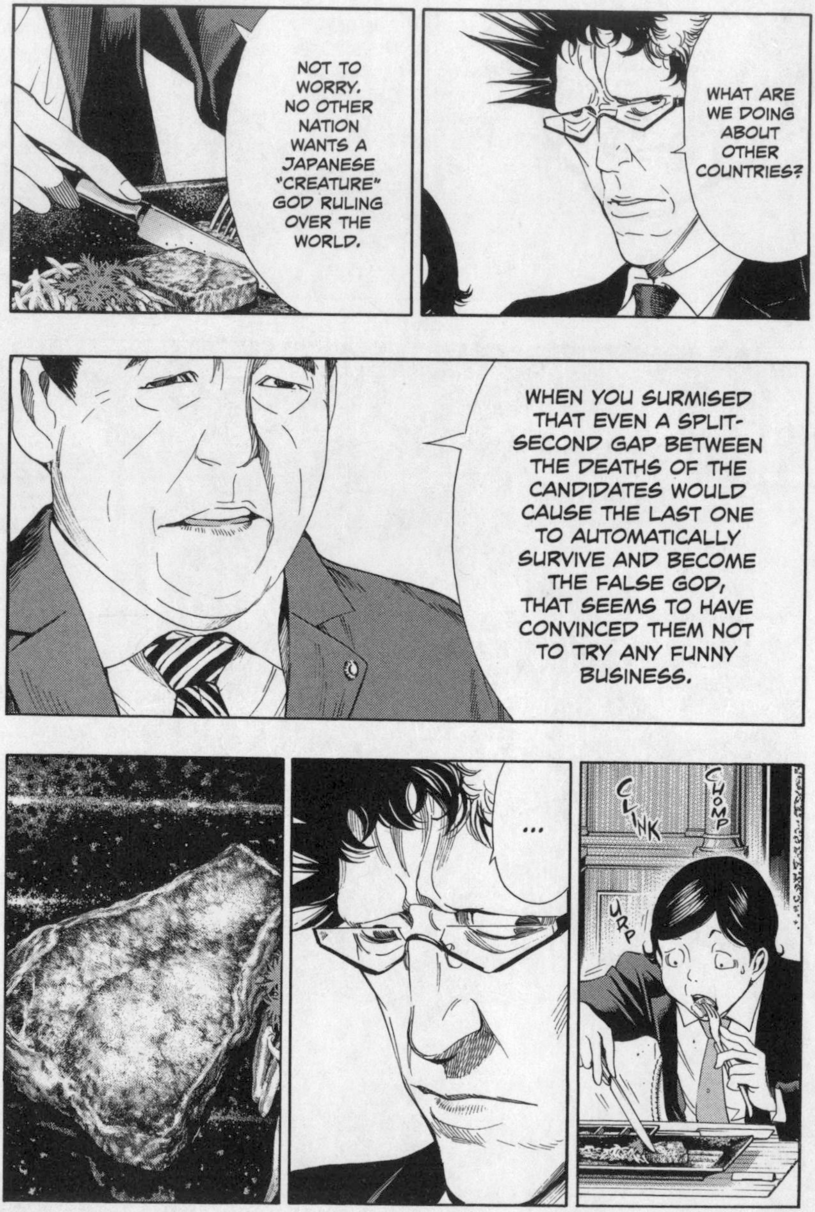
WHAT ARE WE DOING ABOUT OTHER COUNTRIES?
NOT TO WORRY. NO OTHER NATION WANTS A JAPANESE "CREATURE" GOD RULING OVER THE WORLD.
WHEN YOU SURMISED THAT EVEN A SPLIT-SECOND GAP BETWEEN THE DEATHS OF THE CANDIDATES WOULD CAUSE THE LAST ONE TO AUTOMATICALLY SURVIVE AND BECOME THE FALSE GOD, THAT SEEMS TO HAVE CONVINCED THEM NOT TO TRY ANY FUNNY BUSINESS.
CHOMP
CLINK
URP
...

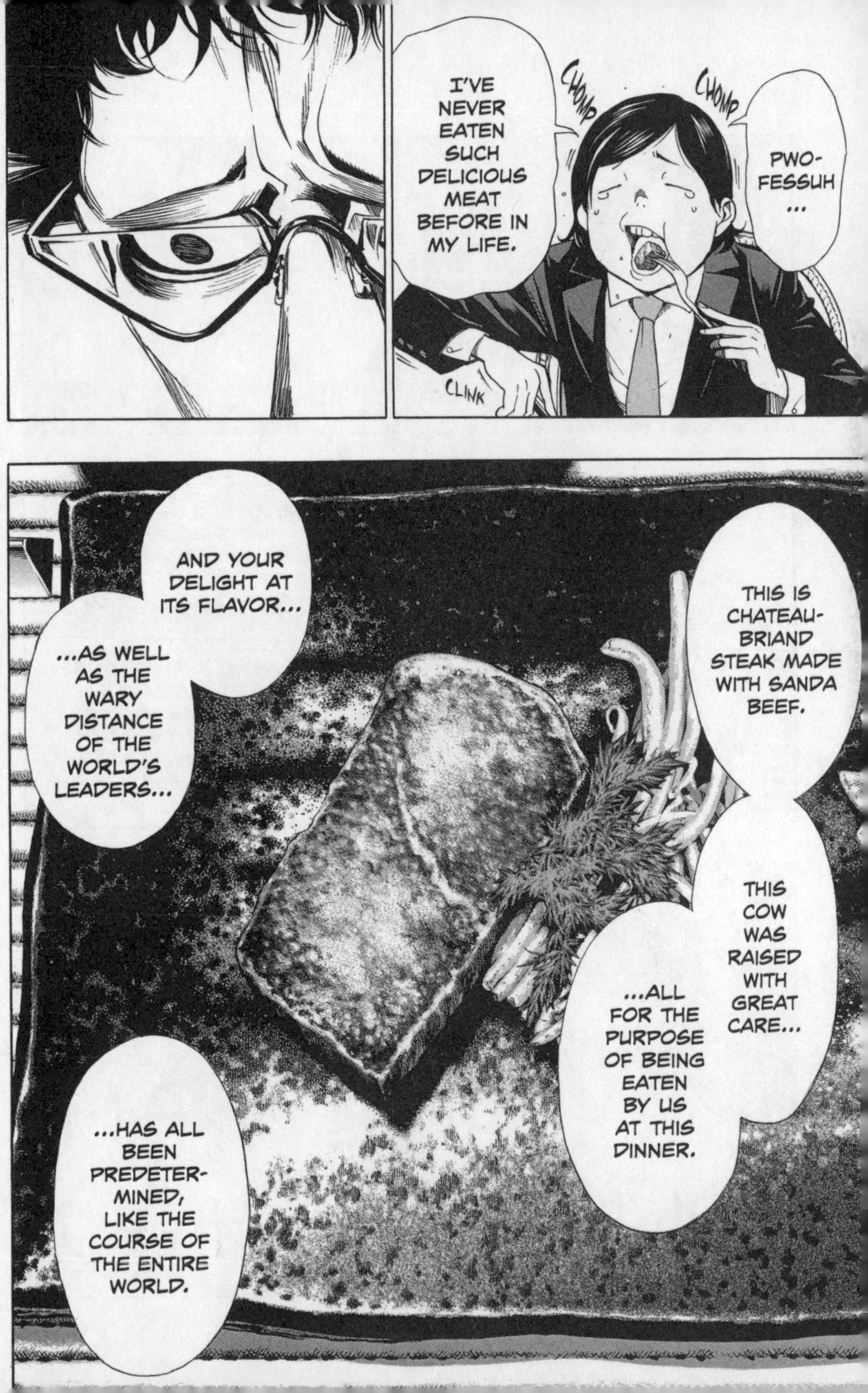
CHOMP
PWO-FESSUH...
CHOMP
I'VE NEVER EATEN SUCH DELICIOUS MEAT BEFORE IN MY LIFE.
CLINK
THIS IS CHATEAU-BRIAND STEAK MADE WITH SANDA BEEF.
THIS COW WAS RAISED WITH GREAT CARE...
...ALL FOR THE PURPOSE OF BEING EATEN BY US AT THIS DINNER.
AND YOUR DELIGHT AT ITS FLAVOR...
...AS WELL AS THE WARY DISTANCE OF THE WORLD'S LEADERS...
...HAS ALL BEEN PREDETER-MINED, LIKE THE COURSE OF THE ENTIRE WORLD.

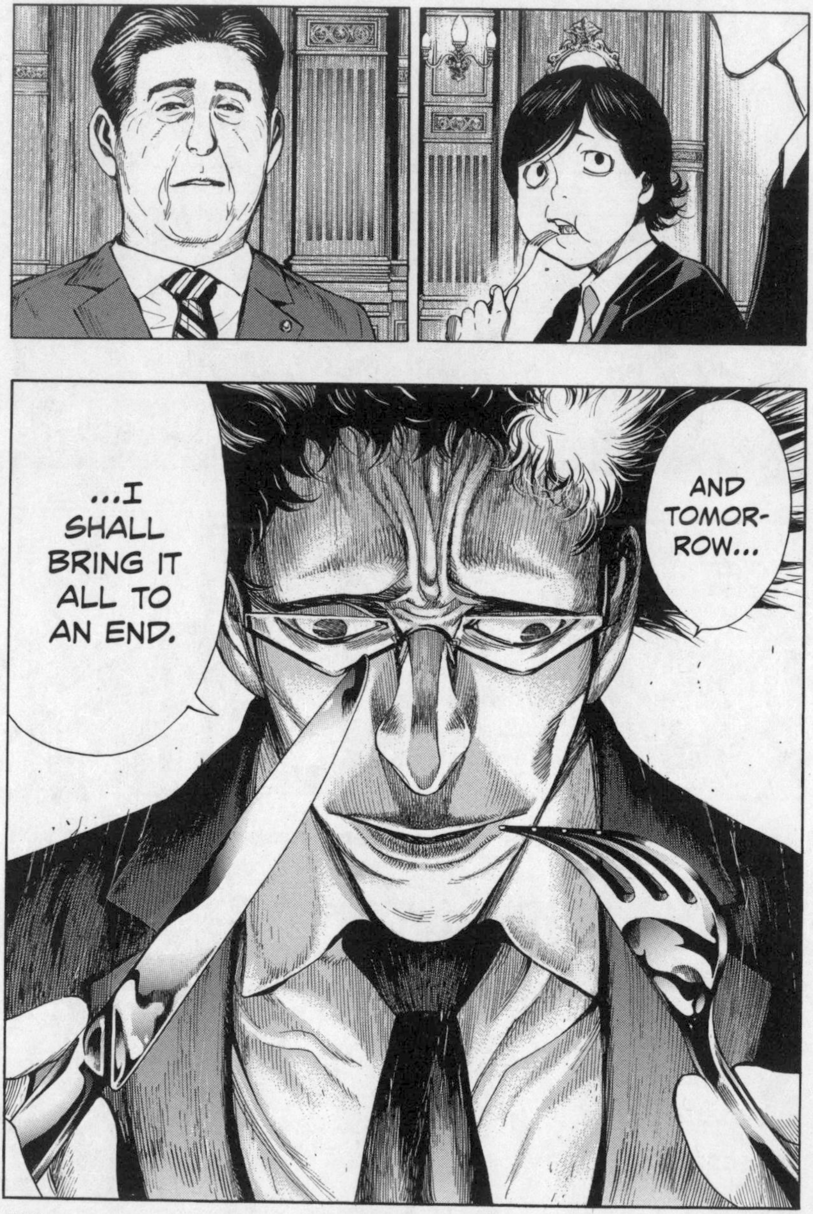
AND TOMORROW...
...I SHALL BRING IT ALL TO AN END.

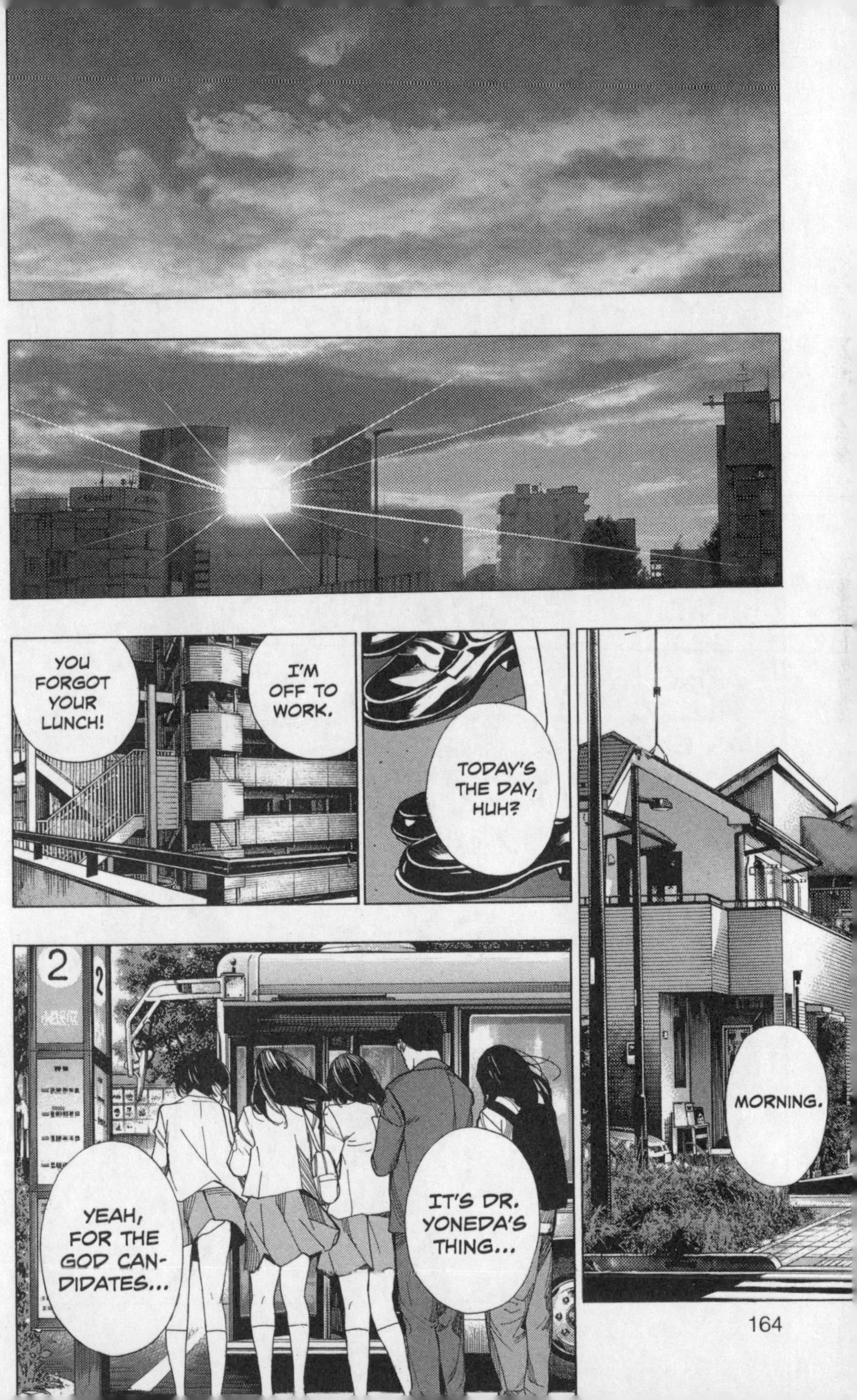
MORNING.
TODAY'S THE DAY, HUH?
I'M OFF TO WORK.
YOU FORGOT YOUR LUNCH!
IT'S DR. YONEDA'S THING...
YEAH, FOR THE GOD CAN-DIDATES...

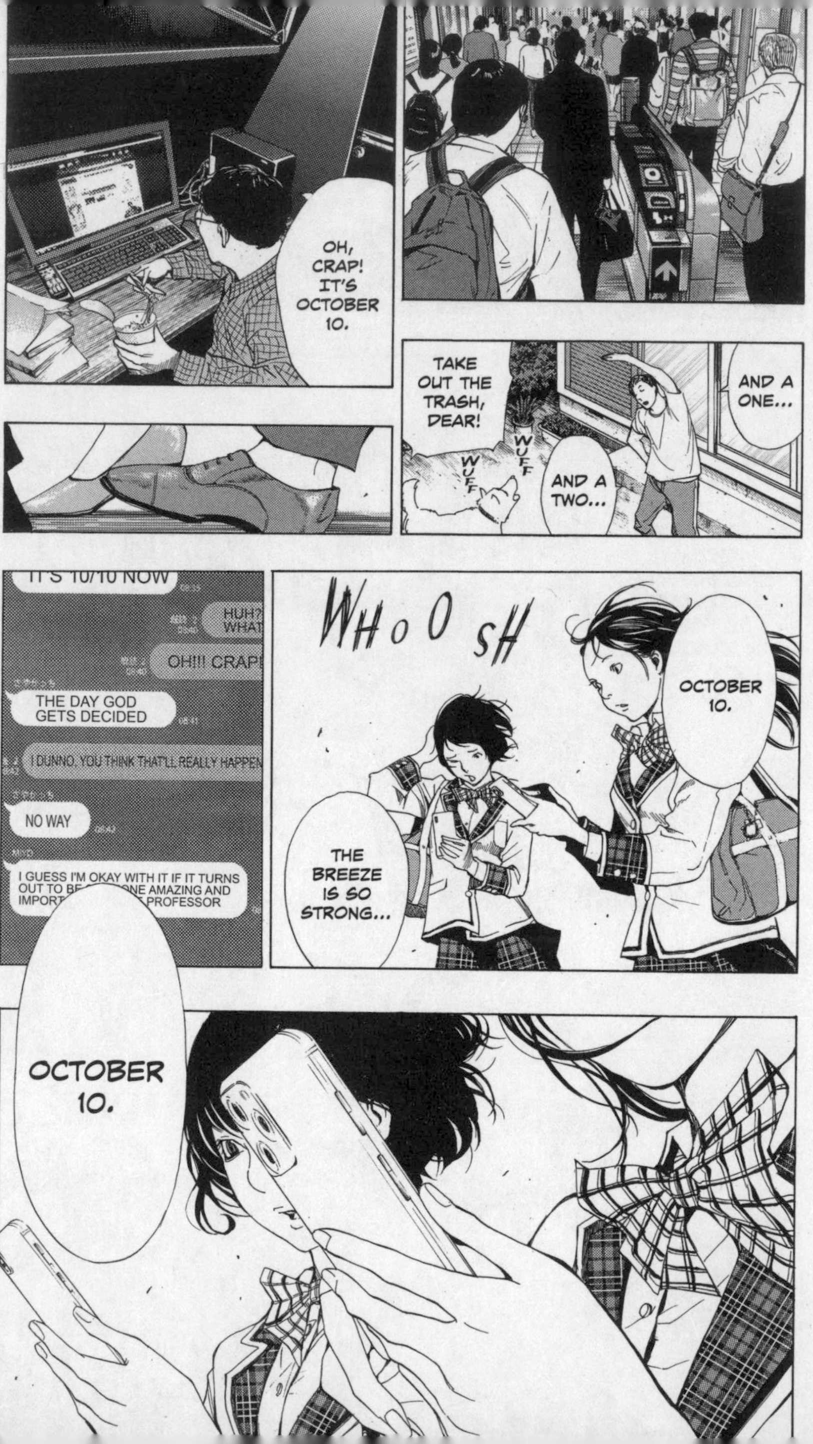
OH, CRAP! IT'S OCTOBER 10.
AND A ONE...
TAKE OUT THE TRASH, DEAR!
WUFF WUFF
AND A TWO...
OCTOBER 10.
WHOOSH
THE BREEZE IS SO STRONG...
IT'S 10/10 NOW
HUH?? WHAT
OH!!! CRAP!
THE DAY GOD GETS DECIDED
I DUNNO, YOU THINK THAT'LL REALLY HAPPEN
NO WAY
I GUESS I'M OKAY WITH IT IF IT TURNS OUT TO BE
ONE AMAZING AND
PROFESSOR
OCTOBER 10.

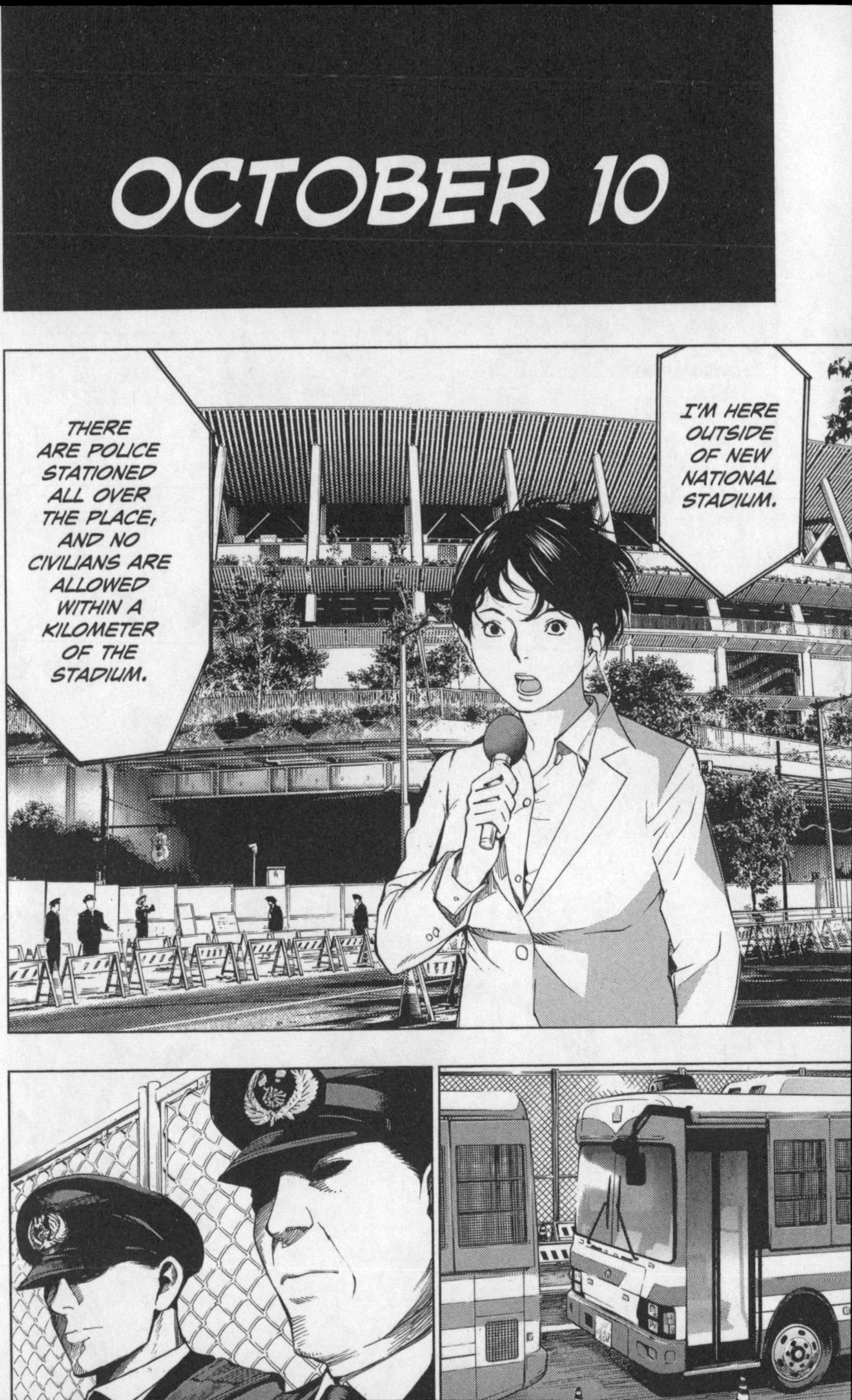
OCTOBER 10
I'M HERE OUTSIDE OF NEW NATIONAL STADIUM.
THERE ARE POLICE STATIONED ALL OVER THE PLACE, AND NO CIVILIANS ARE ALLOWED WITHIN A KILOMETER OF THE STADIUM.

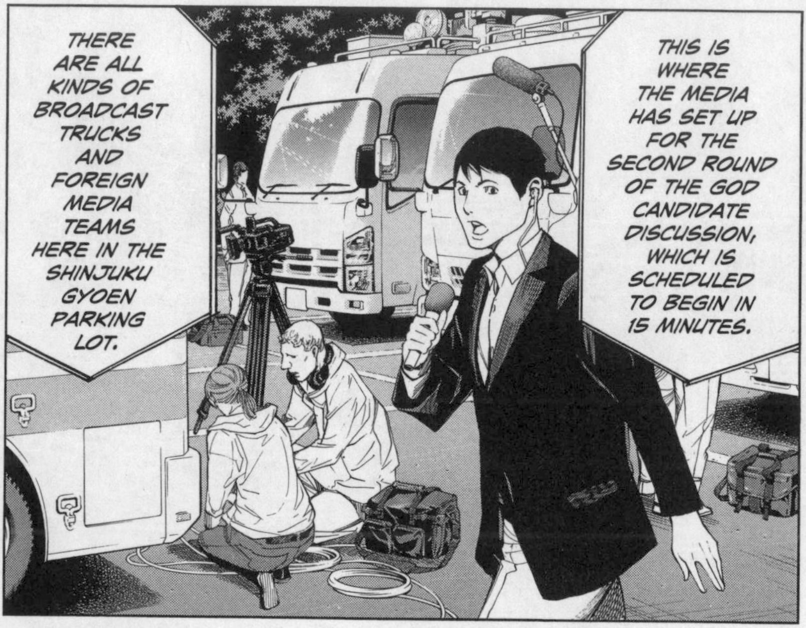
THIS IS WHERE THE MEDIA HAS SET UP FOR THE SECOND ROUND OF THE GOD CANDIDATE DISCUSSION, WHICH IS SCHEDULED TO BEGIN IN 15 MINUTES.
THERE ARE ALL KINDS OF BROADCAST TRUCKS AND FOREIGN MEDIA TEAMS HERE IN THE SHINJUKU GYOEN PARKING LOT.

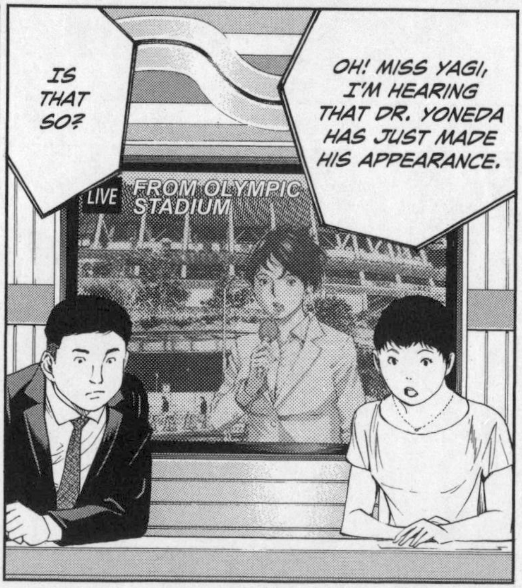
OH! MISS YAGI, I'M HEARING THAT DR. YONEDA HAS JUST MADE HIS APPEARANCE.
IS THAT SO?
LIVE
FROM OLYMPIC STADIUM

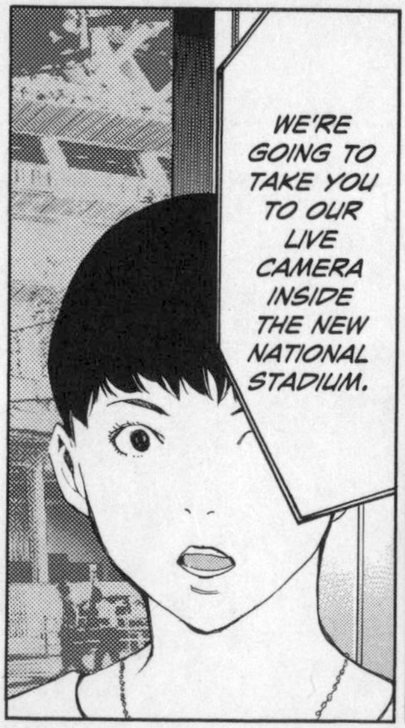
WE'RE GOING TO TAKE YOU TO OUR LIVE CAMERA INSIDE THE NEW NATIONAL STADIUM.

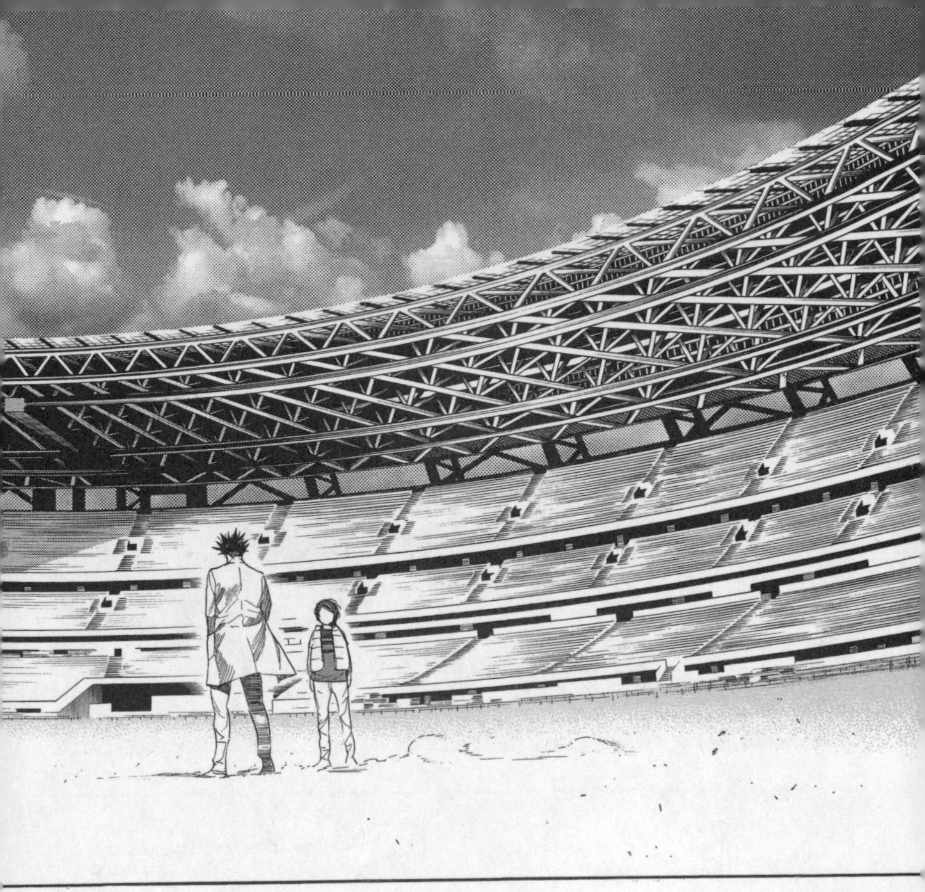
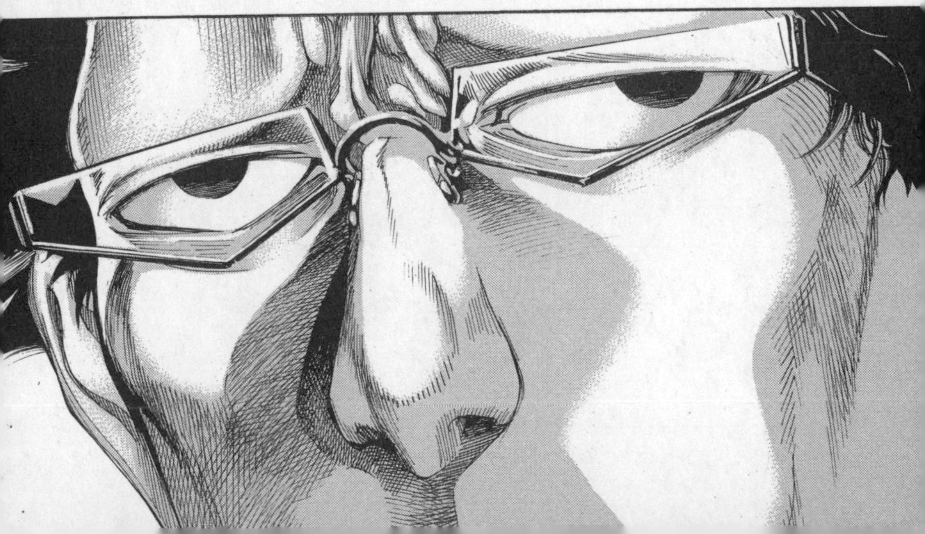

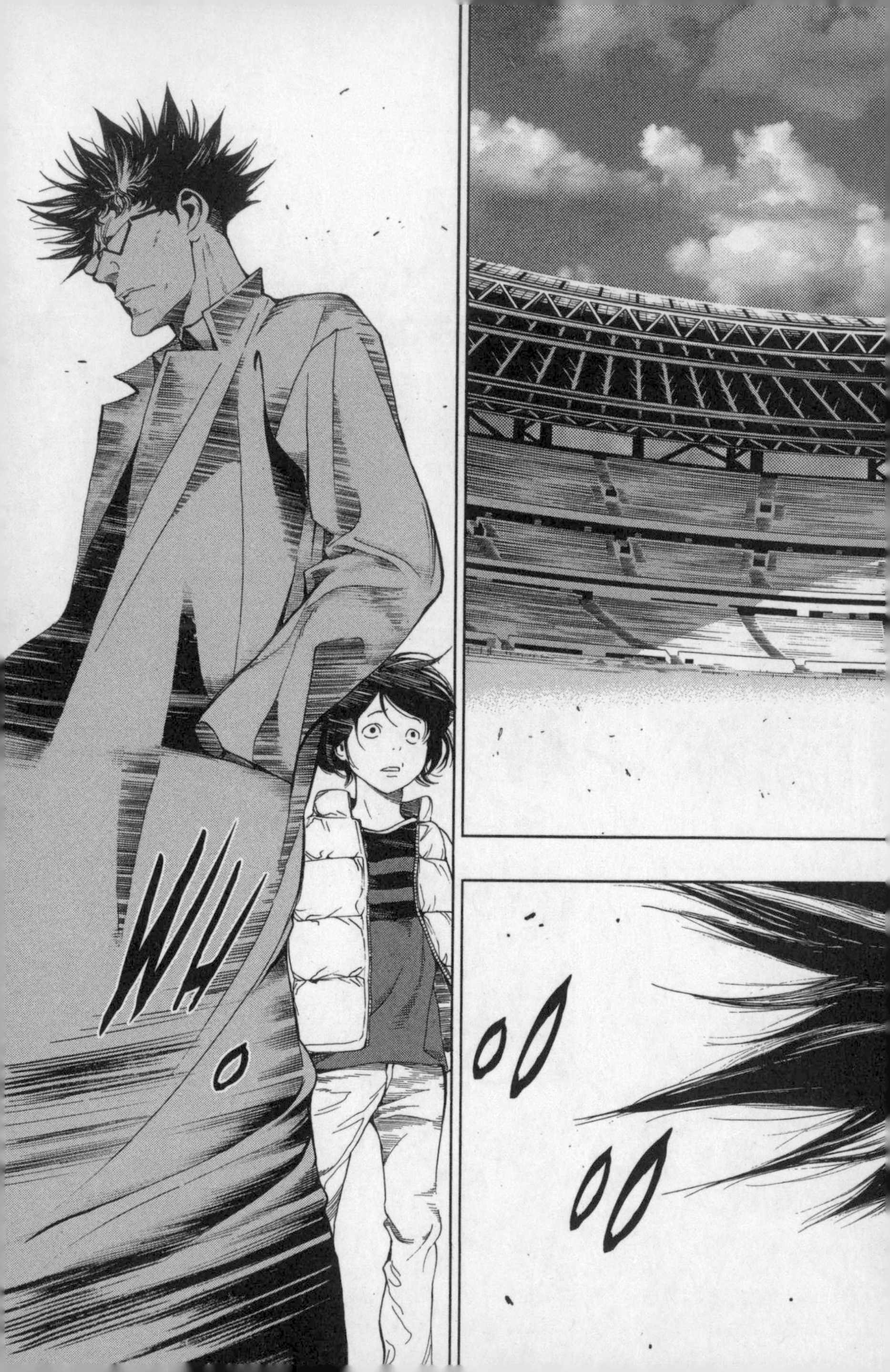
WHOOOOO

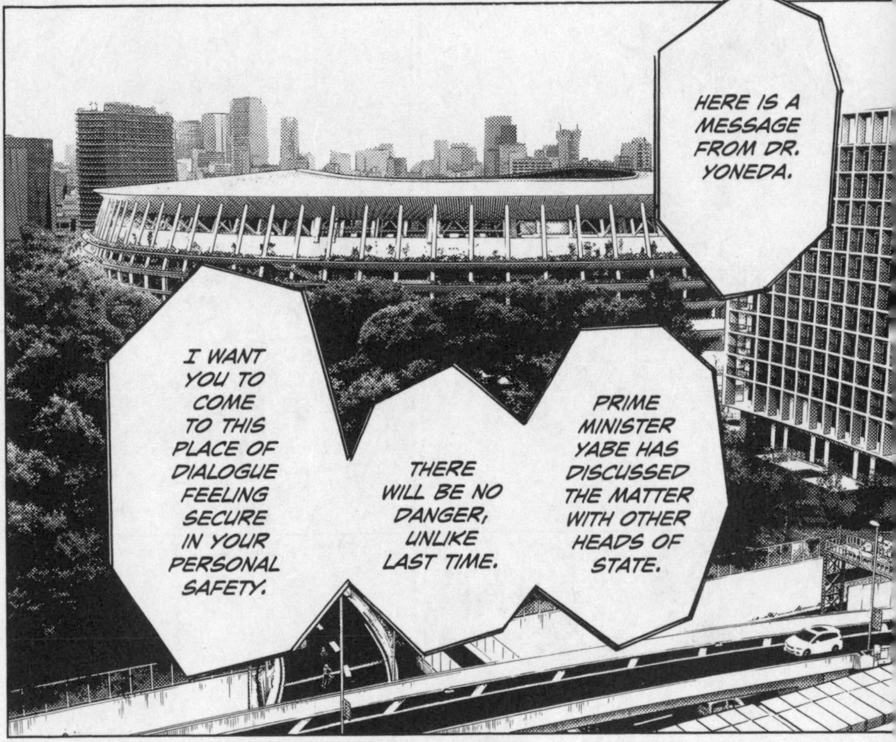
HERE IS A MESSAGE FROM DR. YONEDA.
PRIME MINISTER YABE HAS DISCUSSED THE MATTER WITH OTHER HEADS OF STATE.
THERE WILL BE NO DANGER, UNLIKE LAST TIME.
I WANT YOU TO COME TO THIS PLACE OF DIALOGUE FEELING SECURE IN YOUR PERSONAL SAFETY.

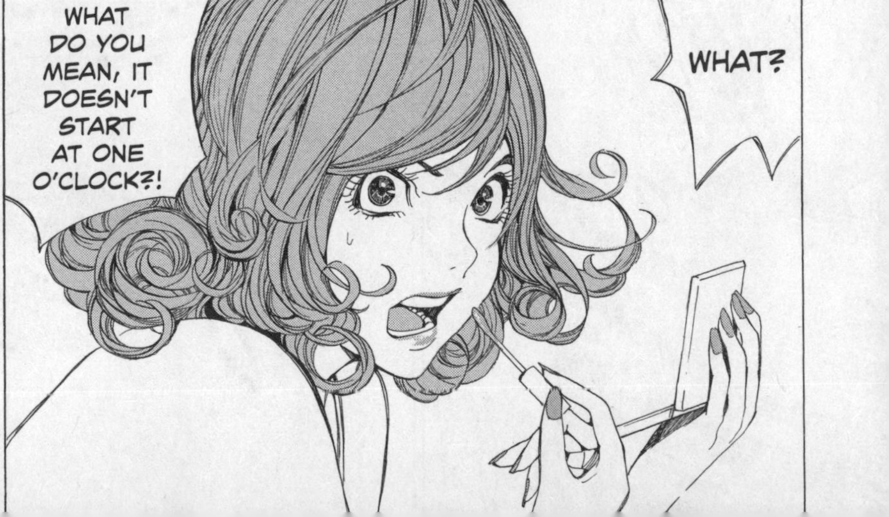
WHAT?
WHAT DO YOU MEAN, IT DOESN'T START AT ONE O'CLOCK?!

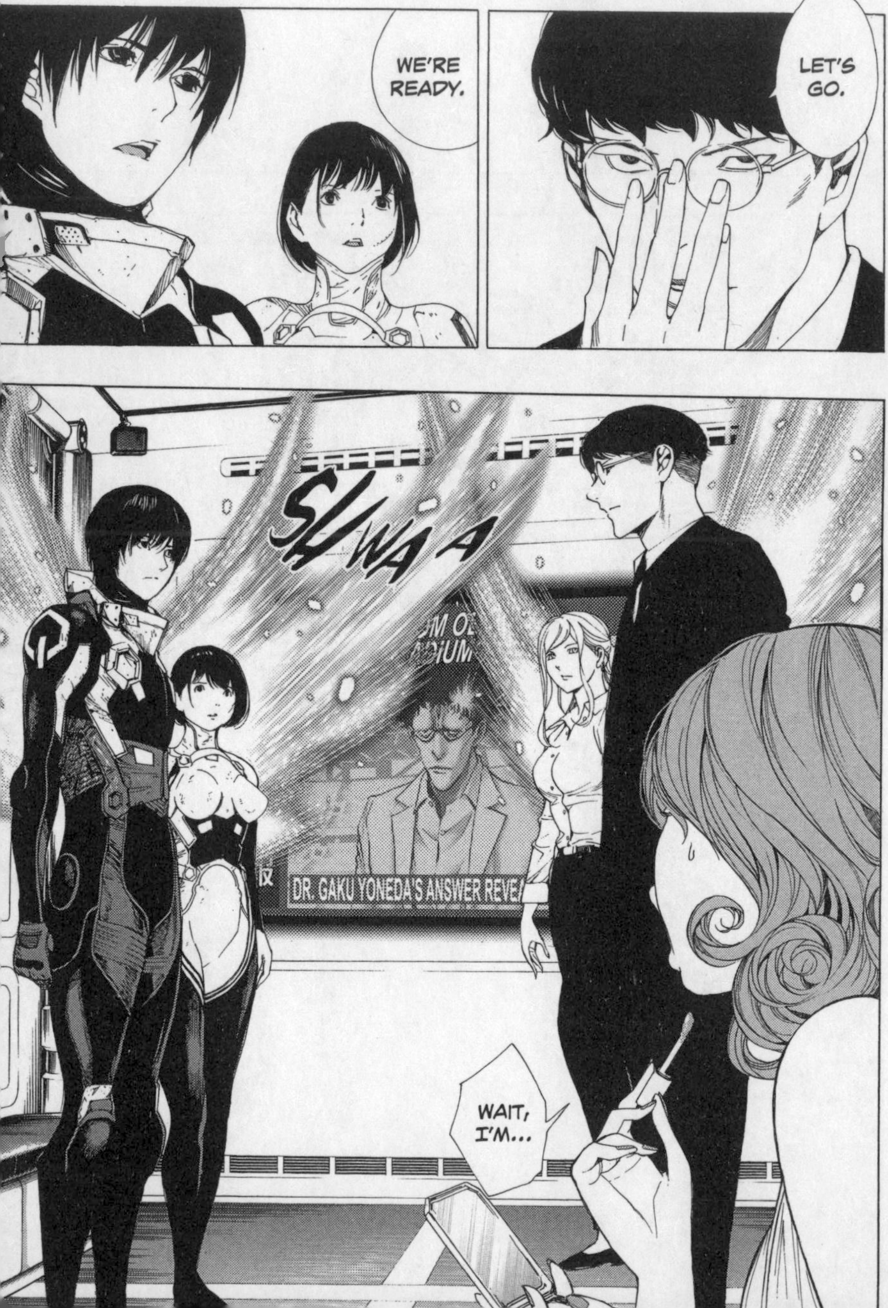
LET'S GO.
WE'RE READY.
SWAA
DR. GAKU YONEDA'S ANSWER REVEA
WAIT, I'M...

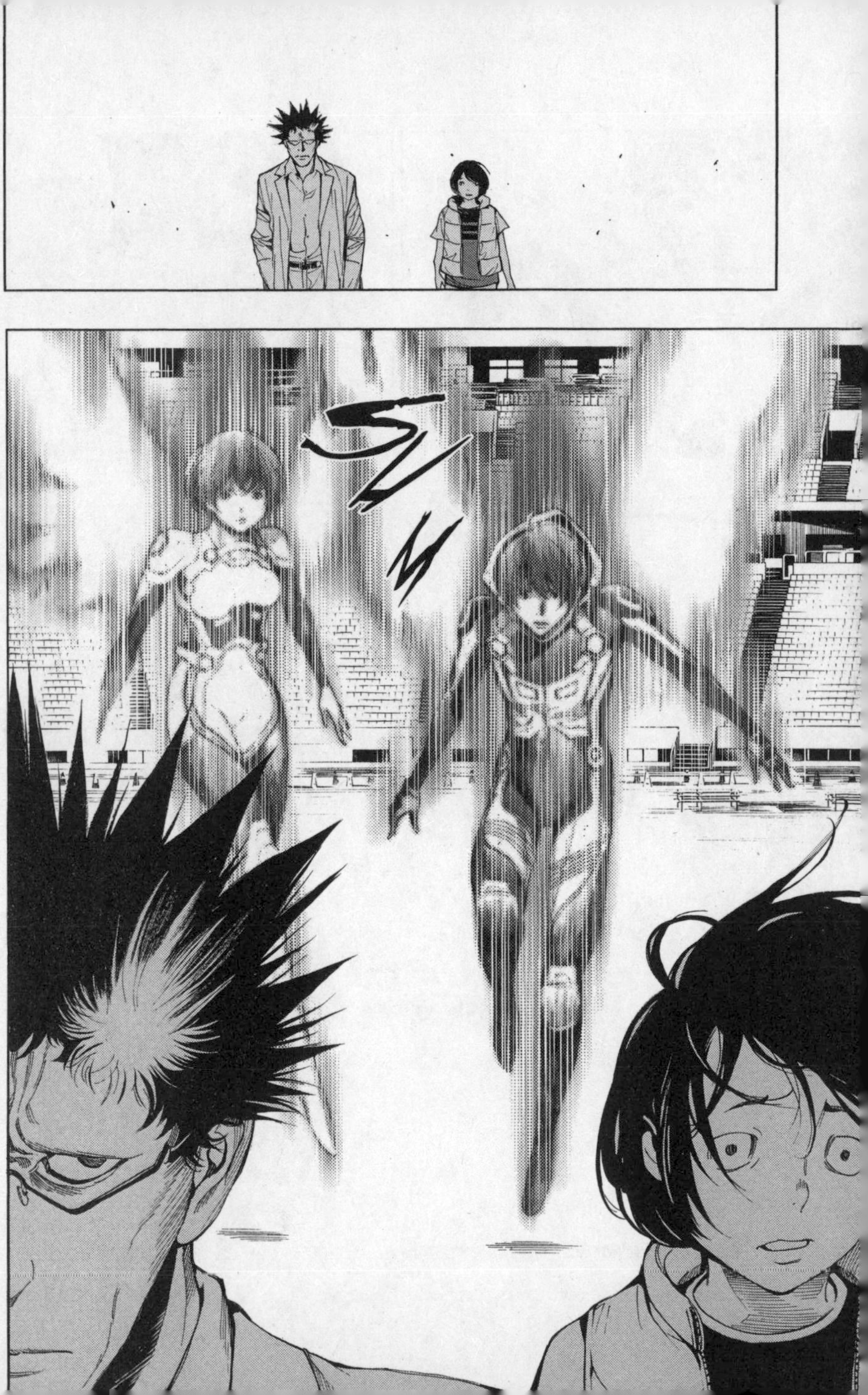
SZM

#47 The Time for Talk

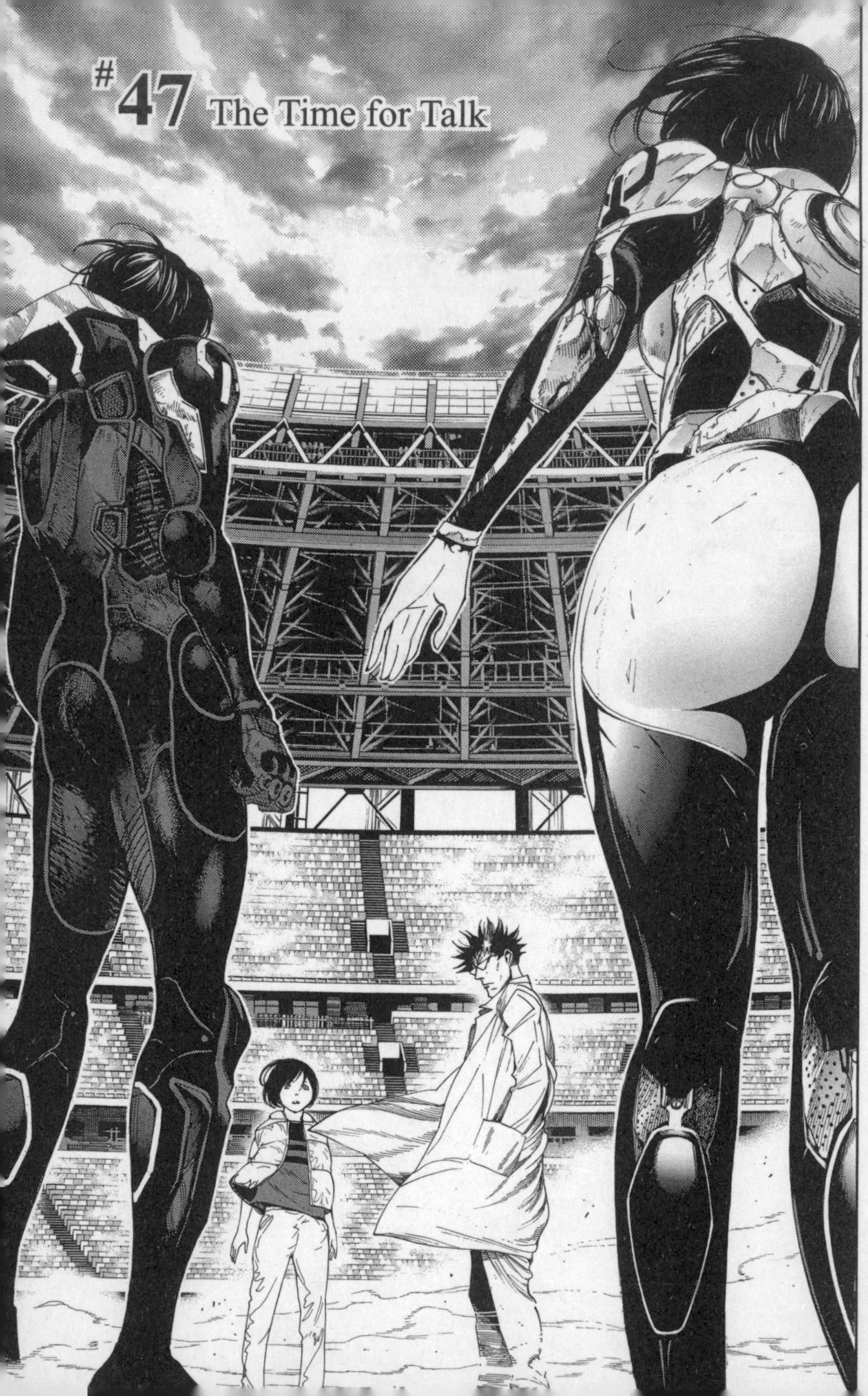

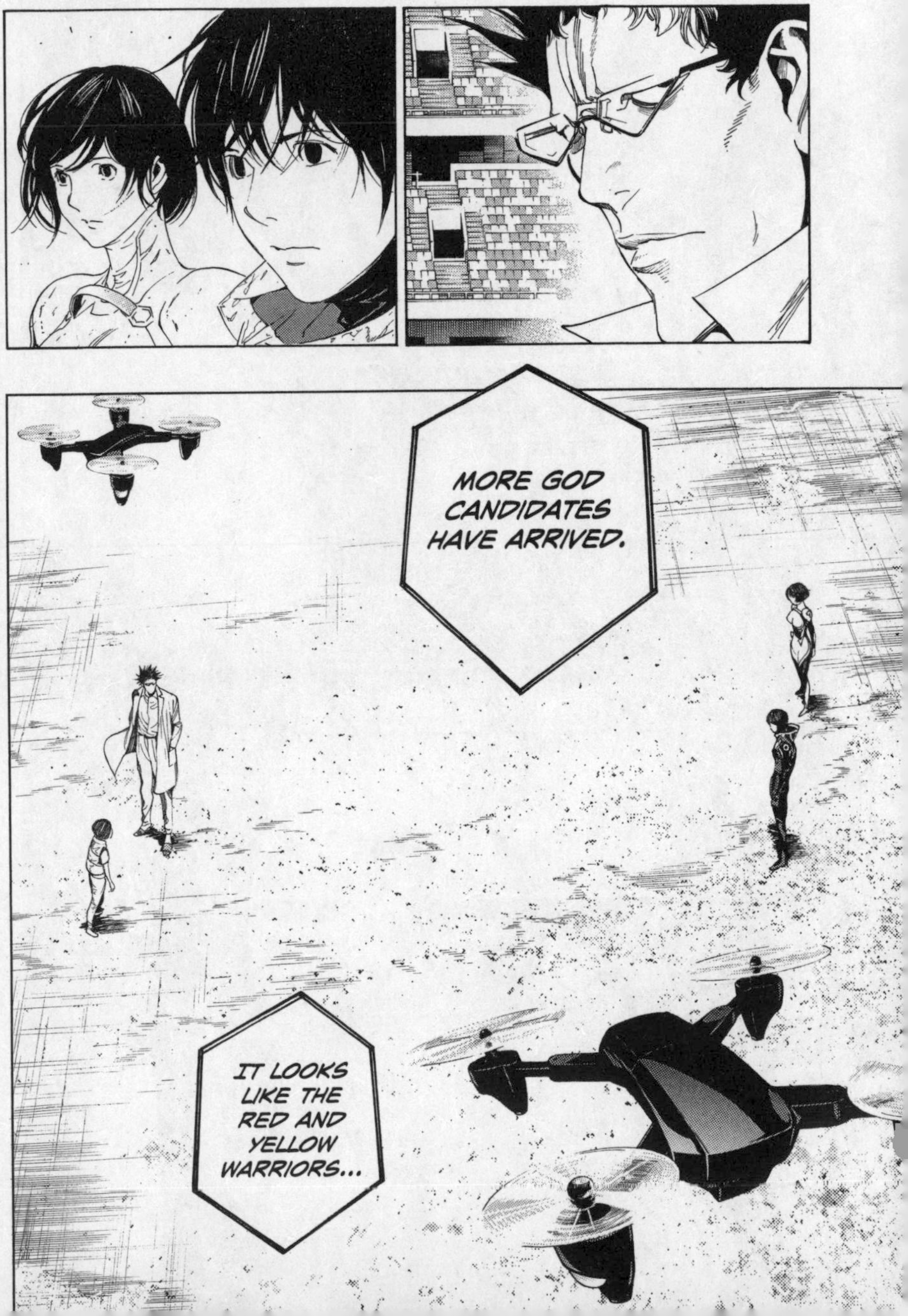
MORE GOD CANDIDATES HAVE ARRIVED.
IT LOOKS LIKE THE RED AND YELLOW WARRIORS...

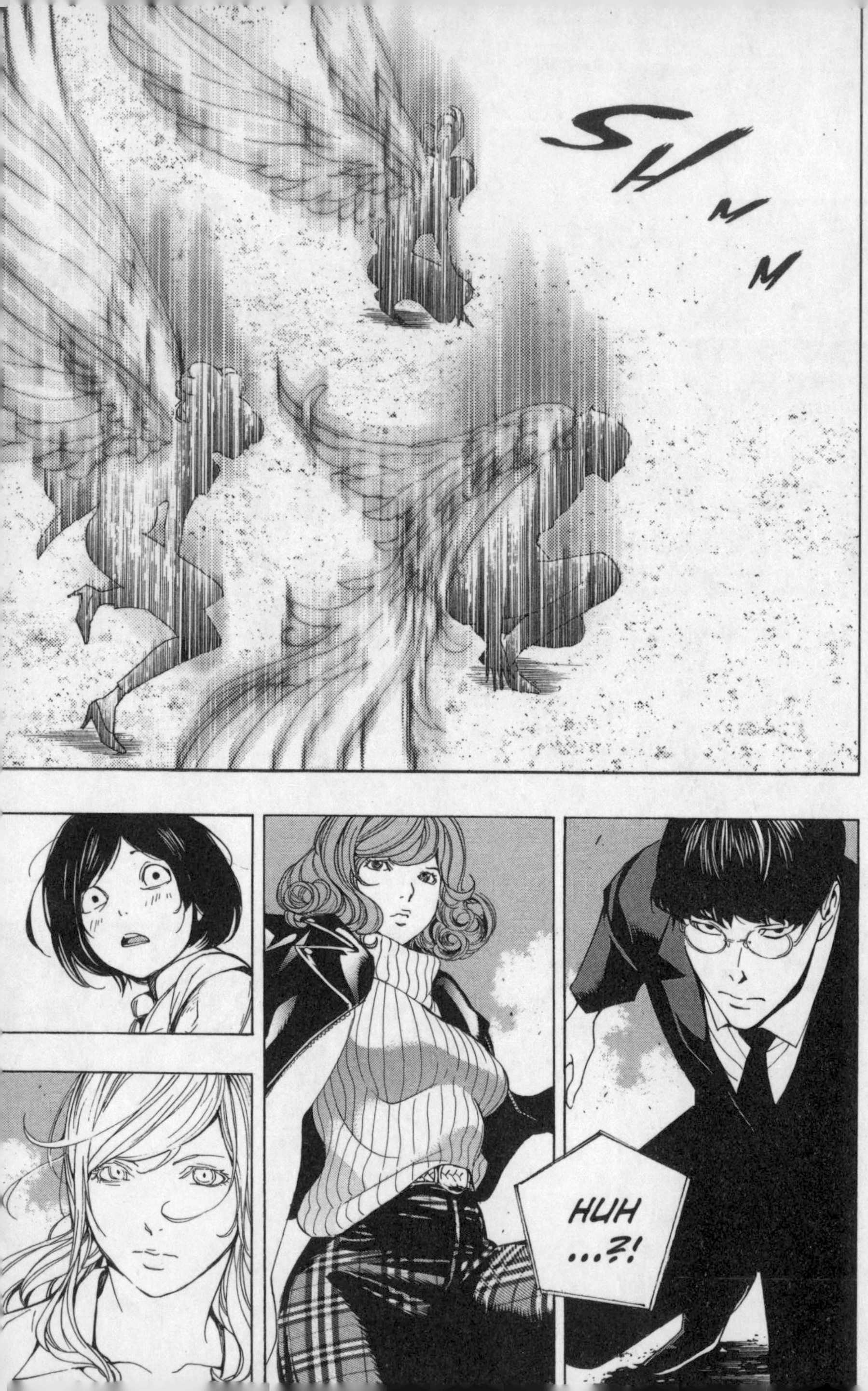
SHMMM
HUH ...?!

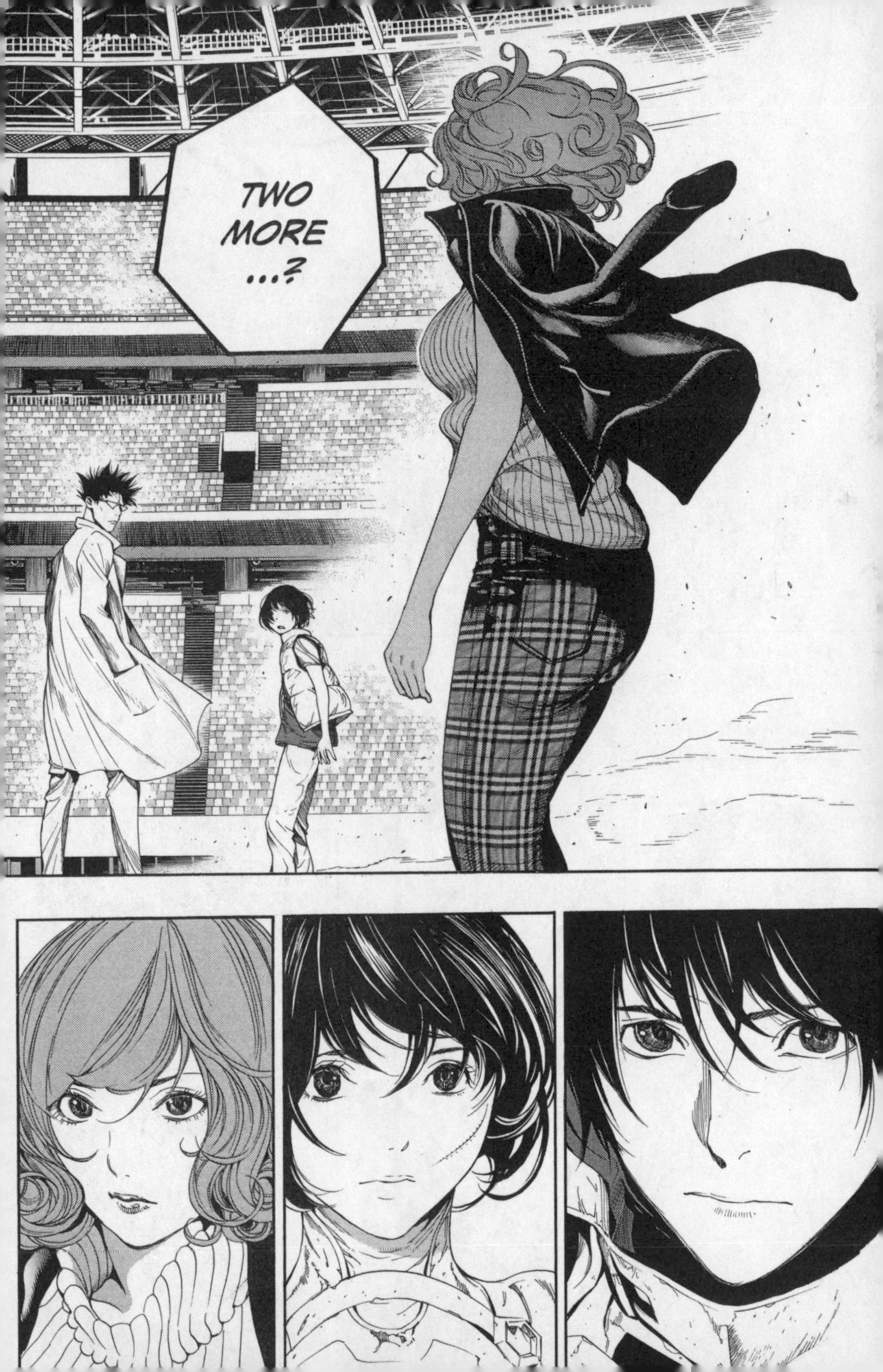
TWO MORE ...?

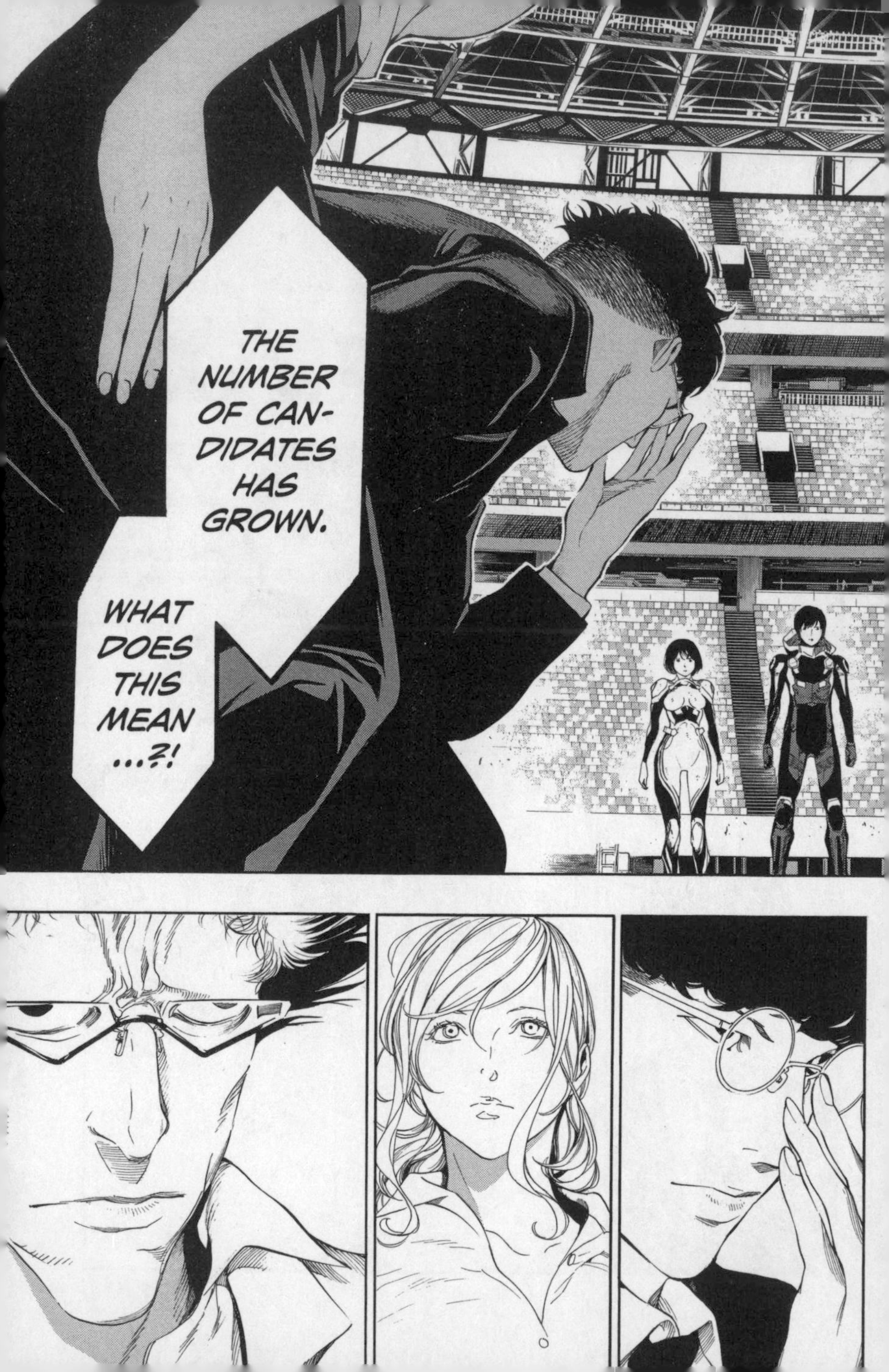
THE NUMBER OF CANDIDATES HAS GROWN.
WHAT DOES THIS MEAN ...?!

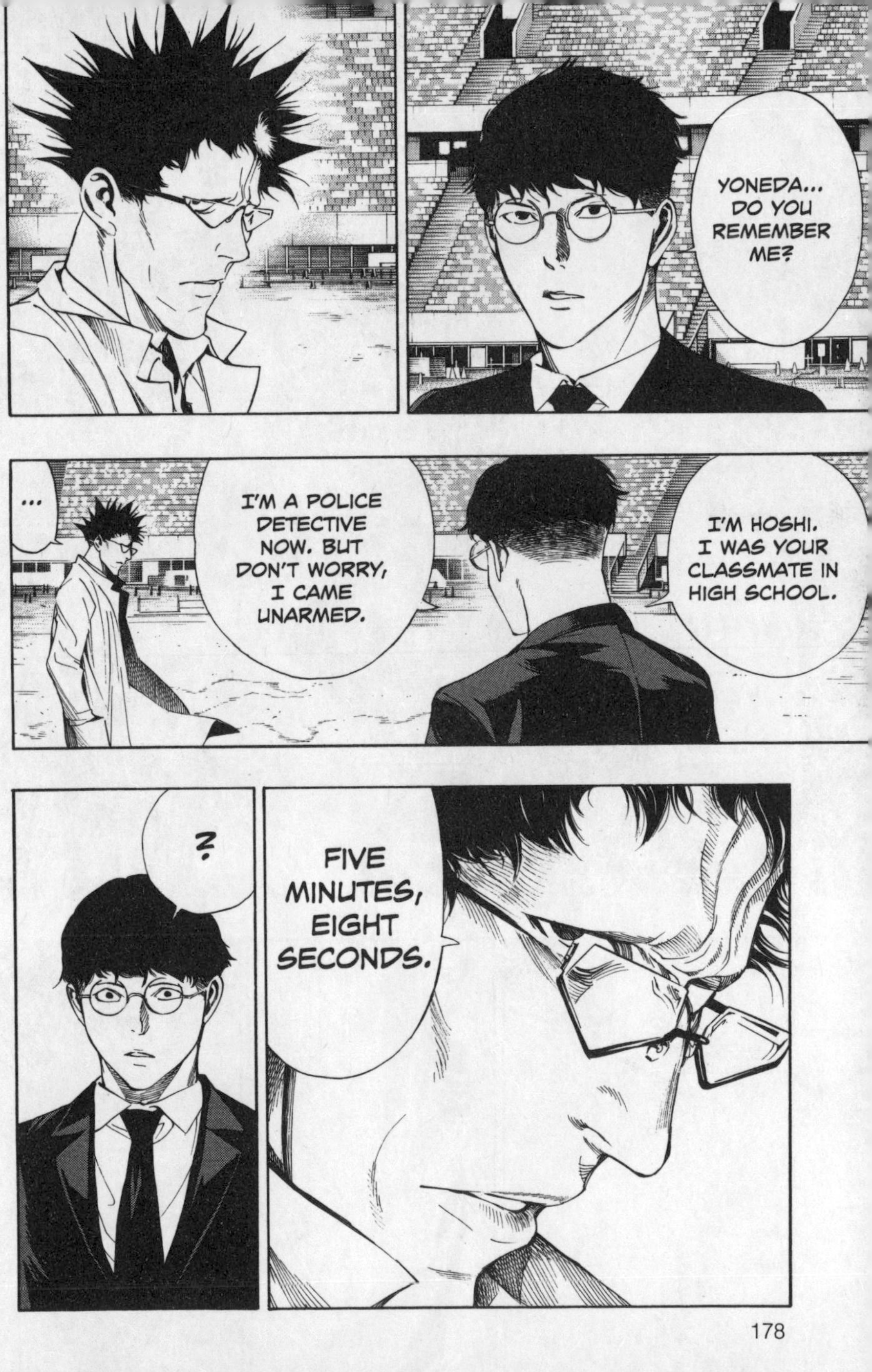
YONEDA... DO YOU REMEMBER ME?
I'M HOSHI. I WAS YOUR CLASSMATE IN HIGH SCHOOL.
I'M A POLICE DETECTIVE NOW. BUT DON'T WORRY, I CAME UNARMED.
...
FIVE MINUTES, EIGHT SECONDS.
?

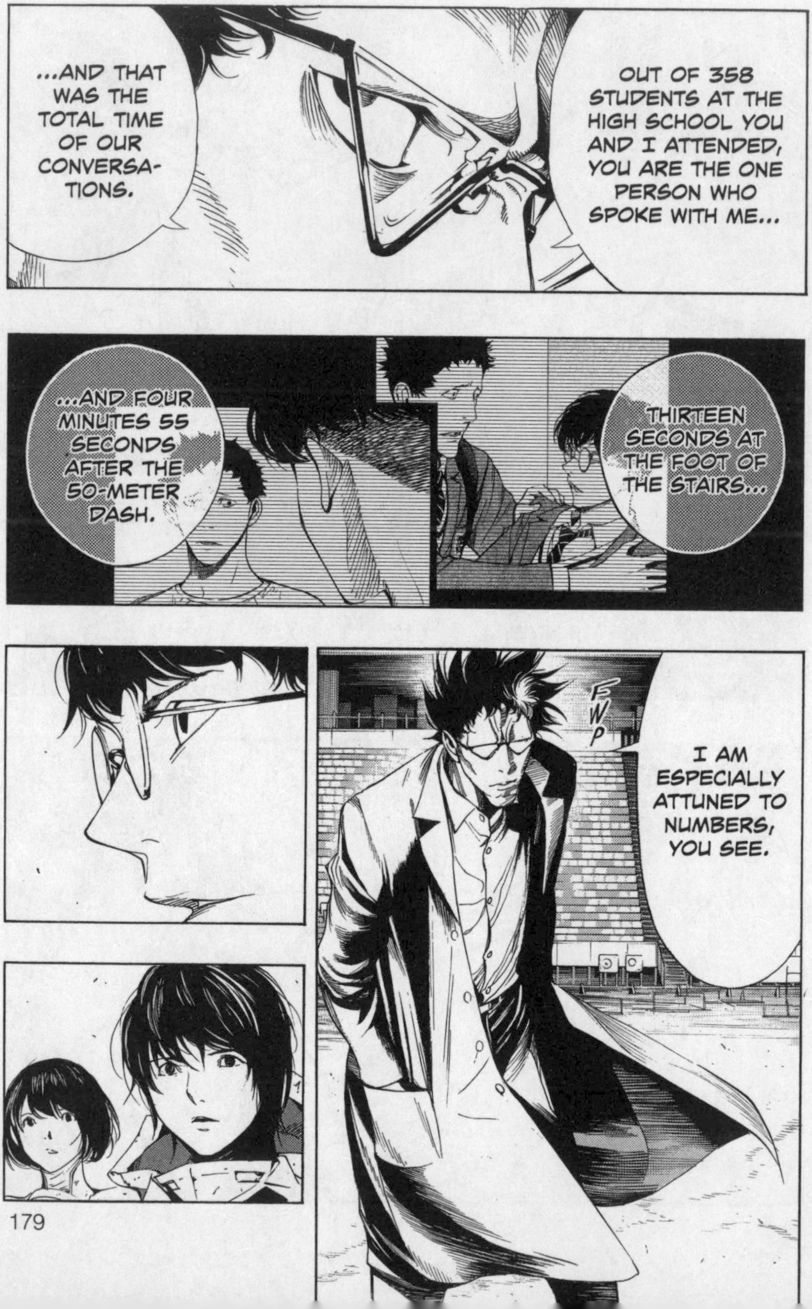
OUT OF 358 STUDENTS AT THE HIGH SCHOOL YOU AND I ATTENDED, YOU ARE THE ONE PERSON WHO SPOKE WITH ME...
...AND THAT WAS THE TOTAL TIME OF OUR CONVERSA-TIONS.
THIRTEEN SECONDS AT THE FOOT OF THE STAIRS...
...AND FOUR MINUTES 55 SECONDS AFTER THE 50-METER DASH.
FWP
I AM ESPECIALLY ATTUNED TO NUMBERS, YOU SEE.

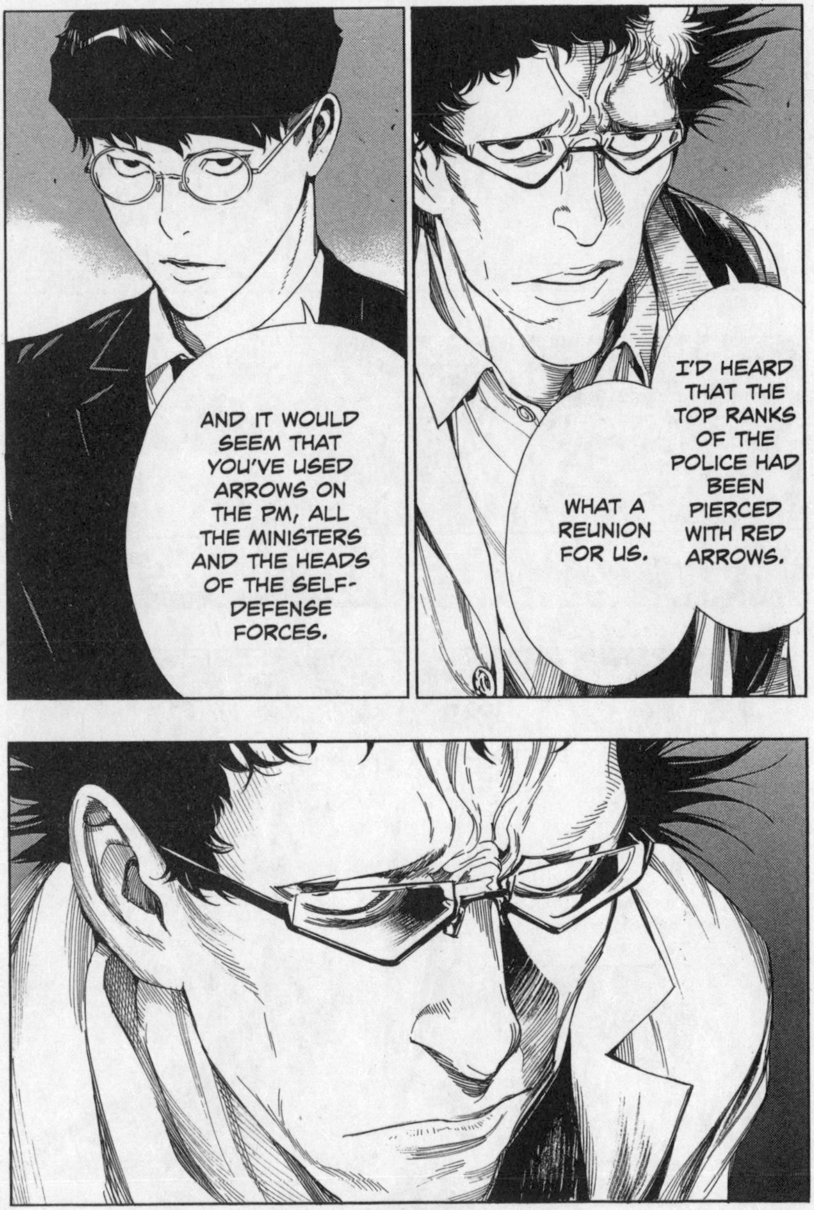
I'D HEARD THAT THE TOP RANKS OF THE POLICE HAD BEEN PIERCED WITH RED ARROWS.
WHAT A REUNION FOR US.
AND IT WOULD SEEM THAT YOU'VE USED ARROWS ON THE PM, ALL THE MINISTERS AND THE HEADS OF THE SELF-DEFENSE FORCES.

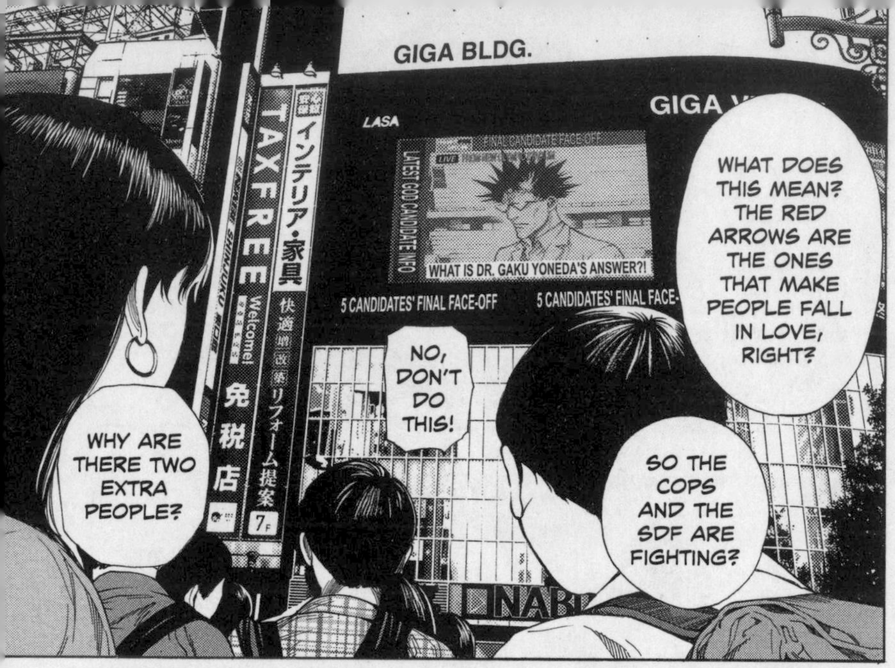
GIGA BLDG.
LASA
FINAL CANDIDATE FACE-OFF
LIVE
LATEST GOD CANDIDATE INFO
WHAT IS DR. GAKU YONEDA'S ANSWER?!
5 CANDIDATES' FINAL FACE-OFF
5 CANDIDATES' FINAL FACE-
WHAT DOES THIS MEAN? THE RED ARROWS ARE THE ONES THAT MAKE PEOPLE FALL IN LOVE, RIGHT?
SO THE COPS AND THE SDF ARE FIGHTING?
NO, DON'T DO THIS!
インテリア・家具
快適増改築リフォーム提案
7F
TAXFREE
Welcome!
免税店
WHY ARE THERE TWO EXTRA PEOPLE?

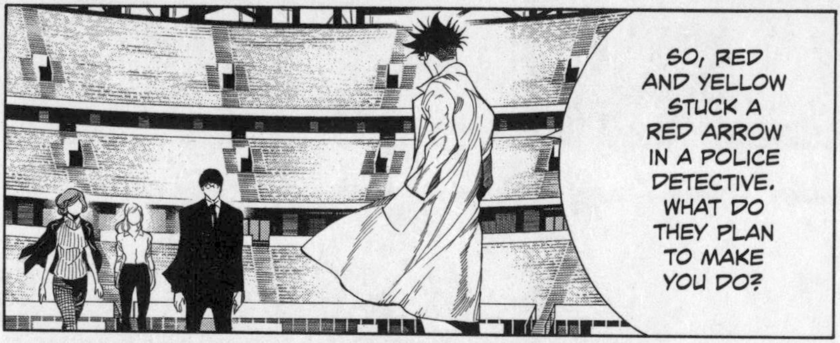
SO, RED AND YELLOW STUCK A RED ARROW IN A POLICE DETECTIVE. WHAT DO THEY PLAN TO MAKE YOU DO?

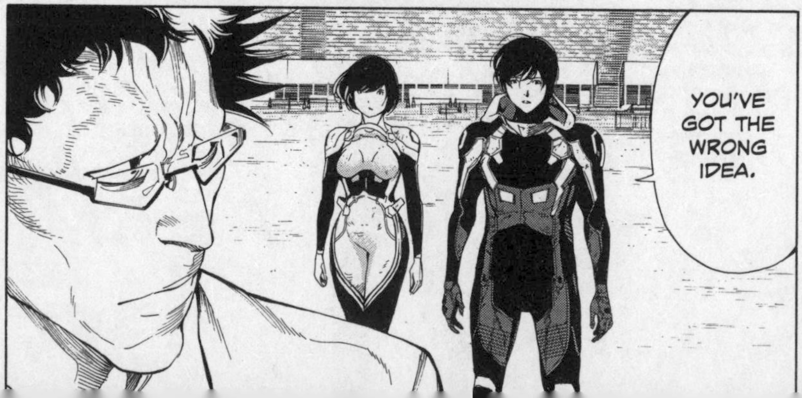
YOU'VE GOT THE WRONG IDEA.

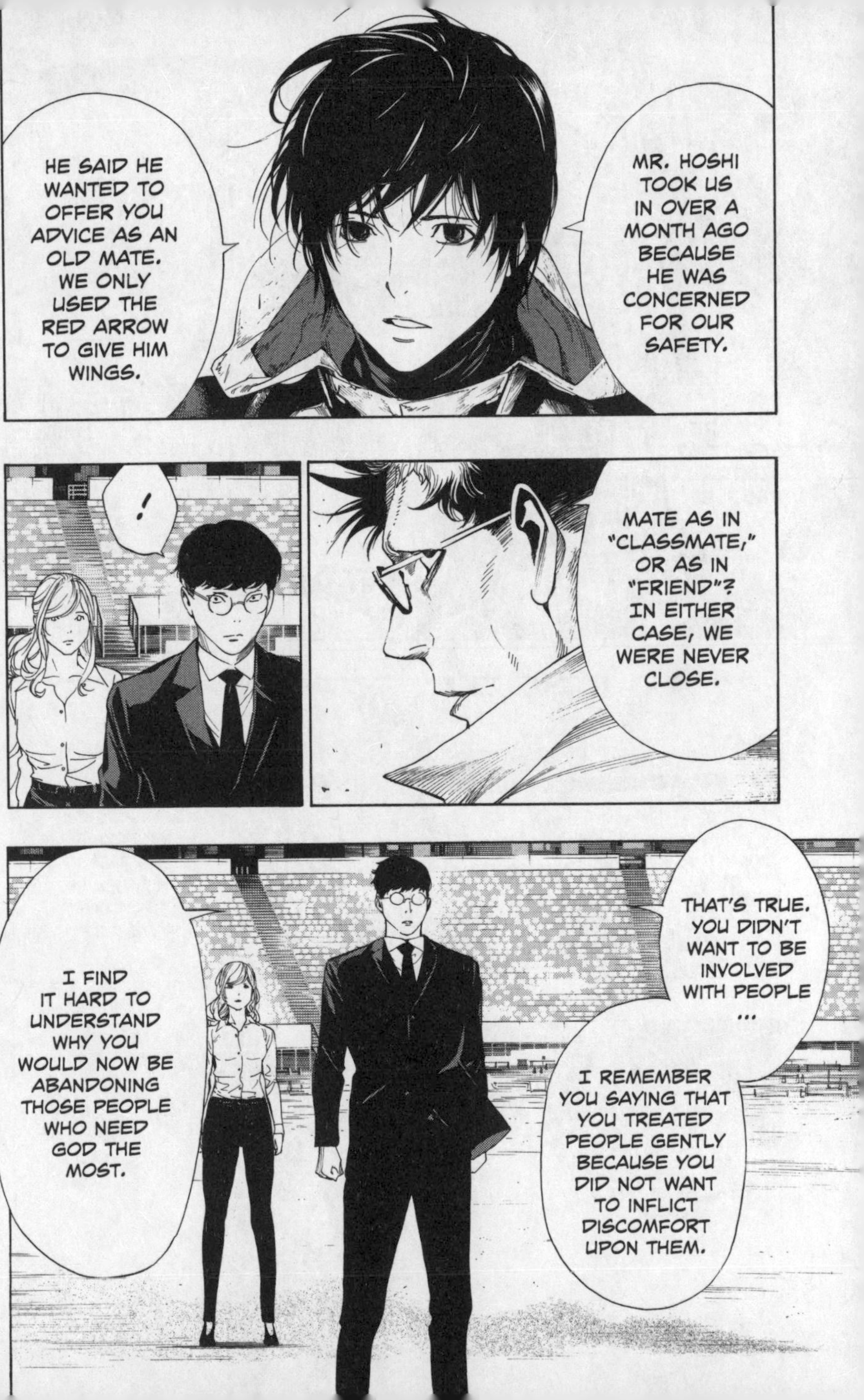
MR. HOSHI TOOK US IN OVER A MONTH AGO BECAUSE HE WAS CONCERNED FOR OUR SAFETY.
HE SAID HE WANTED TO OFFER YOU ADVICE AS AN OLD MATE. WE ONLY USED THE RED ARROW TO GIVE HIM WINGS.
MATE AS IN "CLASSMATE," OR AS IN "FRIEND"? IN EITHER CASE, WE WERE NEVER CLOSE.
!
THAT'S TRUE. YOU DIDN'T WANT TO BE INVOLVED WITH PEOPLE ...
I REMEMBER YOU SAYING THAT YOU TREATED PEOPLE GENTLY BECAUSE YOU DID NOT WANT TO INFLICT DISCOMFORT UPON THEM.
I FIND IT HARD TO UNDERSTAND WHY YOU WOULD NOW BE ABANDONING THOSE PEOPLE WHO NEED GOD THE MOST.

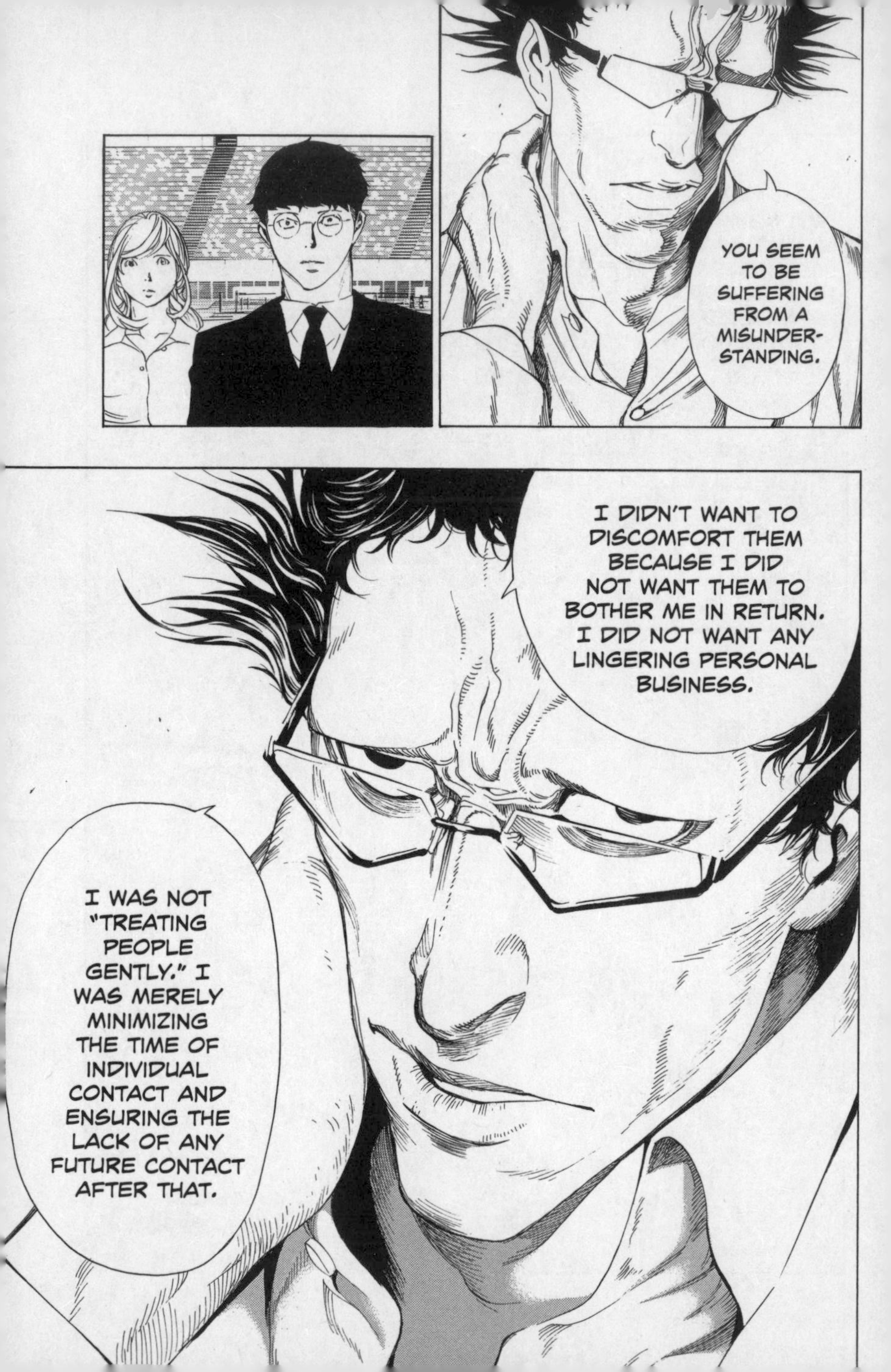
YOU SEEM TO BE SUFFERING FROM A MISUNDER-STANDING.
I DIDN'T WANT TO DISCOMFORT THEM BECAUSE I DID NOT WANT THEM TO BOTHER ME IN RETURN. I DID NOT WANT ANY LINGERING PERSONAL BUSINESS.
I WAS NOT "TREATING PEOPLE GENTLY." I WAS MERELY MINIMIZING THE TIME OF INDIVIDUAL CONTACT AND ENSURING THE LACK OF ANY FUTURE CONTACT AFTER THAT.

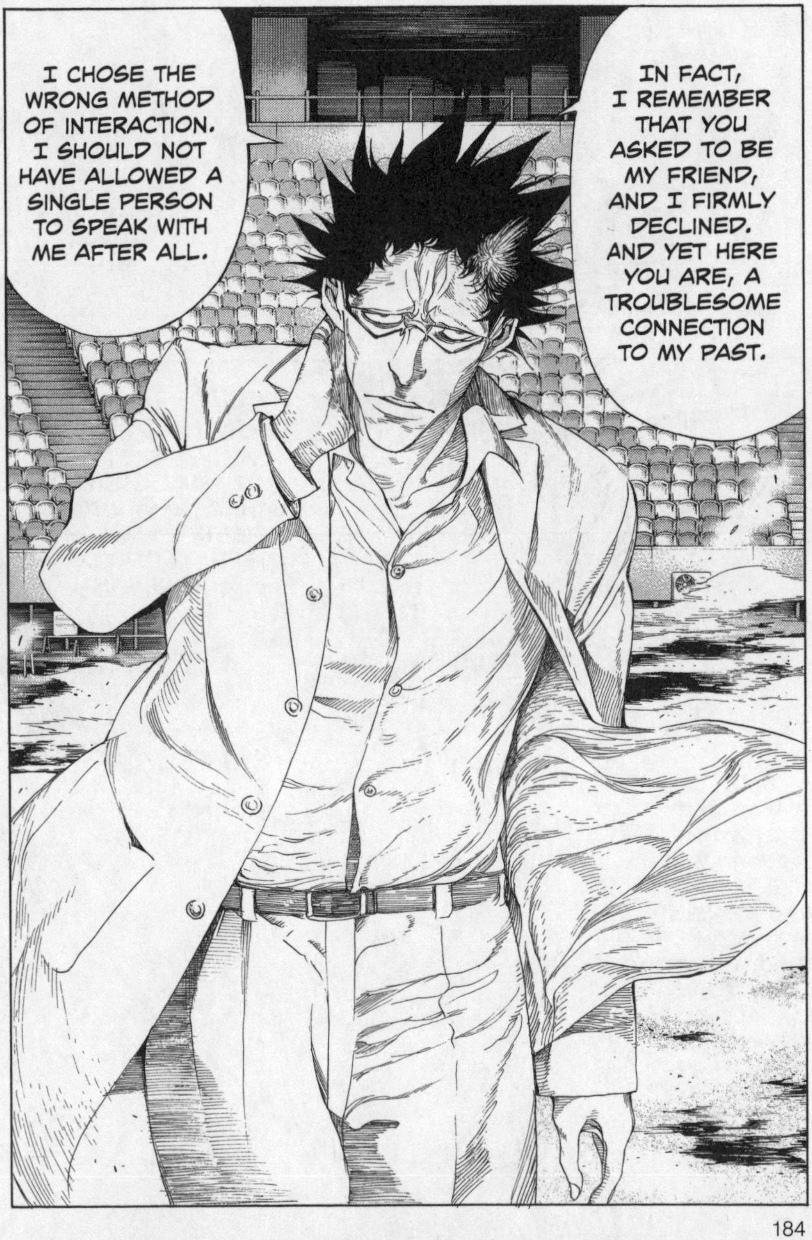
IN FACT, I REMEMBER THAT YOU ASKED TO BE MY FRIEND, AND I FIRMLY DECLINED. AND YET HERE YOU ARE, A TROUBLESOME CONNECTION TO MY PAST.
I CHOSE THE WRONG METHOD OF INTERACTION. I SHOULD NOT HAVE ALLOWED A SINGLE PERSON TO SPEAK WITH ME AFTER ALL.

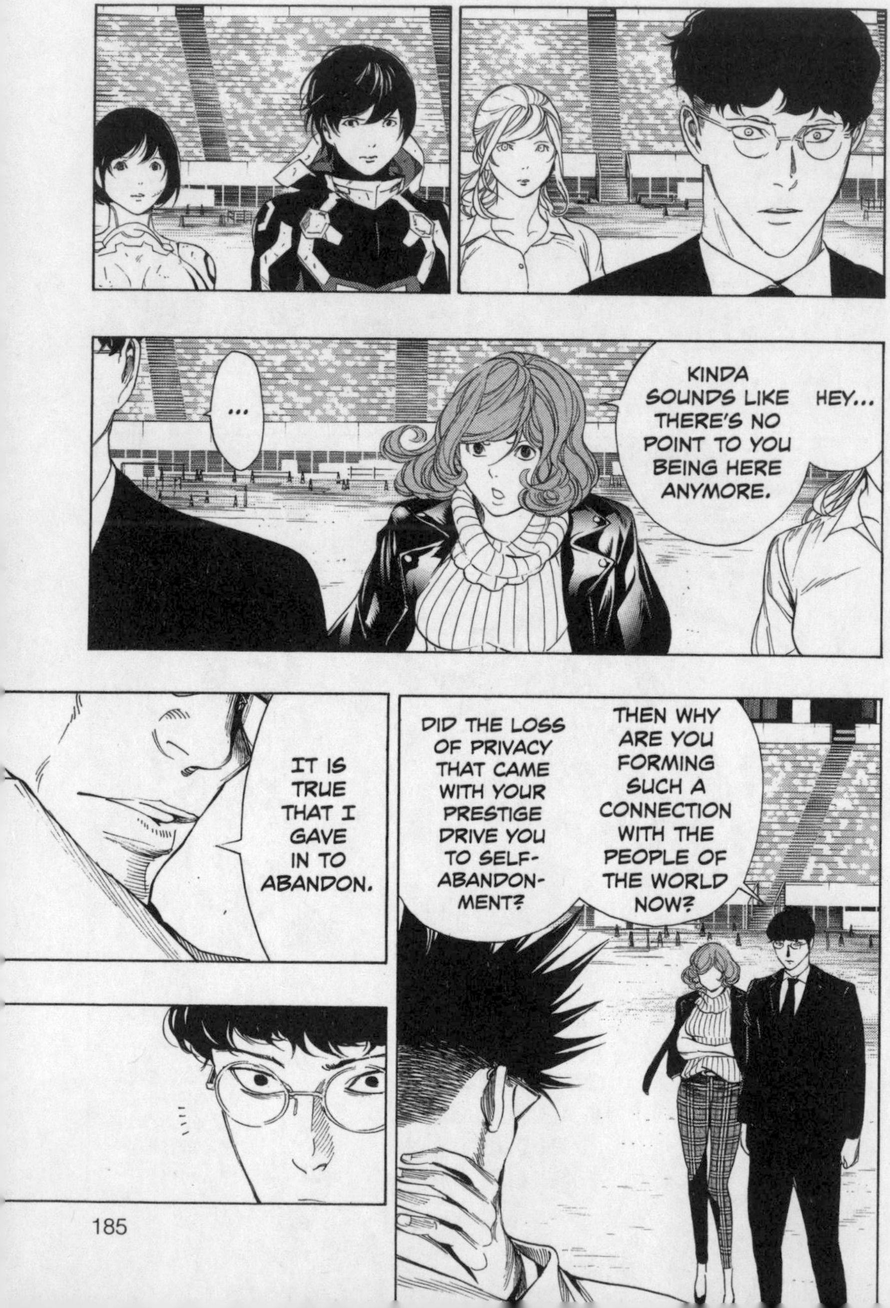
HEY...
KINDA SOUNDS LIKE THERE'S NO POINT TO YOU BEING HERE ANYMORE.
...
THEN WHY ARE YOU FORMING SUCH A CONNECTION WITH THE PEOPLE OF THE WORLD NOW?
DID THE LOSS OF PRIVACY THAT CAME WITH YOUR PRESTIGE DRIVE YOU TO SELF-ABANDONMENT?
IT IS TRUE THAT I GAVE IN TO ABANDON.

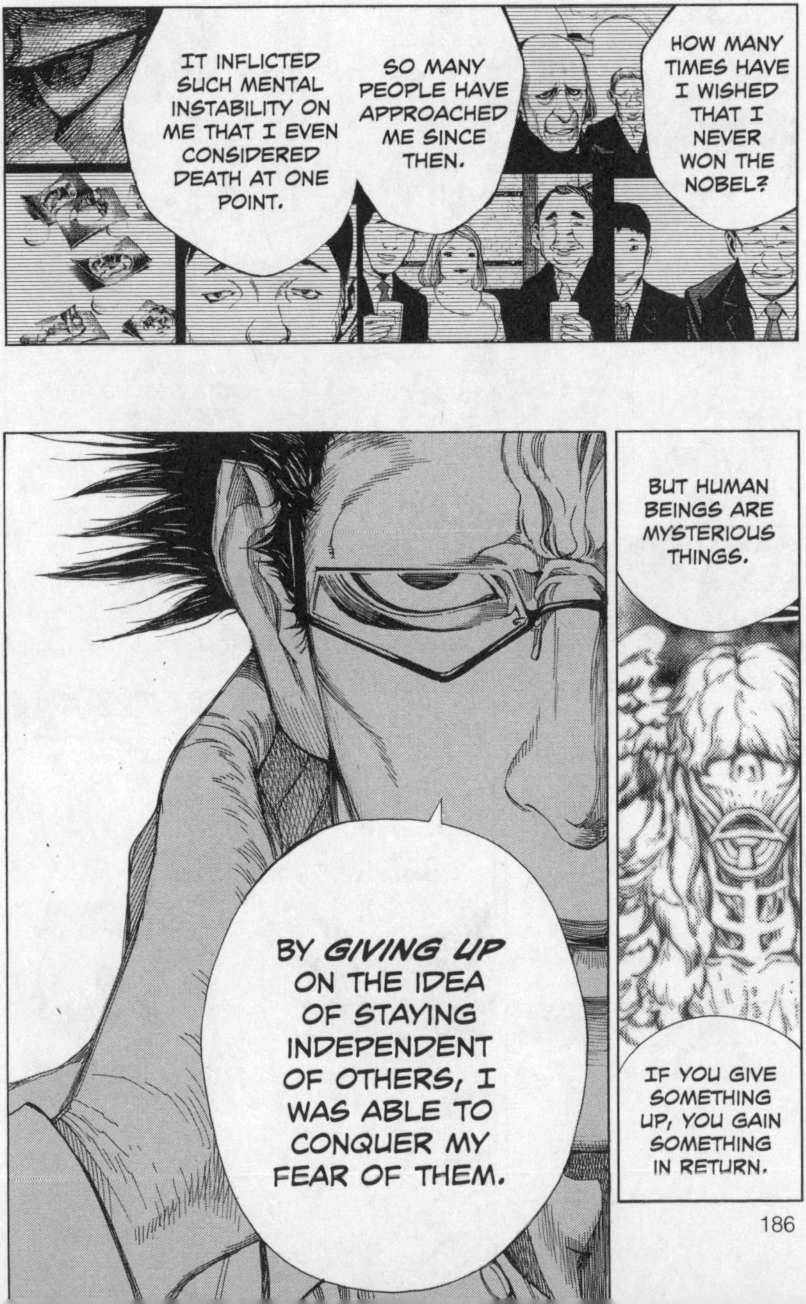
HOW MANY TIMES HAVE I WISHED THAT I NEVER WON THE NOBEL?
SO MANY PEOPLE HAVE APPROACHED ME SINCE THEN.
IT INFLICTED SUCH MENTAL INSTABILITY ON ME THAT I EVEN CONSIDERED DEATH AT ONE POINT.
BUT HUMAN BEINGS ARE MYSTERIOUS THINGS.
IF YOU GIVE SOMETHING UP, YOU GAIN SOMETHING IN RETURN.
BY *GIVING UP* ON THE IDEA OF STAYING INDEPENDENT OF OTHERS, I WAS ABLE TO CONQUER MY FEAR OF THEM.

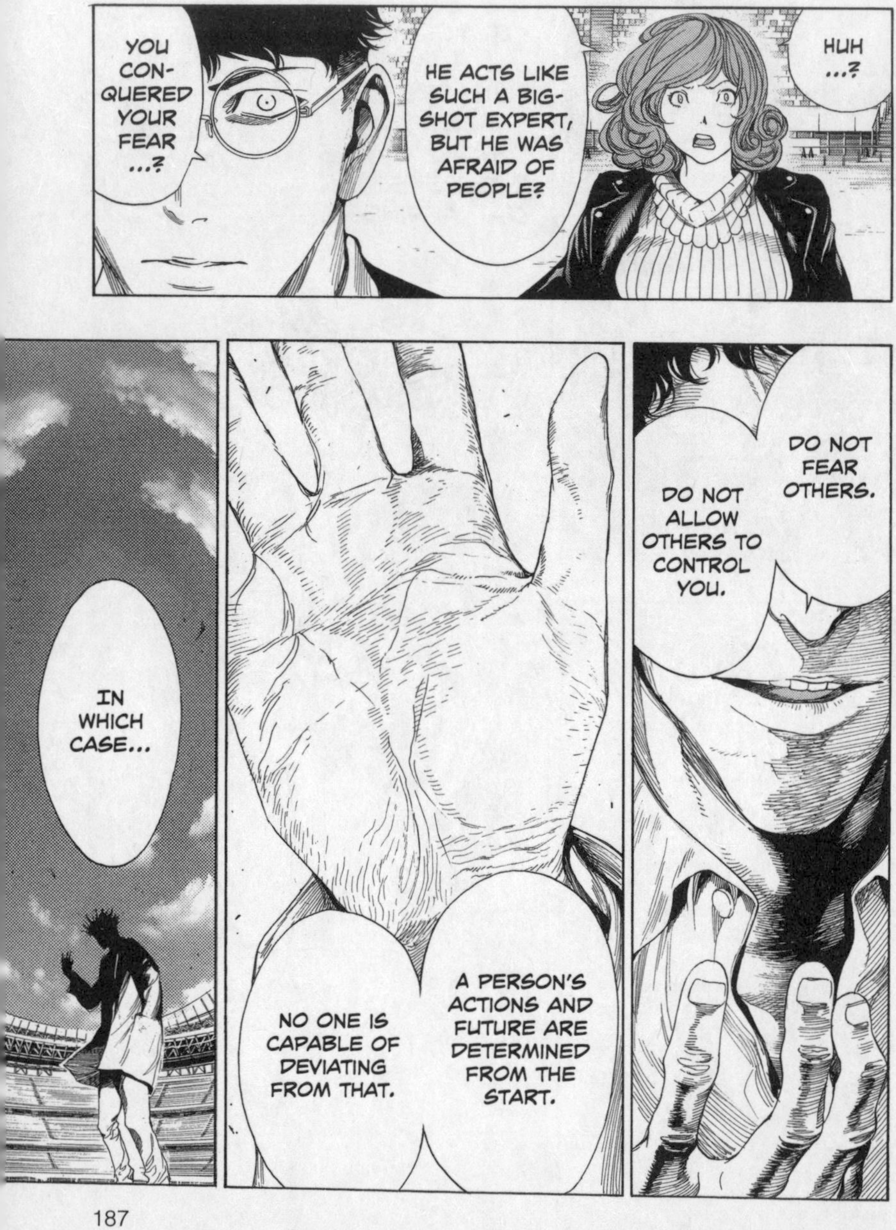
HUH ...?
HE ACTS LIKE SUCH A BIG-SHOT EXPERT, BUT HE WAS AFRAID OF PEOPLE?
YOU CON-QUERED YOUR FEAR ...?
DO NOT FEAR OTHERS.
DO NOT ALLOW OTHERS TO CONTROL YOU.
A PERSON'S ACTIONS AND FUTURE ARE DETERMINED FROM THE START.
NO ONE IS CAPABLE OF DEVIATING FROM THAT.
IN WHICH CASE...

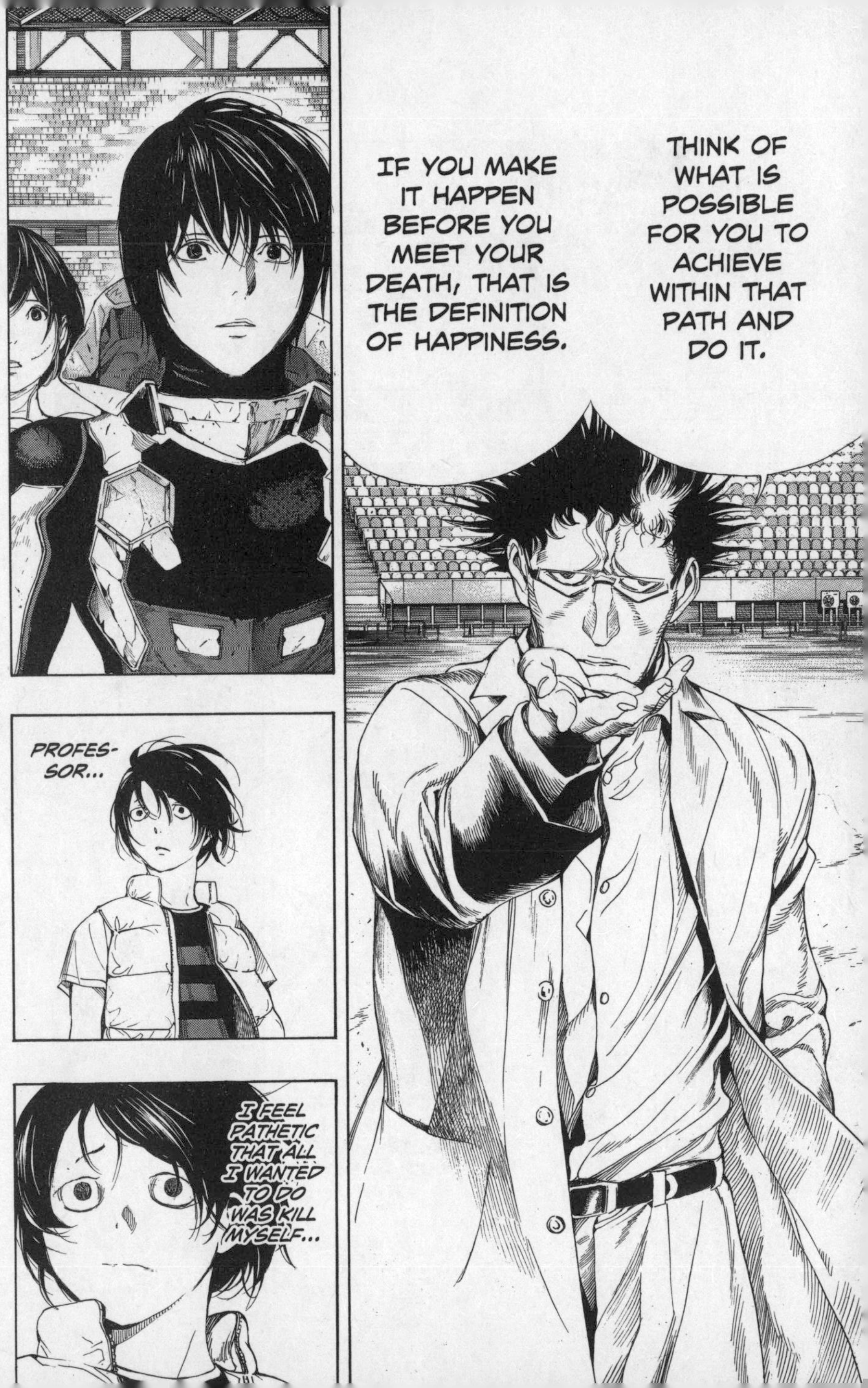
THINK OF WHAT IS POSSIBLE FOR YOU TO ACHIEVE WITHIN THAT PATH AND DO IT.
IF YOU MAKE IT HAPPEN BEFORE YOU MEET YOUR DEATH, THAT IS THE DEFINITION OF HAPPINESS.
PROFES-SOR...
I FEEL PATHETIC THAT ALL I WANTED TO DO WAS KILL MYSELF...

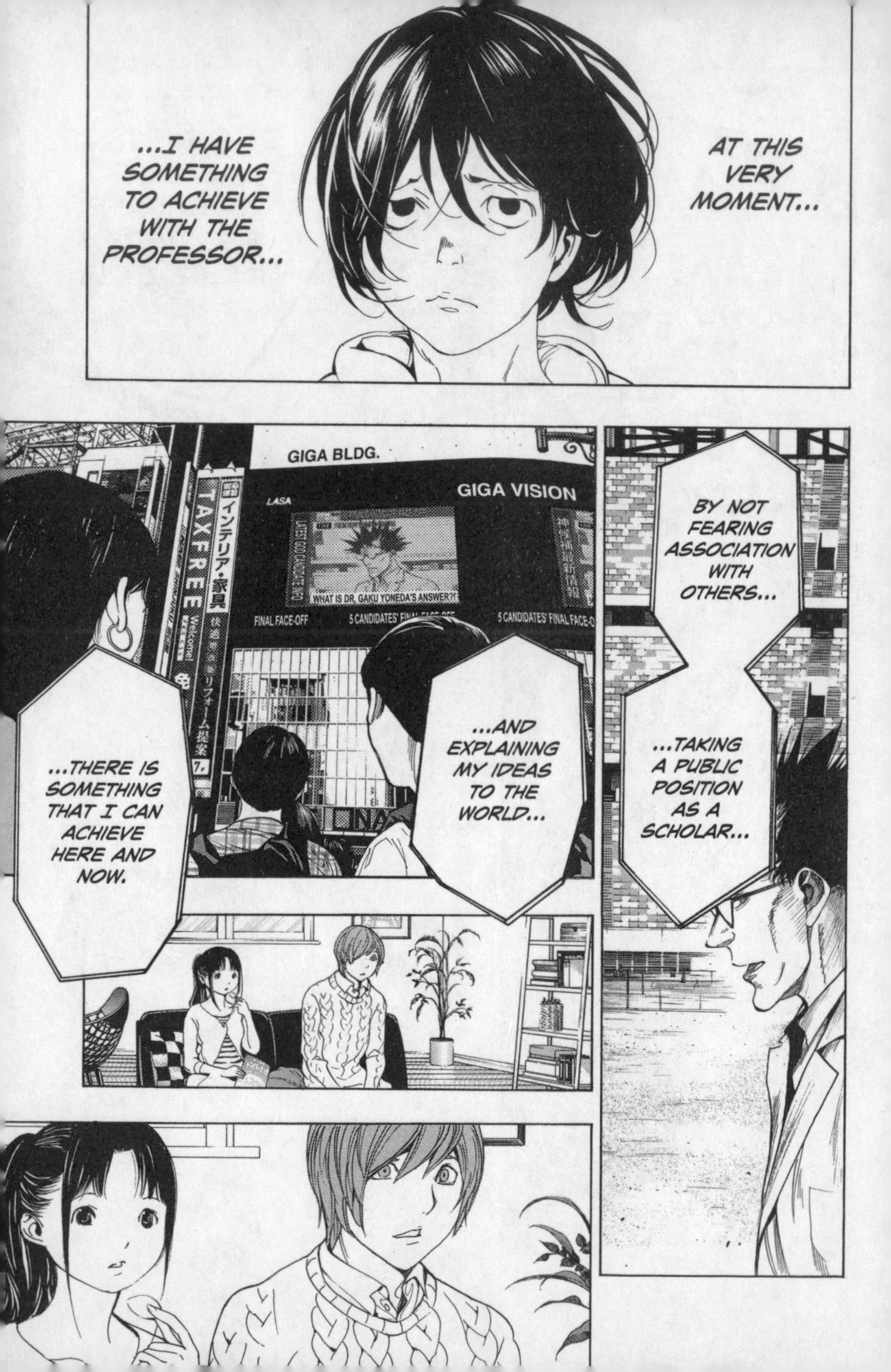
AT THIS VERY MOMENT...
...I HAVE SOMETHING TO ACHIEVE WITH THE PROFESSOR...
BY NOT FEARING ASSOCIATION WITH OTHERS...
...TAKING A PUBLIC POSITION AS A SCHOLAR...
GIGA BLDG.
GIGA VISION
LASA
WHAT IS DR. GAKU YONEDA'S ANSWER?!
FINAL FACE-OFF
5 CANDIDATES' FINAL FACE-OFF
TAXFREE
インテリア・家具
Welcome!
リフォーム提案
...AND EXPLAINING MY IDEAS TO THE WORLD...
...THERE IS SOMETHING THAT I CAN ACHIEVE HERE AND NOW.

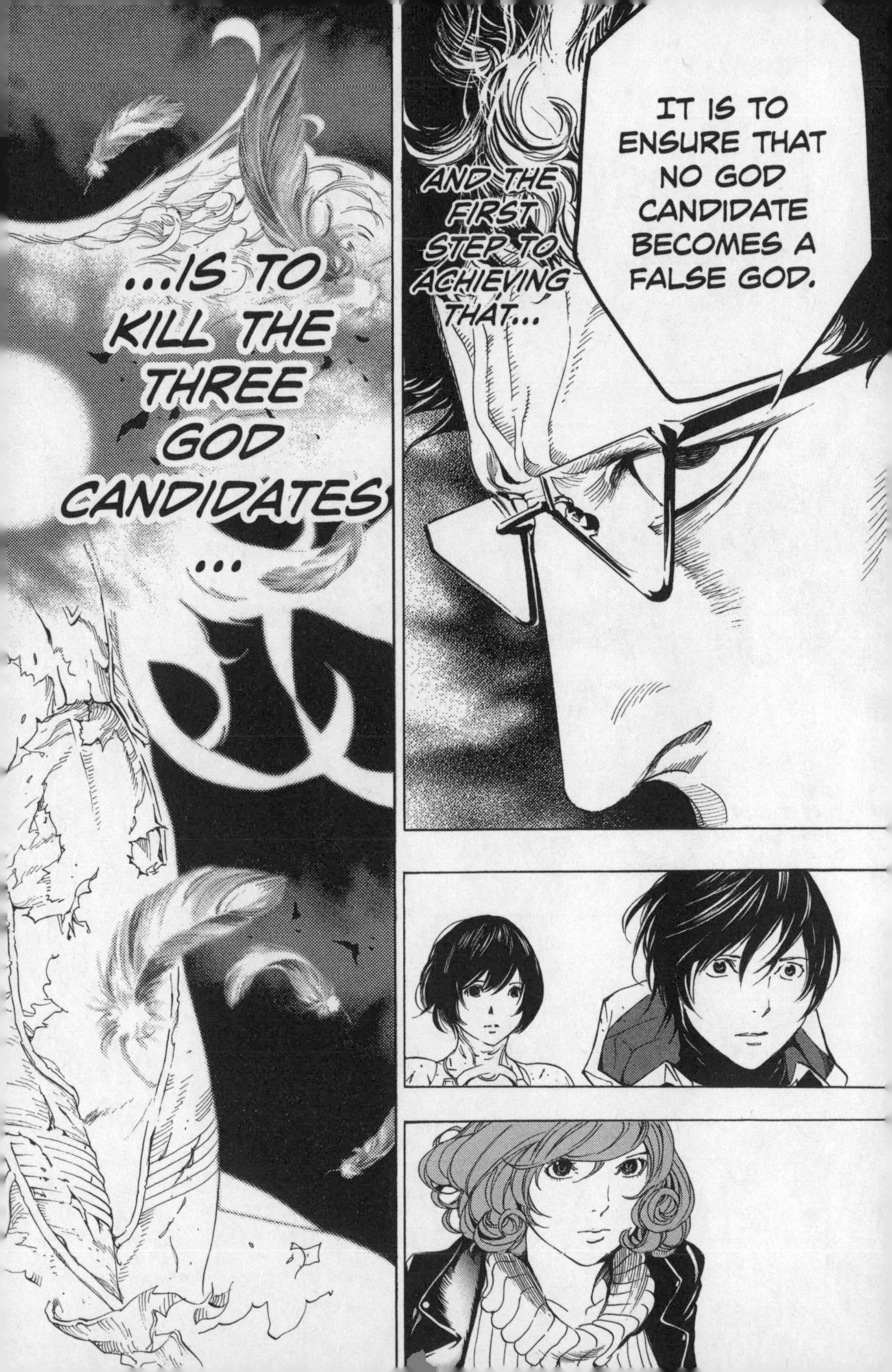
IT IS TO ENSURE THAT NO GOD CANDIDATE BECOMES A FALSE GOD.
AND THE FIRST STEP TO ACHIEVING THAT...
...IS TO KILL THE THREE GOD CANDIDATES ...

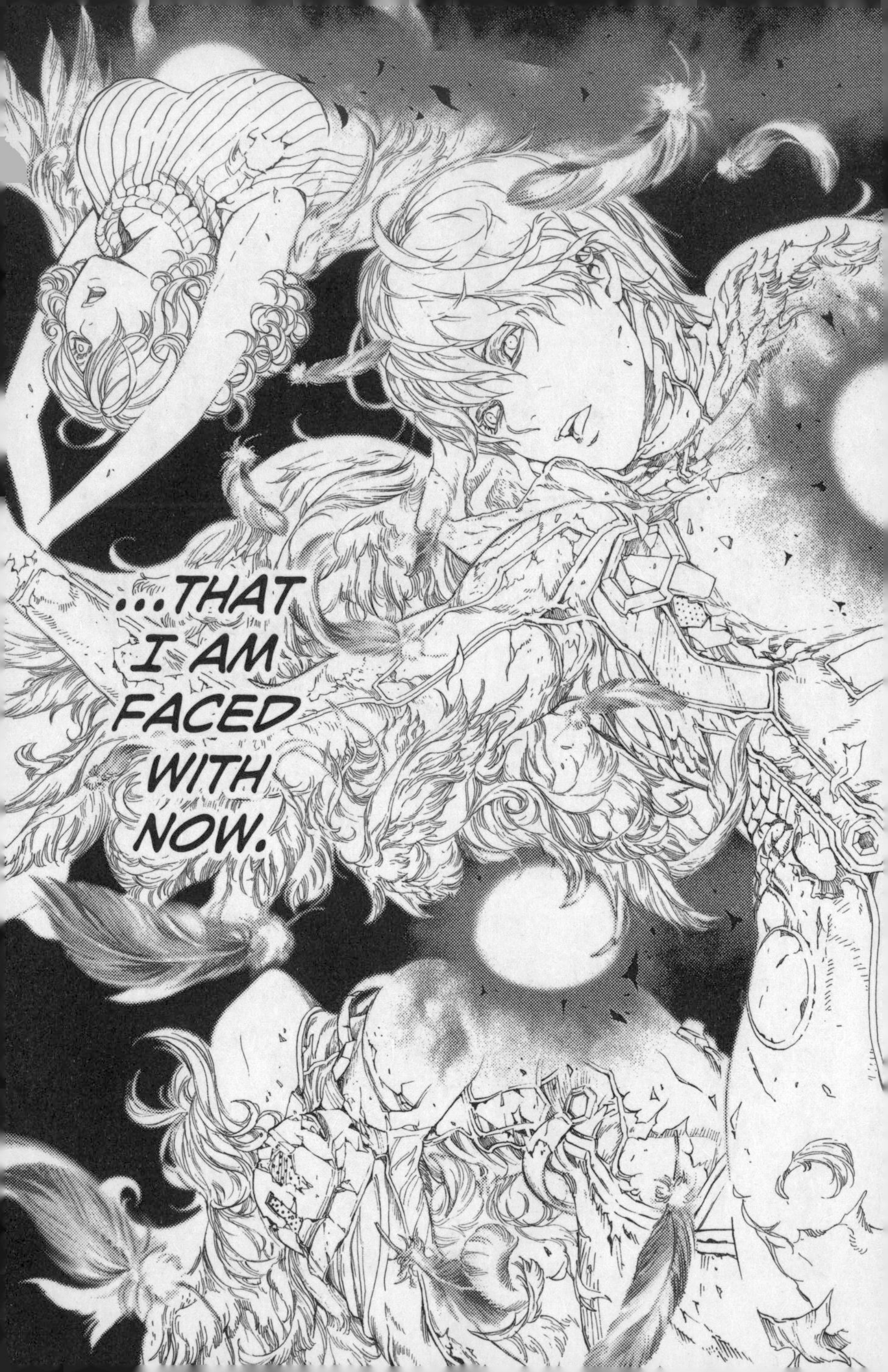
...THAT I AM FACED WITH NOW.

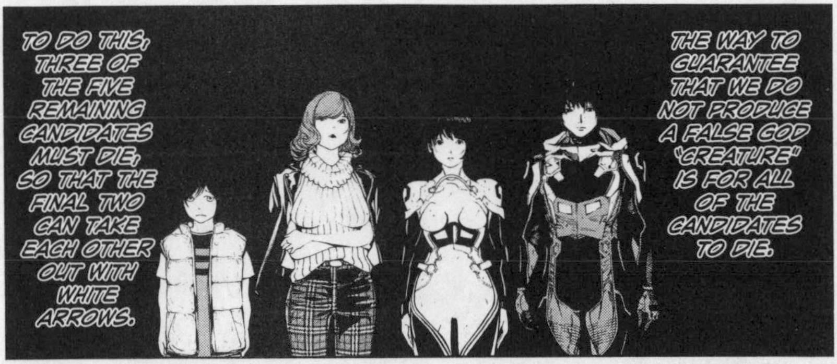
THE WAY TO GUARANTEE THAT WE DO NOT PRODUCE A FALSE GOD "CREATURE" IS FOR ALL OF THE CANDIDATES TO DIE.
TO DO THIS, THREE OF THE FIVE REMAINING CANDIDATES MUST DIE, SO THAT THE FINAL TWO CAN TAKE EACH OTHER OUT WITH WHITE ARROWS.

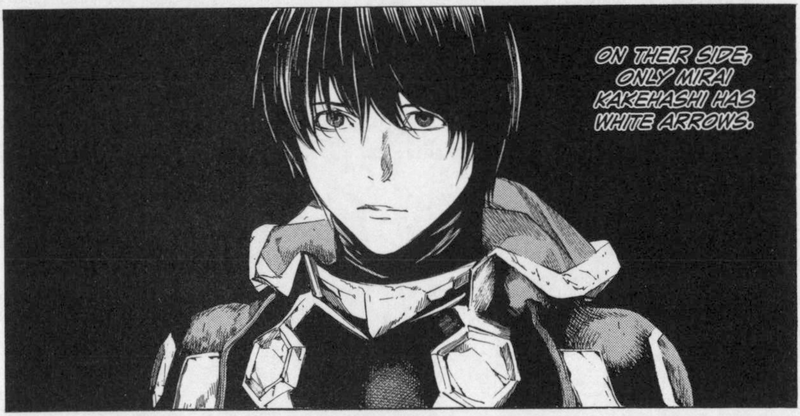
ON THEIR SIDE, ONLY MIRAI KAKEHASHI HAS WHITE ARROWS.

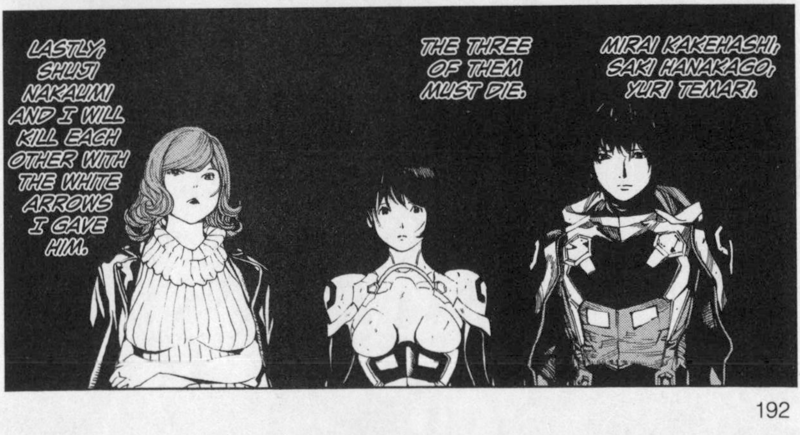
MIRAI KAKEHASHI, SAKI HANAKAGO, YURI TEMARI.
THE THREE OF THEM MUST DIE.
LASTLY, SHUJI NAKAUMI AND I WILL KILL EACH OTHER WITH THE WHITE ARROWS I GAVE HIM.

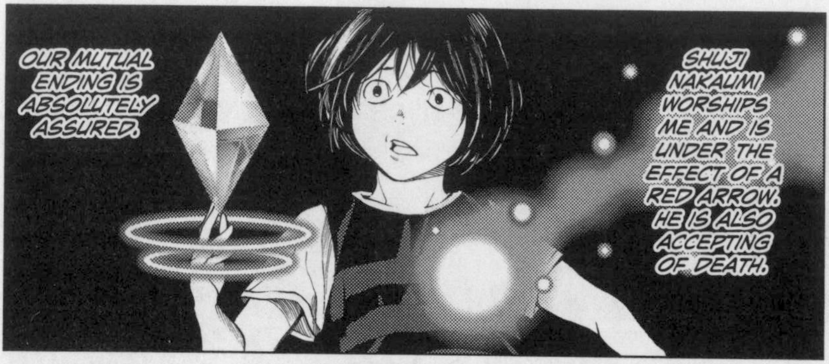
SHUJI NAKAUMI WORSHIPS ME AND IS UNDER THE EFFECT OF A RED ARROW. HE IS ALSO ACCEPTING OF DEATH.
OUR MUTUAL ENDING IS ABSOLUTELY ASSURED.

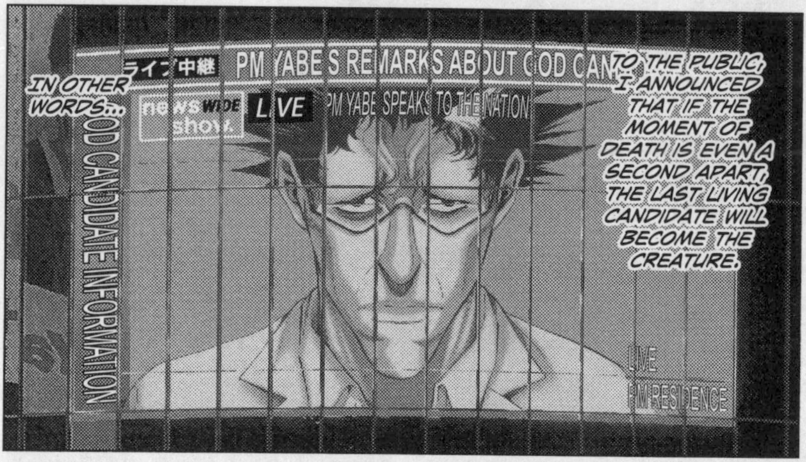
TO THE PUBLIC, I ANNOUNCED THAT IF THE MOMENT OF DEATH IS EVEN A SECOND APART, THE LAST LIVING CANDIDATE WILL BECOME THE CREATURE.
PM YABE S REMARKS ABOUT GOD CAN
ライブ中継
PM YABE SPEAKS TO THE NATION
LIVE
news WIDE show
IN OTHER WORDS...
OD CANDIDATE INFORMATION
LIVE
PM RESIDENCE

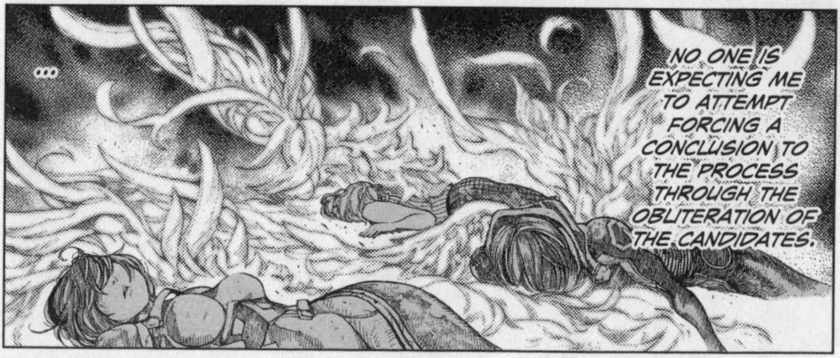
NO ONE IS EXPECTING ME TO ATTEMPT FORCING A CONCLUSION TO THE PROCESS THROUGH THE OBLITERATION OF THE CANDIDATES.
...

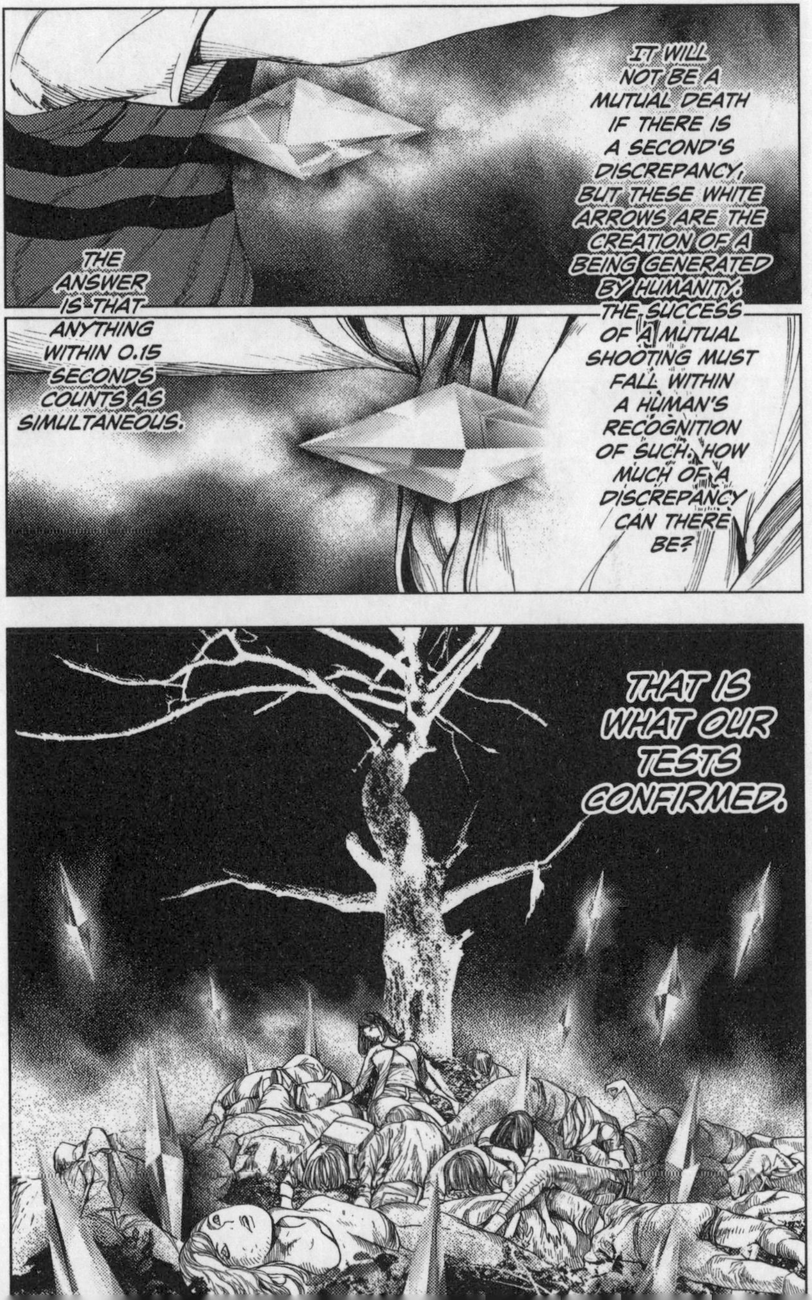
IT WILL NOT BE A MUTUAL DEATH IF THERE IS A SECOND'S DISCREPANCY, BUT THESE WHITE ARROWS ARE THE CREATION OF A BEING GENERATED BY HUMANITY. THE SUCCESS OF A MUTUAL SHOOTING MUST FALL WITHIN A HUMAN'S RECOGNITION OF SUCH. HOW MUCH OF A DISCREPANCY CAN THERE BE?
THE ANSWER IS THAT ANYTHING WITHIN 0.15 SECONDS COUNTS AS SIMULTANEOUS.
THAT IS WHAT OUR TESTS CONFIRMED.

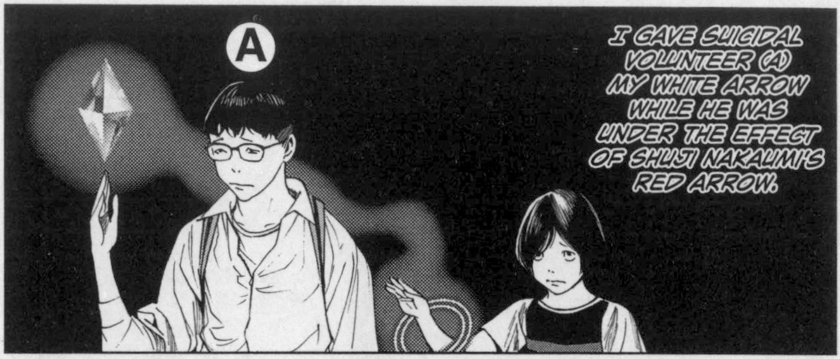
I GAVE SUICIDAL VOLUNTEER (A) MY WHITE ARROW WHILE HE WAS UNDER THE EFFECT OF SHUJI NAKAUMI'S RED ARROW.
A

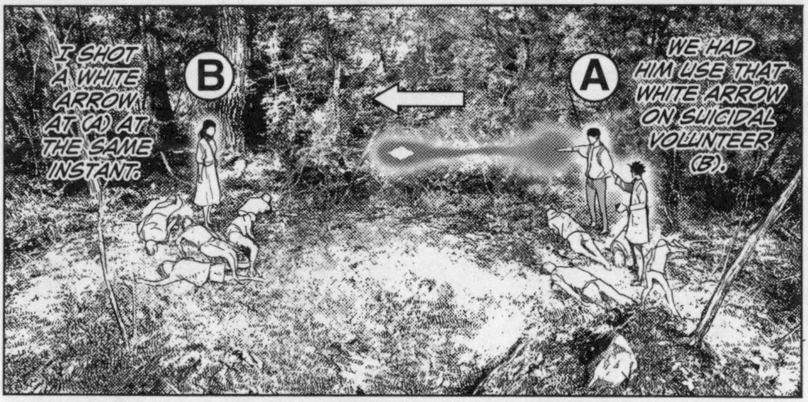
WE HAD HIM USE THAT WHITE ARROW ON SUICIDAL VOLUNTEER (B).
A
B
I SHOT A WHITE ARROW AT (A) AT THE SAME INSTANT.

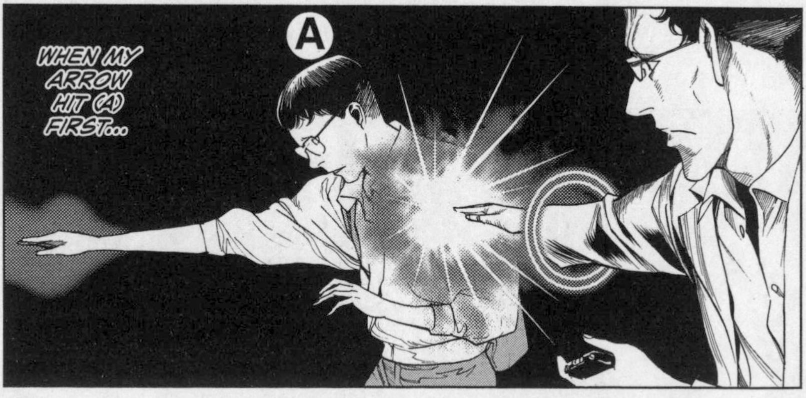
A
WHEN MY ARROW HIT (A) FIRST...

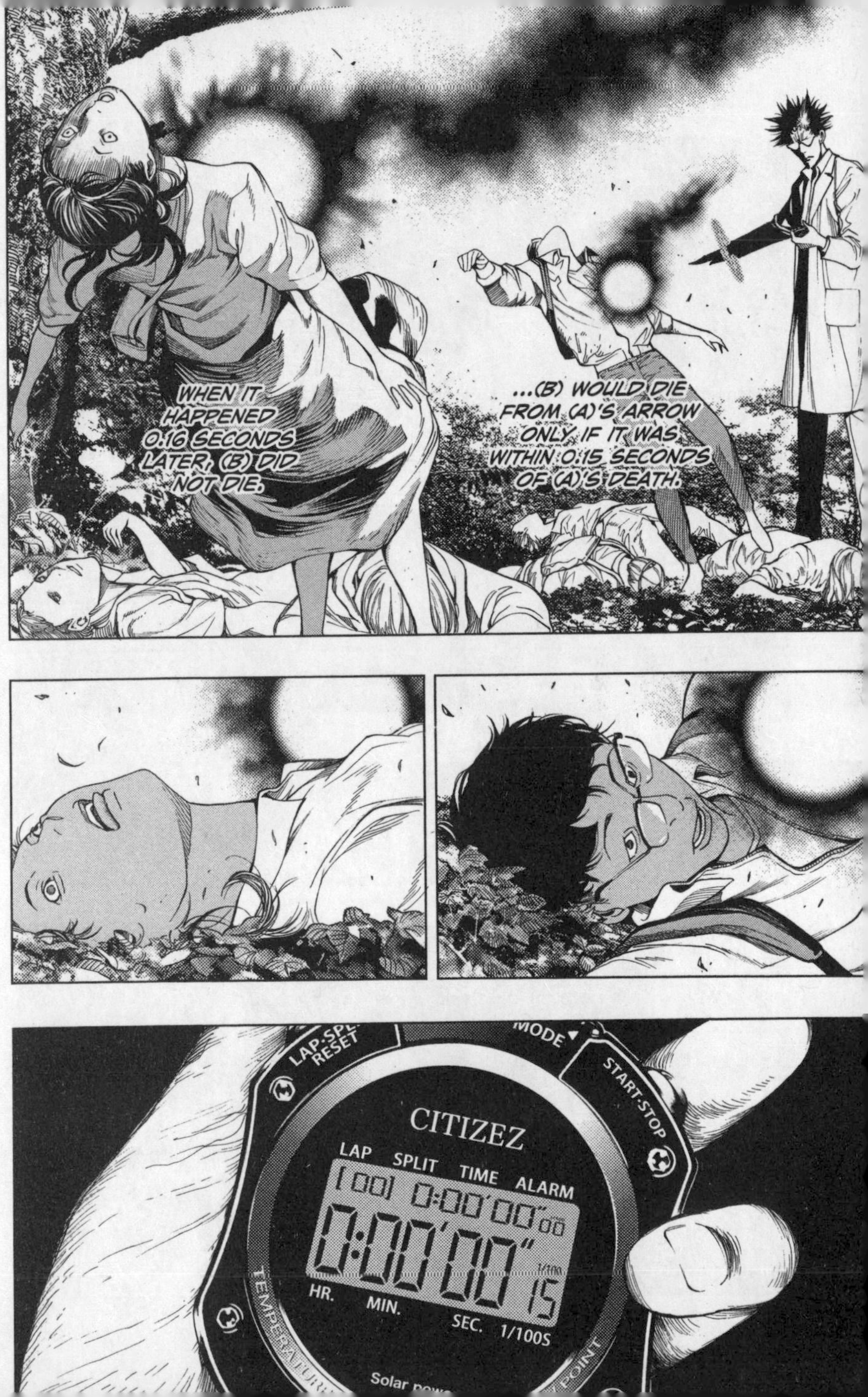
...(B) WOULD DIE FROM (A)'S ARROW ONLY IF IT WAS WITHIN 0.15 SECONDS OF (A)'S DEATH.
WHEN IT HAPPENED 0.16 SECONDS LATER, (B) DID NOT DIE.
MODE
START·STOP
LAP·SPLIT RESET
CITIZEZ
LAP SPLIT TIME ALARM
[00] 0:00'00"00
0:00'00" 15
HR. MIN. SEC. 1/100S
TEMPERATURE

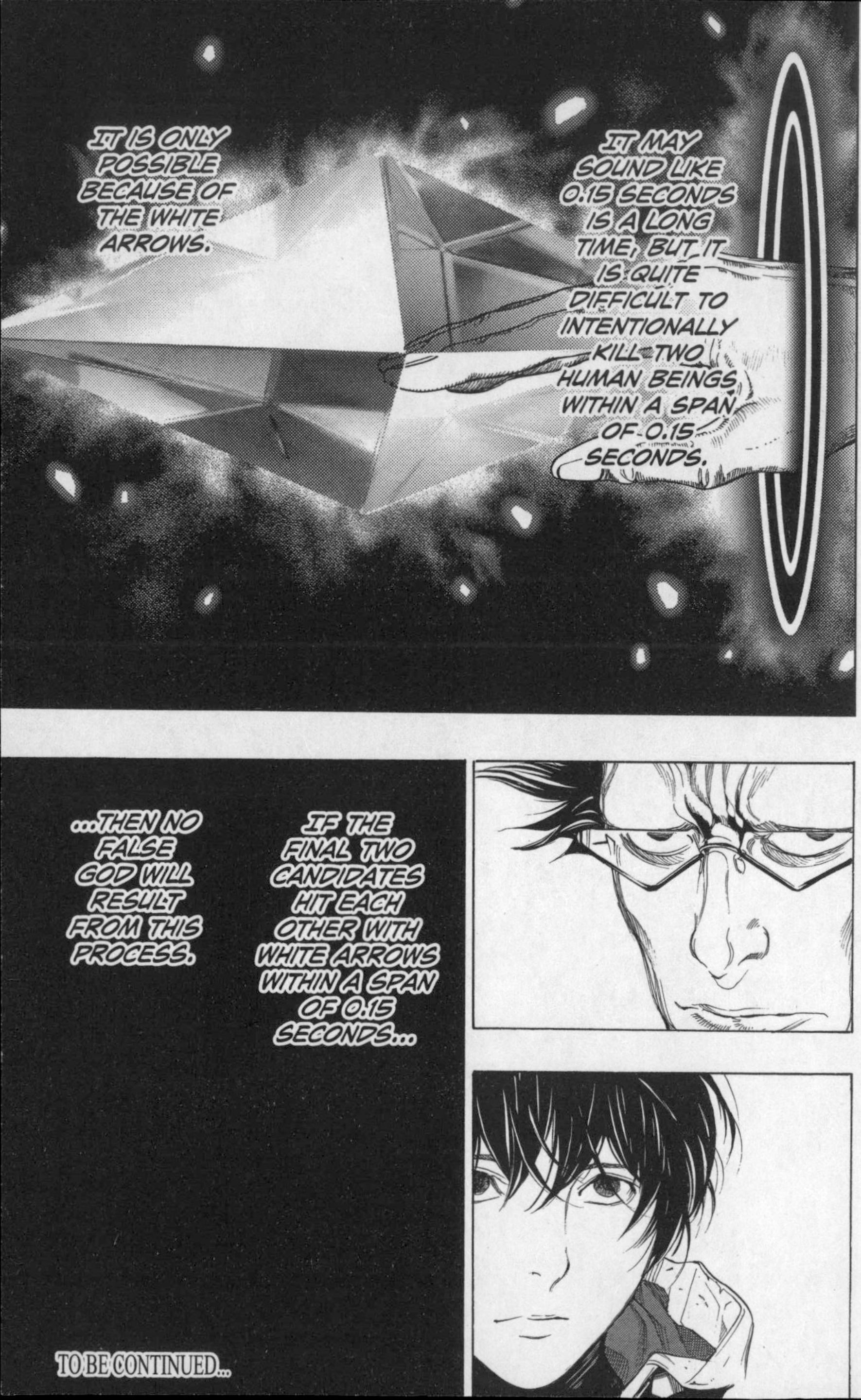
IT MAY SOUND LIKE 0.15 SECONDS IS A LONG TIME, BUT IT IS QUITE DIFFICULT TO INTENTIONALLY KILL TWO HUMAN BEINGS WITHIN A SPAN OF 0.15 SECONDS.
IT IS ONLY POSSIBLE BECAUSE OF THE WHITE ARROWS.
IF THE FINAL TWO CANDIDATES HIT EACH OTHER WITH WHITE ARROWS WITHIN A SPAN OF 0.15 SECONDS...
...THEN NO FALSE GOD WILL RESULT FROM THIS PROCESS.
TO BE CONTINUED...

T sugu mi **Oh** b **a**

○

Born in Tokyo, Tsugumi Ohba is the author
of the hit series *Death Note* and *Bakuman*。.

○

○

○

○

Ta **k** e **sh** i Oba **ta**

○

Takeshi Obata was born in 1969 in Niigata,
Japan, and first achieved international
recognition as the artist of the wildly popular
Shonen Jump title *Hikaru no Go*, which won the
2003 Tezuka Osamu Cultural Prize: Shinsei
"New Hope" Award and the 2000 Shogakukan
Manga Award. He went on to illustrate the smash
hit *Death Note* as well as the hugely successful
manga *Bakuman*。 and *All You Need Is Kill*.

PLATINVM END

VOLUME 12
SHONEN JUMP Manga Edition

STORY **Tsugumi Ohba**
ART **Takeshi Obata**

TRANSLATION Stephen Paul
TOUCH-UP ART & LETTERING James Gaubatz
DESIGN Shawn Carrico
EDITOR Alexis Kirsch

ORIGINAL COVER DESIGN Narumi Noriko

Printed in the U.S.A.

Published by VIZ Media, LLC
P.O. Box 77010
San Francisco, CA 94107

10 9 8 7 6 5 4 3 2 1
First printing, January 2021

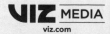
viz.com

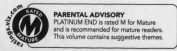

YOU'RE
READING
THE

WRONG WAY!

PLATINUM END
reads from right to left,
starting in the upper-right
corner. Japanese is read
from right to left, meaning
that action, sound effects
and word-balloon order
are completely reversed
from English order.

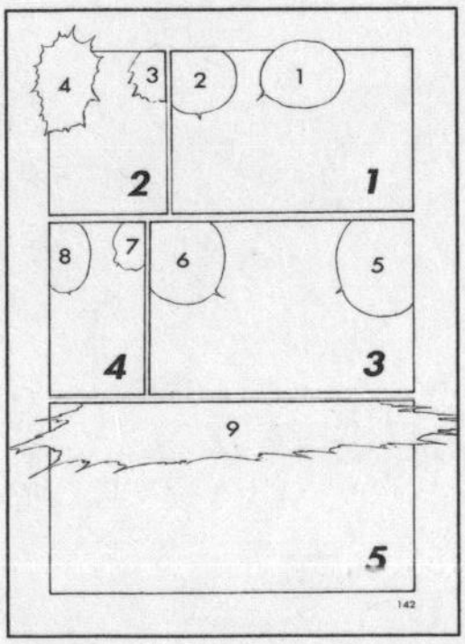

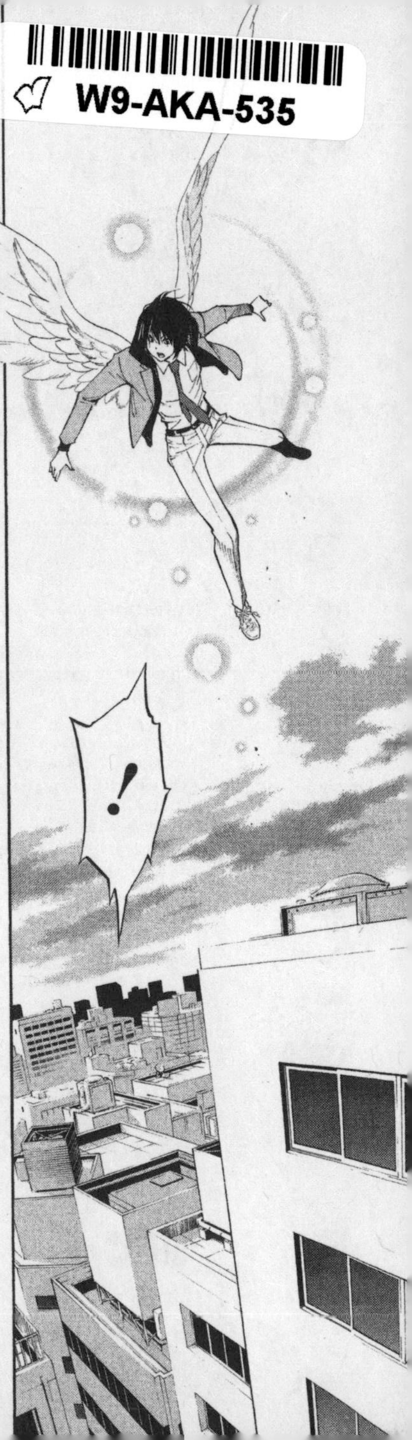
!